Episcopal Wome

Episcopal Women

*Gender, Spirituality, and
Commitment in an American
Mainline Denomination*

EDITED BY
Catherine M. Prelinger

OXFORD UNIVERSITY PRESS
New York   Oxford

Oxford University Press

Oxford   New York
Athens   Auckland   Bangkok   Bombay
Calcutta   Cape Town   Dar es Salaam   Delhi
Florence   Hong Kong   Istanbul   Karachi
Kuala Lumpur   Madras   Madrid   Melbourne
Mexico City   Nairobi   Paris   Singapore
Taipei   Tokyo   Toronto

and associated companies in
Berlin   Ibadan

Copyright (c) 1992 by Oxford University Press, Inc.

First published in 1992 by Oxford University Press, Inc.
198 Madison Avenue, New York, New York 10016

First issued as an Oxford University Press paperback, 1996

Library of Congress Cataloging-in-Publication Data
Episcopal women : gender, spirituality, and commitment in an
American mainline denomination / edited by Catherine M. Prelinger.
p.   cm.   (Religion in America series)
Includes bibliographical references.
ISBN 0-19-507433-5; ISBN 0-19-510465-X (pbk.)
1. Women in the Anglican Communion.
2. Feminism—Religious
aspects—Episcopal Church.
3. Episcopal Church—History—1965–
4. Anglican Communion—History—1965–
I. Prelinger, Catherine M.
II. Series: Religion in America series (Oxford University Press)
BX5968.E75   1992   283'.73'082—dc20   91-46036

1   3   5   7   9   8   6   4   2
Printed in the United States of America

located at the General Theological Seminary in New York. That seminary administered the grant we received.

C. M. P.

Note

1. Frigga Haug, ed., *Female Sexualization: A Collective Work of Memory*, trans. Erica Carter (London: Verso, 1987), p. 282.

of the various articles. We were greatly assisted in these efforts by the keen minds and firm commitments of our two regular consultants, Clarissa W. Atkinson, dean of the Harvard Divinity School, and Sheila Briggs, professor at the School of Religion, University of Southern California. To these two scholars, this project is indebted in ways too many to enumerate.

We are also especially indebted to Paula Nesbitt, then a doctoral candidate in the Department of Sociology at Harvard University. Paula assumed the particularly difficult role of entering the project when it was already fully launched; she graciously accepted the position of statistician and computer adviser to Joanna B. Gillespie's oral history team when professional demands made it no longer possible for Nancy Van Scoyoc, consulting psychologist to Growing Edge Management Consultants, Alexandria, Virginia, to continue in this capacity. Her generous assistance in providing statistical and interpretive insights for the chapter on the clergy was invaluable. Members of the oral interview team included Margaret Woolverton and Margaret Rubel, and to them we are deeply indebted for their fine sensitivity as well as the time and energy they donated to our work.

We also wish to thank the participants who attended our final workshop, held in the spring of 1990 in Princeton, New Jersey. They were: Donald S. Armentrout of the School of Theology, University of the South, Sewanee, Tennessee; Linda J. Clark of the Boston University School of Theology; Pamela Darling of General Theological Seminary; Carolyn D. Gifford, an unaffiliated scholar editing the diaries of Frances E. Willard; William Haugaard of Seabury-Western Theological Seminary; Charles Henery of Nashotah House; Suzanne Hiatt of the Episcopal Divinity School; Sister Jean Knoerle of the Lilly Endowment; William Petersen, Bexley Hall, Rochester Center for Theological Studies, New York; Robert Prichard of the Virginia Theological Seminary; Jean Miller Schmidt of the Iliff School of Theology; Allison Stokes of the Hartford Seminary; Frank Sugano of the Episcopal Theological Seminary of the Southwest; and Ann Swidler of the University of California at Berkeley. They were our first outside commentators, and we are grateful for their suggestions and support.

Finally, we wish to thank the Lilly Endowment, first for the planning grant issued for the year 1987–1988, and then for the major grant that financed our work over the three-year period from 1988 through 1990. Dorothy C. Bass was instrumental in suggesting that we apply for this assistance; she had been encouraged to enter into dialogue with us because of the achievements of the Episcopal Women's History Project,

PREFACE

Collaboration has been a deeply felt feminist goal, one almost always difficult to achieve, particularly in the field of scholarship. I can report that the level of cooperation realized in the production of this anthology was nothing short of remarkable. We adopted a format of procedure that involved three working conferences during the three-year period over which the project extended. At the first two of these conferences, alternate groups of the authors formally presented drafts of their essays; the other authors offered formal critiques. Then we shifted to structured but informal discussion. There was a degree of constructiveness among the critics, and a willingness both to offer and to accept incisive but never negative suggestions, that is rare in academic circles. A level of mutual trust developed that permitted authors to exchange "floppies" and to work materials into their coauthors' contributions. Perhaps we may attribute this spirit of give-and-take in part to the fact that a few of us, at least, do not identify ourselves as academics at all. We are, in fact, a rather heterogeneous group in terms of education and training. We tried to overcome boundaries between the theoreticians and the practitioners, and to learn from one another. Frigga Haug, who edited an anthology in Germany, made a wise comment when she observed:

> Collective projects such as ours, which present each participant with the opportunity of learning, of becoming more skillful both in thinking and writing, and of moving closer to some form of liberation, seem to me to constitute an important element of interpersonal relations. . . . One thing our experience suggests is that work of this kind makes it possible to negate *arbitrary* criteria for hostility—an antipathy based on appearance or behaviour, for example—and thus, perhaps, to negate dislike itself.[1]

As the nature of our volume evolved, we developed a number of common themes that we tried to recapture within the several contexts widely diverse perspectives on the situation of women in the Episcopal Church and the implications of their situation for the future of the tradition. It is, perhaps, in revealing this complexity that the volume comes closest to providing its most accurate insight into gender and mainstream Protestantism in the United States. If that is so, it is Kitty's achievement, a tribute to the quality of mind and spirit that were hallmarks of her leadership.

She is greatly missed.

Cambridge, Massachusetts   *Constance H. Buchanan*
February 1992

FOREWORD

What does a patriarchal religious tradition mean to its "daughters"?
This question fascinated Catherine Prelinger, the editor of this volume.
Her courageous efforts in the face of the cancer that took her life saw
it safely to press.

As historian and feminist, Kitty made the history of Christian culture
in the West since the reformations a particular focus of her scholarly
career. Eager to discover women's lives and their meanings, she knew
that one of the central problems of history is how to hear women's
deeply muffled voices within the languages and institutions of male-
dominated religion—the place where they have been most profoundly
shaped by patriarchal culture and yet also at times have found rare scope
for self-expression.

Kitty was a pioneer in the field of women's history and one of the
loyalties that guided her professional life was her loyalty to women.
While always empathetic, she was never uncritical. Above all, she knew
religion mattered historically to most women and that it still matters to
many; the task is to understand how and with what result. She looked
with equal interest at traditional women for whom religion was sometimes a refuge and at others who found in it a path to personal and
social change.

Had she lived, Kitty would have completed a major study of the female
diaconate in European and American Protestantism, an institution that
provided nineteenth- and early twentieth-century women with resources
for building professional lives in work outside the home. We will not
see that study.

At the request of the Lilly Endowment, she took on the contemporary
project this volume represents, and without her it would not have come
to fruition. The voices of the authors gathered in this volume represent

CONTENTS

    and Festivities   239
    Irene Q. Brown

8. A Woman's Journey toward Priesthood: An Autobiographical
    Study from the 1950s through the 1980s   263
    Sandra Hughes Boyd

III   Images of a New Church   283

9. Ordained Women in the Episcopal Church: Their Impact on the
    Work and Structure of the Clergy   285
    Catherine M. Prelinger

10. The Anthropology of Vitality and Decline: The Episcopal Church
    in a Changing Society   310
    Constance H. Buchanan

11. Theory, Theology, and Episcopal Churchwomen   330
    Margaret R. Miles

    Afterword: Episcopal Women in the Context of American
    Religious Life   345
    Dorothy C. Bass

    Contributors   353

    Index   357

Episcopal Women

Introduction

Catherine M. Prelinger

Mainline Protestantism is the current focus of significant scholarly attention[1]; the popular press has also been attracted by what it calls the shift "from mainline to sideline", or "those mainline blues."[2] Oddly, few so far have addressed the situation of women in the mainline or asked what it may have to tell us about the mainline's widely analyzed "decline." As a category of analysis, gender has been so overlooked in attempts to understand the mainline that little attention has been given even to the proposition, formulated as early as 1977, of the feminization of American Protestantism achieved by the alliance between an influential sector of Northeast American women and their clerical mentors.[3] Nor has an opinion on the prominence of women among the mainline missionaries been ventured.[4]

Most important, there has been little analysis of the ambiguity of women's participation in liberal religious traditions, even as the historical male domination of these has been increasingly recognized. In such traditions, what has been the nature of the religious lives of women? What does women's experience tell us about the limits of the "theological openness, social awareness, and public service" for which, as Dorothy Bass notes in her Afterword, mainline denominations have been known? And, in turn, in what ways might these limits be related to the apparently decreasing ability of mainline Protestantism to continue to offer significant leadership in American society?

Episcopal Women is an effort to look at these questions and the

3

situation of mainline Protestantism through the lens of gender analysis, using the Episcopal Church as a case study. This effort goes beyond reclaiming individual women in the church from historical anonymity to examine religion and gender as part of a broader social fabric. It views gender as a set of socially constructed protocols for male and female behavior—roles in relation one to another. It talks about men and women in terms of pluralities and relationships; issues of universality and historical agency command the center of gender research. Joan W. Scott has articulated the agenda with authority:

> The abstract rights-bearing individual who came into being as the focus of liberal political debate in the seventeenth and eighteenth centuries somehow came embodied in male form and it is his story that historians have largely told. Feminist scholarship has repeatedly come up against the difficulty of including women in this universal representation since, as their work reveals, it is a contrast with feminine particularity that secures the universality of the masculine representation. It seems clear that to conceive of women as historical actors, equal in status to men, requires a notion of particularity and specificity of *all* human subjects.[5]

Scott's conceptualization has immediate relevance to religious studies. Religion has been a prominent force in this culture, defining notions of universality and particularity. Further, it has articulated and legitimated the association of masculinity and femininity with these notions. Few things could be more germane to examination of the universality of the masculine and the particularity of the feminine, therefore, than gender analysis of mainline Protestantism. This tradition, with its gender norms, has been one of the most influential institutions and sacred ideologies shaping North American life.

This volume, then, explores gender as a crucial organizing principle of religious life and thought in liberal Protestantism. The story of the role played by gender, especially of how changes in traditional gender asymmetry in the mainline are related to its widely perceived decline, is both fascinating and important. It is a story which sheds new light not only on mainline women and on the decline of these prominent institutions, but also on the values of the broader society these churches have helped so powerfully to fashion and express.

What is happening to these religious institutions is of acute contemporary significance. They constitute settings in which fundamental issues of social value and meaning in American society are being contested, worked out in part through explicit debate about institutional theology and policy, and in part through less obvious and more gradual processes of institutional change. The denominational conventions of these traditions, which in recent years have made evident the extent to which gender and sexual orientation have become central concerns, draw attention to the level of explicit debate; analysis of institutional dynamics and patterns is required to get at less apparent processes of change.

When gender is brought to bear in systematic examination of these liberal institutions, as in this case study of the Episcopal Church, several things are achieved. We are able to reconstruct the experience of mainstream women in a prominent North American denomination. This experience, in turn, allows us to begin to reconstruct the story of the tradition itself; making women historical subjects reveals the particularity of men as subjects too and necessitates a thorough-going reinterpretation. Beyond this, attention to gender as an analytical category reveals as well the gendered nature of the very institutional structure and practices of this mainline tradition, allowing recognition of the interaction between these and its liberal Christian theology.

Finally, this one institution of the Protestant mainline becomes an instructive case study of the broader debate over gender and its relation to basic social roles and values in the United States today. Whether as contrast or parallel to broader developments, what is happening with this once–culturally prominent tradition helps bring into sharper focus the larger picture of change in society.

Mainline Protestant research to date has focused heavily on leadership, lay as well as clerical, and particularly on national leadership. Most recently, William R. Hutchison's *Between the Times: The Travail of the Protestant Establishment in American, 1900–1960* examines institutions such as the international Sunday School Council, the Federal Council of Churches and National Council of Churches, and the "Reform Establishment." In the book co-authored with Wade Clark Roof, *American Mainline Religion: Its Changing Shape and Future,* William McKinney writes:

> Liberal Protestantism's cultural influence is greater than its lack of vitality suggests. Known for its close ties historically with the northern and eastern establishment, it still is a power and presence of some significance, . . . [T]hree religious groups (Congregational, Presbyterian, Episcopalian) have far more members in the U.S. Senate and House of Representatives than would be expected based on their aggregate sizes.[6]

Denominational leadership here is closely associated with secular rather than spiritual influence, not a method designed to locate the power of women. Likewise, *Between the Times* addresses women in a single essay, "United and Slighted: Women as Subordinated Insiders," also looking

6 INTRODUCTION

at women at the leadership level.[7] When Roof and McKinney project a future for liberal Protestantism on the margins rather than at the center, the authors write:

> For an extended period of American history the group some now think of as Liberal Protestants were the mainline. One might say they established the rules of the American religious game. With legal disestablishment, Congregationalists, Presbyterians, and Episcopalians were forced to admit other teams but they continued to own the stadium. The second disestablishment further reduced their status to the not-unimportant role of umpire. Now for the first time in America, a liberal Protestantism is on the field of play and has to compete with other religious "teams."[8]

The language is revealing. Religion, in every important respect, is a game for men, and men make the rules. Changes in perceived power have to do with power shifts among white men. What is suspect here is not simply the exclusion of white women, and minority women and men, but the conflation of leadership with the entirety of the church. Conclusions are drawn which indeed may be accurately inferred from leadership but say very little about the power and preferences of those in the pews.

Our study deliberately and with intention takes the female laity as its focal point. It nonetheless includes components dealing with leadership; since the focus is on women, our definitions and findings are quite different from those of the mainline consensus. Nevertheless, in their analysis of both laity and leadership these articles do not represent a consensus of their own. Rather, they reflect significant differences. In the section "Historical Perspectives," Mary Donovan examines the major lay women's network in the Episcopal Church and weighs the merits of dismantling an organization which had reaped the rewards of separatism (along with its penalties), in favor of integrated representation in the authority structure. In the section "Images of a New Church," Constance Buchanan's chapter on the anthropology of vitality in the Episcopal church questions the underlying metaphor that equates the increasing absence of young men and the growing presence of women, especially women priests and elderly women, with institutional decline. The interactions of lay women and men in leadership roles within a number of settings, urban and rural, come under scrutiny in respective chapters by Rima Lunin Schultz and Joan R. Gundersen. A chapter on Episcopal women in Texas by Elizabeth Turner compares Episcopal to evangelical women, in their access to and use of secular power. Episcopal women, exploiting the entrée they enjoyed in the community by virtue of their husbands' positions, initiated community-wide philanthropies, while evangelical women focused on projects designed to convert individuals to personal salvation.

"Contemporary Voices" focuses exclusively on the female laity. Joanna Gillespie describes the methodology in her chapter, a reflection constructed from a combination of written questionnaires and oral interviews. Some of the issues she uncovered certainly support conclusions reached by other mainline researchers, but her interpretations are different. Denominational loyalty, for instance, is a consistent theme in earlier studies of the mainstream, one discussed with some sophistication in Robert Wuthnow's *Restructuring of American Religion* and one to which the Roof and McKinney book also returns. Often the concept seems to represent primarily a nostalgia for the past, idealizing a commitment having little to distinguish it from white male bonding to preserve a status quo and limit the access of women and minorities.

The concept of denominational loyalty is rarely used by male authors in a pejorative sense, but the alternative, usually called "voluntarism," is frequently equated to "shopping around"—the expression itself evokes disparagement. Shopping around may quite correctly register consumer preference on a practical as well as theological scale, and the practice is gendered. The church with the program for the elderly or a quality child-care program is understandably the legitimate choice of a contemporary woman, whereas in the heyday of mainline Protestantism middle-class women might have delegated such concerns to a domestic.

"Sheilaism," the practice of individuals leaving organized religion to follow an inner voice first identified by authors of *Habits of the Heart*,[9] is yet another religious attitude which has been assigned highly negative connotations by authors dealing with the Protestant mainline. Although from a feminist perspective, Sheilaism represented the effort of a woman who had experienced oppression in the traditional church to regain her own voice and sense of personhood, Robert Bellah described it as essentially individualistic and narcissistic. Gillespie's research uncovers instances of both voluntarism and Sheilaism, sympathetically understood. What is perhaps more surprising are the many instances of vibrant denominational loyalty among women who either feel they do not recognize the church of their youth, or who feel abandoned by new directions in the contemporary church. They would neither join a different denomination nor leave the church altogether. Irene Q. Brown's chapter is a study of the kind of woman who has absented herself from church attendance but contributes her service to church projects in a spirit of devotional activity. Denominational loyalty has often been achieved through a kind of ironic accommodation on the part of women, a conscious willingness to shut their eyes and ears to certain aspects of church life that men dominate, and to develop their own forms of institutional expression, confident, rightly or wrongly, that they represent the true church in fact if not instrumentally. Joan Gundersen's chapter illustrates this paradox.

Significant minority constituencies are represented in the Episcopal Church, including African-American, American Indian, Hispanic, and Asian: the last, the fastest growing minority, is now thought to number .6 percent of all Episcopalians. Each of these groups is represented among women priests.[10] The black church, discussed in Marjorie Farmer's chapter, is unfortunately the only non-Anglo-Saxon constituency we have been able to include. Another significant lacuna is the absence of a chapter on the charismatic church.

Despite these important omissions, we have reconstructed significant elements of the past and present experience of mainstream women in this one American denomination. Perhaps the most striking feature of the study is the exposure of an acute tension among the authors, one which also reflects the reality of the experience they describe.[11] On the one hand there is the exuberant recognition—even celebration—of women in the Episcopal church. This is expressed in many ways: in their numbers, in the work they perform, often without any acknowledgement, in their financial contributions. There is also now a female presence among the ranks of leadership, for which many, among them authors of this volume, have agitated and strategized for years. But there is deep disagreement about what all of this signifies. Other chapters make it clear that women remain in an impossible situation. How is it that in today's world liberal Protestantism often finds itself in the position of following rather than initiating moral and social consensus? Has the Episcopal Church become a refuge for traditional women? Is the handiwork of church women romanticized when it is really scut work? Several of our authors are acutely skeptical about any real gender change in the church and point to the many instances of institutional oppression which remain within.

Our study looks at a single denomination. Many of the traits that mainline research has targeted among other Protestant denominations, such as the growth of localism and impatience with regional and national bureaucracies, are apparent in the Episcopal Church as well and reflect in part the more vocal participation of women. Our study did not explicitly seek to investigate the stance of Episcopal women on various of the wider sociopolitical questions of the day—ERA, abortion, nuclear armament, environmentalism, El Salvador, and so forth—questions around which special interest groups, often with a nucleus of church members, have been formed. Robert Wuthnow studied the denominational implications of these associations. His conclusion, that in each and every congregation of whatever denomination, some representation of the full spectrum of positions on these issues can be found,[12] parallels our own finding. In each Episcopal congregation, whether predominantly Anglo-Catholic or low church, difference exists across the entire continuum over the volatile theological issues dividing the church in general, particularly over those concerns involving women.

Not only Protestants but Roman Catholics as well will find points of similarity in the Episcopal experience. From the moment ordination for women became an issue in the Episcopal Church, Catholic women have charted the course of women ordinands and weighed for themselves the merits of integration versus separatism. The continued perception of women clergy as the embodiment of maternal rather than priestly authority is one which Catholic nuns view with particular sensitivity. Perhaps they can in reality exercise greater influence through the separate power of their sisterhoods. The disruptiveness of the question of the nature of women's participation is not only similar in both churches, but also linked to other shared structural similarities. In each case the American church is part of a global communion to which in varying degrees it is accountable. While Catholic allegiance to the Vatican is more immediate, the American Episcopal Church is not unaffected by its affiliates in the Caribbean and in Africa, Asia and, of course, the United Kingdom. For the Episcopal Church as for the Roman Catholic, global concerns work almost exclusively in a conservative direction on issues respecting women. This was dramatically apparent at the Lambeth Conference in 1988, where American bishops had hoped to move their British colleagues forward on the path to women's ordination but found the dialogue on women pre-empted by concern, among other things, about polygamy in Africa.[13]

The media would have us believe that the Episcopal Church in North America at the beginning of the 1990s is on the brink of schism. Nothing in our study confirms the imminence of a breach. Like other churches in the Protestant mainline, the Episcopal Church has been losing members. The church went from a high water mark of 3,647,297 baptized members in 1966 to 2,446,050 in 1991. Some of this hemorrhage is more apparent than real, reflecting a definitional change in the meaning of membership. One observer draws attention to the far lower birth rate among middle-class families—the hard core of Episcopalians

—than that of evangelical fundamentalist denominations whose memberships have been increasing dramatically.[14] Wade Clark Roof thinks that the older baby-boomers are returning.[15] The recent Gallup poll summary issue is emphatic in affirming that the decline in Episcopal membership since the 1960s must be explained by "primarily broad societal, lifestyle, and demographic factors that have affected all churches, particularly mainline churches, and not specifically denominational issues (such as, in the case of the Episcopal Church, the changes in the Prayer Book, the ordination of women, inclusive language, and the sanctioning of homosexual relationships)."[16]

Contemporary divisions in the church go back a number of years; certainly the revision of the *Book of Common Prayer* was a significant source of conservative retaliation. The ordination of women, and more recently the elevation of a woman to the episcopacy, has fueled further dissent. The current controversies surrounding homosexuality are offshoots of the focus on women and their place in the sacred order; both represent reaction to the new pluralism within the church. Only with the elevation of women to the priesthood did sexuality assume such a contemporary relevance to the church and require a re-examination of older prescriptions concerning body and spirit, fertility and celibacy, and force the church to examine its role in upholding or subverting societal heterosexual domination. The Philadelphia meeting of the House of Bishops in September 1989 appeared to heal the potential threat from the so-called Episcopal Synod of America, the faction that met at Fort Worth during the previous summer. A statement concluding the meeting affirmed the dissenters as "loyal members of the family" but also reaffirmed the ministries of women through the church. Bishop Paul Moore, earlier in the summer, was more forthright when he said that if the traditionalists "don't like things they should get out"; he was weary of wrangling over traditionalist issues when critical questions of homelessness, disease, and environmental pollution required action.[17] The General Convention of 1988 approved services with inclusive language for trial use and stressed ability and calling rather than gender as a requisite for church leadership.[18]

In theological support of their position, the traditionalists cite the all-male composition of the original band of disciples to disqualify women from the apostolic succession. The House of Bishops invited a powerful counter-argument from British spokesperson and theological secretary to the Board for Mission and Unity, Mary Tanner. Her address centered on what she framed as the process of reception, first exemplified in Christianity by the admission of Gentiles to the church. When Paul made the determination against circumcision a requisite for conversion, a position far in advance of the contemporary church, he decisively altered the future course of Christianity.[19] The theological revisionism of Elizabeth Schüssler-Fiorenza also looks to the very early church:

> In the passion account of Mark's Gospel three disciples figure prominently: on the one hand, two of the twelve—Judas who betrayed Jesus and Peter who denies him—and on the other, the unnamed woman who anoints Jesus. But while the stories of Judas and Peter are engraved in the memory of Christians, the story of the woman is virtually forgotten. Although Jesus pronounces in Mark: "And truly I say unto you, wherever the gospel is preached in the whole world, what she has done will be told in memory of her" (14:9), the woman's prophetic sign did not become a part of the gospel knowledge of Christians. Even her name is lost to us.[20]

The unnamed woman "is the paradigm for the true disciple."[21] Schüssler-Fiorenza cites a myriad of other lost names, misconstrued functions, and masculine nouns and pronouns substituted for generic ones in the course of scriptural transmission. Offices held by women were disguised to suit the institutional demands of a nascent church encroaching upon the customs of a patriarchal society. Schüssler-Fiorenza recommends the hermeneutic of suspicion.

These are compelling theological arguments. History offers others. The Anglican church had its origins in the political establishment of the sixteenth century. The power of the governing class perpetuated itself not through the arrangements of a nuclear family but as a consequence of elaborate and well-conceived alliances of kinship, bonds of clan and links of clientage. Privileged women were not simply the pawns of marriage contracts; they were dynastic representatives prepared by custom and education to act as surrogates for their male relatives.[22] In their persons they embodied the power of the dynasty. Nor was the kinship system confined to the single family who governed. Aristocracy in general reproduced itself in this way, and when commerce augmented land as a source of wealth, male mobility was only feasible if it was grounded in the stability and administrative acumen of female alliances. How does this relate to the Episcopal Church in America? It provides social and economic insight into the tradition of respect for—indeed dependence upon—authoritative and educated women, a tradition perpetuated by the church. For the Episcopal Church, even of the late twentieth century, has not severed its connection to secular leadership; the culture conceived in the upper classes continues to permeate Episcopal culture, augmented as it was so dramatically by the conversions of upwardly mobile capitalists and their families during the era of industrial expansion.[23]

Unwittingly, the Fort Worth Synod of 1989 reflects a quite different tradition, one embedded in the denominations of the Reformation and powerfully reinforced when the Methodists seceded from the Episcopal Church late in the eighteenth century. It is one which has dominated midwestern, middle-class America ever since. This is the culture of the nuclear family. It celebrates the autonomous individual man both in the economy and in evangelical religion, and mutes the service and care he receives at home from wives, sisters, and female servants. The division of social spheres by gendered activities is often enhanced by an assumption of "natural difference," an ideology seldom recognized as a true violation of Christian doctrine.[24]

Does our study of a single denomination shed light on other mainline Protestant denominations? The majority of these chapters do not attempt to generalize beyond the Episcopal Church. Yet a focus on women and an approach that takes gender as a primary category of analysis demonstrates that the Episcopal case offers valuable insight into mainline Protestantism as a whole.

Dorothy Bass, in her Afterword, makes this point. Identifying several themes that emerge in the volume, she argues that the very distinctiveness of Episcopal women's experience offers a crucial vantage point for study of American mainstream Protestantism as a whole. It is useful to call attention at the outset to several of the themes Bass discusses. Most important, within the Episcopal Church changes in the role and status of women in recent decades have led to an especially heated debate over gender, bringing the issues into focus in a way that is particularly sharp and useful for throwing into relief the situation in other denominations. Also, the distinctively sacramental character and tradition of the Episcopal Church helps us to see the religious life of women, a phenomenon that is not as readily discernible in most other Protestant groups. While clearly different from that of other Protestant women, the spirituality of Episcopal women serves as a guide for bringing into focus the religious life of women in the mainline more broadly.

Finally, and perhaps most basic to the whole problem of the mainline and its "decline", the deeper roots of the Episcopal Church in the hierarchical Christianity of the Old World have created an especially deep tension in the denomination between women's subordination and participation. This tension points beyond the situation of Episcopal women to the situation of mainline women in general. It underscores the importance of recognizing that the ambiguity of women's participation in male-dominated churches is a crucial variable that can no

longer be overlooked in assessing the current crisis and the future of
mainline American Protestantism.

Notes

1. Robert S. Michaelsen and Wade Clark Roof, eds., *Liberal Protestantism*
(New York: Pilgrim Press, 1986); Wade Clark Roof and William McKinney,
American Mainline Religion: Its Changing Shape and Future (New Brunswick,
N.J.: Rutgers University Press, 1987); Robert Wuthnow, *The Restructing of
American Religion* (Princeton: Princeton University Press, 1988); William R.
Hutchison, ed., *Between the Times: The Travail of the Protestant Establishment
in America, 1900–1960* (New York: Cambridge University Press, 1989). In this
succession of volumes it is also interesting to see the progression from a denominational press to a small university press, a major university press, and a
distinguished trade press, with its implicit attribution of increased general stature
and importance to the subject addressed.

2. *Newsweek,* 22 December 1986, p. 54; *Time,* 22 May 1989, p. 94.

3. Ann Douglas, *The Feminization of American Culture* (New York: Alfred
A. Knopf, 1977), particularly pp. 165–69, 227–29.

4. Joan Jacobs Brumberg, *Mission for Life: The Story of the Family of
Adoniram, The Dramatic Events of the First American Foreign Mission, and the
Course of Evangelical Religion in the Nineteenth Century* (New York: The Free
Press, 1980); Patricia R. Hill, *The World Their Household: The American Wom-
an's Foreign Mission Movement and Cultural Transformation, 1870–1920* (Ann
Arbor: The University of Michigan Press, 1985); Jane Hunter, *The Gospel of
Gentility: American Women Missionaries in Turn-of-the-Century China* (New
Haven: Yale University Press, 1984).

5. Joan Wallach Scott, *Gender and the Politics of History* (New York: Columbia University Press, 1988), p. 25.

6. Roof and McKinney, *American Mainline Religion,* p. 87. Sixty-seven
members of Congress were Episcopalians, following the election of 1984. There
are approximately 2.5 million Episcopalians in the United States.

7. Virginia Lieson Brereton, in Hutchison, *Between the Times,* pp. 143–67.

8. Roof and McKinney, *American Mainline Religion,* pp. 239–40.

9. Robert N. Bellah, et al., *Habits of the Heart: Individualism and Commitment in American Life* (New York: Harper and Row Perennial Library,
1986), pp. 221, 235.

10. Personal communication from Joanna Gillespie: the "desks" at Episcopal
headquarters, 815 Second Avenue in New York, record only all-minority congregations, not constituencies within mixed congregations. (There is also no
distinctive record designating female and male communicants, one reason our
own statistics are so unsatisfactory.) The "black desk" lists 400 all-black congregations so we can estimate that 4–5 percent of Episcopalians are black, and
1 percent are Hispanic, since there are about 124 Hispanic congregations. There

are about 164 native American congregations as well as 98 Alaskan-Indian congregations, constituting some .8% of all Episcopalians; and the estimate of Asians is .6% of all Episcopalians. For minority women priests, see Mary S. Donovan, *Women Priests in the Episcopal Church: The Experience of the First Decade* (Cincinnati: The Forward Movement Press, 1988).

11. It was Ann Swidler who insistently drew this to the attention of the authors at a conference they sponsored for interchange among themselves and a number of interested invitees at the Henry Chanuncy Center, Princeton, N.J., June 5, 1990.

12. Wuthnow, *The Restructuring of American Religion,* pp. 100–32, 222–40.

13. The Lambeth Conference adopted a hesitant, compromise resolution on making the episcopacy accessible to women. The same conference confirmed polygamy "as a legitimate lifestyle for newly converted Christians" in nations where it is a legal institution. As Bishop Spong explained in his column "The Bishop's Voice":

When one examines the social structure of countries like Sudan, Kenya and Uganda, a number of issues emerge. First, tribal wars, so historically a part of the cultural ethos of this region of the world, regularly decimate the male population, leaving an imbalance in the ratio of women to men. Secondly, the patriarchal nature of local life in those lands has determined that the educational and economic opportunities open to women are extremely limited. Thirdly, and resulting from the first two facts, marriage is the primary means by which women are enabled to be sustained. To keep women in these cultures in the state of unmarriedness would be to compromise their ability to survive, or to drive them into prostitution as their sole means of support. (*The Voice* [Newark, N.J.], October, 1988, p. 2)

14. Bob Libby, "Twenty Years of Shrinkage—Why?" *The Episcopalian,* September, 1988, p. 25. Ken Clark, "Why Have the Sheep Left the Fold?" in *The Rio Grande Episcopalian* (Albuquerque, N.M.), September 1989, p. 4, relying heavily on information supplied by David E. Sumner, argues that birthrate is the only consistent factor in the study of membership. When the birthrate is up, he claims, there is a membership increase seven years later. But he also believes that adult converts account for the major sources of growth. Source for church members: Comparative Statistics of the Episcopal Church, U.S.A., *The Episcopal Church Annual* (Harrisburg, Penna.: Morehouse Publishing, 1992), p. 13.

15. Wade Clark Roof, "The Church in the Centrifuge," *The Christian Century* 106 (November 8, 1989): 1012.

16. George Gallup, Jr., "Overview," *The Spiritual Health* (summary version), pp. 7–8.

17. *The New York Times,* October 1, 1989, p. 31; William L. Sachs, "The Episcopal Synod: Reinforcing Boundaries," *The Christian Century* CVI (August 2–9, 1989): 710–11; "Episcopal Accord," *Ibid.* (November 1, 1989): 977; "Episcopal Family Feud," *Ibid.* (June 21–28): 616.

18. *Journal of the General Convention 1988,* pp. 240–59.

19. Mary Tanner, speech to the House of Bishops, September 23, 1989, *Episcopal News Service.*

20. Elisabeth Schüssler Fiorenza, *In Memory of Her: A Feminist Theological Reconstruction of Christian Origins* (New York: Crossroad, 1983), p. xiii.

21. Ibid., p. xiv.

22. Bonnie S. Anderson and Judith P. Zinsser, *A History of Their Own: From Prehistory to the Present* (New York: Harper and Row, 1988), II:51.

23. Kit Konolige and Frederica Konolige, *The Power of Their Glory: America's Ruling Class: The Episcopalians* (New York: Wyden Books, 1978). According to this study about 3 percent of the American population represented themselves to the Gallup poll as Episcopalians at the time of publication. What they lacked in numbers they made up for in other ways. Episcopalians were the wealthiest, most eastern, best educated and most highly placed professionally of any Christian denomination in the United States. In 1976, 48 percent of all Episcopalians had incomes over $20,000 as compared with 21 percent of the overall population. 43 percent said their occupations were professional or business and 45 percent had gone to college, compared with 25 percent and 29 percent of the rest of the country respectively. Episcopalians were heavily concentrated in the East (45 percent lived there); only 11 percent lived in the Midwest as opposed to 27 percent of the American population. It was (and still is) an urban (or suburban) denomination; one third lived in cities over 1 million people; half in cities over 500,000. Episcopalians were identified with industrialization and with the corporate elite. They displayed a preference for family expansion over missionary activity as a means of religious growth. Demographically speaking, Episcopalians are most like Jews than any other denomination. According to the Konoliges, the Episcopal atmosphere of feeling (their term) has been adopted by non-Episcopalians as the standard for upper-class conduct. The influence of distinctively Episcopalian institutions—the prep school, the male college, the metropolitan club—can hardly be overstated (pp. 27–29). Needless to say, to the serious historian the apparent identity between upper-class values and the Episcopal church makes analysis exceedingly difficult. Where does class end and denomination begin? When gender is factored in, the analytic task is more complicated. Many of the institutions chronicled by the Konoliges no longer exist or exist in a form based, ostensibly, on meritocracy rather than class and gender.

24. The Fort Worth Synod thinks of itself as Anglo-Catholic, but it is closely allied with the Evangelical and Catholic Mission, founded in 1976, and its geographic center is the Midwest. Bishops in the synod include those from Eau Claire and Fond du Lac (Wis.); Fort Worth (Tex.); Quincy (Ill.); and San Joaquin (Cal.). As William L. Sachs remarked:

> Fort Worth unwittingly marked the dissolution of the Anglo-Catholic party—a party that had won its place in the Episcopal Church. The irony, for those at Fort Worth, is that many of the Episcopal priests who now celebrate sung Eucharists in albs and chasubles are women, and that many of the male clergy who respect Anglo-Catholicism also applaud the consecration of a woman bishop. This leaves those who gathered at Fort Worth with only a retrospective sense of purpose. (*Christian Century*, August 2–9, 1989, p. 711).

I

HISTORICAL PERSPECTIVES

The chapters in this section provide historical accounts of the contributions of Episcopal laywomen to church and society, as well as analyses
of the structures that have historically both nurtured and limited their
activities.

In the first chapter, Rima L. Schultz surveys the changing forms of
Episcopal women's activities, from the emergence of strong organizations in the late nineteenth century to shifting, often uncertain, arrangements of the past two decades. Her focus on one diocese (Chicago)
permits her to paint a rich portrait of how a specific social and cultural
setting shaped women's experience of change in their church and in their
own roles. The chapter that follows, by Elizabeth H. Turner, depicts a
very different setting (Galveston), thereby expanding our vision of Episcopal laywomen's activities during the past century. In both chapters,
the social prominence of many Episcopal women emerges as a key
ingredient in their civic contributions, particularly in the earlier twentieth century. Yet it is ironically evident that their activities were restricted by their gender. Rapid social and cultural change since the 1960s,
which has brought issues of gender, race, and class to wider consciousness, has challenged and altered (but not destroyed) many of the structures and themes of laywomen's work described in these two chapters.

The next two chapters focus on the structures within which laywomen
have exercised their considerable, though often subtle, power within
the church. Joan R. Gundersen begins in the setting where almost all
Christians conduct their religious lives: in the local congregation.
Through implicit channels of power forged in their own organizations,
laywomen bypassed male structures to exercise significant influence,

Gundersen argues. Examining women's organizational structures at the national level, Mary S. Donovan detects a similar pattern during much of the church's history. As in the preceding chapters, however, the 1960s emerge as a significant turning point; organized laywomen's abandonment of separatism for integration, a characteristic response to the ethical challenges of that period, significantly altered laywomen's ecclesiastical influence. Both of these chapters prompt reflection upon what has been lost as well as gained amid recent advances of women in church and society.

1

Woman's Work and Woman's Calling in the Episcopal Church: Chicago, 1880–1989

Rima Lunin Schultz

Women's participation in religion has been an impressive source of support for the development and maintenance of what has come to be the institutional structure of the American religious establishment. While women outnumbered men on the membership rolls as early as colonial times, it has only been in the second half of the twentieth century that women have begun to take their place in the governing councils of most of the Protestant denominations. Similarly, women have only recently become ordained ministers in the mainline churches. This recent integration of women into all aspects of worship and institutional life of the principal Protestant denominations comes at a time when these same religious bodies have declining influence in the national culture. Women are "implicated" in the decline or marginalization of church life by critics who point to the feminization of the ministry and national councils, and the rejection of the traditional role of the woman volunteer.

Unquestionably, the nature of women's involvement in organized religion will have much to do with the future viability of religious institutions. Religious institutions have been challenged by the feminists within churches to provide an environment for women that allows them to be equal partners with men in the governance and ministry of churches. In the Episcopal Church since 1970 the barriers have been pulled down one by one. Yet at the parish level women's gains are less evident. At the local level churches are not operating very differently from the pre-1970s model. The main difference is that there are fewer women willing to participate in gender-specific jobs; those who do function in traditional ways suffer the indignities of unappreciated volunteerism. For most middle-class and working-class parishes where budgets are tight, women and men continue to do gender-specific jobs even when other changes such as women's election to vestries and commissions have occurred. Much as in the world of women workers, women now have two jobs in churches: the traditional "jobs" of housekeeping both in the community hall and the sacristy, teaching of the young, and the generalized role of communal socialization (bringing people together); and the new "jobs" of holding vestry and warden positions and participating in commissions and committees, including budget and property (building) committees. The structure of work and the relationships of power and authority in churches, as in society, retain to a large extent patriarchal underpinnings.

The changes in women's roles in the Episcopal Church clearly reflect the social and economic realities of American society. In the late nineteenth century religion became a bridge for women that brought them from the ideal of a sheltered domestic life of the home, which developed in the first half of the nineteenth century, to the public sphere of the workplace, the school, the hospital, the mission, and the social welfare agency. Organized women in the churches of the nation gained managerial experience, which was put to work to accomplish the goals of mission and service. There was a clear relationship between humanitarian and benevolent societies and the religious spirit throughout the nineteenth century. This partnership between the civic (secular) and the religious is most apparent in the Progressive era; social reformers like Jane Addams, Julia Lathrop, Florence Kelley, Vida Scudder, Ellen Gates Starr, and Mary Kingsbury Simkhovitch—the last three Episcopalians and members of the Society of the Companions of the Holy Cross, an Episcopal women's order founded in 1884—acknowledged the strong connection between the religious impulse and the humanitarianism of the late nineteenth century and early twentieth. Jane Addams saw the settlement movement as only one manifestation of a broader Christian humanitarianism at work in the world. Mary Simkhovitch, founder in 1902 of Greenwich House in New York City, realized as a young woman that "that inner sense of God's underpinning had something to do with action. Faith and works, outer and inner, subjective and objective," she wrote, "began to meet, not formally, indeed, but as a process, a natural growth" in her life. Ellen Starr reflected the concerns shared by many Companions in her efforts to bring the personal and the social religious values that guided her into a proper balance. Christianity was the basis for her theories of social reform, not defined by a notion of traditional Christian charity but in the context of a new mental perspective that released Christian faith to reinforce "secular justice, mercy and truth."[1]

The social reform of the Progressive era was inspired by Christian idealism, and the churchwomen whose main involvement remained within religious organizations shared with their reform-oriented sisters a conception of womanhood and a social agenda of good works. Thus, religion both informed the humanitarian spirit of the age and was supported by the political culture that emerged at the close of the century as the Christian volunteer and "educated mother" made it possible for the United States to define and then construct the public service sector of the industrial society.[2] The organized churchwomen systematized the Protestant benevolent impulse and supported the first modern urban agencies of social service. Women had brought an ethical and moral dimension to the political system when they had ventured beyond the domestic sphere to influence public policy in the late nineteenth and early twentieth centuries.[3] This was particularly visible in urban settings such as Chicago and New York. Religious values were integral to the political culture of the time. Habits of benevolence and stewardship were part of the behavior of middle- and upper-middle-class women whether they worked in religious or secular associations.

Throughout the nineteenth century, then, women's willingness to act as "permanent" volunteers made it possible for the ruling men to work in their sphere and have the knowledge that the agencies of social service and social control necessary for social order would be maintained by a staff of unpaid, dedicated workers. Upper-class women began with a belief in Christian stewardship. Progressive reformer Louise deKoven Bowen, treasurer of Hull-House and a leader in the reform of the court system in Chicago, was a lifelong member of St. James Episcopal Church and had been brought up "with the idea that some day [she] would inherit a fortune." She was taught that "the responsibility of money was great and that God would hold [her] accountable for the manner in which [she] used [her] talents." Bowen's volunteerism in church-related and secular settlement work was an extension of her understanding of the Christian use of wealth, and it formed the basis of her religious calling when she taught Sunday school classes and established a club for boys in the neighborhood of St. James parish. As the daughter of a wealthy banker (and the wife of a wealthier one) Bowen's volunteerism fit into the social style of the urban elite in late-nineteenth-century American cities. She was a prominent member of Chicago's ruling elite, and her counterpart could be found in new and old cities across the country.[4]

Women's religious calling was, however, impeded and inhibited by churches run by the patriarchy and based on interpretations of ministry that empowered men and made women subordinate. Thus, pious and devoted women fought for a foothold in "ministry" and were told they could participate only in a calling that was subordinate to the male clergy. As in society as a whole, women who wished to find careers in religious or church work became underpaid, dedicated laborers in the mission and social service fields. Louise Bowen's interests went well beyond the confines of parish life. She was valorized for her civic and political acumen but sought the close-knit involvement of church activities and hoped to bring her talents to St. James. Although she had achieved considerable standing in municipal and national affairs, the rector of St. James pointed this powerhouse in the direction of women's activities long after she was ready for a more central role. She found his lack of imagination regarding her usefulness unsettling and ignored the invitation to assume such a limited and traditional role, while still writing substantial checks to the vestry whenever such donations were needed. In both the growth of the U.S. economy and in the scaffolding of an enormous religious bureaucracy, woman's work—volunteered and inadequately paid—strengthened the male-dominated systems. Except for a minority voice, social reformers and churchwomen alike accepted the limitations of woman's work and calling. The basic power structure and division of labor was not called into question.

These unpaid municipal housekeepers did begin to demand that government accept its responsibility in providing public services that could not be accommodated by the charitable and reform impulses of individuals. Women's demands—for regulation of workplace and home environments, for preventive medicine and a public health policy, for labor laws, for reform of the penal system and creation of a juvenile court— were the result of an understanding that private means were inadequate to meet the needs of an urban industrial society. And the rationale for a great deal of the legislation and reform was the protection of women and children—the weaker and dependent in society—not the perceived equality of men and women.

The merging of religious humanitarianism and practical support of labor causes, for example, was dramatically seen in the experiences of Mary Simkhovitch, Vida Scudder, and Ellen Starr. As young college graduates they had gravitated to settlement houses, where concern for working-class women and female factory workers' protection emerged as major pieces of a new social agenda. Mary Simkhovitch joined fellow Companion Helena Dudley, a member of the first class at Bryn Mawr College and head of Denison House (Boston), in visits to the Social Gospel Reverend W. D. P. Bliss's Church of the Carpenter. There on Sunday evenings the Brotherhood of the Carpenter met for supper and discussion of practical labor problems of the day. The Knights of Labor held meetings of their local federal union at Denison House, which became the center for meeting unemployment crises and for focusing local interest in economic matters. Later the Companions of the Society of the Holy Cross supported the (Episcopal) Church Association for the Advancement of Interests of Labor (CAIL). The Companions' interest in working girls began in the late 1880s and emphasized the reconciliation of classes. Emily Malbone Morgan, leader of the Companions, wrote, "There is a huge and perfectly legitimate field for us to expend our energies and enthusiasms upon. First, in the establishment through our influence of proper state laws as regards child labor. . . . Second, in working slowly but persistently toward better industrial conditions for women."[5]

Even the emergence of a scientific professionalism did not disturb the worldview held by women reformers like Florence Kelley, Jane Addams, Julia Lathrop, Grace Abbott, and all the women associated with their causes. Kelley and her like motivated coalitions of middle-class and working women on the basis of their collective moral outrage about conditions of women and children in factories. The shared understanding of what was "right" and "wrong" came out of the larger and more generalized religious perspective of the American *Zeitgeist* before World War I.[6]

As women became educated about the world beyond the separate sphere, they quite naturally began to prepare for careers in fields of service: medicine, law, public health, social work. It is significant that the membership of the Companions of the Society of the Holy Cross is a veritable roster of women prominent in the field of social work. Patricia Hill's study of women's missionary work points out that at the denominational level women leaders began to imitate men. She writes, "In the larger societies, the officers . . . did work that was not so very different from that done by their male colleagues."[7] Hill says that "[w]ithout quite realizing what was happening, they entered a male professional world." In the Diocese of Chicago, the Woman's Auxiliary leadership by 1911 was proud of its methods of work, which were "becoming more businesslike, more modern, more progressive, with larger grasp and clearer vision." The leaders believed that the results of twenty-six years legitimized the entrance of women into the larger affairs of diocesan social outreach. "Now we find our women attending Parish classes in Sociological subjects, these classes going hand in hand with mission study classes. We want to learn the best ways of working out the Gospel in terms of social service," they wrote, "as well as purely missionary methods. We find this readjustment of method going on in all our progressive branches."[8]

But women did not reevaluate the conceptions about womanhood that they held simultaneously, although there was a gradual shift in tone and policy.[9] Women were no longer asserting themselves solely because of a notion of innate moral superiority; they were lobbying for legislation, entering the political arena, and developing institutional bureaucracies on the basis of their education in these special fields. Many women volunteers were self-educated, and the model of "educated motherhood" became the foundation for women's authority in the Progressive era.[10]

In the nineteenth century, women's demands for more control over women's missionary societies and women's quest for legitimate ways to express a religious call did not conflict with patriarchal institutions but enhanced them. The women in the Diocese of Chicago accepted the patriarchal system and their subordinate place in it. The patriarchal organization of work, which was the foundation of the American capitalist system, continued to channel women in two basic directions: working-class women as a whole continued to inhabit the world of domestic work and low-paying jobs; educated women were funneled into nursing rather than physician careers, classroom teaching rather than educational administration, social casework rather than high-level jobs in the judicial system. And married women in the middle and upper classes were directed toward housework and consumerism, with a segment of their time given to volunteer work.

By the late 1920s the volunteerism of women became detached from the Progressive era's political culture. Women retreated from a reform agenda and accepted a new conception of ideal womanhood, that of the wife-companion. Once more, patriarchal values triumphed and women again fit into the needs of the ruling men and the economic and political system they controlled. The dominance of the private family, the suburban home, and the quest for secure middle-class life placed women subordinate to their husbands and to the male physicians, psychologists, educators, and ministers who had professionalized and taken over areas of service and mission that had once been fields of innovation and influence by women. What is clear is that the changes in society impacted churchwomen and religious institutions also. The erosion of a distinct women's political culture and the retreat into a more private world of family removed a valuable source of female bonding from all women's organizations, including those in churches.[11]

Women's activities in churches underwent very little change through the 1930s to 1950s. In fact, the years of depression and war gave women's volunteerism a boost. In the postwar economic boom the spread of new churches in suburban areas offered opportunities once again for traditional women's volunteerism and reflected the resiliency of the middle-class family with mother at home as the norm, although increased employment of women outside the home was changing social realities.[12] By 1947 female employment had reached wartime levels and was setting new records in the economic boom of the late 1940s and early 1950s.[13] Women were driven back to their lower-paying, less-secure jobs in traditional fields, and most of these women were married. The labor force had changed permanently without a corresponding shift, however, in attitudes toward women. Long before traditional women's organizations fully comprehended what had happened, married women were increasingly fulfilling a new model of wife as helpmate, not pursuing a career but seeking a job to enable families to maintain middle-class expectations. Such a distinction made it possible to ignore the potential outcomes of this serious economic transformation. The complacency of American religious institutions in these decades was a reflection of the general tenor of society.

In the 1960s the new women's movement challenged the support women had implicitly given male-dominated churches. Once again the interdependence of American religious institutions and external social change was clear. Unwilling to accept a separate woman's place or a separate and subordinate conception of ministry, women's demands for equal rights put into jeopardy the continued vitality of religion in the United States. In the last part of the twentieth century feminists call for a complete restructuring of religious institutions, a dismantling of both women's sphere and men's hegemony. Much more is at risk, and traditionalists among men and women feel imperiled.

This chapter looks at the rise and fall of the separate female world of work and calling in the Episcopal Church; and it examines the tensions operating at the parish and diocesan levels. The conflict between traditionalists and modernists in the Episcopal Church in Chicago since the 1960s has been, in many respects, a dispute between those who see women's role as self-sacrificing and altruistic and those who have asked women to put their own interests first. The tensions and strains surrounding this dichotomy can be found in the earliest discussions among auxiliary women as they searched for balance and harmony in their religious lives and church activities and struggled with the image of self-sacrificing womanhood while they attempted to legitimize their new spheres of work. In considering the viability of American Protestantism in today's communities, we need to see if the restructuring of "woman's work" and "woman's calling" has occurred and, if so, what are its consequences for traditional religion.

This chapter explores the way in which women supported and sustained the separate sphere they inhabited. It asks: What did women gain and lose from such subordination and influence? It then takes up the unforeseen changes that occurred as a result of modernization and professionalization within women's separate organizations. It examines the outcomes of such changes not only for women's empowerment (or lack thereof) but in terms of the kind of political, religious, and social values that evolved after the 1920s and asks why patriarchy remained the dominant system in American society. It reflects on how women's innovations are encouraged and then absorbed by the male hegemonic structure.

1880–1920

Nineteenth-century churchwomen's work and its professionalization in such forms as deaconesses, sisterhoods, and female church workers grew out of the conception and social reality of separate spheres.[14] Churchwomen in the Episcopal Diocese of Chicago were able to play an important and expanded role in religion, social service, health care, and education—fields that were considered appropriate extensions of the maternal and moral nature of true womanhood—as long as they accepted subordinate roles and took their direction from male professionals who controlled the churches, missions, hospitals, and schools. The women in Chicago, like their counterparts elsewhere, created a separate structure for woman's work. In this case the woman's structure developed within the boundaries of a diocese that was dominated by a conservative Anglo-Catholic hierarchy.[15]

A core group of middle- and upper-class women—many belonging to families well known in the social and civic life of Chicago—set the tone for woman's work in the Diocese of Chicago in the late nineteenth century. They were the wives and daughters of leading businessmen who, after the Civil War, were involved in the development of industrial and commercial enterprises that eclipsed the more locally based businesses that had characterized the family capitalism of the booster era in Chicago's economic development.[16] The Civil War, which hastened the trend toward a national economy, was a tremendous boon to many manufacturers, bankers, and traders. The new Gilded Age men of business were different from the antebellum boosters, and the city was also a vastly different place. Just as Chicago outdistanced the reach of earlier centers of meat-packing or grain commission—Cinncinati and St. Louis—successful entrepreneurs who came from the smaller and older cities, or were the representatives of large eastern firms desiring western connections, found their way to Chicago, the railroad center of the nation, and the mecca for meat-packing, grain shipping, and wholesale trade. The postwar period was witness to the emergence of large, monopolistic entities in the grain and meat-packing industries. Once transportation and storage facilities as well as meat-processing plants were modernized, consolidated, and specialized, it was possible for ownership to control or dominate the field.

The stakes of business and the material aspects of Chicago life changed radically. "Before the Civil War no mercantile house in Chicago had sales exceeding $600,000; in 1868 seventy-eight firms had a turnover of over a million a year." Marshall Field, starting in 1856, amassed enough to move from clerk to partner by 1860. In 1865 Field started his own store with Levi Leiter and Potter Palmer, all newcomers and upstarts on the scene. By 1866 they were doing $9 million worth of business a year. The firm continued to prosper, and by the time of his death in 1906, Field was one of the wealthiest men in the United States, worth an estimated $120 million.[17]

The post–Civil War millionaires built fashionable homes in the city, and as the managers and directors of the park system, created boulevards and green spaces to enhance the upper-class neighborhoods that were becoming enclaves removed from the industrial and commercial areas as well as from the working-class neighborhoods of an increasingly immigrant population. This same elite obtained the cultural institutions they had come to believe were essential if their city was to achieve its potential greatness commercially and culturally.[18] Relationships among the elite were cemented by clubs such as the Union League, the Iroquois, the Chicago, the Calumet, the Commercial, and for the women, the Woman's Club and the Fortnightly. These clubs did not set the rich apart from the city; they brought their members into webs of relationships that spread the values of the elite, and allowed it a structured way to deal with city life. Rather than having the elite withdraw from the issues of public life, the clubs, though exclusive and proprietary, became the training ground for the upper class. The elite became the arbiter of taste for society as a whole. Collectively, its members shaped the cultural and social space of the city as they were building and controlling the commercial and industrial.

These ruling men not only sat on civic and cultural boards and commissions together, shared private clubrooms and recreation, resided in upper-class enclaves, and dominated the committees of the prestigious Protestant churches they endowed but did business with one another and developed a philosophy of capitalism and corporate life to match the new corporate world they were creating. This philosophy included an approach to the problems of capital and labor, and to questions of immigration, poverty, unemployment, and the social ills stemming from industrialization and urbanization. Fear of the working class, largely immigrant and outside the influence of Protestant churches, mounted in Chicago as labor clashes rocked the city, beginning in the 1870s. From 1873 on, there was more evidence of growing unionism, militancy, and even ideas of anarchy and socialism. A general railroad strike in 1877, the Haymarket riot in 1886, and the Pullman strike of 1894 frightened men of property. Some saw law-and-order methods as the only ones to apply to industrial unrest. Others promoted Americanization programs and patriotism as antidotes for the immigrants' new militancy. There was also a growing understanding among some business leaders that moderate reform measures were required for the survival of American institutions.

The wives of the business elite in postwar Chicago also coalesced into a social group; they joined clubs in the late 1870s and early 1880s, just as their husbands did. But there was a difference. The women adopted courses of study that were rather substantial; classical history, literature, and significantly, new topics, including those of a social and political character, began to provide the foundation for women's self-education and preparation for roles beyond those bounded by earlier notions of a separate sphere. Women who had traditionally confined themselves to voluntary associations and church work now began to expand their scope to include analysis of the social, cultural, and political fabric of the city. These women came from a class of women who by the end of the nineteenth century could begin to contemplate the option of becoming professionals and forgoing marriage and child rearing altogether. By the mid-1880s more young women born in the United States to families of the middle and upper-middle classes were taking advantage of college educations than ever before, but most accepted a model of womanhood that glorified motherhood and domesticity. They had also internalized ideas of altruism and moral feelings. Women were taught that by subordinating themselves to male leadership in church, home, and nation, they were able to best use their influence and inborn talents of nurturing.[19]

Louise deKoven Bowen illustrates this transition. Her mother, a lifelong Episcopalian, had been born within the palisades of the original Fort Dearborn in Chicago. Her grandfather, Edward H. Hadduck, was a government agent who had settled at the fort in 1835. Bowen was the only child of John and Helen Hadduck deKoven. John, a banker, had come to Chicago in 1856. Louise deKoven married Joseph T. Bowen in 1886, and they planned a new home in a neighborhood suitable to their social station. Yet Louise Bowen did not confine herself to the domestic realm; for more than forty years she worked with Jane Addams in Hull-House, most of the time as treasurer and then its president. She was also involved with the Juvenile Protective Agency in Chicago, and was instrumental in reforming the criminal justice system for youthful offenders.[20]

Bowen's sense of social responsibility was acute, reflective of the elite Episcopal social stewardship that was well developed in Chicago by the late 1880s. The Episcopal Church had had a strong relationship to the ruling elite from the earliest days of Yankee settlement. The web of kin and business connections among the Episcopal parishes was substantial, and affiliation with the denomination held the promise of social rank for the new and mobile class of business families establishing themselves.[21] Although the Episcopalians in the city never achieved the numbers or influence of those in New York, Boston, or Philadelphia, the model of an upwardly mobile and influential church characterized Episcopal development in Chicago. Men like Potter Palmer, who came to Chicago from a Quaker background, sought membership in the Episcopal Church soon after business fortunes propelled them into elite circles. Palmer's wife, Bertha Honore Palmer, the undisputed queen of

fin-de-siècle Chicago society and the chairman of the 1893 Columbian
Exposition's Board of Lady Managers, found time to be a member of
fashionable St. James Episcopal Church.[22]

The elite Episcopalians shared a strong sense of social responsibility.
What Episcopalians like William B. Ogden, Joseph T. Ryerson, Walter
L. Newberry, John H. Kinzie, and Isaac N. Arnold were to the life of
antebellum Chicago, such men as Franklin MacVeagh, Nathaniel K.
Fairbank, Edward L. Ryerson, Samuel M. Nickerson, and James Dole
were to the late-nineteenth-century city. Male members of St. James
exemplified the upper-class nature of Episcopal church life in Gilded
Age Chicago: S. M. Nickerson, president of the First National Bank;
B. F. Ayer, general counsel for the Illinois Central; E. T. Watkins,
president of the Chicago Gas Light and Coke Company; S. H. Kerfoot,
real estate magnate; W. K. Nixon, grain commissioner who served as
president of the Chicago Board of Trade; Watson F. Blair, banker;
C. R. Larrabee, treasurer of the Chicago Title Guarantee and Trust
Company; Francis B. Peabody, of Peabody, Houghteling and Company;
George Payson, treasurer of the Western Railroad Association, to mention only a few.[23]

The wives of these men were the leadership of the Woman's Auxiliary
in the Diocese of Chicago. The sense of social responsibility they shared
was expressed by Louise Bowen:

> "I was brought up with the idea that some day I would inherit a fortune,
> and I was always taught that the responsibility of money was great, and
> that God would hold me accountable for the manner in which I used my
> talents. I was, therefore, most eager to learn how to spend what I had in
> a proper way."[24]

At sixteen she began teaching in the parish Sunday school. When she
found that the young men in her classes had little opportunity for recreation, she invited them to her house three times a week to play bil-
liards. Realizing rather quickly that her billiard room "was unequal to
the task of accommodating the young men," she rented a clubhouse for
them, which she described as "the first boy's club in Chicago." Later
she had built a large club for boys at Hull-House, fitted with shops,
games, and poolrooms.[25]

In a similar manner she and Eleanor Ryerson, another young woman
from a socially prominent family, began a program at St. James to teach
little girls domestic arts. The Kitchen Garden Association was one of
the many experiments made by a private organization—a church—that,

having proved effective, was incorporated as a part of city activities. Bowen wrote:

> I heard of the Kitchen Garden Association—of its great usefulness—and we determined to start one in Chicago in connection with the church. We were given the chapel for our labors, and every Saturday we had about one hundred little girls to whom we taught domestic work. The Kitchen Garden consisted of an equipment of little beds about large enough for a big doll. These were fitted up with sheets, pillows, blankets, etc.[26]

The idea of the Kitchen Garden was to teach immigrant and working-class children how to do housework, presumably because their own homes were lacking in appropriate "models." Enmeshed in this project were Bowen's class, religious, and ethnic biases regarding the nature of immigrant and working-class culture in the city. She reflected a combination of charitable impulse, Christian social responsibility, and ignorance about the dimensions of the problems of poverty and social dislocation that beset families in the crowded tenements. Yet it was a beginning of her personal education and growing self-consciousness about urban life. Soon she understood that the homes of the children did not come with perfect beds and complete equipment, and that the problems of socialization and Americanization could not be met by small programs initiated in local churches. She successfully advocated introducing domestic arts education into the public schools.

Louise Bowen became one of the leading Progressive social reformers and fought for the vote for women. Yet she retained many of the characteristics of an elitism informed by values of a religiously inspired social responsibility. Her writings assume church membership and Christian stewardship as a natural aspect of upper-class life. She followed the model of her family in generously giving money and time to church activities. Nor did she see any inherent contradiction in using her influence as a member of the elite toward reforming institutions to enable their adaptation to new conditions. She lived for over thirty-two years on Astor Street, in the heart of the wealthiest section of Chicago, and took pride in utilizing the setting to advance her causes. Her house was the site of all kinds of meetings, from sessions on suffrage to neighborhood gatherings, "where we made appeals for the betterment of conditions in the ward." Her strategy was simple: "We have had many dinners where some scheme of benefit to the city or county has been hatched out behind closed doors. *The meetings have been held here in order not to have anyone know about them*" (italics added).[27]

She remembered when her friend Alexander A. McCormick was made president of the Cook County Board. He told her that he was anxious to appoint "good people as heads of the various county departments," and that "if we could suggest good people he would appoint them." Bowen called together about twenty-five people—heads of settlements, men interested in civic affairs, social workers, and the like—"and we sat all one evening trying to think of good men and women for the various county positions." This kind of informal power brokering suited the style of women of influence, and Bowen personified the connection between elitism and social service. There were other such meetings on, say, education, "where matters were coming up on the School Board which demanded immediate action by citizens." Bowen confided that some of the plans "formed at these dinners or meetings were sprung at large meetings held later and [she] . . . heard people say that they wondered where the plan originated but no one ever gave it away."[28]

She concluded that "when a group of representative citizens come together and use their influence for the making of public opinion, it [is] . . . not so difficult to swing a new project or a reform. . . ."[29] Such a philosophy was extremely applicable to the way in which women were taught to use their influence, even when they did not have the vote. Many elite women in the late nineteenth century thought it preferable to a more aggressive confrontation with the power brokers in society. Because they could exercise a more subtle "power" through social influence, they tended to avoid other kinds of organization and protest. The Woman's Auxiliary leaders stressed their "womanly influence" in their relations with the male-dominated clerical and lay hierarchy of the church, as well as in their interactions with male civic and political seats of power.

Louise Bowen's activities made her unique among elite women, yet even she relied much more heavily on social status and associations than did the more militant women of the Progressive era. The leadership of the Woman's Auxiliary in the Diocese of Chicago lagged far behind the social reformers who were freely speaking out from separatist organizations. Yet the auxiliary members could be brought into the reform movement as an important constituency. Their sense of Christian stewardship and their shared outlook of social responsibility made them receptive to the reforms enunciated by others who were more independent. Few of these newly active matrons questioned the cultural presumptions of women's innate piety, purity, and domesticity. "They moved into America's corrupt and unjust cities not as self-conscious feminists but as 'True Women.' They were, they told husbands, politicians, and industrialists, the conscience and housekeepers of America."[30]

An examination of the cadre of auxiliary leaders provides the beginnings of an explanation for the lack of an independent voice. The manner in which the Chicago branch of the Woman's Auxiliary was organized underscores the domination of bishop and clergy. On October 2, 1884, forty-one parishes were represented at a great gathering in Grace Church, Chicago, called by the bishop of the diocese and presided over by him. Addresses were made by the bishop, the wife of the rector at St. James Church, and a representative of the national organization. The entire first executive board was appointed by the bishop; the rector's wife became president, a position she held until her death in 1887.[31]

Four clergy wives served substantial terms as president of the diocesan branch of the Woman's Auxiliary during the organization's pioneering years. In fact, during the first thirty-one years clergy wives held the office for a total of twenty-one years. The constitution and bylaws of the Woman's Auxiliary made it clear that the bishop had the last word. The constitution could be altered or amended at the annual meeting by a vote of two-thirds of the members present, subject to the approval of the bishop. The president had general charge of the work, under the direction of the bishop. The close relationship of the bishop and auxiliary officers in setting the agenda continued well into the twentieth century.[32]

Diocesan Woman's Auxiliary leaders were comfortable with the bishop as a guide and mentor. The "President's Address" in one annual report emphasized the importance of obedience and loyalty: "Woman's best work is that of influence. The individual must be in the right relationship to her home, to her parish and to her Diocese, then we may look for right and sure results. One discontented, irritable member sets ajar the most perfect plans." Accepting of separate spheres for men and women, the president counseled for peace and harmony in the home, in the parish, in the diocese. Implicit was the woman's conformity to her husband, her priest, her bishop. When each individual fulfilled his and her distinct role, then bishops and clergy could fulfill the great command, "Go ye into the world and preach the Gospel to every creature."[33]

The combination of the concept of women's superior morality and Anglo-Catholic piety endowed ordinary hands-on "woman's work" activities with overt religious symbolism. Auxiliary meetings always began with prayer, and in the parishes women joined guilds—St. Agatha, Dorcas, St. Margaret's, St. Agnes, St. Ann's, St. Monica's—for prayer and good works. Prayer meetings and quiet days were observed with great regularity, and Episcopal women attended church more frequently than communicants of other Protestant denominations, placing greater emphasis on celebration of the eucharist. The increase in parishes accepting more elaborate Anglo-Catholic liturgy and ritual provided an environment dominated by a Christ-Mary typology. Many churches in the late nineteenth and early twentieth centuries added either separate side or Lady chapels clearly focused on Mary or provided alcoves with Marian statuary and candles.

The close relationship of the auxiliary with deaconesses and sisters (the Community of St. Mary) enhanced the religious quality and sentiment of organizational meetings. The Diocese of Chicago's Anglo-Catholicism made it a hospitable place for the work of these religious women. From the mid-nineteenth century onward Anglican women in England and in the Episcopal Church in the United States participated, often in leadership positions, in the revival of religious orders. By the 1880s the Community of St. Mary, formed in New York City in 1865, had sent sisters to dioceses in the South and the Midwest, where bishops and clergy had a more Anglo-Catholic orientation. The Diocese of Chicago—as a result of its growing Anglo-Catholic orientation—was exceptional in its openness to the Community of St. Mary, underscoring the Anglo-Catholic beliefs of the diocesan hierarchy.[34]

The clergy regularly attended monthly auxiliary meetings, often providing the lecture of the day. The organization was separate, but the Anglo-Catholic spirit with its omnipresent male-sacramental imagery of power and female imagery of subordinate, self-effacing service permeated an otherwise female-run enterprise. The undeniable bond between clergy and women must be appreciated when analyzing the nature of female leadership in this diocese. The bonding was a product of the strong sacramental and sacerdotal conception of the male ministry that dominated the thinking of laity and clergy. Women's loyalty to priests and bishops would create intense conflict and anguish in regard to women's ordination in the 1970s.[35]

Woman's work in Chicago in the 1880s was influenced by several new trends in both religion and social thinking. The first was the movement in the Episcopal Church to develop national agendas for church work, both at home and abroad. The General Convention's structuring of the Woman's Auxiliary to the Board of Missions was energized by the efforts of two sisters, Mary Abbot Twing and Julia Emery, who had brought about a great change in women's position in the Episcopal Church. They took the message of woman's work to dioceses throughout the country.

Frequent visits to Chicago meant that the diocesan Woman's Auxiliary leadership was intimately in touch with a national leadership group.[36]

Similarly, the diocesan presidents of the Chicago branch visited parishes regularly and initiated new branches. One president remembered many visits to out-of-town parishes, "where they had never so much as heard whether there be a Woman's Auxiliary." She added the presidents had "their trials with objecting and indifferent clergy," but they found out who the missionary women were, and learned to whom they might turn for support and counsel.[37]

Day and evening meetings were held monthly, often assembling upward of 150 to 200 women.[38] Missionary priests and women church workers gave talks to stimulate interest and educate local women about domestic and foreign activities. Letters were exchanged between the New York office and local auxiliary officers, setting an agenda for giving. The organizational push broadened the network of women and brought to the parish level information and concern about church life that strengthened women's missionary commitments. Increases in the United Thank Offering and in support of missionary activities in the first forty years of the Woman's Auxiliary demonstrated its success.[39]

A remarkable feature of this period of organization building for the Woman's Auxiliary was the concurrent expansion of women's groups on the parish level. Each parish had a varied assortment of guilds, societies, and often, a branch of the auxiliary. Young women participated in a junior auxiliary. Membership of the various groups was small, and there was room for different women to assume leadership roles. Rather than thwarting women's work, this arrangement seemed to contribute to more woman's finding the right niche for themselves.

Within the world of woman's work there were three major goals: prayer, study, and mission (action). Prayer connected women to the paternalistic scheme of a male-dominated religion and enhanced feelings of loyalty and obedience to the institutional church. Study met women's intellectual needs. Women attended regular lectures on the missionary fields delivered either by guest speakers (often missionaries back from their posts) or auxiliary members themselves. No meeting was complete without a time for prayer and a time for instruction on some aspect of the work of the church. Often when women gathered to do work, for example, to sew or prepare food, one of the group would read while the others did their particular chores.

Study brought to the auxiliaries a world of ideas and an awareness of the needs of people other than themselves. Women were frequently admonished by their own leaders to have a mental map of the world on which to locate where missionaries were stationed. They were told to visualize missionary work in order to be more motivated to support it. Mission, the third goal, was the natural outcome of prayer and study.

Characteristic of this generation was that all women involved in church work participated in a very direct way: famine in Africa, floods in Central America, a fire in a church school in South Dakota—all occasioned immediate and direct action. Supply boxes were filled with clothing, food, and other necessities. Money was also collected, but the sense of personal involvement that came from sewing for children in a missionary school on an Indian reservation was immeasurable. Small and large projects were measured in daily deeds done by hand. Women did not wait for crises, however. Auxiliary groups and guilds took on support of the mundane as well as the exotic. The ideal was daily prayer, daily study, and daily good works—a litany for many devoted churchwomen.

Clergy saw the great potential of women, and carefully guided them to work the clergy deemed appropriate. In the context of the dominant ideology—that woman's work was to be an extension of their maternal and subordinate nature—women were prohibited from lay leadership or ministry in the major Protestant churches.[40] Yet women went beyond the gender-specific boundaries the culture imposed. The organizational strength developed by women's religious actions—the results of prayer, study, and mission—in an unexpected way eventually pushed women out of domesticity into public life. The rise of the deaconess movement is an example of the relationship of women's inward piety and worldly pragmatism. The search for ways to serve God through charity and sacrifice propelled women to demand a more public role in the church.

The tension between femininity and feminism surfaced in the disjunction between the clergy's traditional conceptualization of the role of women and the ideas of female vocation expressed through the rebirth of the order of deaconesses and the reemergence of sisterhoods in the nineteenth century.[41] The debate in the Episcopal Church over the theological and social meaning of deaconesses and sisters found both sides accepting the cultural formulation of separate spheres but arriving at different models of behavior and different understandings of gender roles. Let us examine the deaconesses first. "By establishing the deaconess as a recognized profession for women in the Church," Mary Donovan tells us, the male leaders "imagined they could direct women's natural nurturing tendencies into work that would enhance the Church's ministry." The clergy saw the deaconess as a religious extension of the ideal of true womanhood: "a woman who would be pious, pure, submissive, and domestic, who would simply substitute obedience to the priest or bishop for obedience to a husband." But the deaconess, unlike the deacon, had no liturgical functions.[42]

Deaconesses and sisterhoods were fundamentally different. The former did not take lifelong religious vows and were viewed as another kind of women church workers. Their purpose, according to the church fathers, was limited to performing services to the church community as nurses, social workers, and visitors to inmates in hospitals, prisons, and other institutions. They functioned under the supervision and direction of diocesan bishops and were not required to live in communities with other deaconesses. They were unmarried women who could, because of a life change, leave the order; in fact, most churchmen conceived of deaconesses as relatively impermanent church workers. Members of the church hierarchy viewed the motivation of the deaconess as like that of the social worker or nurse. Those who favored deaconesses were far more likely to accept the prevailing role definition of women and to regard them as in need of men's control and direction.[43]

Deaconesses, too, believed that their profession was the religious extension of ideal womanhood, giving a public voice to their higher moral sensibility. Still, in their minds and hearts they had taken vows of lifelong service that excluded marriage. Not only were they professional church workers, educated in Scripture and theology as well as housekeeping and nursing, but they *acted* as persons with a religious vocation. Trained (generally by other deaconesses) to be capable professionals, they chose, when possible, to live in deaconess houses and to observe daily devotional schedules designed to enhance personal piety and Christian discipline. They wore nunlike habits and believed that the ceremony that "set them apart" was their ordination rite.[44]

The Episcopal Church's ambivalence about deaconesses derived from an inherently contradictory, gender-based position on ministry. The Canon on Deaconesses in 1889 included the provision that a "deaconess may at any time resign her office," presumably in order to marry. Because most deaconesses believed they were ordained ministers who had made lifelong vows, the provision was generally seen as confusing or downright offensive. What did "laying on of hands" mean when deaconesses were set apart by bishops? The deaconesses asked for clarification time and time again as they stood at the threshold of an authentic ministry but were unable to take the step across.

The ill-defined status of deaconesses was particularly poignant in a diocese such as Chicago. Here the contradictions were dramatic: an Anglo-Catholic diocese that stressed religious vocation and devotional practices to an extreme was inhospitable to the deepest strivings of these women because of the deep fear among clergy and bishops of a feminine "invasion" of the priesthood. Anxiety about women's ordination was also shared by many women who were unable to accept the concept of a female priest.[45]

The issue of femininity and feminism was even more dramatic in the development of sisterhoods. There was, among many men and women, strong opposition to sisterhoods because their communities conjured fears of the Romanizing tendencies flourishing in Anglo-Catholic parishes where the influence of the Oxford Movement and Romanticism had taken root.[46] Resistance to such ideas and ritual innovations made it difficult for the first sisterhood in the United States to give full expression to the ideal of a religious community for women. Aware of the Episcopal Church's hostility to monastic orders for women, Anne Ayres and the Reverend William Augustus Muhlenberg—founders in 1852 of the first sisterhood—proceeded very slowly with organization of the Community of the Holy Communion in New York City. They emphasized that the community was devoted to charity but took no lifetime vows. As Mary Donovan describes them, "Community life revolved not around a schedule of religious devotions but around the sisters' charitable acts and services."[47]

With the founding in 1865 of the Community of the St. Mary—begun by members of the Community of the Holy Communion dissatisfied with its devotional limitations—sisterhoods distinguished themselves from the deaconess movement. Under lifetime vows, the sisters of the Community of St. Mary lived in autonomous communities. They created a more intense devotional routine and withdrew to a more ordered religious life, with worship services scheduled throughout the day. (Although the bylaws expressly stated that irrevocable vows were not required, the sisters made such professions privately to a confessor.) Donovan assesses the work of the sisterhoods as essentially a groundbreaking role, opening up new occupational possibilities.

> As pioneer women professionals, the nuns were generalists—specialists would follow later—but they proved that women could manage large institutions, supervise employees, and develop educational and rehabilitative programs. At the same time, however, their tendency toward self-effacement, their threefold vows of poverty, chastity, and obedience, and their dedication to service tended to obscure their accomplishments, so that they did not serve as role models for a secular generation of women.[48]

The evolution of woman's work in local churches also tells the story of female striving for a more public role in religion. By the 1850s in

Chicago—and prior to the volunteer work undertaken by woman during the Civil War—there was a strong outreach to the needy by Episcopal ladies' parish aid societies, and the clergy generally supported these efforts. Forms of social Christianity were practiced long before the Social Gospel movement. The leaders of the Woman's Auxiliary in the 1880s were women who already had enriched parish life through their involvement in local charitable and educational projects. Women at St. James, Grace, and Trinity—Chicago's three oldest Episcopal parishes—had pioneered mission Sunday school classes, mothers' meetings, infant crèche schools, and sewing and industrial classes, and had distributed aid to the sick and indigent.[49]

Only a small number of urban women, however, had the freedom and education to search for meaning and calling in the volunteer work that they did for the church. The vast majority of working-class women were the objects of the middle- and upper-middle-class women's ministrations. Educational initiatives and day-care centers were designed to bring middle-class values to the working class and immigrants of the cities.[50]

For the women at the top of the diocesan auxiliary's organizational pyramid, women's separatism did not appear to bring about independence. But they profited from their privileged status relative to other women both inside and outside the church community. Valued as exemplary and devoted Christians, they had the attention and confidence of the male hierarchy. The women leaders regularly helped pay for the bishop's urban programs but never used money as a way to challenge the status quo. They derived an enormous sense of personal and group accomplishment from such subsidies; indeed, they felt privileged to make the programs possible. More than this, they were told that they *were* doing the Lord's work. It was a heady relationship for faithful and devoted women.

Acknowledging women's achievements, including those that were innovative and progressive, still does not address issues of power and authority. The degree of woman's influence and empowerment is difficult to measure. Between 1890 and 1920, however, the initiatives taken by women leaders to establish the urban agenda of the Episcopal Church in Chicago meshed very well with the goals of the male hierarchy. It is a subtle question whether or not women were really in the driver's seat or whether they were able to carry out this agenda because men found it appropriate and useful.

Like Jane Addams, the church women were schooled in ethical and religious values and knew enough about the world and its problems to worry about living a life that was productive and socially responsible. The women who composed the leadership of the Woman's Auxiliary did not follow Addams and other social reformers of the Progressive era into the settlement houses of Chicago's slums, but they supported the embyronic social, educational, and charitable agencies of the church. They were enthusiastic about child care for working mothers, for example, and applauded women's new professional roles in social work and nursing. They were the main financial backers of the Episcopal sisters and deaconesses who ran the orphanages and day nurseries, and ministered to the poor in the public county hospitals and penal institutions.[51]

The deaconesses and the sisters were the link between the middle- and upper-class women and the poor women in the city; the former regularly reported on their work in the city to auxiliary members, and the latter raised money to continue the work.[52] In 1888 the Community of St. Mary—called to Chicago the year before by the diocesan bishop—established a branch of its order. It was welcomed by such leading socialites and clubwomen as Mrs. Nathaniel K. Fairbank, Mrs. Corning Judd, and Mrs. George H. Wheeler, who soon organized a group of laywomen joined "in strong and spiritual bonds to assist the sisters by alms and prayers."[53] By 1925 the group, the St. Frances Guild, had two hundred associates including Lydia Hibbard and Mrs. Wheeler who made substantial contributors to St. Mary's Mission House.

The elite women were impressed that many of the sisters were wealthy, educated women who had followed literally the injunction to give all their possessions to the poor while they served the faith they had chosen. The example was so powerfully presented that the associates volunteered at the mothers' meetings held for the neighborhood women who used the social services and outreach provided by the Companions of St. Mary in buildings adjacent to the Episcopal Cathedral of Saints Peter and Paul on the impoverished West Side.[54] Ellen Gates Starr, one of the cathedral communicants and a resident of Hull House, addressed the working-class women and the upper-class associates at a mothers' meeting in 1912; her text the "Shrines of St. Francis Assisi and the Franciscan tradition."[55] The elite women, then, were witnesses to the Franciscan tradition in its modern configuration through the examples of the sisters. The glow from the reflected spirituality clearly warmed them and privileged them to engage in an idealism beyond their own social world. The sisters and social reformers like Starr graciously accepted their support and participation.

The mothers' meetings were very much in keeping with the settlement

house approach. The working-class and poor women in the neighborhood brought their babies to the meetings; the sisters and elite women
cared for the infants while the working women engaged in sewing and
other activities. Instruction regarding health and home matters was part
of the discussions planned by the sisters as a way of influencing the
women. The neighborhood women were encouraged to help with the
home duties of needy neighbors, to visit the neighborhood sick, and to
pass along what they were learning. This was community building in a
Christian context. Although the sisters did not require church membership, they clearly emphasized a worldview that was Christian and
middle class. They also trained young girls in all household duties, taking
them for that purpose into their own mission house, again with a view
toward moral as well as practical education. Children in the orphanage
run by the sisters were encouraged to attend the local public schools;
to remove the stigma of orphan status, the sisters and the guild associates
saw to it that each child had individualized clothing that did not resemble
institutional garb.

The Mission House, then, functioned as a settlement house in the
neighborhood; the guild meetings, boys' and girls' clubs, and mothers'
meetings were held in the noninstitutional environment of the sisters'
residence. The belief and hope were that the interactions there would
help bring into being the harmonious relations sorely needed. Park
outings and recreational days were scheduled throughout the year. And
in the summer the children of St. Mary's Home were taken to the sisters'
summer house in Wisconsin.

St. Mary's Mission House included a dispensary, physician's office,
and space for children on the first floor. The second floor provided a
reception room, space for assembly and worship, and classrooms. The
sisters' quarters were on the third floor. The sisters began a kindergarten
and a day nursery, ministered to the sick, and helped the poor in many
ways. They also established a refuge for girls who had taken "their first
downward step." Within a decade permanent child-care facilities for
orphans, half-orphans, and the children of working mothers had been
established by the diocese, and were being run by the Companions of
St. Mary and paid for by members of the Woman's Auxiliary and other
women's guilds.[56]

The Companions of St. Mary functioned more independently than
did deaconesses. Sister Frances controlled the life of the Mission House
and was completely in charge of the direction and placement of the
sisters in her charge. The rules of the order were those imposed by the
Community of St. Mary and had developed from the sisterhood's hi-

erarchy rather than from the male-dominated church organization. The order had its own network of training for work in the world, as well as for the contemplative life that provided an interior space that gave a great degree of spiritual autonomy to the women. In Chicago its activities were legally separate from those of the diocese, and in 1890 the sister-hood was incorporated in Illinois as a not-for-profit corporation known as St. Mary's Mission Society. Thus, the order held title to property, real and personal, and received gifts, donations, and legacies. St. Mary's Home for Children and Free Dispensary for the Poor was chartered under the laws of Illinois in 1901.[57] But the sisters could not have survived in Chicago without the help of elite women who completed the circle of sisterhood.

In Chicago the outreach work to the immigrants and the poor within the city limits could not have been accomplished without the financial backing of the Woman's Auxiliary and other women's guilds, such as the St. Frances Guild associated with the Companions of St. Mary. At one point, for example, the Woman's Auxiliary was supporting almost completely the salaries of three deaconesses who assisted in city missions working among the poor in hospitals and prisons. The deaconesses were aided also by the Companions of St. Mary. In fact, it was the Woman's Auxiliary that provided funds for an organized approach to city mis-sionary work beginning in 1892; theretofore nothing systematic had been done to provide services for Episcopalians in hospitals, prisons, and other public places. Again and again the bishops in Chicago came to the Woman's Auxiliary for monies to maintain these services. When the St. Mary's Home for Children had outgrown its facilities, one of the members of the auxiliary sold her jewels valued at $8,000 for the new building fund. Women's fund-raising was an essential ingredient in this work, but it was also the self-sacrificing activities of sisters and deacon-esses, often underpaid and inadequately supported, that made such endeavors possible.[58] Churchwomen, sisters, deaconesses, and reli-giously inspired social reformers formed a powerful alliance that was crucial for the Episcopal Church's outreach in Chicago during the late nineteenth and early twentieth centuries.

The religious motivation for social work—the pursuit of social holi-ness, as Ellen Gates Starr characterized it—was open to innovation from the secular field. Efforts to bring more professional approaches to social problems were inaugurated after 1905, when a new diocesan bishop and his cathedral staff embraced the Social Gospel agenda.[59] Between 1905 and 1920 churchwomen were drawn into the political culture of the Progressive era as a result of their involvement with working-class women and children. Kindergartens, day care and infant schools, mothers' meetings, and the like were all part of the reform agenda. Kathryn Kish Sklar has pointed out the importance of religion and moral traditions as underpinnings of the political culture of Progressive women reformers before 1920.[60]

The concern for social justice of the churchwomen in the Diocese of Chicago had a religious basis. When auxiliary members set up the Providence Day Nursery—patterned on a program pioneered by Presbyterian women in Chicago—they did so from the moral authority of their religious convictions. They had been taught that they had a Christian duty to feed the poor and spread the gospel to the unconverted, and had come to believe that they could construct institutions and programs to make the world better. The cadre of professional social workers and the leadership of churchwomen had, by the first decade of the twentieth century, brought Progressive programs and political legislation to the attention of the Woman's Auxiliary.

Following the General Convention's request that diocesan social service committees be organized, the Diocesan Convention in Chicago appointed a Committee on Christian Social Service in 1908. It was clear from the reports to the convention the next year that a substantial part of the Social Gospel message had filtered down to the local level.[61] The City Mission staff in the 1890s had the limited goal of evangelizing and serving the inmates and patients of penal, charitable, and medical institutions; by 1910 the staff was serving as the nucleus of a broader connection with civic, social, philanthropic, and educational institutions. The cathedral church and the diocesan institutions were still the center of mission outreach, but now the work included Christian social settlement work, day nursery and kindergarten classes, and work with parents and young women and men in the neighborhood. The servicing of individuals in penal and charitable institutions was still carried on, but the focusing of services to the community and neighborhood manifested the change in orientation. Chase House, the church's social settlement, reflected the community orientation; it was the first neighborhood social center of the church to have no connection with a particular parish.[62]

Churchwomen were encouraged to unite with political groups to secure passage of legislation for a Saturday half-holiday for the employees of Chicago retail stores, and to work to obtain fair wages and hours for labor. Articles in the house organ of the church, *The Diocese of Chicago,* called for an end to sweatshops and child labor. "Children do not become criminals and degenerates from choice," the editor argued, "but because they can not help themselves." The message was brought to parishes through the social service committees appointed by local rectors—always two women and three men—with the rector as ex-officio chairman. There were thirty-six parochial social service committees by 1914.[63]

The influence of the national church was apparent in the coordinated effort, but it was local women's guilds and societies that had carried out neighborhood programs in parish houses from the 1880s. When the national council of the Episcopal Church set its social service agenda, the Woman's Auxiliary members were ready to merge their programs with that of the church, which, after all, was what the women had been doing. Prayer, study, and mission (action) had paved the way for the articulation of pragmatic social programs and reform legislation by auxiliary members.

How much the new work competed with the more traditional missionary-related projects needs to be considered. Immediately apparent was the new competition among women with different plans and different definitions of what constituted woman's work and calling. The introduction of the social service agenda also meant that volunteers and professional workers rubbed shoulders more frequently. The interactions threatened the privileged position of the volunteer and restricted her area of expertise and control. The pattern was becoming a typical one in American society. Women's activities often produced innovative programs and raised the consciousness of the public. Before long the process of professionalization occurred, and areas once the domain almost entirely of women were "mainstreamed" into the masculine system and men gained control. It is not surprising that our image of the Social Gospel movement is dominated by the male leadership—the preachers in major urban centers. The women who were responsible for the earliest "institutional" uses of Protestant churches in cities—parish houses that were really proto-settlement houses—are unknown.

Part of the problem was related to the image women volunteers in church work had of themselves. Auxiliary leaders in Chicago believed that women's silent, invisible grace created the atmosphere in which women could do their best work. *Best work* was defined by women as influence, persuasion, and control. One president of the Woman's Auxiliary admonished members to go "about their Father's business" by promoting the missionary activities of the church under the direction of the clergy.[64] For this generation the quintessential model for woman's work was the Sisters of St. Mary. "So quietly, unobtrusively do they move in and out of the Mission House . . . that one must be often there and really a part of the work to realize its worth and its growth." Sister Frances seemed clothed in humility, obedience, and activity. "If we believe in our bishops, our clergy, and that is why we are here today, why we are the Woman's Auxiliary, each baptized person must ask herself, How can I help?"[65]

The well-intentioned auxiliary women looked to the church hierarchy for their authority. The moral agenda for social change under the banner of the Social Gospel provided the common ground for Episcopal women and the male hierarchy. It made possible a conjoining in support of legislation for children and women, for example, that cut across gender and class divisions. Deaconesses, sisters, priests, auxiliary members, and working-class mothers who brought their children to the day nurseries and sewing classes could align with social reformers. It was an extraordinary coalition that had as an underlying thread a religiously derived conviction about morality and justice for women and children. A reform movement came from the merging of religious sentiment and awakened social conscience within the context of woman's separate sphere. In the process women's organizations were becoming more modern and professional, taking on aspects of the masculine model.

The first changes in women's organizations resulted from maturation and bureaucratization. The leadership infrastructure began to express itself in more bureaucratic terms. Similarly, denominations began to develop national structures with central headquarters and departments to direct church work, including mission and social service, the fields most associated with traditional woman's work. The changes were the product of the larger changes associated with modernizing tendencies.[66] Along with modernization and professionalization, changes in the political culture of both men and women occurred after World War I as Americans pulled away from the reform agenda of the Progressive era.

1921–1960

The retreat from reform in the decades after World War I by a whole range of Americans was paralleled by a loss of direction within women's Protestant organizations. Sklar writes that "after 1920 Florence Kelley and her closest colleagues . . . continued to emphasize moral themes and count on the support of religious institutions." But women's political culture after 1920 had taken on a less-value-laden bureaucratic tone.[67] There is an important connection between the breakdown of the liberal theology that had integrated the sacred and the secular prior to World War I and women's redefinition of their place and their work in American society.

The reordering of women's traditional church work was the result, in part, of the efficiency and competence of women leaders and their new organizational knowledge. The leaders of women's societies quite naturally embraced professional models of behavior as their own organizations developed. They encouraged coordination of the grass-roots efforts and tried to impose methods of systematic giving and an acceptance of common objectives or priorities to bring the small units into line with what were becoming national women's bureaucracies.[68]

A change in the interactions between the rank and file and the leadership came with the new professionalism. Women volunteers at the state and national levels and women active primarily in local churches were growing apart in their approach to church activities. The leaders felt the rift and blamed themselves for many of their new troubles. Harmony was called for, but clear signs of confusion and disharmony persisted. Auxiliary meetings became forums for the discussion of the proper role of women. Some complained that committee work was stressful, and often led to poor feelings about it. Women worried about the proper way to serve the church.[69]

The leadership found it increasingly difficult to deal with local initiative and the proliferation of guilds and societies—some with overlapping membership and agendas. Local women's groups traditionally had made their own decisions about which missions or charities to support. Parish aid societies distributed food, fuel, and clothing to needy neighbors during winter months, and in well-endowed city parishes, elaborate neighborhood outreach programs had developed over the years. The decisions about such endeavors were made on the local level, and the women had considerable influence in church affairs even though they did not sit on the vestry or serve as delegates to the annual diocesan convention. A balance had been achieved at the local level. Originally, the local branches of the Woman's Auxiliary were simply another women's group.

As the auxiliary enlarged its scope and adopted a more comprehensive vision of its work, there were efforts to combine women's work at the local level. Duplication of fund-raising activities competed with the goals of the auxiliary, so its leaders discouraged local gift-giving and cautioned local women not to become too involved with specific missionary projects or individual missionaries. The activist women—the Woman's Auxiliary officers—increased their personal visitations to parishes, began meeting in private homes, and tried to reconcile the conflicting demands on women at the parish level by merging guilds and auxiliaries. In short, the officers wanted local women to give up any work that was outside the auxiliary's programs and agenda priorities.[70]

Women were told by clergy in the Diocese of Chicago that professional social service was becoming too fashionable, too materialistic, and superficial. It was secular activity that could never be a substitute for true religious feeling and personal devotion. This attitude was summed up by the motto of the Cathedral Shelter and Guild Woman's Auxiliary: "This is true greatness: to serve unnoticed and to work unseen."[71] Women were asked to sublimate their personalities and personal achievements; the inadequacy of their gifts and the endless need for more sacrifice and obedience to the cause of mission was stressed.[72] There was, of course, an inherent contradiction here. Volunteers were controlled by the model of self-sacrifice. Meanwhile, social agencies took their direction from the professional trends of the male model. Soon women volunteers were directed to form guilds or auxiliaries to social agencies. They were marginalized to being fund-raisers rather than social innovators.

Changes were occurring regardless of the relatively static role model of the self-sacrificing volunteer presented to women. The national church had begun the reorganization of auxiliary work in 1919, and one of the first responses was from Chicago's bishop, who told the auxiliary women very plainly what their duties and privileges were. He warned against the tendency to overbroaden auxiliary work—women should remain within their own sphere—and declared that the "Woman's Auxiliary ought to let well enough alone."[73] Women were on the verge of having more personal options; the Nineteenth Amendment was a harbinger. In terms of church polity, women were to have representation on the Board of Missions for the first time since formation of the Woman's Auxiliary. The bishop's impulse to contain women within their traditional sphere was typical of the male hierarchy in Chicago. But trends in the national church carried the day, and the Woman's Auxiliary in Chicago followed the lead.

Again, innovation of policy and program was at the heart of the matter. The well-educated volunteer wanted an expansive role and the national church seemed to be encouraging it. The local bishop sensed the autonomy this portended and tried to stave it off by promoting traditional woman's work. Modernization was a two-edged sword for women. To reject the new trends excluded women from the emerging center of social service, and they had come to believe in the need for professionalization. On the other hand, by adopting the new model, they risked giving up their greatest means to influence: their special claim to a moral authority as women.

Diocesan Woman's Auxiliaries were told that the competing and sometimes conflicting structures involved with woman's work in the church at the parish and diocesan levels needed reorganization. As discussed above, women leaders were already attempting to bring about some degree of conformity among the local branches. The Woman's Auxiliary board in Chicago adopted the Church Service League plan advocated by the national council. Five fields of service—parish, community, diocesan, nation, world—were to be federated rather than merged, so as to provide a better foundation.[74] Woman's work continued to be reshaped by national and diocesan attempts to coordinate professional and volunteer groups in the fields traditionally the domain of the auxiliary.

In 1923 the Chicago branch of the auxiliary accepted the suggestion of the national auxiliary to separate the Social Service Department from the Woman's Auxiliary. Social Service would have a closer relationship with the bishop and council—the male leadership group in the diocese—and still retain a link with the auxiliary.[75] Five years later the deaconess aid committee of the Woman's Auxiliary was discontinued, and that work incorporated into the Social Service Department. This created dissension, for some auxiliary members feared a loss of control; bit by bit items from the gender-segregated agenda of the auxiliary were incorporated into church departments where men and women worked together.[76]

Some women saw this integration of woman's work into the general work of the church as threatening to their position; they preferred the status quo to the more open-ended and perhaps more competitive environment of the church departments, where not only men but professionals would make policy together with the auxiliary representatives. The privileged subordination of the upper-class women bound them to a position of inequality in church councils; but it conversely assured them moral authority in their own sphere and a special relationship with the clergy that neither men nor female professional church workers could achieve. This moral authority was directly related to the voluntary nature of their ministry. The service of love, the sacrifice of love, and the vigilance of love were qualities associated with women's voluntary efforts, rather than were competence, expertise, and training. Women were told that the more selfless their contribution, the better the gift. But women were also assured of a privileged position if service and sacrifice held sway over special expertise and training. To relinquish the former in the quest for organizational modernization risked the latter.

The integration of woman's work into the mainstream of the church's organizations took a long time to accomplish.[77] It was implied in the 1920 statement by the National Council that the Woman's Auxiliary was an auxiliary to all departments of the church. At the time parish councils were being organized all over the country and men were being enlisted more actively in the service of the church. Fear was expressed lest these councils of men and women "tend toward the eventual disintegration of the Auxiliary."[78] The plan to collapse woman's work into the main body of the church did not include giving women equal status in church councils, where they could not vote. Nor could they be delegates to diocesan conventions or the General Convention. Integration actually meant that activities once controlled by women in their separate sphere would now be controlled by men, but women would continue to do the work.

Resistance to reorganization came not from men but from *women*. Ideally, once women were no longer in spheres separate from men's, they could expand into the full scope of church work. In practical terms, the shift meant that women would be dealing with more bureaucracy and supervision. Their work was the same but it had been reclassified as the church's agenda of social service.

Attempts to develop a modern administrative system and to create a comprehensive urban social service network were cut short by the economic upheaval of the 1930s. Traditional women's activities flourished during the depression years as auxiliary members rallied to subsidize the severely diminished budgets of the diocesan institutions. The self-effacing qualities of women volunteers that had strong roots in the Chicago diocese were strengthened by these years of hardship and economic retrenchment.[79] At the parish level a similar effort was made by the women. In rural parts of the diocese the social services were performed almost entirely by deaconesses who traveled by car and brought some relief to communities.[80]

For women in the Diocese of Chicago, the 1930s and 1940s represented a socially conservative period in which the male hierarchy became defined nationally as an ingrown and conservative group concerned with defense of Anglo-Catholic traditions. The Woman's Auxiliary leadership had little involvement with interdenominational activities, except for such efforts as Red Cross and USO work during the war years. Photographs taken during these decades impress the viewer with the staid and conservative qualities of women volunteers: hats and gloves at all times and a routine of teas, fund-raising balls, bazaars, and bake sales. What is missing from the record is the political involvement that had been such an important part of the women's sphere in the pre-1920 era. Women now were functioning more and more as fund-raisers remote from the agencies and settlement houses being run by professional directors and staffs. Society pages were replete with illustrated accounts of prominent Episcopalians doing "charity work." The image of the respectable matron running the church bazaar had replaced the women reformers of the Progressive era. Additionally, the consumer culture had crept into parish life; fashion shows, luncheons, and social engagements were regularly included in churchwomen's organized activities.[81]

Post–World War II prosperity energized women's activities, and in keeping with the retreat from the Progressive agenda and the new ideal of wife-companion, the suburban exodus gave women volunteerism new life. The growth of new parishes in new Chicago neighborhoods as well as in the suburbs provided women with opportunities to create separate organizations along the lines of traditional models or to seek out new formulations. Women chose the former, and there is substantial evidence that parishes begun in the 1930s through 1950s were initiated and sustained primarily by the customary women's fund-raising activities.[82]

We must wait until the 1950s for the Woman's Auxiliary to begin to take stock of itself as an organization. This makes sense in terms of the pattern of growth in the diocese itself. In 1953 a new bishop arrived in Chicago with plans to bring the Episcopal Church to the suburbs; a plan to buy property and support new missions inaugurated a more vigorous phase of church life. This agenda for construction and expansion was linked to the national church's concern with membership figures. A parallel call for growth in women's activities was touched off by the National Executive Board of the Woman's Auxiliary's 1954 study of the goals of woman's work. A decision was made to focus on diocesan boards; in 1956 teams of national board members and staff planned on-site visits with Woman's Auxiliaries in dioceses throughout the country.

The Chicago auxiliary participated in the series of Parish Life Conferences inaugurated by the national Woman's Auxiliary to implement a policy of bringing women's work into the center of church affairs. The message was clear: men and women were asked to coordinate programs together, and a lay ministry *without* a gender-specific orientation was the stated goal. A subtext of the integration of men's and women's activities, it appeared, was concern among church leaders that church members were less involved in church work than before. This coordination was part of the larger issue of evangelism and commitment.[83]

If women were to participate fully in the life of the church, the reorganization required that real changes had to occur from the parish level to the highest governing group, the General Convention, allowing women voting and representation rights. Such political rights had evolved very slowly. A few dioceses granted women the right to vote in parish and diocesan meetings and to serve on vestries or as delegates to the diocesan convention, but not until the 1950s was there any widespread movement in this direction. Mary Donovan tells us that as late as 1961, women served on vestries in only 31 of the 104 dioceses, and they were elected as delegates to only 47 diocesan conventions. The 1934 General Convention provided that four women, nominated by the Woman's Auxiliary, serve on the National Council (along with twenty-eight men), but even they were elected by a General Convention that excluded women deputies.[84]

Chicago women waited until the 1960s to serve on vestries, and the majority of parishes did not move in this direction until the 1970s. Participation in the annual convention of the diocese and in diocesan committees such as the Diocesan Council was also slow, but by the 1970s a sprinkling of women had assumed leadership roles. They tended to be women who had a high degree of visibility in the traditional women's organization, now renamed Episcopal Churchwomen.

By the 1960s Episcopal women in Chicago appeared to have changed their organizational structure but not their traditional gender-specific activities. There were, also, basic membership problems that reflected the deeper societal patterns affecting the participation and integration of women in religion. Any organization that aimed to be inclusive of all women in the diocese had to accommodate both traditionalists and modernists—the two major divisions among women that had emerged by then. The leaders of Episcopal Churchwomen—officers and directors of the diocesan board—continued to be predominantly white, middle-class homemakers, staunch proponents of traditionalist remedies for modern problems. Unwilling to change their modes of volunteerism, they functioned in ways that excluded groups of women. One illustration of their inflexibility was the increasingly rigid response of the ECW board to the scheduling problems of working women.

Working women had been attending evening meetings since the late 1920s, and in the 1960s working women asked for added flexibility in this regard. Instead, the traditionalists moved to eliminate the evening division. This was at a time when more and more women were entering the labor force, which precluded their participation in daytime meetings, and attendance at the annual conventions was dropping substantially. The 1960 annual report of the Chicago ECW documented the erosion of woman's work and participation, acknowledging the serious stresses on women from family, work, and community demands, but counseled women to budget their time in order to meet "Christian obligations." Yet there were few concrete steps taken to make that possible for employed women.[85]

Resistance to accommodating change in the structuring of women's involvement in the church typified the ECW board's response to altered circumstances. Working women found it increasingly difficult to approach the board because its meetings were held during their working hours, and the inauguration of two-day annual conferences for churchwomen in 1961 further alienated employed women. The traditionalists looked forward to the event held at a resort-type site as an excursion to conduct business and also to socialize; the modernists resented the large chunks of time such leisurely scheduling imposed.[86]

The traditionalists' refusal to accede to working women's demands was partly the expression of the unwillingness of white, middle-class volunteers to open up leadership positions to women of different races and economic backgrounds. Policy-making at the diocesan level was shared by a relatively small and homogeneous group of women. For some time there had been a few representatives from the black parishes; these women typically tended to be even more upwardly mobile than their white counterparts. In fact, the only women able to participate in the daytime meetings and at the annual conferences were those with means and time to spare. The issue of privilege remained a significant aspect of woman's work in the diocese.[87]

1961–1989

Two major trends continued in the 1960s and 1970s: woman's work was increasingly integrated into the general work of church commissions and departments, with women and men *together* encouraged to establish lay action departments. The United Thank Offering became one of the last programs that could be identified with woman's work. The second trend had to do with a reevaluation of women's calling. That old-fashioned word was itself not used, but in its place one heard *ministries, careers in the church,* and *vocation.* Parish women were told by the national bureaucracy that separate woman's work no longer had a place in the church. Directives and study guides were sent to diocesan ECWs with the message that they should begin to phase themselves out. "We are increasingly emphasizing full time professional work in the Church in its true prospective [*sic*]," Episcopal Churchwomen was told in 1963 by the head of the Division of Christian Ministries. "There is but one ministry. That is the ministry of OUR LORD, JESUS CHRIST. This is the vocation of all baptized persons—our vocation as Christians."[88] Reversing long tradition, "Some are called to the ordained ministry. Some are called to be College Workers or Christian Educators, or nurses, or doctors, or engineers, or wives and mothers. There is no difference in essence. There is difference in function."[89]

The pressure to transform both the form and the substance of woman's work and calling was unending in the decade of the 1970s. Although individual parishes might dig in their heels, the ECW was unable to avoid dealing with the new conditions. In 1970 its annual convention topic was "Women's Lib: Who Needs It? What's It All About?" A panel asked, "Does 'the Movement' Affect Churchwomen?" No one really needed to be told what "the Movement" was all about. The new thinking about women had permeated every aspect of society. The media and the churches, as well as all other organizations, were deeply involved in the dialogue. Women were now telling *one another* that they were individuals who had rights not just to employment opportunities and education but to self-realization. After decades of a theology of self-lessness, of submission and subordination, of tireless work behind the scenes, of accepting influence rather than power, women who had viewed church groups as one of the last remaining places they could assume traditional roles were told by the leadership to think about themselves in more personally ambitious and aggressive ways.

For the generations of women born between 1910 and 1930 who were in leadership positions in the 1960s the messages were foreign and threatening. They had been the women in the diocesan organizations that first dealt with the restructuring of woman's work begun in the 1940s and culminating in 1959. Most now lived in new parishes in the suburbs; those who remained in city parishes witnessed changes in the demography and economic conditions of their neighborhoods. Issues of race, class, and employment differed remarkably along the suburban-urban axis.[90]

While diocesan and national agendas were encouraging a rethinking of women's roles, women were still doing this traditional work in parishes—work that was becoming more demanding as the women available to do it grew fewer. This was especially true in new missions and fledgling parishes as well as older, marginal parishes. The Triennial Resolution of 1967—"That the General Division of Women's Work and its committees be encouraged to enter into such new structures, in connection with other departments and units of the Executive Council, as seem appropriate to discharge the responsibilities and functions now vested in the division and/or the respective units"—was more easily stated than implemented. Parish life was far less amenable to change. The activities of the Executive Council, now subsumed under different departments, still remained the burden, on the local level, of women volunteers.

The board of the ECW continued to reflect the leadership style and ideological point of view of the more traditional woman. Itself a bureaucracy with parliamentary procedures and rules as well as deeply embedded customs, the diocesan ECW suffered the new restructuring but was unable to "remake" itself. Not that it did not try. A great deal of time and energy went into leadership training, self-evaluation seminars, and conflict-resolution training. There were women in the parishes who resented allocations of money for such activities. The president of a suburban parish women's group protested the 1970 diocesan ECW budget because it seemed "unduly extravagant" during "these days of violent social tensions" to spend $1,000 yearly toward the training of the sixteen board members. The group hoped "that the necessary qualities of leadership and sensitivity might be sought in potential Board members and not developed after their selection. We are, therefore, deducting the percentage of our Fair Share [local chapter tithe to diocesan ECW budget] that would be used for 'Training' and adding this to our contribution to Episcopal Charities." The board of a women's group in another suburban church withheld a portion of its Fair Share for the same reason.[91]

A good part of the ECW's problem was the lack of agreement regarding the role of the church in the world. Some clergy challenged the heart of the leadership group—a core of women who now were substantially representative of the more suburban parishes—that it would be tragic if they were "really an organization to preserve a suburban home-centered church, hardly aware of the existence of the technological world and the main realities of the secular city, particularly the secular inner city." The ECW was told to confront the problems of the inner city, if its members believed in any gospel at all.[92]

Criticism of the ECW came from women who wanted to have the organization confront such issues as abortion, racism and poverty, civil rights, women's rights, and women's ordination. The last two were subjects of vital concern to the new feminists and also to the national church. The ECW board, however, was made up of socially conservative women unwilling to open up the decision-making process on the controversial and divisive questions that were important to most women. When asked to take a stand on issues of the day, the board declined, asserting that it was not a policy-making body. When the national church encouraged dioceses to participate in the 1978 Task Force on Women in the Church, Chicago's ECW diocesan board hesitated; when women from one of the parishes in the diocese volunteered to participate, board members discouraged them and ultimately rejected this local initiative.[93]

An important aspect of the disharmony of the 1960s and 1970s was the lack of connection to a religious and social worldview such as that which had typified the political culture of the Progressive era. Women of that era were able to do "good works" not just because they believed they were of a superior moral nature or accepted their "place" in the cosmology of sex roles but, more to the point, because they agreed on what constituted "good works." In the post–World War II decades the earlier traditions that had identified actual social programs with the task of building the Kingdom of God came under criticism. As Robert Wuthnow puts it, "[T]he kingdom of God became a vision of hope, rather than a plan for society."[94]

Wuthnow suggests that by the 1960s a whole new set of alignments in religious outlooks began to appear: divisions developed across denominational lines along a liberal versus conservative political continuum. By the late 1960s and early 1970s there was a great deal of diversity and division on social and political issues within *every* denomination that entered congregational life and polarized the membership of many churches.

Episcopal women demanded that the ECW take positions, provide leadership, and enter the fray. One woman called for the diocesan ECW to be "unafraid of controversy, to be true to the great principles embodied in the best of Christian traditions, to set goals and to work toward them." Critical of the ECW for "merely mark[ing] time," or tending "to one's housekeeping," she called for women "to lead, to be guides, to open new doors, to provide new opportunities."[95] Other women resented the board's withholding of information about the national church. They wanted to be informed about all the programs and plans.[96] But women could not find common ground nor could they agree about an agenda of social action.

Not only were the women at odds with one another but an underlying tension existed between those in the pew and the national leadership.

Revisions in the *Book of Common Prayer*, acceptance of women's participation in all levels of church governance, and in 1976 the vote in
General Convention approving the ordination of women to the priesthood were structural changes. The "new breed" of clergy had been, on
the whole, considerably more liberal than the men and women in the
pews. Civil rights and antiwar activities by the clergy pushed some Episcopalians out of the churches. The call for direct aid for black economic
development, for example, had been answered by the national church
in a dramatic and proactive fashion. The national ECW responded in a
similar manner and shocked many women in the pews. Many traditionalists did not recognize their own churches.

During the late 1960s and the 1970s the ECW began to come apart.
This was a response to efforts by national and diocesan church leaders,
including the bishop of Chicago, to dismantle gender-specific church
work and to include men and women in lay ministry.[97] The merging of
separate women's work into the mainstream of church life was encouraged at the Triennial Meeting of the Women of the Church held in the
fall of 1964.[98] Given the option, many parishes in the Chicago diocese
voted to dismantle the separate-sphere ideology, and whole parish chapters of the ECW resigned.[99]

The dismantling of parish chapters of Episcopal Churchwomen indicated that for many the organization no longer met the needs of
women. In some cases lack of membership at the local level reflected
changes in life-style and interests. Women chose other ways to participate. Some found greater meaning in small prayer groups or Bible
study; others were elected to local vestries or parish committees and
saw no purpose in working with a separate women's group. The growth
of special-purpose groups allowed women with specific concerns—abortion, women's ordination, world hunger, peace and justice, race relations—to deal directly with matters of conscience outside the local parish
or even their own denomination.[100] Women could also participate on
diocesan commissions or committees and ignore both the local and the
diocesan ECW. Freed from the concept of woman's work, women could
also find sisterhood in groups that did not have to be connected to their
churches.

In the Chicago diocese the ECW traditionalists began to feel like the
disenfranchised and unrepresented, even though the ECW continued to
be the official voice of churchwomen and appointments to commissions
or committees by the male hierarchy tended to be made from the ranks
of the ECW board and officers.[101] One issue brings the conflicts into
dramatic relief: women's ordination to the priesthood. It is not surprising

that the women in this diocese found it difficult to deal with the growing support for the ordination of women that was emerging in the Episcopal Church in the late 1960s and early 1970s. Chicago women had strong bonds of fidelity and loyalty to Anglo-Catholic priests and bishops. Many of the most ardent antagonists of women's ordination came out of this diocese. But most significantly, Chicago's bishop consistently voted against women's ordination throughout this period whenever the issue was raised in the House of Bishops.[102] The overwhelming guidance from clergy opposed the ordination of women.

For the ECW to take a stand in favor of ordination, then, would have required the organization's leaders to take a very independent and difficult position: for the first time they would have had to go against the patriarchy. The traditionalists retained their privileged status by joining with the antiordination forces, and not confronting the male leadership. At its annual convention in May 1973 the ECW passed a resolution by a large majority directing the women delegates to the General Convention to oppose the ordination of women.[103] Delegates to the annual convention by self-selection represented the more traditional churchwomen who continued to identify with the women's organization, but did they represent the majority of Episcopal women in the Diocese of Chicago? When a debate was proposed on the issue, the ECW board took no action and allowed the suggestion to die on the vine.[104]

Many women found it almost impossible to deal with the conflict that any open discussion of women's ordination was certain to engender. Christian women were not supposed to be confrontational; the model of submissiveness and self-effacement that had been operating for so many generations offered no acceptable way for them to be assertive and to argue with one another. Nor did these churchwomen know how to disagree with their clergy and bishops. One ECW president had to explain to a member why the organization was *obliged* to confront controversial social and political issues: As "caring Churchwomen . . . we should be as knowledgeable as possible in the issues that face our 'Christian Sisters' in the business world or as homemakers, as well as in the internal affairs of our Church today." The modest proposal of the ECW board then being considered was for the women's convention to take the opportunity "to exercise their Christian love for others through learning and sharing." No one was pressing for action; women were simply being encouraged to talk things over.[105]

Such phrases as "caring Churchwomen," "Christian Sisters," "Christian love," and "learning and sharing" were, in themselves, ways to sidestep the real feelings of women in the church. They actually helped women avoid their own deepest pains and frustrations and the anger that traditional volunteer women felt about the changes going on in their church. But the very fact that they had been socialized into a model of behavior that emphasized harmony and, when conflict arose, cautioned silence and personal prayer meant that their emotional and psychological vocabulary had no words or phrases to deal with the new circumstances. The advice that women need not agree with someone to walk together with them was acknowledgment that the bonds of sisterhood had, in reality, been severed. New bonds would have to be forged.

Many clergy in the Diocese of Chicago were not part of the "new breed," or embraced parts of the liberal agenda and rejected others. There was enough disagreement, however, with the national leadership to legitimize insubordinate feelings among parishioners. Traditionalists were given "permission" by parish priests and the diocesan bishop to withhold personal support of some changes while remaining in the church. In fact, the bishop's approach to the ordination of women became a model of passive resistance to the new policy. He opposed the ordination of women at the diocesan convention in October 1976 and voted three times in the House of Bishops against it on grounds of custom and lack of ecumenical consensus. He felt that the step taken at the General Convention in 1976 was premature at best.

Nevertheless, the bishop recognized the authority of the General Convention to legislate for the Episcopal Church. He told his people, "[A]s Bishop of the Diocese, I will concur in the request of the Standing Committee and the Commission on Ministry. I will not speak to prevent canonically ordained and licensed women from functioning or serving this Diocese, nor, if qualified under the Canons, from being ordained here." He then explained that he would not personally officiate at any ordination of women to the priesthood but would allow his suffragan to do so. "Each of us must act as God the Holy Spirit guides his or her conscience. It is my hope that my own decision in this matter, which is likewise based on conscience, will be accepted by all members of the Diocese."[106]

Initially, the Standing Committee of the Diocese of Chicago endorsed two qualified women candidates to the priesthood; a change in the committee's membership in October 1977 reversed the majority and stymied women's ordination in the diocese for several years. Now the diocese found itself in an extraordinary position: the diocesan bishop would not *personally* ordain a woman candidate but would allow his suffragan to do so, and he would recommend qualified candidates to the Standing Committee, the only body of the diocese with the charge of approving or disapproving candidates to the priesthood. But the Standing Committee had no intention of voting for women candidates. The stalemate represented the hierarchy's position.[107]

What followed was a difficult period—through the 1980s—and again a compromise was worked out that informally circumvented the national policy of the church: a "back-door" ordination of Chicago's women candidates. The diocesan bishop presented the credentials of qualified women candidates to bishops in dioceses with committees hospitable to ordaining women. The women deacons would become canonically resident in the host diocese (though physically they could remain in the Chicago diocese) and, after an ordination ceremony performed by the "substitute" bishop and clergy and a proper waiting period, would be transferred back to the Diocese of Chicago and there be allowed the full rights and responsibilities of a priest.[108]

The journey from seminary to priesthood became, for some women in the Diocese of Chicago, a long and lonely spiritual quest, a form of "exile" from one's spiritual roots. Commenting on one such candidate, a sympathetic priest remarked on "the silent suffering and subtle martyrdom of women in this Diocese" who struggled to achieve their own true ministry.[109] This Anglo-Catholic priest was himself torn between his love for and devotion to the diocesan bishop and his feelings for a woman candidate who had served faithfully and well as a deacon under his supervision. Transferred to a distant diocese through the "back-door," the woman achieved ordination in 1980. She had been the first woman to attend Seabury-Western Theological Seminary in 1970 and had been ordained to the diaconate in June 1975; her ordination took sixteen months.[110]

Ironically, the model of submissive and subordinate womanhood fit this process quite well. Once more women were to be silent in their suffering and await the permission of men. Early in her struggle, the pioneering woman priest had been told to "keep on praying and hoping and trusting."[111] Women were not to fight for beliefs or take actions on their own behalf. Throughout this period the ECW in Chicago made no public statements for or against the arrangement. The bonds of sisterhood were already damaged between women traditionalists and modernists within the organization. Now, added to the disharmony were deep and generally unstated feelings of anger that women who sought the priesthood (successfully or not) felt when they faced the ECW.

Although the ECW had made no direct statement, members elected as their new president in 1978 a woman who opposed the ordination of women and had been in positions of authority in the diocesan power structure—by reason of her long-standing volunteerism with the ECW—to slow down the ordination process in the diocese. One board member in 1978 encouraged the board to set up an educational program to discuss women's ordination. Still accepting of the role of dutiful and obedient womanhood, she suggested a program that was "constructive . . . noble and non-emotional" as a way to promote healing where there was pain and confusion. A dread of conflict and the inability to accept the authentic feelings of anger that go along with change continued to win the day.[112]

There is no question that the divisions that happened over women's ordination in the Chicago diocese were crucial, but, ironically, by the mid-1980s women priests had been accepted in many parishes of the diocese. With the new diocesan bishop, the diocesan staff now reflects a positive attitude toward inclusion of women at the highest levels of church policy-making. But "organized womanhood" has suffered considerable damage at the diocesan level. The ECW diocesan board flounders as it attempts to find its "work" and "calling" in an age when distinctions and boundaries between women and men have been blurred. Some observers have even raised the question of whether or not the ECW in its present configuration is workable.

The resurgence of women's guilds and societies at the parish level, however, points to a significant change in the attitudes of both traditionalists and modernists.[113] The former have found that local parish activities are where intergenerational tensions among women can be approached and resolved. The latter have discovered the need for bonding with other women *aside* from a particular cause or mission, or fundraising activities. Even in parishes where men and women have performed all of the church work together for almost two decades, women have decided to meet for companionship and to explore ways of spiritual growth. If there is any single thread that runs through the expressions of sisterhood of women in the liberal and conservative camps, it is the interest in prayer, the emphasis on personal faith, and the thirst for a female context for many aspects of devotional life.

In 1988 several women began the program "Hearing Women's Voices" in the Diocese of Chicago. After years of rejection of issues that might further divide women, these churchwomen—some from the ECW traditionalist flank and others who have not participated in the ECW—decided to take an accounting of woman's work and woman's calling. After honoring the past, the second year of the program launched a diocesan-wide survey of women to allow many different voices to be heard. An acceptance of pluralism and a will to find a way to work with differences are apparent. The steering committee chose the format of an eucharistic celebration for a conference and designed the liturgy of the day to reflect the variety of women's personal spiritual journeys in search of callings in the church. Both the Anglo-Catholic traditions so strong in this diocese and a newfound comfortableness about women's determination to be more autonomous combined in the service.

Women have become more visible in the diocese at all levels and in all ministries. There are still significant organizational conflicts, and the difficulties of volunteerism plague individual women as they strive for balance in their lives. Nor is there real agreement about the mission of Christianity in the world today. The litany of prayer, study, and mission (action) that energized organized womanhood in the late nineteenth and early twentieth centuries no longer informs the daily life of most Episcopal women or sets the boundaries of their activities. A hollowness at the center reflects the plight of the traditional denominations. The great edifice of institutions remains intact, but it is not clear to what purpose the energies of Christians are to be applied. All the organizational life still evinces a lack of direction. One hundred years ago women were key to the development of a Christian agenda of work in the world. It is unclear whence leadership for the construction of a new agenda will come. Without a new agenda women's integration into the body of the church cannot hope to solve the larger issues that continue to confront religion in the United States.

Notes

1. Jane Addams, *Twenty Years at Hull-House* (New York: 1910), pp. 95–97; Vida Dutton Scudder, ed. *Letters to Her Companions by Emily Malbone Morgan* (Adelynrood, South Byfield, Mass.: Society of the Companions of the Holy Cross, 1944); Mary Kingsbury Simkhovitch, *Here Is God's Plenty* (New York: Harper & Brothers, 1949), p. 158; Ellen Gates Starr, "College Settlement Work: Hull-House," *Society of the Companions of the Holy Cross,* Fourth Paper (1895).

2. Whether or not the Progressive movement was a conservative defense of capitalism or a truly liberal attempt at transformation continues to be argued among historians. The way in which women (those underpaid and those not paid at all) fit into the occupational structure of the new service sector appears to lend support to those who see the Progressive era as a triumph of conservatism. Yet the social feminists and the organized churchwomen were idealists in search of healing in society—some were obviously more radical than others.

62 HISTORICAL PERSPECTIVES

Were they preserving the old order or ushering in a new age of social justice? Rather than give an answer for the collective spirit of women, it seems appropriate to reply for the churchwomen in Chicago: they clearly upheld traditional virtues as their model of behavior—family, God, social order—but they were willing to use modern strategies and to form partnerships with government, regulate business, and reform the environment for those ends.

3. Barbara J. Berg, *The Remembered Gate: Origins of American Feminism: The Women and the City* (New York: 1978); Nancy F. Cott, *The Bonds of Womanhood: "Woman's Sphere" in New England, 1780–1835* (New Haven: Yale University Press, 1977); Carroll Smith-Rosenberg, *Religion and the Rise of the American City: The New York City Mission Movement, 1812–1870* (Ithaca: Cornell University Press, 1971); Mary P. Ryan, "The Power of Women's Networks: A Case Study of Female Moral Reform in Antebellum America," *Feminist Studies* 5 (1979): 66–85; Barbara Welter, "She Hath Done What She Could: Protestant Women's Missionary Careers in Nineteenth-Century America," *American Quarterly* 30 (1978): 624–638. For information about antebellum women's benevolence in Chicago, see parish files for Grace Church (1850), St. James Church (1834), and Trinity Church (1842), in Archives, Episcopal Diocese of Chicago; see especially minutes and papers from St. James Sunday School and Parish Aid Society, and reports of women's work from nineteenth century: Eliza Voluntine Rumsey, "Recollections of a Pioneer's Daughter," MS; Agnes Reynolds, "Laura Houghteling Reynolds," MS. See also Louise deKoven Bowen, *Growing Up with a City* (New York: Macmillan, 1926).

4. Bowen, *Growing Up*, p. 51.

5. Scudder, *Letters to Her Companions*, pp. 64–65.

6. Kathryn Kish Sklar, "Religious and Moral Authority as Factors Shaping the Balance of Power for Women's Political Culture in the Twentieth Century" (Paper delivered at the Jane Addams Conference, Rockford College, Rockford, Illinois, October 1989), p. 1.

7. Scudder, *Letters to Her Companions*, p. 102; Patricia R. Hill, *The World Their Household: The American Woman's Foreign Mission Movement and Cultural Transformation, 1870–1920* (Ann Arbor: University of Michigan Press, 1985), pp. 62.

8. Hill, *The World Their Household*, pp. 93–94; Mrs. Frederick Greeley, "Address at Auxiliary Dinner," *Diocese of Chicago* (1911), pp. 7–9.

9. Anne Firor Scott, *Making the Invisible Woman Visible* (Chicago: University of Illinois Press, 1984), p. 203; Hill, *The World Their Household*, pp. 84, 92; Sheila M. Rothman, *Woman's Proper Place: A History of Changing Ideals and Practices, 1870 to the Present* (New York: Basic Books, 1978).

8. Rothman concludes that "the political consequences of the concepts of educated motherhood were nowhere more evident than in the passage of the Nineteenth Amendment." Rothman, *Woman's Proper Place*, p. 127. Also Hill, *The World Their Household*, p. 5.

10. Rothman, *Woman's Proper Place*, p. 177; Barbara J. Harris, *Beyond*

Her Sphere: Women and the Professions in American History (Westport, Conn.: Greenwood Press, 1978), especially the discussions of the Shepherd-Towner program and the birth control movement. Women are innovators and then lose out to masculine hegemony. Also J. Stanley Lemons, *The Woman Citizen: Social Feminism in the 1920s* (Urbana: University of Illinois Press, 1973).

11. Initially, relatively few of the new female workers were native-born, middle-class white women; the vast majority were immigrants and blacks. Harris, *Beyond Her Sphere*, p. 104. At the same time, achievements for women in the professions were small, and women remained a tiny, isolated minority in all of the learned professions even though the percentage of women in college rose.

12. Ibid., pp. 154–155.

13. Ibid.

14. Olive Anderson, "Women Preachers in Mid-Victorian Britain: Some Reflexions of Feminism, Popular Religion and Social Change," *Historical Journal* 12 (1969): 467–484; Joan Jacobs Brumberg and Nancy Tomes, "Women in the Professions: A Research Agenda for American Historians," *Reviews in American History* 10 (June 1982): 275–296 (Bromberg and Tomes emphasize that "within the nineteenth-century woman's sphere, unpaid work outside the home became a route to self-respect and power oftentimes involving a lifetime commitment to a single organization or cause" [p. 285]; Cott, *The Bonds of Womanhood;* Mary Sudman Donovan, *A Different Call: Women's Ministries in the Episcopal Church, 1850–1920* (Wilton, Conn.: Morehouse-Barlow, 1986); Harris, *Beyond Her Sphere;* Hill, *The World Their Household;* Rosemary Skinner Keller, Louise L. Queen, and Hilah F. Thomas, eds., *Women in New Worlds* (Nashville: Abingdon Press, 1982); Scott, *Making the Invisible Woman Visible;* Welter, "She Hath Done What She Could," pp. 624–638.

15. Should this separate women's organization be termed a "parallel church"? I agree that woman's work was separate and that the Woman's Auxiliary was a full structure existing apart from the Episcopal Church. Mary Donovan quite accurately defines this women's organizational structure as separate, unequal, and apart. I think the word *parallel* implies some kind of equality, and I have trouble with any implicit assertion that women's organizations were equal to the organization of the church.

16. Rima Lunin Schultz, "The Businessman's Role in Western Settlement: The Entrepreneurial Frontier, Chicago, 1833–1872" (Ph.D. diss., Boston University, 1985).

17. Frederick Cople Jaher, *The Urban Establishment: Upper Strata in Boston, New York, Charleston, Chicago and Los Angeles* (Urbana: University of Illinois Press, 1982), p. 476.

18. Helen Horowitz, *Culture and the City: Cultural Philanthropy in Chicago from the 1880s to 1917* (Lexington: University of Kentucky Press, 1976).

19. Addams, *Twenty Years at Hull-House;* Harris, *Beyond Her Sphere;*

Rothman, *Woman's Proper Place;* Anne Firor Scott, Introduction to *Democracy and Social Ethics,* by Jane Addams (Cambridge: Harvard University Press, 1964).

20. Rima Lunin Schultz, *The Church and the City: A Social History of 150 Years at Saint James, Chicago* (Chicago: Cathedral of Saint James, 1986), pp. 126–127, 141–142.

21. Ibid., pp. 120–124.

22. Ibid., pp. 125–126.

23. Ibid., pp. 120–121.

24. Bowen, *Growing Up,* p. 51.

25. Ibid., pp. 48–50.

26. Ibid., p. 51.

27. Ibid., pp. 22–23.

28. Ibid., pp. 23–24.

29. Ibid.

30. This is a quotation from Carroll Smith-Rosenberg, *Disorderly Conduct: Visions of Gender in Victorian America* (New York: Knopf, 1985), pp. 173–174. Here Smith-Rosenberg in a fascinating chapter, "Bourgeois Discourse and the Progressive Era," summarizes the chapter "Woman's Movement and Socialism, 1870–1900," in Mari Jo Buhle, *Women and American Socialism, 1879–1920* (Urbana: University of Illinois Press, 1981), pp. 49–53.

31. John Henry Hopkins, *The Great Forty Years in the Diocese of Chicago* (Chicago: Centenary Fund of the Diocese, 1936), p. 140; Schultz, *The Church and the City,* pp. 133–134.

32. "Minutes," Woman's Auxiliary, Chicago, 1884–1930; Report of the Chicago Branch of the Woman's Auxiliary, 2 October 1884–29 May 1888, pp. 16, 15; the Reverend Dr. Clinton Locke, "Woman as a Citizen" (preached at the Fourth Semi-Annual Meeting of the Woman's Auxiliary, Chicago, 4 October 1888); Woman's Auxiliary Fifth Annual Report, May 1889, p. 5; "President's Address," Thirteenth Annual Meeting of the Woman's Auxiliary, Chicago, 1897—all in Minutes, Executive and Regular Meetings, Woman's Auxiliary, Chicago, 1895–1929, Woman's Auxiliary Papers, Episcopal Churchwomen of Chicago Archives. See also Mrs. Florence Greeley, "Notes and Reminiscences of the Woman's Auxiliary," *Diocese of Chicago* (January 1917, February 1917) (hereinafter Woman's Auxiliary Papers, Episcopal Churchwomen of Chicago Archives cited as WA Papers; Episcopal Churchwomen of Chicago Archives cited as ECW Archives).

33. "President's Address," Sixteenth Annual Report, Woman's Auxiliary, Chicago, 1900, WA Papers.

34. Sister Mary Hilary, *Ten Decades of Praise: The Story of the Community of Saint Mary during Its First Century, 1865–1965* (Racine, Wis.: DeKoven Foundation, 1965).

35. Rima Lunin Schultz, "The Making of an American Church: A Study of Leadership, 1834–1945" (manuscript, 1988), Episcopal Diocese of Chicago. Also

"Correspondence," 1970–1979, Episcopal Churchwomen of Chicago Papers, EWC Archives (hereinafter cited as ECW Papers).

36. Sixteenth Annual Meeting, Woman's Auxiliary, Chicago, 31 May 1900; Special Meeting, Woman's Auxiliary, Chicago, 17 January 1905; "Resolution: Memorial to Miss Julia C. Emery," Regular Meeting, Woman's Auxiliary, Chicago, February 1922; Annual Report, Woman's Auxiliary, Chicago, May 1888—all in WA Papers. Hopkins, *The Great Forty Years,* p. 140.

37. Mrs. Frederick Greeley, "Fiftieth Anniversary Woman's Auxiliary," *Diocese of Chicago* (November 1934); "Minutes," Regular Meeting, Woman's Auxiliary, 6 January 1910, 3 February 1910, WA Papers.

38. "Minutes," Regular Meeting, Woman's Auxiliary, 6, April 1898; Officers' Conference, Woman's Auxiliary, Chicago, 17 February, 1916; "Minutes," Regular Meeting, Woman's Auxiliary, 2 March 1916—all in WA Papers. Hopkins, *Great Forty Years,* p. 150.

39. Hopkins, *The Great Forty Years,* pp. 140, 150–151, 154.

40. Lois A. Boyd and R. Douglas Brackenridge, *Presbyerian Women in America* (Westport, Conn.: Greenwood Press, 1983); Donovan, *A Different Call;* Hill, *The World Their Household;* Scott, *Making the Invisible Woman Visible.*

41. Deaconess Mary Truesdell, "The Deaconess Office and Ministry" Executive Committee of the National Conference of Deaconesses, 1952, Deaconess Papers, Episcopal Diocese of Chicago Archives. Hereinafter Archives Episcopal Diocese of Chicago cited as EDC Archives.

42. Donovan, *A Different Call,* pp. 88, 90. For information on the German Lutheran deaconess movement see Catherine M. Prelinger, *Charity, Challenge and Change: Religious Dimensions of the Mid-Nineteenth-Century Women's Movement in Germany* (Westport, Conn.: Greenwood Press, 1987). The deaconess activities at Kaiserswerth were noted by Protestants in the United States who were inspired to restore the diaconessate. See Catherine M. Prelinger and Rosemary S. Keller, "The Function of Female Bonding: The Restored Diaconessate of the Nineteenth Century," in Rosemary S. Keller, Louise L. Queen, and Hilah F. Thomas, eds., *Women in New Worlds: Historical Perspectives on the Wesleyan Tradition,* vol. 2 (Nashville, Tenn.: Abingdon, 1982).

43. Michael Hill, *The Religious Order: A Study of Virtuoso Religion and Its Legitimation in the Nineteenth-Century Church of England* (London: Heinemann Educational Books, 1973), p. 271.

44. Minute Book, Chicago Chapter of Deaconesses; Photographic Collection, Chicago Chapter of Deaconesses; Minute Book, Deaconess Society of St. Stephen—all in Deaconess Papers, EDC Archives.

45. In 1931 the Deaconess Canon was changed: the stipulation that deaconesses must be unmarried or widowed was deleted. This change was evidently made by the General Convention without prior consultation with the deaconesses, most of whom disliked the alteration because it was based on an under-

66 HISTORICAL PERSPECTIVES

standing of the vocation that they did not share. The Episcopal Church discontinued the order in 1970, allowing women to enter the diaconate as men did, but with the important exception that provisions related to the priesthood did not apply to women. Phyllis Edwards, a longtime deaconess resident in the Diocese of Chicago, was outspokenly in favor of women's ordination, going against the formal positions taken by the Episcopal Churchwomen of the Diocese of Chicago. "Minutes," October 1931, Chicago Chapter of Deaconesses, Deaconess Papers, EDC Archives, reflect disagreement with the deletion of the phrase "married or widowed" along with the intention to lobby for its restoration. Phyllis Edwards, "Letter to House of Bishops," August 1974, "Correspondence," ECW Papers. See Donovan, *A Different Call*, pp. 93, 98; Truesdell, "The Deaconess Office and Ministry," pp. 25ff.; Lecture Notes, Central House, ca. 1960s, Deaconess Papers, EDC Archives.

46. John Shelton Reed, " 'A Female Movement': The Feminization of Nineteenth-Century Anglo-Catholicism," *Anglican and Episcopal History* 57 (June 1988): 226–227. See Sister Hilary, *Ten Decades of Praise.*

47. Anne Ayres, *The Life and Work of William Augustus Muhlenberg* (New York: Harper & Bros., 1880), pp. 254–255, 256; Alvin W. Skardon, *William Augustus Muhlenberg* (Philadelphia: University of Pennsylvania Press, 1971), pp. 129–130; Donovan, *A Different Call*, p. 33.

48. Donovan, *A Different Call*, p. 50.

49. Schultz, *The Church and the City*, pp. 154–157, 145–151; Box 1 and Box 2, Trinity Church Papers, EDC Archives; *Trinity Church Chronicle* (Trinity Church, Chicago), January 1893–January 1898; Box 1, Grace Church Papers, *Grace Church Visitor* (Grace Church, Chicago), 1893–1899, 1900–1905.

50. Louise deKoven Bowen, *Speeches, Addresses, and Letters Reflecting Social Movements in Chicago*, 2 vols. (Ann Arbor, Mich: Edwards Brothers, 1937), 2: 789–791; Smith-Rosenberg, *Religion and the Rise of the American City;* Rothman, *Woman's Proper Place;* Christine Stansell, *City of Women: Sex and Class in New York, 1789–1860* (New York: Knopf, 1986).

51. Bishop William E. McLaren, "Address to the Woman's Auxiliary," 4 October 1888; Annual Report, Woman's Auxiliary, Chicago, 1889; "Report," Twelfth Annual Meeting, Woman's Auxiliary, Chicago, 28 May 1896, pp. 39–40; "Monthly Meeting," Woman's Auxiliary, Chicago, 7 March 1901—all in WA Papers.

52. "Minutes," Woman's Auxiliary, Chicago, 6 February 1902, 3 April 1902, 1 October 1903, 3 March 1904, 5 May 1904, 5 October 1905, 8 November 1906; "Minutes," Executive Meeting, Woman's Auxiliary, Chicago, 5 November 1914, February 1916, 2 March 1916–all in WA Papers.

53. *Chicago Herald*, 2 September 1888.

54. Bishop William E. McLaren, "Reminiscences," *Diocese of Chicago* (January 1893).

55. *Mission Work* (Chicago: Diocese of Chicago), March 1912, p. 7.

56. "Cathedral," *Diocese of Chicago* (September 1890); *Year Book of the*

Cathedral of Saints Peter and Paul and City Missions (Chicago, 1912), pp. 45–46; Report of St. Mary's Home for Children, Chicago, 1894–1899, St. Mary's Home File, EDC Archives; "St. Mary's Home for Children," *Diocese of Chicago* (February 1905).

57. "Memorandum in the matter of St. Mary's Mission Society," n.d., Community of St. Mary File, EDC Archives.

58. *One Hundred Years. 1884–1984* (Chicago: Episcopal Churchwomen, 1985), pp. 12–15; *Diocese of Chicago* (October 1911): 7–9, (February 1910): 9; Fifteenth Annual Report, Woman's Auxiliary, Chicago 1899; "Minutes," Monthly Meetings, Woman's Auxiliary, 7 March 1901, 6 February 1902; 1 October 1903, 3 March 1904, 8 November 1906, 2 March 1916, 12 May 1921, WA Papers.

59. With the election of Charles Palmerston Anderson as the fourth bishop of Chicago in 1905, the Episcopal Church in Chicago began to move toward embracing a Social Gospel agenda. See Schultz, "The Making of an American Church."

60. Kathryn Kish Sklar, "Religious and Moral Authority as Factors Shaping the Balance of Power for Women's Political Culture in the Twentieth Century" (Paper delivered at the Jane Addams Conference, Rockford College, October 1989), p. 21.

61. *Diocese of Chicago* (April 1910): 10.

62. Deaconess Helen M. Fuller, "The Work of Our Church Institutions. Chase House," *Diocese of Chicago* (December 1922): 22–23; *Living Church* (28 September 1920, 1 February 1921); pamphlet printed by Chase House (Chicago, 1923), Chase House Papers, EDC Archives.

63. *Diocese of Chicago* (April 1910): 10; "Report of the Committee on Christian Social Service," *Journal of the Proceedings of the Convention of the Diocese of Chicago* (Chicago, 1914), p. 61; "Minutes," Regular Meeting, Woman's Auxiliary, Chicago, 5 February 1920, WA Papers.

64. Greeley, "Fiftieth Anniversary Woman's Auxiliary."

65. "President's Address," Sixteenth Annual Report, Woman's Auxiliary, Chicago, 1900, WA Papers.

66. Lois A. Boyd and R. Douglas Brackenridge, *Presbyterian Women in America* (Westport, Conn.: Greenwood Press, 1983). Hill, *The World Their Household.*

67. Sklar, "Religious and Moral Factors," p. 12. See also Paula Baker, "The Domestication of Politics: Women and American Political Society, 1780–1920," *American Historical Review* 89 (1984): 620–647.

68. See Hill, *The World Their Household;* Boyd and Brackenridge, *Presbyterian Women.*

69. "Minutes," Regular Meeting Woman's Auxiliary, Chicago, 6 February 1913; Officers' Conference of the Woman's Auxiliary, Chicago, 17 February 1916; "Minutes," Regular Meeting Woman's Auxiliary, Chicago, 2 March 1916, 29 March 1917, 2 May 1917; "Minutes," Annual Meeting, Woman's Auxiliary,

Chicago, 30 June 1918; "Minutes," Regular Meeting Woman's Auxiliary, Chicago, 8 April 1920, WA Papers.

70. "Minutes," Special Board Meeting, Woman's Auxiliary, Chicago, 31 May 1928; "Minutes," Executive Board Meeting, Woman's Auxiliary, Chicago, 3 October 1929, WA Papers. Patricia Hill found this in her study of the women's foreign mission societies of the mainline denominations; *The World Their Household*, pp. 98, 108. "Minutes," 31 May 1928; 3 October 1929, WA Papers.

71. *Cathedral Shelter Mission* (September 1928), p. 11.

72. "Minutes," Regular Meeting, 11 April 1901, 5 November 1915, 2 December 1915, 6 January 1916, 2 November 1920, February 1916; Officers' Conference of the Woman's Auxiliary, Chicago, 17 February 1916; "Bishop's Address," Annual Meeting, Woman's Auxiliary, Chicago, 25 May 1916; "Minutes," Regular Meeting, Woman's Auxiliary, Chicago, 8 April 1920, 20 November 1920, WA Papers.

73. "Minutes," Woman's Auxiliary Meeting, Chicago, 4 November 1920, WA Papers.

74. "Minutes," Annual Meeting, Woman's Auxiliary, Chicago, 7 February 1923, WA Papers.

75. "Minutes," Special Board Meeting, Woman's Auxiliary, Chicago, 31 May 1928, WA Papers.

76. Triennial Report, 1955–1958, WA Papers.

77. Ibid.

78. "Minutes," Executive Meeting, Woman's Auxiliary, Chicago, 2 December 1926, WA Papers.

79. A representative project of this era was one called Friendly Farms; women from all over the diocese came to St. James Parish House during the summer of 1932 and put up 12,000 cans of fruit and vegetables supplied by the rural parishes and missions. The goods were sent to the diocesan institutions.

80. Schultz, *The Church and the City*, pp. 205–210; Bishop Wallace Conkling Papers, 1941–1953; Diocesan Financial Papers, including Centenary Fund Papers (1930–1940), Bishop and Trustees Minutes (1930–1939), Diocesan Council Correspondence (1932–1940), Ways and Means (1938–1943), Committee of Seven (Refinancing the Debt) (1938), Finance Committee Minutes (1928–1933), Diocesan Mission Papers, including Town and Country Papers (1934–1965)—all in Deaconess Papers, EDC Archives.

81. "Society in Chicago," *Chicago Daily News*, 10 December 1947, 11 March 1950, p. 11; *Chicago Sunday Tribune*, 2 April 1961; "Fashions and Fancy," *Chicago Daily News*, (n.d.) December 1947; Mrs. Olga Houle, Letter to Parishioners, St. Chrysostom's Church, Chicago, 23 February 1955. The Business and Professional Woman's Guild at St. Chrysostom's met in evenings at Parish House for dinner and programs. For example, on 18 January 1954, Miss Marion A. McKinney, director of the Woman's Travel Department of the Union Pacific Railroad Company, talk, "Travel without Fuss and Feathers"; McKinney dem-

onstrated, with a miniature suitcase and doll models, how to pack three-weeks' travel wardrobe in one suitcase.

82. *100 Years, 1884–1984* (Chicago: Episcopal Churchwomen, 1984), pp. 31, 42, 47–48, 51, 55–56, 64–65, 76, 79.

83. "Program of the Women of the Church, 1956–57," Woman's Auxiliary, New York, 1 May 1956; ECW President to Miss Armstrong, 29 May 1957—both in WA Papers.

84. Donovan, *A Different Call,* p. 173. Not until 1967 did the General Convention finally allow women to serve as deputies to it; women were seated only in 1970, when this vote was affirmed—over fifty years after the acceptance of women as deputies had first been proposed. That same convention finally granted the women who served as deaconesses a status equivalent to that of male deacons: membership in the first order of ministry.

85. 1960 Annual Report of the Chicago ECW sent to Miss Frances M. Young, executive director, General Division of Women's Work of the National Council; "Minutes," Diocesan Board, Episcopal Churchwomen, Chicago, 5 October 1960, 7 December 1961, 6 December 1962, all in ECW Archives.

86. "Board Minutes," ECW, Chicago, 3 March 1960; 5 October 1960; 7 December 1961; 6 December 1962, all in ECW Archives.

87. The most dramatic example of the tension occurred when ECW chapters at various black parishes joined with black clergy and confronted the diocesan ECW board on the issue of representation of blacks in 1973. The board had selected a slate of all-white nominees to be delegates to the ECW Triennial Convention. The black clergy and women demanded better minority representation. The ECW board had responded that its procedures for selecting the slate had been "legal," according to the bylaws. This response was met with resentment and anger among local ECW chapters in black parishes. Several severed their ties with the diocesan ECW. The conflict eventually came to the annual diocesan ECW convention, where nominations of blacks for delegate positions were made from the floor. The outcome was to add one black name to the slate. Many felt it was not much of a victory and that race relations were at a very low level in the diocese among the ECW women. Several ECW chapters, like the one at Trinity Church, Chicago, never returned to the diocesan ECW organization. Mrs. Charlotte Alderson, president, to ECW presidents and the clergy of the South Deanery, 19 April 1973; The Revs. Henri A. Stines, Raymond S. Mitchell, and Charles Granger to Mrs. Charlotte Alderson, 25 April 1973; The Rev. Charles I. Granger, Jr., to Mrs. Charlotte Alderson, 23 April 1973; "Minutes," ECW Executive Meeting, 5 April 1973, ECW Archives.

88. Mrs. Robert Rodenmayer, Division of Christian Ministries, Episcopal Churchwomen of Chicago, 1963, ECW Archives.

89. Ibid.

90. Correspondence Files, 1968–1975; Cathedral of St. James; *Cathedral Newsletters,* 1961–1979; Change to Missionary Status, 1930, Church of the Epiphany; Correspondence and Papers, 1956–1973, Church of the Epiphany,

Chicago; Financial Papers, 1934–1964, Church of the Epiphany; Correspondence and Papers, 1960–1973, Trinity Church, Chicago—all in EDC Archives. See also Schultz, *The Church and the City.* These materials evidence the problems of three parishes in Chicago; they have differing resources but all face dislocations and change as a result of urban/suburban changes. On the other side, materials from new suburban parish files tell the story of growth and the problems involved with these decisions. See parish files for St. Anskar, Rockford; St. David, Aurora; St. Dunstan of Canterbury, Westchester; St. David, Glenview; St. Hilary, Prospect Heights; St. James the Less, Northbrook, all in EDC Archives.

91. Mrs. J. W. to ECW President, 1970; P. S. to ECW, 13 January 1970—both in Correspondence Files, ECW Archives.

92. The Reverend Canon Eric James, "Keynote Address," Annual Convention, Episcopal Churchwomen, Chicago, 1969, ECW Archives.

93. K. G. to ECW President, 2 April 1978, Correspondence Files, ECW Archives.

94. Robert Wuthnow, *The Restructuring of American Religion: Society and Faith since World War II,* pp. (Princeton: New Jersey: Princeton University Press, 1988), p. 139.

95. E. B. to ECW President, 8 December 1975, ECW Archives.

96. Rockford Emmanual Church ECW to ECW Board, 20 November 1973, ECW Archives.

97. Bishop Francis G. Burrill, "Address," Annual Convention, Episcopal Churchwomen, Chicago, 10–11 June 1964, ECW Archives.

98. Resolutions Regarding Critical Analysis of Organizational Structure of Episcopal Churchwomen, Triennial Meeting, St. Louis, Missouri, October 1964, ECW Archives.

99. Correspondence Files, 1970–1979, ECW Archives.

100. Wuthnow, *Restructuring of American Religion,* pp. 122–123; 126–127.

101. "Minutes," Standing Committee, 4 June 1969, 19 October 1971, 8 May 1974, EDC Archives.

102. Bishop James W. Montgomery, "Statement on Ordination of Women," 29 December 1976, EDC Archives.

103. "Resolutions," Annual Convention, Episcopal Churchwomen, Chicago, May 1973; Diocesan ECW Treasurer to President, ECW, St. Paul's by-the-Lake, Chicago, 24 September 1973, Correspondence Files, ECW Archives.

104. S. E. G. to ECW 10 May 1973; ECW Diocesan Secretary to S. E. G., 13 June 1973, Correspondence Files, ECW Archives.

105. Diocesan ECW President to D. H., 25 March 1971, Correspondence Files, ECW Archives.

106. Montgomery, "Statement on Ordination of Women," EDC Archives.

107. *Advance Magazine* (April 1978):5.

108. Ibid.

109. The Reverend R. L. Whitehouse to the Right Reverend John B. Coburn,

Bishop of Massachusetts, 15 July 1978. This letter was shared with me by the Reverend Nancy Grace Van Dyke Platt, to whom I am grateful for her openness in allowing me to know the details of her "exile" from her own diocese during the sixteen months she awaited ordination to the priesthood and endured the "back-door" policy.

110. Bishop John B. Coburn to Bishop James W. Montgomery, 6 June 1979; Mrs. Patricia C. Nason, administrative assistant to Bishop Coburn, to Nancy Platt, 17 October 1979; Letter Dimissory of the Reverend Nancy Grace Van Dyke Platt, from the Diocese of Chicago to the Diocese of Massachusetts, 20 November 1979; transfer from Diocese of Massachusetts to the Diocese of Chicago, 4 November 1980; received in Chicago by Bishop Montgomery, 17 November 1980. All the material noted here was shared with me by the Reverend Nancy Platt and are her personal papers.

111. Suffragan Bishop Quintin Primo, Chicago, to Nancy Platt, 25 June 1973, shared with the author by Nancy Platt.

112. K. G. to D. A., Holy Saturday 1978, Correspondence Files, ECW Archives.

113. Carol Rutledge and Ann Hallet to "Dear Sisters in Christ," St. Hilary's Church, Prospect Heights, Illinois, 15 August 1987; "A New Concept and Beginnings for ECW's and Christian Women's Groups," *Clerica*, (Chicago; March 1987). "Report on Women's Activities," Women of St. Paul's Church, Rogers Park, Chicago, 1984. "St. James Cathedral: A Shining Star," *Anglican Advance* (September 1989).

2

Episcopal Women as Community Leaders: Galveston, 1900–1989

Elizabeth Hayes Turner

Soon after Galveston entered the twentieth century it became a victim of the 1900 hurricane, at that time the worst natural disaster to have occurred in North America. Although suffering from the loss of an estimated 6,000 lives and two-thirds of its structures, the city began immediately to restore, rebuild, and reorganize.

The efforts of various women's groups were essential to the process, and in every community-oriented endeavor Episcopal women were among the organizers and the officers. This was not a new phenomenon in Galveston. From the end of the Civil War onward Episcopal women had assumed a leading role in community building, contributing more women to the ranks of civic leadership than any other religious institution. Why this should be true at the western extremities of the Old South is explained in part by the religious and social structure of the island city, by the tradition of Episcopal women in nineteenth-century benevolent enterprises, and by the church's teaching that a life of faith generates a transforming social ethic. Against a background of southern traditionalism and conservatism, this chapter attempts to explore the reasons why Episcopal women came to assume a dominant role in the Galveston's secular civic activities, to demonstrate how this interest in public activism coordinated with their parish involvement, and to show that although over time changes have taken place in women's social activism, spiritual motives have remained the guiding principles in their community involvement.

The notion that Episcopal women became the dominant force in civic activism is a concept at odds with accepted historical assumptions concerning the rise of women leaders in the New South. Scholarship explaining their emergence from their homes into civic and reforming activities has concentrated on the role of the Methodist Episcopal Church, South. The origins of a progressive movement for women southwide are said to be the women's home and foreign missionary societies established by Methodist women in the 1870s. In the following decade Frances Willard, president of the Women's Christian Temperance Union, toured the South and encouraged women, mostly from the evangelical churches,[1] to form unions, creating an alliance for the first time with a national women's organization. Motivated to engage in public reforming activities through basic human compassion and perfectionist theological tenets, and yet frustrated by unresponsive legislatures, southern evangelical women found that they needed the vote to effect their plans. By linking temperance to suffrage, scholars have helped to explain how an overwhelmingly evangelical South produced women who entered the ranks of the reformers, eventually reaching a feminist position regarding equal franchise and later establishing interracial cooperation and an equal rights agenda.[2]

The broad interpretive sweep may have been true for areas of the South where evangelical churches predominated numerically or at the state level, where individual women leaders may have followed a path from the WCTU to suffrage societies. But the South is far more varied than many have supposed or even have asserted, and no single paradigm suffices. In Galveston Baptist and Methodist churches were relatively small at first, the WCTU remained weak, and issues of class and elitism based on a thriving port economy led to economic and racial separation in women's organizations and civic leadership. Issues of economic superiority allowed privileged Episcopal (and in somewhat fewer numbers Presbyterian and Jewish) women to step into a majority of leadership positions in women's secular organizations. For reasons that shall be explained, women active in this city's progressive secular organizations came not from the Methodist Episcopal Church, South, in any great numbers but from the Protestant Episcopal Church.

Discovering why women from some denominations rather than others tended to fill leadership positions in civic affairs early in the city's history begins with an explanation of urban population and economic dynamics. Galveston more nearly resembled the port cities of Charleston, Mobile, and New Orleans in social and religious composition. In terms of economic vitality, however, it competed favorably with such interior cities as Atlanta, Nashville, Birmingham, and Dallas.[3] Like its older sister cities, Galveston maintained its economy principally through cotton factoring and shipping, businesses that led to the rise of other entrepreneurial enterprises: banking, merchandising, railroad construction, insurance, and cotton and flour mills. Accompanying the strong entrepreneurial base was the rise of iron works, utility companies, electric trolleys, a public school system (1881), and a branch of the University of Texas Medical School (1891). Small shops, dairies, fishing businesses, drayage and livery services, mortuaries, and many more of the accoutrements of a thriving city provided income for hundreds of families. Galvestonians by 1891 boasted that theirs was "the wealthiest city in the world of its size."[4]

In September 1900 Galveston's economic supremacy received a fatal blow from hurricane winds and thirty-foot waves. No amount of rebuilding, determination, or urban restructuring could win back the heady prosperity of the 1890s. Houston in 1914 dredged a port of its own and became the principal exporter of Texas's new-age commodity: oil. Galveston did not share in the spoils of the oil patch; instead, it capitalized on its coastal advantages to become the premier resort city on the Texas Gulf Coast. Tourism, a first-rate medical school, fishing, shipping, insurance companies, and military installations managed to save Galveston's economy; by 1980 it was a slow-growing average middle-sized city of 62,000.[5] For the most part investment capital left for more lucrative opportunities in other parts of the state. A few families whose fortunes had been made in the pre-storm era turned their wealth into twentieth-century foundations that aided the John Sealy Hospital, charities, medical research, and historic preservation.[6]

To discover how many women from the various denominations became civic activists, I gathered the names of women officers of various secular and semireligious women's organizations between 1880 and 1920. To these were added all of the church and synagogue women's societies and several organizations to which both men and women belonged, such as the United Charities and the Red Cross. The next step was to evaluate and categorize the secular organizations according to their goals and purposes stated in constitutions, charters, minutes, newspaper articles, and city directories. Organizations purely social in nature were not considered for this study, but those that directed their energies toward

community building, helping dependents regardless of religious affiliation, or promoting women's education or rights were seen to be advancing southern women into public life and were therefore considered
activist. The selected organizations fell into six classifications: benevolent institutions; auxiliaries; ethnic and immigrant women's aid societies;
patriotic and hereditary organizations; art, music, and literary clubs;
and civic associations. In all, forty-six church and synagogue societies
and twenty-seven semireligious and secular groups were chosen for
study.[7]

The next step involved becoming acquainted with the women who
served as officers of each organization. City directories were the most
useful source in this regard, but at times they were incomplete. Club
records when available filled in, as did newspaper clippings and state
histories of associations. Eventually I was able to extract from the general population for the years 1880 to 1920 a discrete group of 370 women
activists.

To establish their identities further, I added their husbands' names
when appropriate and searched for biographical information, such as
birth and death dates, place of birth, arrival in and departure from
Galveston, wedding date, number of children, number of servants, military service, education for the women, and community and political
affiliations for the men. This information was collected from community
books, blue books, obituaries, and manuscript census records for 1880,
1900, and 1910. Church affiliation was gleaned from church directories,
vestry and deacon minutes, and church histories. City directories provided the addresses and occupations for the years 1880, 1890, 1900,
1910, and 1921. Including the men, the number of Galvestonians under
consideration was close to 650. With establishment of the database it is
possible to estimate each woman's social status, count how many women
were involved in activist organizations, and ascertain their religious
affiliations.

In terms of denominational preference the Episcopal churches attracted the majority of the city's elite. The wealthiest of all congregants
in the years between 1880 and 1920 belonged to Trinity and Grace
Episcopal churches.[8] Ownership and directorship of the highly lucrative
cotton and transport companies, banks, law firms, mills, and import
business were in the hands of families whose education and upbringing
had prepared them for a life of elegance and refinement. Many came
from New England, the mid-Atlantic states, Virginia, and South Carolina. And most preferred to worship in the liturgically elegant Episcopal
churches. Even in antebellum days, the single most successful church

on the island in terms of numbers and prosperity was Trinity Episcopal Church.[9] It follows, then, that this denomination contributed the greatest number of men and women civic leaders to the community.

Although hovering at approximately 5 percent of the city's religious population, and 3 percent of the city's total population, 136 (36.7 percent) Episcopal women contributed to community leadership (Table 2–1). The Episcopal churches fostered more women leaders than any other denomination. Their representation among the 370 women activists, moreover, was seven times higher than their denominational representation in the city. Undoubtedly, a sense of noblesse oblige motivated their actions because ample incomes, leisure, and servants freed them from the confines of domestic duties. But a theology of grace, good works, and service carried over into community life in a way that liberated upper-class Episcopal women for work beyond their homes but still within the woman's cultural sphere.

Presbyterian women constituted the second-largest group of activist women in Galveston. Women members of the First Presbyterian Church and its mission churches were staunchly Calvinist in their worship; serious, hard-working, and on the whole, prosperous, they belonged largely to the upper and upper-middle classes. Rather than retiring into church life, Presbyterians saw community needs as a form of mission, an extension of Christian servanthood, and perhaps more than any other denomination, exhibited a desire to remain vital to the community despite fewer communicants.[10] Reflecting these concerns, Presbyterian women accounted for 54 (14.5 percent) of Galveston's 370 activist women.

Among the evangelical Protestant denominations, the Methodists, both northern and southern denominations, vied for numerical superiority. In terms of economic standing, however, southern Methodists began the century as solid middle-class citizens but became more prosperous over time. Baptists, probably because their denominational strength lay in rural churches, grew slowly in Galveston, their members drawn largely from the middle and lower-middle classes. As Baptists came to dominate the South, Baptists in Galveston began to increase as well, in 1960 surpassing all other denominations. Southern Methodists and Baptists made up approximately 5 percent of the churched population at the beginning of the century, and their numbers of women activists (Baptist, twenty-one; Methodist, thirty-nine) equaled or, in the case of Methodists, exceeded their denominational representation.[11]

Lutherans, who used German in their worship services until 1894, were the largest group of foreign Protestants. They made a significant

Table 2-1. White Churches and Activist Women by Denomination in Galveston, 1880–1920

Denomination	1890		1906		1916		Activist Women	
	Number	Percent*	Number	Percent	Number	Percent	Number	Percent
Baptist	734	5.3	534	2.5	1,220	5.2	21	5.6
Catholic[†]	8,200	55.1	14,872	70.2	11,299	48.6	20	5.4
Disciples of Christ	50				379	1.6	3	.8
Episcopal[†]	670	4.8	1,278	6.0	815	3.5	136	36.7
Jewish	650	4.7	200[‡]		1,000	4.3	36	9.7
Lutheran	787	5.2	758	3.5	1,152	4.9	7	1.8
Methodist, North	841		681		798			
Methodist, South	439	3.5	627	2.9	1,300	5.5	39	10.5
Presbyterian[§]	485	3.5	475	2.2	617	2.6	54	14.5
Unknown							50	13.5
Other	892[†]		1,932[†]		4,642[†]		4	1.0[‖]
Total Denominations[†]	13,748		21,157		23,222		370	
Total Population	29,084		34,355		41,863			

*Percent of churched populace. [†]Includes black congregants. [‡]Heads of families only. [§]Northern and Southern.
[‖]Christian Science = 1 and Swedenborgian = 3.

Sources: U.S. Census Office, Report on Population of the United States at the Eleventh Census: 1890, Part I (Washington, D.C.: 1895), p. 705; U.S. Census Office, Report on Statistics of Churches in the United States at the Eleventh Census: 1890 (Washington, D.C.: Government Printing Office, 1894), 112–13; U.S. Bureau of the Census, Religious Bodies: 1906, Part I (Washington, D.C.: Government Printing Office, 1910), pp. 381, 442; U.S. Bureau of the Census, Religious Bodies, 1916, Part I (Washington, D.C.: Government Printing Office, 1919), pp. 337, 405–407. Activist women were officers of Galveston organizations with community-building missions; officers were compiled from organizational records, city directories, and associational histories.

cultural impact on the island community, but their numbers were small and their economic position, with the exception of a few individuals, generally middle class. Lutheran women, although from families of skilled artisans and professionals, were among the most reluctant to enter leadership ranks. Only 7 (1.8 percent) were found among the 370 women civic activists, suggesting that patriarchal customs, lack of skills in speaking English, and immigrant status may have inhibited their ability to assume public roles.[12] Perhaps another reason that Lutheran women were fewer is that many financially successful Lutherans either converted to the Episcopal faith or married members of the Episcopal Church.

Jewish congregants composed 5 percent of the religious population by 1916, but among activist women the 36 Jewish women represented nearly 10 percent. A number of extremely wealthy Jewish families practiced community philanthropy, and the congregation as a whole with its outgoing and beloved Rabbi Henry Cohen, shepherd of the congregation for fifty years, found Galveston a hospitable environment for charitable deeds and assimilation.[13]

In terms of denominational predominance, Galveston, like its sister port city of New Orleans, was overwhelmingly Catholic. Historically, the city hosted Catholic immigrants from Germany and Ireland who filled the ranks of the working classes as dockworkers, cotton loaders, fishermen, and petty entrepreneurs. Only occasionally did a Catholic family enter the ranks of the city's professional or grand entrepreneurs. Because civic leadership in the New South depended on status, Catholic women were at a decided disadvantage in joining the ranks of women activists. Catholic institutions did not encourage women's secular activities, and Protestant civic leaders displayed little interest in including them in benevolent and civic affairs. Consequently, Catholics, the majority of residents on the island, contributed only 20 (5 percent) of the 370 women community leaders.[14]

Galvestonians tended to sort themselves by congregation according to class. Methodists and Baptists filled the ranks of the middle classes; wealthier citizens preferred the Episcopal and Presbyterian churches. Inevitably, acceptance into positions of civic leadership hinged on class standing, and this was no less true for women whose status depended on their husbands or other male relatives. Civic leaders came from the elite classes; middle-class to lower-middle-class women came to civic leadership in smaller numbers, chose not to participate, or were, especially in the nineteenth century, not included. Toward the middle of the twentieth century, class categories tended to blur, and though historical elitism resides with the older churches on the island to this day, no single church has the corner on wealth. Still, patterns of community involvement for Galveston women have traditionally resided with those congregations—Episcopal, Presbyterian, and to a lesser degree Jewish—that have maintained elite status and have traditionally supported secular civic reform.[15]

Two of the most important assumptions of this chapter are that women reformers in Galveston responded to urban problems as they saw needs arise, and that Episcopal women, although participants in conservative southern cultural traditions, experienced fewer obstacles to their entrance into urban problem solving. Several factors that prevented southern evangelical women from immersing themselves in urban problems stemmed from the denominations' provincialism, their overwhelmingly rural nature, and their emphasis on a theology of personal salvation. The largest Methodist and Baptist churches in Galveston were affiliated with the Southern Baptist Convention and the Methodist Episcopal Church, South.

The rural nature of these denominations and their "all-pervading poverty" diminished evangelical concerns over urban problems. In 1916, 92.4 percent of Baptists and 89.8 percent of Methodists resided in rural areas across the South. Since their separation in the 1840s from national denominations, Methodists and Baptists lacked experience with churches and communicants in northern cities or with theological schools outside the South.[16] Urban expansion in the South, although steady, created challenges for evangelical southern churches later than it did for national churches. In 1906 Methodists laudably responded in Galveston to the influx of immigrants from eastern Europe, but their efforts at some form of relief for the needy came thirty years after Episcopal women had established poor relief societies. Last, a theology of personal redemption motivated evangelicals to see cures for society's ills in evangelism, conversion, and individual transformation. Their missions were directed toward saving souls particularly in foreign mission fields, with only the belated recognition that "it was sometimes necessary to support social reform programs."[17]

Episcopal parishes in the South, on the other hand, relied on their connection to a national church for inspiration, guidance, and for models of progressive action with regard to urban problems. Mary Donovan has pointed to the fact that Episcopal women created models for ministry in urban settings that both offered them "a broader range of activities than in most other denominations" and provided examples for their southern sisters.[18] Episcopal doctrine that emphasized good works and responsibility for the poor, particularly in the context of community, encouraged women to minister to those in need. Donovan has also remarked that Episcopal women shared a "unique attitude toward social service," wherein laywomen assumed active servanthood, following Christ's commandment to minister to the poor and suffering. Evangelism leading to conversion and possible membership was not their primary concern. And witnessing, so popular among evangelical sects, was left to the priests. Women educated others, organized, and served, only later insisting on theological training to carry on that side of ministry.[19] Donovan writes primarily about the role of women within the church, about their enormous impact on the acceptance and implementation of programs designated as part of the social gospel movement.

Equally arresting are the ways in which Episcopal women used their church training to carry programs to the community: programs of amelioration, relief, civic betterment, woman suffrage, and improved race relations. Edgar Gardner Murphy, priest and spokesman for the Episcopal Church, while ministering in Texas, preached that service and sacrifice to the community good were ideals to which those who made up the privileged classes or "wealth-worthy" should give priority. He believed that philanthropy should be personal, an ecclesiastical form of the gospel of wealth that did not necessarily challenge the hierarchy of the social classes but that called for a caring distribution of resources to ameliorate suffering. How much of Murphy's theology found its way to the hearts and minds of Episcopal women in Galveston is difficult to determine, but his theology fit well with southerners' conservative notions of social concern.[20]

The involvement of Episcopal women in community activism began with the founding of Trinity Church Guild in 1875 and continued well into the twentieth century. The guild's primary goal was in outreach to the poor, and it was one of the few charitable organizations on the island that practiced systematic, sustained poor relief to the city's stranded, unemployed, sick, poor, and aged.[21] Presbyterian women formed a similar society in the 1880s, but other poor relief societies, such as those organized by the Lutherans and the Jews, primarily helped their own members. Methodist and Baptist women, in an extension of evangelism, by the 1880s had organized home and foreign missionary societies.[22] Although raising money for missionaries and for missions, whether home or foreign, did educate Christian women in needs beyond their provincial world, it did not necessarily bring them into direct contact with urban ills. Too many missionary societies met in protected church parlors as they planned the ways and means of mission funding. By contrast, Trinity Church Guild began not as an auxiliary to missions but as a benevolent society, a poor relief agency that interviewed the poor, visited them in their homes, evaluated their needs, and raised the money to support them through sales of handcrafted items.

Other legacies for Episcopal women resulted from direct contact with the urban poor. A coalition of men and women of various faiths established the Galveston Orphans' Home, and by 1900 women had founded the Letitia Rosenberg Woman's Home, another orphanage, and a free kindergarten for children of factory workers. Although the boards of lady managers were accorded representation by members of all the white churches, Episcopal, Presbyterian, and to a lesser extent Jewish women dominated them.[23] The boards constituted a female hierarchy, a religious voluntary elite among whom status was as important as piety. The members' responsibilities as caretakers of orphans, aged women, and children from the factory district were commensurate with their status in the community, and though they may have used the boards for their own social purposes, there is no doubt that they also advanced their own roles as semipublic servants while allowing broader application of women's domestic values. Most important for women's twentieth-century activism, benevolent institutions served as training bases for future civic involvement, and they remained under female dominance, aided by various forms of community support, until the 1970s, when social service agencies co-opted their functions.

In the halcyon years of the 1890s elite women ventured into the world of secular women's clubs. The Wednesday Club, the Echo Club, the Ladies' Musical Club, and numerous patriotic and hereditary women's organizations—the Daughters of the Republic of Texas, the Daughters of the American Revolution, and the United Daughters of the Confederacy—emerged to grant women a separate but elevated world of refinement. The organizations differed entirely from benevolent institutions; they were not charities. And although they differed from one another as well in purpose and mission, they shared a commonality in bringing well-to-do women together for self-improvement and the building of esteem. Education was a common theme throughout each of the clubs, whether that meant learning Brahms's *Requiem,* Shakespeare's *Julius Caesar,* or the true history of Texas independence.[24]

The nineties proved to be a wellspring decade for women as it brought them together in greater numbers than ever before, and focused on their self-improvement or artistic development. Episcopal women were fortunate to have open to them opportunities for service and leadership in parish guilds, which served both the parish and the poor; on boards of lady managers of benevolent institutions; and in women's literary and

artistic clubs. Episcopal women dominated nearly every women's organization founded before the turn of the century (Table 2–2). Galveston
white women in the 1890s, through women's church societies, boards
of lady managers, and women's clubs, were preparing themselves for
even more active civic roles in the Progressive period. But they learned
their first lessons in civic leadership through crisis.

On September 8,1900, the most destructive hurricane ever to reach
the North American continent slammed into the unprotected island,
thence carrying its deadly winds and rain across the nation, finally blow-
ing itself out over the Atlantic Ocean. For fifteen hours Galvestonians
endured the maelstrom, awaking as if from a nightmare to a city with
over 3,500 of its structures demolished and approximately 6,000 (nearly
18 percent) of its 38,000 citizens drowned. Removal of debris and dis-
posal of bodies were problems that pressed for immediate attention.
After efforts at burial failed, authorities decided to burn the bodies in
great funeral pyres; the ordeal lasted for six weeks. Sheltering the homeless and dispensing clothing, food, and medicines fell to the hastily
devised Central Relief Committee and the Red Cross.[25] A call to the
nation's charity brought generous gifts to help in relief and restoration.[26]
Within three weeks telegraph service, electricity, water, and transportation had been restored and business had returned to near normal.[27]
Within a year the city had also created a city commission form of government, probably the most significant urban structural reform to
emerge in the Progressive era. City commission became a model for
hundreds of cities across the nation, and put Galveston on the map as
a "progressive city."[28]

Women's Secular Organizations, 1900–1920

Galveston women who were eager to bring their talents to bear mobilized for action. Those who had performed acts of charity through the
women's societies of their churches and synagogues, through boards of
lady managers of benevolent institutions, and who had organized wom-
en's clubs drew upon the concept of a national network of women's civic
organizations to meet the crisis. In March 1901 survivors of the storm
created the Women's Health Protective Association (WHPA), a civic-
minded women's club, that first tended to the reburial of victims of the
hurricane whose bodies had been improperly interred, committed themselves to revegetating the denuded island, and agitated for and worked
toward a cleaner, healthier environment.

TABLE 2-2.   Activist Women's Membership in Select Women's Clubs by Church Affiliation, 1890–1920

Affiliation	Wednesday Club		Ladies Chorus		DRT		DAR		UDC	
	Number	Percent	Number	Percent	Number	Percent	Number	Percent	Number	Percent
Episcopal	41	46.59	32	66.6	23	44.23	28	62.22	17	38.64
Presbyterian	11	12.5	6	12.24	9	17.31	3	6.67	6	13.64
Unknown	10	11.36	2	4.08	6	11.54	3	6.67	6	13.64
Catholic	7	7.95	1	2.04	3	5.77	3	6.67	9	20.45
Methodist	7	7.95	1	2.04	5	9.62	2	4.44	3	6.82
Baptist	5	5.68	1	2.04	4	7.69	5	11.11	3	6.82
Jewish	4	4.54	4	8.16	1	1.92				
Christian Church	1	1.14								
Lutheran	1	1.14	1	2.04						
Swedenborgian	1	1.14	1	2.04	1	1.92	1	2.22		
TOTAL	88	100%	49	100%	52	100%	45	100%	44	100%

Note: DRT = Daughters of the Republic of Texas; DAR = Daughters of the American Revolution; UDC = United Daughters of the Confederacy.

Sources: Activist women members of women's clubs were compiled from club records, club histories, club directories, blue books, church directories, and women's church and synagogue associational records.

By 1913 sanitation had replaced beautification as the association's major focus. The women demanded from city government compliance with the 1907 Texas Pure Food and Drug Act. The battle to enforce sanitation on dairies, markets, meat markets, and groceries continued through 1917, until the outbreak of war diverted their attention. The WHPA, with its coterie of highly motivated progressive women, fought for and won updated city building ordinances, regular inspection of food producers, elimination of breeding grounds of flies and mosquitoes, regular medical examination of schoolchildren, the establishment of public playgrounds, hot-lunch programs, and well-baby and tuberculosis clinics.[29] In a flurry of public activity, domestic politics had become public policy.[30]

Still, the WHPA was typical of women's progressive clubs across the country, and was the first in the city open to all white women "of good character."[31] Although the club democratically elected its officers each year, leaders from women's groups in the 1880s and 1890s constituted the majority of leaders. Experience, status, and ambition put a majority of Episcopal and Presbyterian women at its helm.[32] Of the six women presidents of the WHPA in the years between 1901 and 1919, four were members of Trinity Church. The most striking evidence of the influence of Trinity Guild, as opposed to the parish alone, can be seen in the histories of these four presidents: Mrs. Joseph Clark, Mrs. Bertrand Adoue, Mrs. George D. (Jean Scrimgeour) Morgan, and Dr. Ethel Lyon Heard. Three of the four belonged to Trinity Guild; Mrs. Adoue served as its president from 1875 to 1883, Mrs. Clark became president of the guild in 1918, and Jean Morgan belonged to both Trinity and Grace Episcopal sisterhoods and served as president of Grace Episcopal's sisterhood in 1901. Ethel Lyon Heard, a physician, city pathologist, suffragist, and member of Trinity Church waged the "Better Baby Campaign," instructed citizens in first aid through the YWCA, and fought city government over enforcement of the Pure Food and Drug Act. All of these women held positions of prominence in the community, three by virtue of their husbands' careers and their own volunteer careers, one through her own professional life.

The storm marked the beginning in Galveston of civic work for white women of all classes, and heralded the advent of a progressive women's community made up of organizations such as the WHPA, the Women's Christian Temperance Union (WCTU), the Galveston Equal Suffrage Association (GESA), the Juvenile Protective League, Mothers' Clubs, and the Young Women's Christian Association (YWCA).[33] In many ways the first two decades of the twentieth century became women's decades, as they organized to protect the health, physical well-being, and equal rights of women and children. Episcopal women continued to lead in the purely secular organizations as executive officers and as members of the boards of directors.

Because of the open nature of these organizations, Methodist and Baptist women were no longer underrepresented in secular women's groups on account of class and status, yet they did not compose a majority of the officers of the secular progressive women's groups. Evangelical women and Episcopal and Presbyterian women continued to divide not only on issues of class, which however subtly still persisted, but on type of organization. No Episcopal women, for example, entered the officer ranks of the WCTU, which was composed almost entirely of Methodist, Baptist, and a few Presbyterian women.[34] And evangelical women preferred primarily to join Christian associations. In other words, women from evangelical Protestant churches, if they entered the public sphere at all, tended to confine their activism to organizations where Christianity guided the organizing principle.[35] The one women's organization in which Episcopal, Presbyterian, Methodist, and Baptist women met in nearly equal numbers as members of the board of directors was the YWCA. The obvious Christian emphasis of the organization attracted members of evangelical churches to the board, but Episcopal and Presbyterian women, no less ardent in their desire for a structured program of Christian emphasis and protection for young women, backed the organization with funds, volunteer labor, and officers. In fact, a wealthy Episcopalian, Cornelia B. (Mrs. J. C.) League, donated $200,000 for the completion of the YWCA building in 1924.[36]

The Galveston Equal Suffrage Association, the most "radical" in terms of women's rights, was also dominated by women of the Episcopal and Presbyterian faiths. Ten of twenty-four identifiable officers between the year of its founding, 1912, and 1920 were Episcopal; four were Presbyterian; two were Methodist; and one was Baptist.[37] Indicating the nearly nonexistent link between suffrage and the WCTU, only one suffrage officer maintained membership in the WCTU. Tension between the two groups was so strong that in 1915 she resigned from the GESA over perceived scorn on the part of suffragists toward WCTU leaders. The truth is that Galveston suffragists and WCTU members moved in different circles bound by religion and economic status.[38]

Increasing professionalization also tended to be found more often among women of the nonevangelical churches. Of twenty-four identifiable suffragist officers, nine were professionals: a librarian, a physician (Dr. Heard), and two teachers all of the Episcopal faith, as well as one

Presbyterian real estate agent made up over half the group. And, interestingly, of the ten Episcopal women who were suffragists, six belonged to women's societies within Trinity or Grace parishes; two were
presidents of these societies. Episcopal women were better able than
even the Presbyterians to maintain membership in both secular civic
and Christian civic organizations while continuing their strong involvement in women's parish life. The reason rested upon the fact that Episcopal women, inheritors of the traditions of the servant church,
reconciled their faith and the needs of the secular world more successfully than did women of the evangelical churches.[39] And at no time did
the parish lend women the support they needed better than during the
1920s.

Parish and Civic Life, 1920–1930

On April 3, 1919, the Reverend Raimundo de Ovies, an Englishman
of Spanish descent, arrived in Galveston to become Trinity Episcopal
Church's fifth rector. During the years that de Ovies ministered in Galveston (1919–1927), the parish became more businesslike in its structure,
and for the first time acknowledged openly that the congregation stood
for service to the community.[40] The message was broadcast in hundreds
of different ways, but none more forcefully than through the creation
of the Church Service League, an organization designed by the national
church, transmitted through the Diocese of Texas, and implemented by
scores of parishes across South Texas. It was the Episcopal answer to
a United Charities, and served as a channel and a clearinghouse for the
many and varied organizations (mostly women's groups) that existed at
the parish level.

The Church Service League represented the culmination of the "progressive" spirit in Christian life. Once Episcopal women became actively
engaged in community affairs during the years between 1900 and 1920,
their work in the community and in church work that affected lives
outside the parish did not end with the passage of suffrage or the demise
of the Wilson era. Rather the progressive spirit continued, at least until
the Great Depression.[41]

The enthusiasm for the creation of its Church Service League at Trinity came initially from Mrs. Clinton S. Quin, wife of the newly elected
bishop coadjutor of the Diocese of Texas, who was responsible for
encouraging the new plan in all Texas parishes.[42] Trinity responded with
alacrity, and on May 20, 1921, de Ovies called a meeting of women

active in parish organizations to create a parish league. He prophesied that "the Church Service League would become the most powerful organization in the Church," which, except for vestry control, it did. Then Mrs. Quin spoke about the league's purpose. "She said that it came into being with the Nation Wide Campaign," and that its purpose was to federate—"in order to prevent overlapping—all women's organizations in the church and to help every woman to 'line up' for service."[43]

The concept of the Church Service League followed vaguely along the lines of a rationalization of church processes. Orderliness and an efficient approach to the "business" of the church began with the administrations of both Quin and de Ovies. Trinity's new rector compared "the work of the Church in the Parish to the working of a large corporation," and called it "God's Business." In his schema the parish was the corporation, the rector was its business manager, the vestry its board of directors. Heads of departments were the Sunday school superintendent, the officers of the guilds, societies, and brotherhoods, and the organist and choirmaster. The working force was made up of teachers, choir members, ushers, and members of parish organizations. The corporation's goal was to work toward "Christian, modern, efficient SERVICE to the Community," with "Trinity Church the most influential organization for GOOD in the State of Texas."[44]

For the rector, the Church Service League offered another opportunity to whip the congregation into shape and to head it off into deliberate (as opposed to haphazard) community service. For the women's organizations, it provided much more: an overarching organizational structure to help them implement their many tasks, and a concerned and interested body "above" them in the diocese and the national church reminding them that their efforts were not seen by God alone. For women who made community relations their voluntary careers, the league brought two added benefits: first, a deliberate and open policy of furthering God's work in the community outside the parish, and second, accountability. Every organization within the league submitted a report of its activities, an accounting of its involvement not just within the parish but in the community, the diocese, the nation, and the world. The groups that had given time only to the parish were at least shown a model of a larger ministry and given leave to think about, and perhaps act on, their Christian duties beyond the churchyard.[45] This in itself would have been quite enough to encourage the spirit of corporate efficiency, but there was more.

Within the Church Service League four standing committees were

formed that reported to the diocese and acted as spurs to the service
"line up":[46] Education, which handled the programs for the year; Publicity, which kept track of the parish calendar, telephoning, and press
releases; Recruiting, which brought in volunteers and encouraged baptism, confirmation, and parish membership; and, significantly, Social
Service. The primary task of the Social Service Committee was to report
on community problems such as public health and the need for district
nursing, to visit the sick in hospitals, to introduce Americanization (for
mainstreaming recent foreign arrivals), and to oversee recreation.[47]

From the beginning Jean Scrimgeour Morgan chaired the Social Service Committee. As the parish's foremost progressive activist, she had
for years led the way toward civic involvement.[48] From 1908 to 1915
she had served as president of the Women's Health Protective Association; while doing that she began selling Red Cross Christmas seals
for the Texas Anti-Tuberculosis Association. She worked through the
war years for the Red Cross, and then, under its auspices, in 1919
founded the Galveston Public Health Nursing Service, which sent nurses
to the poor and sick. She continued her affiliation with all of these
organizations and became a member of the board of directors of the
YWCA.[49] Probably no one better represented Trinity Episcopal Church
in civic affairs; Morgan never forgot her Christian roots. In an address
to the women of the church she proclaimed that "the responsibility rests
upon us to give as much at least to the community as we receive from
it. If we are using up more than we give we are parasites, and parasite
and Christian are contradictory terms." "Christian Social Service is the
Church at work; it is Christ in action through us."[50]

The league's Social Service Committee served as an arm to the community, its members touching those areas of life that were public and
secular. Morgan's reports of these efforts read like a community activity
list. "Nearly every organization for good work among the poor, and
others, is made up largely of members of Trinity Church, or those who
are Episcopalian."[51] Trinity women were listed in no fewer than twelve
of the city's leading civic groups in 1921, and in 1925 of the twenty-
seven clubs that Protestant women were able to join, ten were presided
over by Episcopal women.[52] Eleanor Thompson, the only woman to win
election to the Galveston School Board of Trustees in 1917, was at the
same time president of Trinity Guild.[53] Women from Trinity continued
to fill the boards of lady managers for the two orphans' homes, the
woman's home, and the first free kindergarten. They continued to be
active in the Women's Civic League (formerly the WHPA), and because
so many had been suffragists, the League of Women Voters. For many,

these activities represented an obligation to the community that came with their wealth and prestigious position. But noblesse oblige alone does not account for the overwhelming numbers of Episcopal women in civic affairs or for the quality of their servanthood. Also at work was an Episcopal theology that affirmed serving humanity in its many areas outside the church and in its variety of needs. Although Trinity's priests and women leaders had evinced this position from the 1870s, only in the 1920s with the coming of de Ovies, the diocesan emphasis on service, and a national church campaign—the culmination of progressivism— did the parish make public avowals to work even more diligently for the community.[54]

The call to community service was internalized differently by various parish members. Some saw it as a way finally to integrate women's volunteer work with men's, ending rigid separations between men's and women's associations. The Red Cross, United Charities, and the school board were first steps for women into volunteer working relationships with men. Others, remaining securely within a woman's sphere, found their place of service within secular women's organizations such as the Women's Civic League, the League of Women Voters, and the YWCA. And some parish women who had no desire to secularize their efforts at all found the parish organizations sufficiently service oriented to meet their call to activism. That is why the Church Service League of the 1920s marks a watershed period in the life of the church. For once the worlds of secular and religious efforts were engulfed in a wave of di-ocesan and national approval. But it could not last.

The minutes for the Church Service League of February 16, 1928, state that "the new Executive Board for Women's Work in the Diocese would no longer be responsible for promoting the Parish Organization of C.S.L. or Parish Council." The organizations within the parish would not change, but there would no longer be a diocesan emphasis on a parish clearinghouse such as the CSL had been. Although Trinity's Church Service League continued for several more months, it too did not survive the coming of the depression years.[55]

The extinguishing of the CSL, which occurred at the national level as well, left the parish with little supervision over community efforts by its members, and outreach efforts become difficult to trace. Still, depression woes in 1930 led the Reverend Edmund H. Gibson to open the city's only soup kitchen, staffed by men and women volunteers. From the time of its opening in November to its closing in February 1931 after "conditions [had] definitely improved," the kitchen served 25,000 meals, supplied 200 persons with clothing, and found jobs for more than 100 people.[56] It was ecumenically supported by donations from all "religious faiths and creeds." One other attempt to minister directly to the needs of the working poor was the founding in 1934 of Sunshine Cottage, a community center on the island's West End. Kindergarten classes and lessons for older children were directed briefly by a team of parish women. The soup kitchen and Sunshine Cottage were two of the last evidences of hands-on outreach to the poor by the parish.[57]

Secular and Church Societies, 1930 to the Present

After 1931 emphasis on community activism among the women's parish societies declined. There are reasons other than the demise of the Church Service League or the advent of the depression for this. First, the rising emphasis on foreign mission support from the diocese diverted attention away from poor relief. In 1903 Trinity had inaugurated a chapter of the Woman's Auxiliary to the Board of Missions, presided over in its early years by Mrs. Charles Aves, the rector's wife. The group coordinated with the national church efforts to spread the gospel world-wide. It also included every baptized woman on the church rolls, making it a predecessor to Women of the Church. Deflecting interest away from poor relief and into missions, study, and prayer was in some ways a means of compensating for the co-optation of poor-relief efforts by secular agencies, and also a means of harnessing women's efforts into serving the agenda of the women's component of the national church. The Woman's Auxiliary came to resemble missionary societies in all of Galveston's other Protestant churches, which at the same time were also pulling in among themselves, dividing into circles, reading and learning about missions, and receiving guidelines from women's agencies at the denominational level.[58]

The shift of women's church societies away from direct aid to the poor gave churchwomen fewer opportunities for the church to work through them in the community. Trinity Guild and others, such as the Ladies Aid Society of the First Presbyterian Church, thirty years earlier had begun to shift their work away from charity to the poor outside the parish and concentrate instead on the parish alone. The storm was the ostensible cause, but eventually governmental and secular agencies began to serve the community's welfare needs thereby supplanting church-women's charity. County Commission minutes indicate an increase in aid to indigents between 1900 and 1920.[59] The founding of the United Charities in 1914, which acted as a clearinghouse for relief work, brought under one agency a form of systematic social welfare. Its creators were men active in the commercial life of the city, but its first board of directors, representing various denominations, was composed of five men and two women from the community. The two women, Margaret Sealy Burton and Sally Trueheart Williams, were members of the Episcopal and Presbyterian churches, respectively. Soon after its organization, United Charities hired a professional woman administrator, who coordinated the efforts of at least twelve church benevolent societies and petitioned the county commissioners for aid to individuals in need.[60]

Public health agencies, some of them founded by Episcopal women, oversaw visiting nurses, well-baby clinics, and hot-lunch programs in the schools. John Sealy Hospital, named for its Episcopal benefactor, became the city's charity hospital, and by the 1920s, Jennie Sealy Smith, a longtime member of Trinity Guild, had funded and built a women's hospital.[61] Churchwomen interested in serving the poor sought nomination to the boards of directors of separate charitable institutions or to federated agencies.

The city's economy suffered setbacks during the 1920s and 1930s that went beyond depression-era doldrums. Cotton, the king of exports for Galveston in the years before World War I, no longer drove the Texas economy. Its replacement, black gold, had passed the city by. The Spindletop gusher in 1901, which inaugurated the Texas oil boom, came as Galveston was still prostrate from the 1900 hurricane. Houston in 1914 completed dredging the Buffalo Bayou for a deep-water port, leaving Galveston with little but leftover shipping business. Furthermore, the city's growth did not keep up with burgeoning towns to the north and west. Had none of these economic vicissitudes beset the Gulf Coast city, the guilds and ladies' aid societies still might have reverted to primary parish care, but the economy did not attract the upwardly mobile, and thus the churches began to suffer a lack of funds. They needed their women's groups to find the ways and means to keep the churches open.

The outcome of this retreat from direct involvement in urban and social problems by parish societies was a long period of introversion for parish workers. No program to address the increasingly obvious problem of discrimination in employment, housing, and schooling for black citizens of Galveston was set forth.

Episcopal churches were not alone in their retreat from the more pressing problems of urban life. Few churches in Galveston were able to square off against the South's number-one social problem: segregation. Southern women, constrained by custom and traditions of conservatism, often feared the white community's contempt for fostering egalitarian ideas. To fulfill their obligations to the city, then, Episcopal and Presbyterian women sought "safe" outlets for their Christian outreach. Women gave over 4,000 hours of volunteer service to John Sealy Hospital, and served on the boards of the County Welfare Association, Junior League, and the Red Cross.[62] Women of all denominations visited shut-ins, hosted church dinners, clothed orphans, supported seminary students, and raised money for missions. Because they contributed to the domestication of churches in the twentieth century, they filled the space assigned them in the nurturing roles of homemaker, nurse, and teacher, always providing the personal, caring touch. "Every [women's] circle was allotted a 'shut-in' to cheer up by visiting. These sick people were taken small gifts, plants, and cookies," read a Presbyterian Women of the Church report in 1967. Personal ministry constituted for women an important segment of "work devoted to the service of Christ and His Church. . . . [63]

Pressed into a kind of retreat to home life in the post–World War II era, most laywomen responded as though nurturing, domesticity, and personal ministry within the parish were natural callings. Traditional explanations exist for why women, who had greatly augmented the labor force during the war, should be content with homemaking roles in family and church. These rest on the supposition that increased materialism, retirement from the twenty years of social and political upheaval, return of men from the war, the attraction of a wife-companion model, and pseudoscientific studies showing women to be "naturally" domestic had enticed white women to retreat to the suburbs.[64] Churches, benefiting from the nation's return to traditional values, received a spurt of new growth as families enrolled their little ones on cradle rolls. Most of the older churches in Galveston reached their peak of growth during the 1960s. But they successfully avoided contact with minorities in blighted urban areas, though no more than ten blocks away (Table 2–3).[65]

Personal ministry, although an essential part of church life, was not conducive to focusing on the most pressing of societal problems. Racial discrimination, the major issue of the 1950s and 1960s, was not addressed in any systematic manner by white churchwomen. That is not to say that white Christian women completely ignored the problem of race relations, but southern customs of public separation, especially for women, made interaction with blacks in solving the dilemma of discrimination, poverty, and undereducation difficult. Churchmen and churchwomen often saw opportunities for Christian service *to* blacks instead of *with* blacks. In the late 1930s one Presbyterian woman, head of the

TABLE 2-3.　Membership in Four Galveston Churches, 1900–1980

Year	Trinity Episcopal	First Presbyterian	Moody Memorial Methodist	First Baptist
1900	611		348	
1910	902	453	629	
1920	627	576	904	
1930	1,164		1,121	
1940	1,370		1,101	
1950	1,474		997	
1960	1,661		1,336	2,346
1970	1,247	626	1,169	2,543
1980	1,063	770	1,074	1,796

Sources: Journals of the Annual Council of the Protestant Episcopal Church in the Diocese of Texas, 1900–1980; Journals of the Annual Sessions of the Texas Conference of the Methodist Episcopal Church South, 1900–1980; Minutes of Session, 1910 and 1920, of the First Presbyterian Church, Galveston, Box 1, First Presbyterian Church Records (Rosenberg Library, Galveston); Session's Annual Statistical Report, The Presbyterian Church in the United States, 1970 and 1980 (First Presbyterian Church, Galveston); *Minutes of the Annual Session of the Galveston Baptist Association, 1960–1980.*

Christian Social Service committee, taught "a weekly Bible class to a group of Negro women in the West End," awarding each of them a book at the end of the year. Some of the circles sent clothing and money to Stillman College, a black Presbyterian school in Tuscaloosa, Alabama.[66] Among Episcopalians in Galveston, white and black clergy and laypeople conducted the Summer Conference and School of Religion for blacks in 1948 at St. Augustine Episcopal Church. And at the 1961 Annual Diocesan Meeting held in Galveston, the more than one thousand delegates focused on "modern industrial urbanization, the special challenge it offers and how it can best be met."[67]

Problems of integration had long concerned the bishops of the Diocese of Texas. As early as 1933 Bishop Clinton S. Quin had worked to achieve integrated diocesan camps for black and white children but found strong opposition. He included without incident for the first time in 1938 black clergy in the Clergy Conference. Fortunately, black parishes had always been given voting rights in the Diocese of Texas, and by the 1950s the diocese had formed the Bi-Racial Committee, which included black and white clergy.[68]

Not until Bishop John E. Hines (who had served as bishop coadjutor of Texas from 1945 to 1955) took the reins in 1956 did civil rights receive the determined push that it needed within the diocese. National events such as *Brown* v. *Board of Education,* the Montgomery bus boycott, and federal troops in Little Rock, Arkansas, exerted their influence on concerns over integration within the diocese. Hines presided over the

1958 and 1959 Diocesan Councils in which delegates voted to integrate the diocesan high school in Austin and to desegregate diocesan summer camps gradually. St. Stephen's School in Austin admitted its first black student in 1961, but not without concerted opposition from conservatives within the diocese. In fact, Hines, having come into authority in the midst of tremendous social upheaval, was left beleaguered and wearied by those in the diocese who dreaded changes in the social order. In 1958 the Diocesan Development Fund Campaign had failed, in part due to the lack of belief in the bishop's social programs. The 1960 Report on the State of the Church found the conditions of the church fractious, disheartening, distorted, dissonant, and temporal, and recommended that the diocese fall to its knees in self-examination. Hines and his supporters were accused by some in the diocese of communist aims in consequence of calls to remove racial barriers from all diocesan institutions. Despite the opposition, at the 1963 Diocesan Council the Department of Christian Social Relations spoke out for an end to racial prejudice in the parishes.[69]

Against this background of unrest and agitation the Galveston Episcopal community—black and white—struggled to come together. By their own admission members of Trinity Church found the transition to social equality difficult. Yet a turning point came for them when a few individual women members of Trinity participated in the civil rights marches and in the sit-in at Walgreen's Drugstore in 1960. Meanwhile the parish desegregated in 1962 and Trinity Church School did so at about the same time. The three most active and vocal clergy in the integration transition were Rabbi Henry Cohen, a lifelong advocate of ethnic and religious tolerance and racial equality; Father Dan O'Connell of St. Mary's (Roman Catholic) Cathedral; and the Reverend Edmund Gibson of Trinity Episcopal Church.[70] Although desegregation of schools, lunch counters, recreation centers, and public transportation proceeded fairly smoothly in Galveston, the problem of dealing with inequalities in economic opportunities, housing, and past patterns of discrimination that had left older generations of minorities disadvantaged still needed to be addressed. Progress in this direction was begun in great measure not by white Episcopal women but by members of St. Augustine of Hippo Episcopal Church, traditionally a black congregation dating back to its founding in 1885 and its acceptance as the first black mission in the diocese in 1886.

St. Augustine Episcopal Church began with a group from the British West Indies who had been members of the Church of England and were accustomed to electing their own vestry and receiving ministrations from black clergy. Their independent spirit continued through the years, in part because lay delegates were granted full voting privileges in Diocesan Council meetings. The mission was served by both black and white clergy at various times, but in 1954 the mission received the Reverend Fred Sutten, a white Texan, who changed dramatically the nature of Episcopal outreach in Galveston.[71]

Sutten's concern for "the socially deprived" led him in 1955 to mobilize the congregation to establish St. Vincent's House, at first a chapel and settlement house, in a predominantly black area of Galveston. His initial goal was to bring forth a center of Christian light in a neighborhood devoid of churches and even playgrounds for children. He was aided in this endeavor by his parishioners, especially the Associated Women of St. Augustine, and by Episcopal communicants in Beaumont, Texas, his hometown. Both men and women of Trinity and Grace Episcopal churches also supported St. Vincent's early on, and eventually parishes on the mainland helped, as did contributions from the United Fund. The diocese helped meagerly at first while in the midst of its own financial dilemma and at the beginning of its long period of social unrest. St. Vincent's House survived, however, to become an official agency of the diocese in 1984.[72]

Against formidable lassitude on the part of the white community, black Episcopalians created in St. Vincent's a home "dedicated to enlarging the opportunities for mental, physical, and spiritual development of the children in the area." By 1964, with the dawning of the Great Society's war on poverty, Galvestonians of all races came to realize that St. Vincent's, the only settlement house in the Diocese of Texas, had been ahead of its time in dedicating itself to the advancement of minority children. At first St. Vincent's offered recreation—body building, ballroom and modern dance classes, home economics, and varied supervised sports—in an abandoned grocery store. Two years later a small tract of land and a metal building were purchased, where recreation, worship, and counseling took place.[73]

Over time the services offered at St. Vincent's expanded in experimental fashion as the directors reached out to various agencies in the community for help. In 1969 the center, staffed by Vista volunteers and by students and teachers from the University of Texas Medical Branch, at Galveston, opened a family health clinic to provide screening examinations for all ages. St. Vincent's provided the only free venereal disease treatments in Galveston, which in 1970 led the "major U.S. cities in the incidence of syphilis." In conjunction with the Gulf Coast Regional Mental Health-Mental Retardation Center, it opened a methadone treatment program along with counseling and therapy for heroin addicts. The following year a tutoring program for middle and high school students ensued, with cooperation from school administrators and students. In 1973 the clinic added a mental health counseling program, a legal aid service, adult education classes, and a preschool—and operated on a budget of $230,000. After the downturn in the Texas economy in 1985, St. Vincent's added a food bank, a clothing closet, a transportation program, and direct aid to families.[74]

Not all of these programs have continued. The methadone treatment program has been transferred to another location, and legal aid ended with the demise of the Vista program. But St. Vincent's current director, Alfreda Houston, a black native Galvestonian, professional social worker, mother of eight, and longtime member of St. Augustine's, has commented that the center often initiated programs, taking advantage of federal, state, and community funds, then gave them up to other agencies with better funding or larger facilities. In other words, St. Vincent's has served as an experiment station in the field of urban problem solving in much the same manner as the Church Service League of the 1920s. When a program worked and could be maintained as effectively by other agencies, then St. Vincent's moved on to other innovative approaches to the dilemmas of current poverty.[75] By 1989 St. Vincent's had raised enough funds through a matching grant from the Episcopal Foundation to build a new center, larger and more accommodative.

Support from various agencies—the diocese, the Episcopal Foundation, the United Way—has been supplemented by donations from various churches. At first only Episcopal churches contributed to St. Vincent's or believed in its future. Eventually representative congregations of all faiths, especially Temple B'nai Israel, gave support. Some churches held back until recently; white Baptists and black Baptists have been slow in lending their support.[76] But since 1969 the Women of the Church of Trinity Episcopal have been supporting St. Vincent's with a sizable annual donation from its budget, and in recent years women members of Trinity have been elected to the Board of Trustees for St. Vincent's.[77]

No other facility with as many different features for the advancement of the poor has existed or currently exists in Galveston.[78] That this particular social service center should be an extension of the Episcopal Church means that outreach in this city has come full circle in the past one hundred years. In this new age, however, black churchmen and churchwomen made the initial move toward relief and aid to inner-city youth. White Episcopalians, slower to respond, were hampered by southern customs that preferred to ignore the acute needs of blacks. But through the urging of Father John Donovan, Bishop Roger Cilley, the Reverend J. Scott Turner, and Mary MacGregor, lay ministry coordinator of Trinity Episcopal Church, women congregants have also come full circle to understand their mission to the whole community and to rely on St. Vincent's as their benevolent outreach. St. Vincent's House is for Trinity Church akin to the guilds and ladies aid societies at the turn of the century and to the Social Service Committee of the Church Service League of the 1920s. At last this congregation has rediscovered "its role as the servant church" in rendering aid to the poor.[79] Undoubtedly, these events have challenged white Episcopal women to see black churchwomen as partners in the amelioration of the slum environment. And just as important, this ministry has revitalized the church community.

Following closely upon the cooperation of black and white Episcopal churches in an inner-city project came advances in the position of women within the community[80] Organizational life for women in the 1950s had been confined almost entirely to separate clubs and leagues. Episcopal women continued to hold positions of leadership in these groups, for example, eighteen presidents (about one-third of all presidents) of the Junior League over the years were members of Trinity Episcopal. Segregation of women on community boards was by no means rigid or complete; women had served on various charitable and philanthropic boards such as those for the Rosenberg Library and the United Way. And Episcopal women have continued to be elected to the school board; the first woman member, an Episcopalian, won her office in 1917. In keeping with the city's search for an economic renascence, Episcopal women have served on the city planning commission and the Galveston Historical Foundation. They have been instrumental in the early efforts toward historic preservation, particularly of the Strand, the city's historic commercial district.[81]

Parish life for women changed dramatically after 1970. The full integration of women into positions of leadership in the community, the march of women toward full- and part-time careers outside the home, the continuous agitation for women's rights in the 1970s, the advance of women within the denomination at the national level, and the admittance of women to the priesthood all combined to bring about the gradual and peaceful admission of women to offices within the parish. In 1974 the congregation elected its first woman to the vestry; since then the parish has had two women senior wardens, and women have come close to dominating the affairs of the parish. The consensus among parish leaders, however, is that a vestry needs the balance of both men and women.[82] Generationally, Trinity women recognize that men die off and women stay on, creating an imbalance of sorts that can be righted only by a conscious effort to keep men actively participating in parish affairs.

Trinity women have applauded the integration of women into traditional male areas of church life, including assembling together at the Diocesan Council meetings and the accession of women to the priesthood, but their parish has not yet experienced the ministry of a woman priest. Despite the integration of women into male offices, they have also sought to retain their own organizations; such traditional women's organizations as the Altar Guild, the Daughters of the King, and prayer groups have provided opportunities for service in a spiritual setting.[83] Often these societies are filled with women in their older years who are making the transition from career retirement to volunteer service for the parish.[84] The availability of women's groups within the parish is as important to women now, especially for retirees, as it was at the turn of the century.

Conclusion

Episcopal women of Galveston have been influenced most profoundly in their actions both in parish life and in civic endeavors by three factors: denominational ties to a national church with an episcopal structure based on the tenets of scripture, tradition, and reasoning; compassion and a desire for service stemming firm privilege, economic security, and constituency in the upper classes; and southern customs of conservatism and traditionalism.

One of the most important facets of the Episcopal Church in the South and certainly in Galveston has been the ability to ground itself in scripture and yet remain imbedded in the secular world, providing a positive force in a changing world. In part southern parishes have benefited from a national episcopal system and its adoption of Social Gospel ministry in the late nineteenth and early twentieth centuries. Episcopal women in Galveston, although living in the midst of southern conservatism, were the beneficiaries of the example and influence of their northern sisters in areas of social outreach.

In Galveston, Presbyterians and Jews, although fewer in number, maintained an equally impressive openness to secular change, incorporating into their missions an agenda of social justice. As the Methodist

Church entered the twentieth century, a program of social concern, especially among its women, emerged out of the denomination, with modest effect upon Methodist women in Galveston. By 1939 and the unification of the Methodist Church, this church resembled a mainline Protestant church, showing fewer of its southern evangelical roots. Methodist women have placed more women in ministry than other denominations in the South, yet Methodist laywomen in this city have traditionally avoided secular involvement until quite recently. Baptists, who have remained separate from their northern coreligionists, converted more southerners to their ranks than any other denomination. Traditional Baptists still preach a message of otherworldliness that tends to compartmentalize their worldview, allowing them to endorse enthusiastically spirituality in church but finding fewer modes of application for society. Only slowly have Baptists in this century entered into programs of social Christianity.[85] The past decade, however, has witnessed a major about-face for the denomination as "inerrantists" and biblical literalists have gained control of its governing boards, pushing back the gains made by socially conscious theologians in the seminaries, by laywomen in positions of church leadership, and by women in ministry.

From 1900 until World War II class and status exerted important influences on women's participation in secular civic activism. The fact that one or two Baptist and Methodist women of privileged families participated as readily as the scores of well-to-do Episcopal, Presbyterian, and Jewish women, suggests that economic station had at least an equal bearing on women's secular activism as religious affiliation. At the beginning of the century Episcopalians, on the whole, had been the beneficiaries of more temporal wealth than had members of other denominations. This resulted in more leisure time for its women members; fewer of the married women were tied down with domestic chores, and fewer single women were engaged in working careers. Compassion for those less fortunate and denominational support of social outreach worked together: noblesse oblige and theology joined hands to create a coterie of progressive-minded Episcopal women. Women activists mainly from the Episcopal, Presbyterian, and Jewish congregations merged into officership of women's organizations—their admission was based on class, denominational approval, and leadership interest and talent. After World War II rigid hierarchical status rankings began to give way as movements toward a more democratic society emerged. Nonetheless these same churches still rendered more women into public activism than others.

In the years before 1960 women participated in civic affairs for the most part solely through women's organizations. The separate-sphere nature of women's social involvement created a white women's community based on civic activism. This worked in their favor until sometime in the 1920s. Up to that point sisterhood, common goals, and the relative unresponsiveness of government to social problems propelled female civic activists into municipal housekeeping and even suffrage. Evidence of the progressive spirit in the parish was manifested in the Church Service League, which up to that time was the church's most concerted unified outreach program. Once domestic politics became public policy, however, women's groups found their goals for public service co-opted by professional social workers and social service agencies, leaving them in organizations that although useful to the community offered no substantive society-changing agendas. Organizations such as the League of Women Voters and the Junior League continued to train women for civic responsibility, but they found few solutions to the real problems of discrimination against blacks and women. Here southern customs of segregation and conservatism impinged on women's groups in Galveston. Yet, the civil rights movement forced a shift in women's orientation, helped them focus on change in a positive way, and offered opportunities for community activism among women of all races in both women's organizations and in integrated groups such as the Community Action Council and through the church's own St. Vincent's House.

In the 1970s as women sought careers outside the home, their participation in parish life changed to reflect their altered status. When women broke down barriers to equality in the workplace, the parish also accepted women's equal governing rights. Some would contend that out of the separate women's organizations grew a feminist spirit that inveighed against the strictures of their place apart. But there is no evidence that these southern women strode in to demand participation. Trinity women insist that the battles for equality of women in parish life occurred at some other level or in some other region of the country. Refusing to accept the labels "liberal" or "feminist," they perceive integration for blacks in business and for women in positions of authority in the parish as quiet, just, and without rancor. Southern customs of gradualism and denials of feminism have followed Galveston Episcopal women into parish life, where they believe that alterations in women's parish roles occurred as a result of the changes in women's family, professional, and working roles, not as a consequence of a strident spirit.

Episcopal women in Galveston have always been influenced by social currents, by a theology that looks outward as well as inward, and by a sense of their own position in community life. This assurance, backed by a practical active Christianity, has tended to shape their involvement in secular affairs as well. Because they share the conservatism of the region, white Episcopal women have struggled with the traditions of segregation and paternalism that have kept them from facing issues of discrimination for blacks or for themselves at the movements' beginnings. The same church, however, inspired by progressive bishops, sent messages of hope to black Episcopalians in Galveston and eventually (albeit belatedly) lifted the proscriptions against the integration of blacks and women into full participation in the life of the church. Episcopal women of both races have shown patience with the authoritarian remnants of a patriarchal institution. This makes it possible for women like Alfreda Houston, who says she remains an Episcopalian because white members are willing to admit their past errors, and Mary MacGregor, who worked at the diocesan level for the full participation of women in the church, to cooperate on the needs of the community in a Christian context. Without acknowledging the role of feminism in their lives, Episcopal women active in both secular and parish activities have been motivated by an abiding sense of social justice and by their own sense of mission stemming from a long tradition of women's real contribution to community and parish life.

Notes

1. For a definition of evangelical Protestantism, see Joel A. Carpenter, "Evangelical Protestantism," in *Encyclopedia of Religion in the South,* ed. Samuel S. Hill (Macon, Ga: Mercer University Press, 1984), pp. 239–244.

2. Dewey W. Grantham, *Southern Progressivism: The Reconciliation of Progress and Tradition* (Knoxville: University of Tennessee Press, 1983), pp. 200–201; Jean E. Friedman, *The Enclosed Garden: Women and Community in the Evangelical South, 1830–1900* (Chapel Hill: University of North Carolina Press, 1985), pp. 111–118; Anne Firor Scott. "Historians Construct the Southern Woman," in *Sex, Race, and the Role of Women in the South,* ed. Joanne V. Hawks and Sheila Skemp (Jackson: University Press of Mississippi, 1983), p. 107; Anne Firor Scott, *The Southern Lady: From Pedestal to Politics, 1830–1930* (Chicago: University of Chicago Press, 1970), pp. 144–148; Ruth Bordin, *Frances Willard: A Biography* (Chapel Hill: University of North Carolina Press, 1986), pp. 113–115; Barbara Leslie Epstein, *The Politics of Domesticity: Women, Evangelism, and Temperance in Nineteenth-Century America* (Middletown, Conn.: Wesleyan University Press, 1981), pp. 118–121; Joseph R. Gusfield, *Symbolic Crusade: Status Politics and the American Temperance Movement* (Urbana: University of Illinois Press, 1970), p. 89; Paula Baker, "The Domestication of Politics: Women and American Political Society, 1780–1920,"

102   HISTORICAL PERSPECTIVES

American Historical Review 89 (June 1984):638. See also Jacquelyn Dowd Hall, *Revolt against Chivalry: Jessie Daniel Ames and the Women's Campaign against Lynching* (New York: Columbia University Press, 1979), pp. 22, 25, 36, 66, for a discussion of the significance of the WCTU to the Texas woman suffrage movement and of Methodist mission societies to interracial cooperation.

3. Urban historians have been mindful of the differences between southern cities both in their growth rates and in their cultural and social values. See Don Harrison Doyle, "Urbanization and Southern Culture: Economic Elites in Four New South Cities (Atlanta, Nashville, Charleston, Mobile) c. 1865–1910," in, *Toward a New South? Studies in Post–Civil War Southern Communities,* ed. Orville Vernon Burton and Robert C. McMath, Jr. (Westport, Conn: Greenwood Press, 1982), pp. 11–36; Don Harrison Doyle, *New Men, New Cities, New South: Atlanta, Nashville, Charleston, Mobile, 1860–1910* (Chapel Hill: University of North Carolina Press, 1990), chap. 1; Elizabeth Hayes Turner, "Women, Religion, and Reform in Galveston, 1880–1920," in *Urban Texas: Politics and Development,* ed. Char Miller and Heywood T. Sanders (College Station: Texas A & M University Press, 1990), pp. 75–95.

4. "Galveston and Deep Water," pamphlet, p. 11, in Subject Files (Rosenberg Library, Galveston), quotation; David G. McComb, *Galveston: A History* (Austin: University of Texas Press, 1986), pp. 99, 112; *Galveston Daily News,* 11 April 1942; for banking, 16 June 1926, 4 July 1926, 9 March 1930, 1 October 1932, 23 September 1931, 8, 9, September 1958 (historical articles); for cotton, 7 November 1915, 5 September 1920, 1 October 1927, 1 September 1929, 21 March 1930, 11 April 1942, 11 September 1942 (historical articles); for the Port of Galveston, 11 June 1906, 11 April 1917; for merchants, 22 July 1922, 22 July 1923, 4 July 1926, 1 September 1927, 26 April 1932, 9 September 1958, 21 February 1971, *Galveston Tribune,* 14 September 1932 (historical articles); for railroads *Galveston Daily News,* 16 December 1928, 31 December 1933 (historical articles).

5. McComb, *Galveston,* pp. 182,188.

6. Most notably the Sealy, Moody, and Kempner families.

7. The semireligious and secular organizations include Galveston Orphan's Home, Letitia Rosenberg Home for Women, Lasker Home for Homeless Children, Johanna Runge Free Kindergarten, the Jewish Free Kindergarten, Wednesday Club, Echo Club, Art League, Histrionics Society, Ladies Musical Club, Daughters of the American Revolution, Daughters of the Republic of Texas, United Daughters of the Confederacy, Colonial Dames, Daughters of the War of 1812, Hospital Aid Society, Woman's Cooperative Association, Council of Jewish Women, Mothers' Clubs, Women's Health Protective Association, Galveston Equal Suffrage Association, Women's Christian Temperance Union, Young Men's Christian Association Auxiliary, Young Women's Christian Association, United Charities, Red Cross.

8. For a study of the social standing of the activist women and their families in Galveston I have relied on Max Weber's tripartite definition of social power—

economic status, political power, and prestige—and have concluded that the most salient dimension of his definition for women is social status or prestige. By combining variables that indicate economic position and status, I have created a status index that roughly indicates social standing. When matched with religious preferences, most Episcopalians are listed in the top one-third of the status index. Max Weber, *The Theory of Social and Economic Organization* (New York: Oxford University Press, 1947), p. 428; Weber, "Class, Status, Party," from *Max Weber: Essays in Sociology,* trans. and ed. H. H. Gerth and C. Wright Mills (New York: Oxford University Press, 1946), chap. 7.

9. Earl Wesley Fornell notes that "the now venerable Trinity Church, founded in 1841 and directed for several decades by Benjamin Eaton, was the most successful Protestant [church] on the Island during the mid-century." *The Galveston Era: The Texas Crescent on the Eve of Secession* (Austin: University of Texas Press, 1961), pp. 79–80. The best study of the Episcopal Church in Texas is the two-volume history by Lawrence L. Brown, *The Episcopal Church in Texas, 1838–1874* (Austin: Church Historical Society, 1963), and *The Episcopal Church in Texas: The Diocese of Texas, 1875–1965* (Austin: Eakin Press, 1985).

10. For a history of Presbyterians in Texas, see *Echoes from the Past: A Brochure of Brief Historical Sketches Connected with Presbyterianism in the South and Its God-given Work in the World* (Galveston: Presbytery of Brazos, 1936).

11. For histories of Baptists in Texas, see Robert A. Baker, *The Blossoming Desert: A Concise History of Texas Baptists* (Waco: Word Books, 1970); John W. Storey, *Texas Baptist Leadership and Social Christianity, 1900–1980* (College Station: Texas A&M University Press, 1986). Histories of Texas Baptist women in mission work include Inez Boyle Hunt, *Century One, A Pilgrimage of Faith: Woman's Missionary Union of Texas, 1880–1980* (n.p: Woman's Missionary Union, 1979); Patricia Summerlin Martin, "Hidden Work: Baptist Women in Texas, 1880–1920" (Ph.D. diss., Rice University, 1982). Histories of Methodists in Texas include Olin W. Nail, ed., *History of Texas Methodism, 1900–1960* (Austin: Capital Printing Co., 1961); Walter N. Vernon et al., *The Methodist Excitement in Texas: A History* (Dallas: Texas United Methodist Historical Society, 1984).

12. There were exceptions; Johanna Runge, wife of a German cotton factor who worked his way to the top, opened the city's first free kindergarten for factory children. Neither her name nor her husband's can be found on the Lutheran rolls, although their daughter Julia was baptized in the Lutheran Church. Minutes [Protokoll-Buch]. First Evangelical German Lutheran Church, January 1893 to 1912, Rosenberg Library, Galveston (microfilm). See also H. C. Ziehe, *A Centennial Story of the Lutheran Church,* 2 vols. in 1 (Seguin: South Texas Printing Co., 1951), 1:70–71, 2:146–148; *A Brief Review of the Past and Survey of the Present of the First Evangelical Lutheran Church of Galveston* (Galveston, 1925), p. 19; *One Hundredth Anniversary of the First Evangelical Lutheran Church* (Galveston, 1950), pp. 55–59.

13. For histories of Jews in Texas, see Henry Cohen, David Lefkowitz, and Ephraim Frisch, *One Hundred Years of Jewry in Texas* (Dallas: Jewish Advisory Committee, 1936); University of Texas Institute of Texan Cultures, *The Jewish Texans* (San Antonio: University of Texas Institute of Texan Cultures, 1974).

14. Galveston's Catholic population has traditionally been Anglo, not Hispanic. For information regarding non-Hispanic Catholics in Texas, see Carlos E. Castaneda, *Our Catholic Heritage in Texas, 1519–1936,* 7 vols. (Austin: Von Boeckmann-Jones Co., 1958), 7: 285, 361–365; Sheila Hackett, *Dominican Women in Texas: From Ohio to Galveston and Beyond* (Houston: Sacred Heart Convent of Houston, Texas, 1986); Priests of the Seminary, comps., *History of the Diocese of Galveston and St. Mary's Cathedral* (Galveston [1922]); Catholic Youth Organization, *Centennial: The Story of the Development of the . . . Diocese of Galveston* (Houston: Catholic Youth Organization, 1947); Galveston *Daily News,* 26 February, 2 April 1922.

15. Samuel S. Hill, Jr., "An Agenda for Research in Religion," in *Perspectives on the South: Agenda for Research,* ed. Edgar T. Thompson (Durham, N.C.: Duke University Press. 1967), pp. 195–213.

16. Grantham, *Southern Progressivism,* p. 22; Kenneth K. Bailey, *Southern White Protestantism in the Twentieth Century* (New York: Harper & Row, 1964), p. 7 (quotation). See also David Edwin Harrell, Jr., "Religious Pluralism: Catholics, Jews, and Sectarians," in *Religion in the South,* ed. Charles Reagan Wilson (Jackson: University Press of Mississippi, 1985), p. 70; C. Vann Woodward, *Origins of the New South, 1877–1913* (Baton Rouge: Louisiana State University Press, 1951), pp. 449–451, puts the percentage of Baptists and Methodists in the rural South in 1915 at 82 percent.

17. Bailey, *Southern White Protestantism,* p. 22 (quotation). For an especially insightful critique of southern evangelical churches, see Samuel S. Hill, Jr., *Southern Churches in Crisis* (New York: Holt, Rinehart & Winston, 1966). See also John Lee Eighmy, *Churches in Cultural Captivity: A History of Social Attitudes of Southern Baptists* (Knoxville: University of Tennessee Press, 1972); Rufus B. Spain, *At Ease in Zion: Social History of Southern Baptists, 1865–1900* (Nashville: Vanderbilt University Press, 1961).

18. Mary Sudman Donovan, *A Different Call: Women's Ministries in the Episcopal Church, 1850–1920* (Wilton, Conn.: Morehouse-Barlow, 1986), pp. 5,9.

19. Ibid., p. 16.

20. Ralph Luker, *A Southern Tradition in Theology and Social Criticism, 1830–1930: The Religious Liberalism and Social Conservatism of James Warley Miles, William Porcher Dubose and Edgar Gardner Murphy* (New York: Edwin Mellen Press, 1984), p. 308.

21. William Manning Morgan, *Trinity Protestant Episcopal Church, Galveston, Texas, 1841–1953* (Houston: Anson Jones Press, 1954), pp. 564–565.

22. Constitution and By-Laws of the Ladies Aid Society of the First Pres-

byterian Church, Galveston, Texas, n.d., Minutes of the Ladies Aid Society of the First Presbyterian Church, Galveston, 1893–1909, Treasurer's Report of the Ladies Aid Society of the First Presbyterian Church, Galveston, 1893–96, all in First Presbyterian Church Records, Rosenberg Library, Galveston. *A Brief Review of the Past and Survey of the Present of the First Evangelical Lutheran Church of Galveston; One Hundredth Anniversary of the First Evangelical Lutheran Church; Constitution and By-Laws of the Ladies Hebrew Benevolent Society of Galveston, Texas* (Galveston, 1903); Minutes of the Ladies Hebrew Benevolent Society, 1879–1918 (Congregation B'nai Israel, Galveston); A Stanley Dreyfus, "The Hebrew Benevolent Society. A Saga of Service," (typescript), A. Stanley Dreyfus Papers, Rosenberg Library, Galveston; Mrs. J.E. Murphy, "The History of Methodism in Galveston, 1839–1942," (typescript), Moody Memorial Methodist Church, Galveston. See Vernon E. Bennett, *An Informal History of the First Baptist Church, Galveston, Texas* (Galveston, 1970); Minutes of the First Baptist Church of Galveston, 1866–83 (microfilm), Rosenberg Library, Galveston; "Women's Work in the First Baptist Church, Galveston, Texas" (typescript), First Baptist Church, Galveston.

23. *Charter and By-Laws of the Galveston Orphans' Home* (Galveston, 1913); Minutes of the Board of Lady Managers, 1885–1913, Galveston Orphan's Home Records, Rosenberg Library, Galveston; *Charter, Constitution, and By-Laws of the Society for the Help of Homeless Children of Galveston, Texas* (Galveston, 1894); The Woman's Home Charter, August 10, 1893, Minutes of the Board of Lady Managers, 1894–1911, both in Letitia Rosenberg Woman's Home Records, Rosenberg Library, Galveston; Minutes of the Board of Lady Managers, 1904, Lasker Home for Children Records, Rosenberg Library, Galveston; "Mrs. Johanna Runge" (typescript biography), Subject Files, Rosenberg Library, Galveston.

24. "The Wednesday Club of Galveston, Texas," compiled in 1948 by Corinne Smith and revised in 1978 by Mrs. Elizabeth Head, Mrs. James E. Johnson, and Mary Tramonte (typescript history), in the possession of Elizabeth Head, Galveston; *Fifty Years of Achievement: History of the Daughters of the Republic of Texas* (Dallas: Banks Upshaw and Co. [1942]), pp. 15–17; city directories, 1891–1900; Megan Seaholm, "Earnest Women: The White Woman's Club Movement in Progressive Era Texas, 1880–1920 (Ph.D. diss., Rice University, 1988), p. 190. For a general history of the women's club movement see Karen J. Blair, *The Clubwoman as Feminist: True Womanhood Redefined, 1868–1914* (New York: Holmes & Meier, 1980).

25. Herbert Molloy Mason, Jr., *Death from the Sea: Our Greatest Natural Disaster, The Galveston Hurricane of 1900* (New York: Dial Press, 1972), pp. 90, 107, 110, 116, 194, 198, 209–10, 217–218, 221; John Edward Weems, *A Weekend in September* (College Station: Texas A & M University Press, 1957), 145; McComb, *Galveston,* pp. 124–128, 134; "1900 Storm Meetings. September 9, 1900–September 14, 1900," City Council Minutes, Galveston City Hall, Gal-

veston; Clarence Ousley, *Galveston in Nineteen Hundred* (Atlanta: William C. Chase, 1900), pp. 255–264.
    26. Ousley, *Galveston in Nineteen Hundred* p. 259; McComb, *Galveston,* p. 134; Mason, *Death from the Sea,* pp. 222–226.
    27. McComb, *Galveston,* p. 132; Mason, *Death from the Sea,* p. 230.
    28. Bradley Robert Rice, *Progressive Cities: The Commission Government Movement in America, 1901–1920* (Austin: University of Texas Press, 1977), p. xiv; Richard G. Miller, "Fort Worth and the Progressive Era: The Movement for Charter Revision, 1899–1907," in *Essays on Urban America: The Walter Prescott Webb Memorial Lectures,* ed. Margaret Francine Morris and Elliott West (Austin: University of Texas Press, 1975), pp. 89–121; James Weinstein, "Organized Business and the City Commission and Manager Movements," *Journal of Southern History* 27 (May 1962):166–182. For a discussion of urban structural reform and the South, see Samuel P. Hays, "The Politics of Reform in Municipal Government in the Progressive Era," *Pacific Northwest Quarterly* 55 (1965):157–169; Samuel P. Hays, "The Changing Political Structure of the City in Industrial America," *Journal of Urban History* 1 (1974):6–38; Howard N. Rabinowitz, "Continuity and Change: Southern Urban Development, 1860–1900," in *The City in Southern History: The Growth of Urban Civilization in the South,* ed. Blaine A. Brownell and David R. Goldfield (Port Washington: Kennikat Press, 1977), pp. 109–10; Blaine A. Brownell, "The Urban South Comes of Age, 1900–1940," ibid., pp. 141–142.
    29. *Galveston Daily News,* 3 March 1901. The WHPA was a member of the Texas Federation of Women's Clubs from 1902 until 1908, Galveston *Daily News,* 3 December 1902, 12 May 1906, 8 April 1908, 11 December 1920.
    30. Baker, "The Domestication of Politics," p. 638. Marlene Stein Wortman, "Domesticating the Nineteenth-Century American City," *Prospects: An Annual of American Cultural Studies* 3 (1977):531–572; Grantham, *Southern Progressivism,* pp. 200–208.
    31. Galveston *Daily News,* 3 March 1901.
    32. Turner, "Women, Religion, and Reform in Galveston, 1880–1920," pp. 88–89.
    33. *Galveston Tribune,* special edition between 17 March and 18 March 1915.
    34. Membership lists for the WCTU are scanty, but city directories, articles, and general histories show no Episcopal women among them.
    35. The findings show that of twenty-seven voluntary organizations studied between 1880 and 1920, two had percentages of women from evangelical Protestant churches of 50 percent or higher: the Woman's Christian Temperance Union and the Young Women's Christian Association. Prohibition legislation and the protection of young women, accompanied by a Christian message, drew more followers from among Baptists, Methodists, and, by 1914, Disciples of Christ than from all other denominations combined.
    36. Statement of Trustees Building Fund of Y.W.C.A., March 1925, Galveston YWCA Records, Rosenberg Library; *Galveston Tribune,* 22 September 1924.

37. To discover the suffragists' religious affiliation, church and synagogue records and directories have been thoroughly searched, along with any existing women's church and synagogue society records. Three remain unidentified (or unchurched); the other suffragists were Lutheran (1), Jewish (1), Catholic (1), and Swedenborgian (1). See also Larry J. Wygant, " 'A Municipal Broom': The Woman Suffrage Campaign in Galveston, Texas," *Houston Review* 6, no. 3 (1984):117–134; *Galveston Tribune,* special edition, 1915.

38. Mrs. J.S. Sweeny to Annette Finnigan, 26 March 1915, Jane Y. McCallum Papers, Austin Public Library, Austin. Among the rank and file only one Methodist woman transcended the breach between the Galveston Equal Suffrage Association and the WCTU.

39. Hill, *Southern Churches in Crisis,* p. 197. Hill notes also that Episcopal sacramental theology is far less likely to worry about sacred-secular, church-Kingdom distinctions.

40. Morgan, *Trinity Protestant Episcopal Church,* pp. 115–134, 238, 550; Vestry minutes, 1919–1927, Trinity Episcopal Church, Trinity Episcopal Church Records, Rosenberg Library, Galveston, hereinafter cited as TEC Records; Church Service League Papers and Reports, TEC Records. For a too-brief discussion of the Church Service League of the Diocese of Texas, see Brown, *The Episcopal Church in Texas,* 2:100–101.

41. J. Stanley Lemons makes the point that many Progressive era women's activities continued beyond the Wilson era into the 1920s. Lemons, *The Woman Citizen: Social Feminism in the 1920s* (Urbana: University of Illinois Press, 1973).

42. Church Service League minutes, July 18, 1923, File 16, Box 3, TEC Records, hereinafter cited as CSL minutes.

43. CSL minutes, 20 May 1921, File 16, Box 3, TEC Records.

44. Vestry minutes, February 24, 1919, TEC Records.

45. In 1921 these parish groups joined the CSL: Church Periodical Club, Daughters of the King, Woman's Auxiliary to Missions, Trinity Church Guild, Altar Guild, Girls' Friendly Society, Young People's Service League, Church School, Choir, Cemetery Committee, Font Roll, and United Thank Offering committee. At the diocesan level the organizations belonging to the CSL contributed funds to diocesan projects such as Grace Hall (a dormitory for women at the University of Texas at Austin), Camp Allen for young people, and prayer books. Missionary boxes were sent to various out-of-state projects like St. John's Hospital, Albuquerque, New Mexico. At the the world mission level the CSL donated to a Japanese relief fund, sent kimonos to Japan, supported two women missionaries in China, and sent goods to Japan and Mexico for missions there. Annual Report of Trinity Church, Galveston to the Church Service League, Diocese of Texas, 1923, TEC Records.

46. From the beginning the Church Service League of the Diocese of Texas was headed by Anna (Mrs. Percy) Pennybacker of Austin. Pennybacker's endorsement of the league was of tremendous advantage to the diocese. She had served for years in women's clubs, becoming president of the Texas Federation

of Women's Clubs and finally president of the General Federation of Women's Clubs in 1912.

47. Church Service League, Executive Committee Meeting minutes, May 25, 1921, TEC Records.

48. Morgan did not support votes for women, even though most suffrage officers were Episcopalism.

49. Morgan, *Trinity Protestant Episcopal Church*, pp. 428–431.

50. Report of the Social Service Department to the Church Service League, 21 December 1922, TEC Records (first quotation); Jean S. Morgan, "Social Service in the Parish," (manuscript; speech presented to the Woman's Auxiliary of Trinity Episcopal Church, 21 October 1932), Morgan Family Papers, Rosenberg Library, Galveston (second quotation).

51. Report of the Social Service Department to the Church Service League [1921], TEC Records.

52. Episcopal women belonged in 1921 to the Red Cross and its Nursing Service, Social Service Club, Galveston Orphan's Home, Woman's Home, Playground Association, YWCA, YMCA Auxiliary, United Charities, Hospital Aid Society, Anti-Tuberculosis Association, and PTA; Report of the Social Service Department to the Church Service League [1921]. Episcopal women in 1925 presided over Colonial Dames, DAR, Daughters of the Republic of Texas, League of Women Voters, Merrie Wives, PTA, Red Cross Nursing Service, Wednesday Club, and YWCA; Galveston League of Women Voters, "Directory, Women's Organizations, 1925–1926," Pamphlet File, Rosenberg Library, Galveston.

53. Eleanor Roeck (Mrs. James E.) Thompson, was a suffragist, wife of a prominent physician, and the mother of eight children. By 1923 the Men's Club had joined CSL. Annual Report of Trinity Church, Galveston to the Church Service League, Diocese of Texas, 1923, TEC Records.

54. The Reverend Raimundo de Ovies, speaking to the members of the CSL, had this to say about community service: "If you will make this [enlistment of more members in the CSL] the object of your fall and winter campaign, only God Himself knows what service we may be able to render both the Parish and Community; and for you shall be that greatest of all blessings 'Well done, thou good and faithful servant' of our Lord's." Raimundo de Ovies to the Church Service League, 20 July 1922, File 19, Box 3, TEC Records. See also Hill, *Southern Churches in Crisis*, p. 196.

55. CSL minutes, February 16, 1928, Box 3, TEC Records.

56. *Galveston Daily News*, 28 February 1931 (quotations); Robert C. Cotner et al., *Texas Cities and the Great Depression* (Austin: Texas Memorial Museum, 1973), p. 150; Morgan, *Trinity Protestant Episcopal Church*, pp. 554–555.

57. Morgan, *Trinity Protestant Episcopal Church*, p. 562.

58. Donovan, *A Different Call*, chap. 6, pp. 173–75. The most important facet of the Woman's Auxiliary was its link to the women's arm of the national church, which had been developing since the 1870s. As an ambitious and energetic national women's parallel church developed, Episcopal women at the

parish level soon benefited from the influx of national information and diocesan-level commitments to women's activities. The long-term outcome of affiliation with this parallel movement was integration by women into church governing systems at the General Conference and the eventual ordination of women priests.

59. Minutes, County Commissioners Court, Galveston, Texas, 1900–1920.

60. In 1916 the United Charities disbursed $10,680 in aid and found work for 150 unemployed. In the two years between 1914 and 1916 it helped 2,300 transients and 984 family cases. *Galveston Daily News*, 7 May 22, 23, 15 August, 17 September 1914, 3 November 1916; Constitution, United Charities of Galveston, Morgan Family Papers, Rosenberg Library, Galveston, Mary E. Wood to Jean S. Morgan, 4 November 1916, *ibid.* Mary Wood's religious affiliation is not known.

61. McComb, *Galveston*, pp. 167, 190.

62. Report of Women of the Church to the Synod of Texas, Presbytery of Brazos, 1960–1967, First Presbyterian Church Records, Rosenberg Library, Galveston; hereinafter cited as FPC Records.

63. Ibid.

64. Sheila M. Rothman, *Woman's Proper Place: A History of Changing Ideals and Practices, 1870 to the Present* (New York: Basic Books, 1978), pp. 224–228; William H. Chafe, *Women and Equality: Changing Patterns in American Culture* (Oxford: Oxford University Press, 1977), pp. 48–49.

65. The Methodists in the postwar period built a new church, Moody Memorial Methodist, at the west end of the city, effectively leaving the inner city for the suburbs.

66. Report of the Christian Social Service Committee, 1938–1939, 1939–1940, 1960–1967, FPC Records.

67. Sixteenth Annual Summer Conference and School of Religion, 30 June–21 July 1948, program, Parish Scrapbook 1940s (Trinity Episcopal Church); *Texas Churchman* 64 (January 1961):1 (quotation).

68. Brown, *The Episcopal Church in Texas*, 2:106–107, 136.

69. Ibid., 2: 241, 243, 247, 251, 251, 261–262, 270–272. See also *Journal of the Diocese of Texas*, 1960.

70. Interview with the Women of the Church, Trinity Episcopal, represented by Mary MacGregor et al., 21 April 1989, tape recordings in the possession of Trinity Episcopal Church; McComb, *Galveston*, pp. 210–214.

71. Morgan, *Trinity Protestant Episcopal Church*, pp. 673–677; Brown, *The Episcopal Church in Texas*, pp. 9–10, 233–234.

72. Interview with Alfreda Houston, Director of St. Vincent's House, 26 July 1989. (quotation), *Galveston Daily News*, 27 July 1967.

73. "A History of St. Augustine's Parish: 1884–1990," (St. Augustine Parish, Galveston); *Galveston Tribune* 5 September 1963; *Galveston Daily News*, 17 August 1965.

74. *Galveston Daily News*, 21 October 1969, 3 March 1970, 11 June 1970

(quotation), 10 December 1970, 29 March 1973, 26 October 1973, 17 February 1974.

75. Interview with Alfreda Houston.

76. Ibid.

77. Interview, Women of the Church, Trinity Episcopal Church; Women of Trinity Episcopal Church, Annual Reports, 1969 to 1987 (Trinity Episcopal Church, Galveston). From 1969 until 1973 the WOC (Women of the Church) allotted on average $500 to St. Vincent's House. From 1982 until 1987 the WOC donated $1,000 annually to help defray the expenses of the summer lunch program. In 1983 the WOC reported that it "took pride in being the impetus behind the Diocesan WOC's contributing $500 toward St. Vincent's House, and for making St. Vincent's House a regular budgeted item for an annual $1,000 contribution from the Diocesan WOC. 1983 Annual Report, Women of Trinity Church, Trinity Episcopal Church.

78. The most needy clients in this era of modern poverty are women and children. Interview with Alfreda Houston.

79. The Reverend J. Scott Turner, associate rector of Trinity, presided over the Board of Trustees for St. Vincent's House. Through his solicitations to corporations and the Episcopal Foundation, he raised $750,000 for a new building, now finished. It is painted a bright yellow and festooned with a large white cross, both symbols of hope in a dreary section of Galveston. Interview with Mary MacGregor, 9 August 1989, Trinity Episcopal Church, Galveston. Hill, *Southern Churches in Crisis,* p. 196 (quotation).

80. On the subject of the advancement of southern women, Nancy Cott states: "Among the generalizations prompted by reviewing the South in the history of women's rights, none opens more vistas than the thought of the unprecedented potential of harnessing the efforts of black and white women together." Cott, "The South and the Nation in the History of Women's Rights," in *A New Perspective: Southern Women's Cultural History from the Civil War to Civil Rights,* ed. Priscilla Cortelyou Little and Robert C. Vaughan (Charlottesville: Virginia Foundation for the Humanities, 1989), pp. 11–19, quotation on p. 18.

81. Interview, Women of the Church, Trinity Episcopal Church.

82. *Galveston Daily News,* 20 February 1974: interview, Women of the Church, Trinity Episcopal Church.

83. Dorothy Middleton, "History of the Daughters of the King" (typescript), Trinity Episcopal Church.

84. Interview, Women of the Church, Trinity Episcopal Church.

85. Storey, *Texas Baptist Leadership and Social Christianity, 1900–1980,* pp. 172–218.

3

Women and the Parallel Church: A View from Congregations

Joan R. Gundersen

The Episcopal Church today has an asymmetrical structure correspond-ing to the roles available for laymen and laywomen. The roots of this asymmetry lie in the changing ways laywomen have related to their parishes and their national church, as individuals and collectively. The implications of these structural relationships for the church today require exploring the origins of the asymmetry, for the church cannot assess its current direction until it more fully understands the perceptions and experiences of the laity.[1] The Episcopal Church shares this asymmetry with many other denominations, although the particulars of the arrange-ment are dependent upon the specific polity and history of a denomi-nation and congregation.[2] Thus, exploring the relationship of women in and to the Episcopal Church may help us understand American religion in general.

It is my contention that women first developed a separate parish-based sphere for their activities within the church. Excluded from tra-ditional structures, women redefined parish life to place women at the center of activities that they oversaw through their own organizations. Hence, congregations contained two structures, the "official" parish controlled by a male vestry and clergy, and the "women's church" con-trolled by women's organizations.[3] In the late nineteenth century and early twentieth women completed a parallel church structure by adding

levels of organization corresponding to the diocesan and national structures controlled by males. However, national and diocesan church policies simultaneously changed so that the horizontal division of religious
work into a woman-centered parish and male-centered national church
was undermined, thereby muting women's separate powers while semi-
incorporating women into the male structures. The process of incorporation has continued in the twentieth century without adequate exploration of women's separate ministries. The result is an asymmetrical
church in which women work both in "church" organizations and in
separate "parallel" women's organizations.

Two hundred years ago, when the national church rose from the ashes
of the old established Anglican Church, parish life was minimal. A parish
was a place one came to worship on Sunday. Collectively, as a parish,
most laymen and -women were consumers of worship but not direct
participants in parish activities except through the responses of the liturgy. Occasionally, ministers would teach catechism to the youth, a
handful of congregations had choirs, and of course, a small group of
men met as the vestry to handle the temporal affairs of the parish. The
new national church (and the formative diocesan conventions) did make
room for laymen's participation, most notably in the House of Delegates.[4] But since most laymen had a limited role in parish life, perhaps
voting once a year in a parish meeting, the opportunities for the typical
layman and -woman were similar.

Although laymen and -women had very few ways to participate collectively as parish members, there was a rich lay spiritual life fostered
through the family and in small groups. Devout families said prayers
daily at home, read from the Bible, argued religion, taught their children
(and slaves and servants) and met in small prayer groups. This last was
a legacy from the Methodist movement, which was then just separating
from the church. The home also served as the base for important rituals
that marked the milestones of life: birth (and baptism), marriage, and
burial. Clergy fought long and hard in the eighteenth century to return
baptism, the central rite of church membership, to the church physically.
To the extent that the ministers succeeded in holding baptism at the
church building, they often had to agree to private baptism (that is,
keeping it a family rite) rather than one of congregational witness.[5] The
other rites would not move to the church for at least another hundred
years.

Between 1780 and 1830, however, the church experienced a transformation that can be sketched only with broad strokes in this chapter.
Women began to work collectively, inventing a parish life that was an
extension of the home. That they did so at a time when men's and

women's roles were increasingly separated helped to determine the relative roles of men and women within this new collective life. Women's roles centered around home, family, and morality; men claimed the world, work, and politics. Whether the church was a male or female sphere was not predetermined, despite deeply ingrained theological misogyny and women's exclusion from the ordained ministry and church governance. Parish and philanthropic activities did not fit into the existing organizational structure, and thus women could define these in ways that made them extensions of women's sphere.

Parish life in the nineteenth century became a web of activities drawing people toward the church. In this development women took an active part. As Sunday schools developed, women served as the teachers and often financed them.[6] Ladies' social circles, guilds, benevolent societies, sewing societies, and missionary societies raised money for good works associated with the church. Many churches, parish halls, hospitals, orphanages, schools, and missions (both foreign and domestic) were built through women's fund-raising in a local parish. By the 1830s these institutions were clearly visible in parishes all around the nation.[7]

Fund-raising provided women with a form of collective power. By 1836 clergy could not afford to ignore women's needs in a parish, as the young priest Frederick Goodwin learned to his chagrin. Goodwin had to leave his work in Prince George County, Maryland, when the women of his church did not provide a subscription to his salary. His diary records no reason for the women's actions other than the women had heard he might leave and thus were unwilling to provide the subscription that would raise his salary to an acceptable level. However, that diary reveals a young clergyman who often left his women parishioners unnamed while including men's names, stressed women's submission, and was more interested in male conversion and male Bible groups. The women had good reason to wish him gone. Goodwin's experience reveals the boundaries of action and power within a small parish. The vestry officially controlled the finances of the church, and officially hired and paid the minister. Women's fund-raising, done collectively, became discretionary funds that might be pledged to vestry operations, and hence seem subordinate and auxiliary to male control. Women, however, did not turn over all their revenues to male boards, and they could withhold their usual pledge. Despite vestry efforts to capture discretionary control of the funds by having the women pledge the money to the vestry, women's organizations retained control of most of their funds and followed their own plans of disbursement.[8] By the late nineteenth century women's financial role in the hiring of clergy was a given in many parishes. In some cases women then took the lead. For example, in 1893 the women of St. Thomas' Church in Providence, Rhode Island, formed a committee to raise money for the expressed purpose of hiring a priest. When the money was raised, they also dictated the choice of minister to the vestry.[9]

A guild organized to raise money for an Episcopal church often preceded the formation of a parish in numerous frontier towns of the Midwest and Pacific Northwest.[10] The budgets these groups controlled were substantial. The financial records of All Saints Church, Northfield, Minnesota, for example, show that as late as 1930 the guild budget was as large as the vestry budget. Because a major portion of the vestry budget was committed to clergy salary and nondiscretionary items such as heat and light, the women actually controlled most monies spent on program and improvements. Scattered parish records suggest that All Saints was not unusual among small or rural parishes.[11] In larger, wealthy congregations, such as Trinity Church in New York, St. James Parish in Chicago, or St. James Church in Richmond, women's organizations had less direct power because vestries or male officers of corporations controlled more of the funds, but women still created spaces for themselves.[12]

Although such financial control was important, women's fund-raising activities had another more important effect. The activities themselves fostered community and became an essential part of parish life. The parish suppers, ice cream socials, silver teas, and other social events were more than fund-raisers, they were parish events that brought together a part of the community. Preparing for a bazaar, a night of amateur dramatics, or cleaning up after a Sunday school picnic were as important in building community as was the event itself. Women literally made room for themselves in the parish by refocusing the parish on activities familiar to women: sewing, cooking, working with small children, hostessing, and the like. Men might aid in these duties, but women could take the lead because they were essentially female roles. As Morgan Dix, rector of Trinity Parish, New York, noted in the 1878 parish yearbook, "There are things that ought to be done here, which women can do a great deal better than men, and some which men cannot do at all, and which will never be done unless women do them. . . ."[13]

The importance of parish social life in small communities, where most Americans lived until after 1900, cannot be overemphasized. As one San Diego woman concluded, "St. Luke's was part of our *every*day life."[14] Although men created a male world of fraternal organizations, taverns, and political clubs, women and church activities provided the largest single source of "polite" or family social opportunities. The women of frontier Northfield, for example, did not found a traditional guild in 1858, they formed a "Ladies Social Circle" that allowed men to attend their meetings at double the dues of a woman and without any voting rights. The women literally cashed in on the desire of men on the frontier to enjoy women's company. According to Joseph Kett, churches sponsored 70 percent of one Indiana town's social events in 1910.[15]

Evidence of the impact of their parish work on women's self-perceptions cannot be quantified, but there are revealing indications of the empowerment that women received through this work of servanthood. Consider the tongue-in-cheek letter written by the Sewing Circle of Grace Church, Tilden, Alabama, to one of their members whose impending marriage would require her to move away. They protested, "We have a prior claim upon you which we can not have set aside, and should any one attempt to infringe upon our rights, he must expect dire vengeance in the way of censure, protestations, and lamentations from an indignant and injured community."[16]

Interviews with older women in parishes often spark crystal-clear memories of work parties held years before. In 1964, for example, newspaper columnist Nell Phillips commented on the finding of a 1906 All Saints Guild Cook Book, "The women of the Church getting the recipes ready often met at our house and I can still see how eager they were to make this cook-book a success." Margaret Starks, the daughter of Nell Phillips, could recall the specific work assignments of women in a bazaar she had helped organize over thirty years earlier. Older women interviewed as part of the Lilly Project research remarked on the loss of companionship when women stopped sewing and working together in church guilds.[17] The report issued in 1988 of the Committee for the Full Participation of Women in the Church further supports the importance of community-building in women's religious lives. The survey concluded: "The interpersonal aspects of congregational life—the potential for developing friendships, the mutual support which can result from shared work and worship—are of greater importance to women than they are to men, or at least that women are more aware of (or willing to mention) their need for such companionship within the church."[18]

The invention of parish community life required the literal reconstruction of churches. Church architecture originally provided no place for any of these activities. Eighteenth-century churches were strictly halls for worship, with possibly a small addition to house church records and vestry meetings. Even the famous and often-used plans of architect

Richard Upjohn published in his carpenter plan book in the middle of the nineteenth century provided only for a room for worship and a rectory.[19] As parish community life grew, however, space had to be found for its activities. Sunday school rooms, guild halls, church parlors, rehearsal rooms for choirs, kitchens—all became a part of the basic church plan. The church was literally remade into a home that women proceeded to decorate with their handiwork.[20]

The terminology for these church facilities and women's work reveals the ways such activities helped to create a conceptual framework of a domesticated church. Parlors and kitchens were now found in both homes and churches, and women acted as hostesses in these rooms. Although the national church and clergy might like the imagery of "daughter" to describe women's roles (Daughters of the King, "loving daughters of the church"), laity sometimes referred to "Mothers of the Church." Since church "fathers" referred to ordained men, the use of "mother" for the women who ran parish life creates an intriguing parallel.[21] Thus a "mother" of the church could sit in a (church) parlor sewing (for a missionary box) as she planned a (parish) dinner. Her role was domestic, but her activities actually provided a major community-building event for the congregation and an important contribution to evangelism.

The domestic imagery also invaded the chancel through the work of the altar guild. Women washed and sewed linen for, and decorated and set, the Lord's table. In a 1949 article significantly titled "The Lord's Housekeepers," a Rhode Island woman articulated the power that this imagery granted women to assert claims in areas from which they were otherwise barred.

> The Altar Guild is unlike any other guild of the Church, in that it offers to women a high and unusual privilege. It may have been with a touch of wistfulness that we women envied the youngest altar-boy, performing duties denied to us and perhaps unconscious of his good fortune. But the work of the Altar Guild gives to women the honor of important service in sacristy and sanctuary—the only opportunity given us for service there. . . . [22]

This passage draws on the domestic imagery under challenge by 1949 in the nation at large. In earlier years such comment would not have included a mention of women's exclusion from other roles.

Official ministries for women also reflected the invention of parish life and its extension to social service. The nineteenth century did develop religious orders for women while denying them the ordained ministry. Deaconesses, sisters, missionaries, and paid professional lay workers all worked in extensions of the ministry of the parish community. They ran schools, orphanages, and hospitals, supervised Christian education, did parish calling and social work, and ran church music programs. Similarly, as the church developed structures of organization to link women to the diocese and the national church, the structures continued to focus on the new areas of ministry developed by women.[23]

By the mid-nineteenth century women's parish work had transformed the church, and created a set of parallel structures with responsibility for much of the new ministry. While men met at annual parish meetings, women often met in adjoining rooms for annual meetings of guilds. Women's Auxiliary meetings were held in conjunction with diocesan and national conventions. In larger, wealthier parishes, and at the diocesan and national levels, these parallel structures remained in a shadow cast by the official church.[24]

In smaller parishes, however, the women's groups might overshadow the vestry. Mrs. H. C. O'Ferrall, for example, in 1888, after noting women's contributions to the congregation, called the church in Chatfield, Minnesota, a "womens [sic] Church."[25] In Rhode Island there were a number of small unincorporated Episcopal congregations because there were not enough male members to serve as corporation officers. Similarly, in the missionary district of the Platte, some congregations depended on women as delegates to conventions and as officers because there were not enough interested men. In some Rhode Island and Minnesota parishes by 1900 vestries turned to women to serve as parish treasurers even though women could not sit on the vestry.[26] Given women's success with church financing, it is not surprising that vestries might turn to them as treasurers. In the case of Northfield, the only two women to serve as parish treasurer (over seven decades apart) simultaneously held office as treasurer of the women's guild.[27]

Despite all the emphasis on ordained ministry, women also conducted religious services in isolated areas before 1900. Caroline Smyser of rural Glyndon, Minnesota, for example, began holding services in her home for her family. Soon others joined her family in worship, and Bishop Henry Whipple licensed her as a lay reader to regularize the situation. Anson Graves in Nebraska licensed Bertha Graves as a lay reader at about the same time. Several Rhode Island parishes began as gatherings of people for worship in the homes of women who conducted services in the absence of clergy. In addition, numerous parishes have their origins in missions served by deaconesses who read services for the faithful few who had gathered.[28]

Reaction to women's prominence in parish life resulted in a number of changes in the late nineteenth century and early-twentieth, changes that slowly tried to incorporate, control, or subordinate women's organizations to the official church, and to reassert a leadership role for males in the parish.[29] The changes were incremental, and their timing depended on the individual parish and diocese. Official views and theoretical models of church structure defined women's organizations and ministries as peripheral and males' ministries as the "real" church, but actual power and women's perceptions, especially at the parish level, might vary considerably from this official vision. In fact, before 1920 there were indications that the official church considered adopting the parallel church structure by granting women access to the official church through a system of delegates from the women's structures to various boards and conventions. Mary Donovan's book, *A Different Call,* details the failure of this to happen nationally, but some parishes and dioceses formally adopted elements of the parallel structure.

One factor in the incorporation/subordination of women's separate structures was the slow extension of the franchise (and even slower extension of officeholding) to women in male-dominated structures. Women first received the parish vote, then the right to attend the diocesan convention as delegates, and finally delegate status in the House of Deputies. Between 1890 and 1920 many dioceses granted women the right to vote in parish meetings. Many women, however, chose not to use their franchise. In Rhode Island, for example, a survey taken three years after women gained the right to vote in parish meetings, showed that women in only half the parishes were using their right; in the rest, the idea of parallel churches was strong enough that women continued to see the guilds as their church structure.[30]

The right to hold office followed at an even more deliberate pace. In each case or office, women initially voted to fill offices they could not legally hold. For example, women began voting in parish meetings in Minnesota in the 1890s, but not for another sixty years could they sit on vestries. The Diocese of Minnesota began admitting women as regular delegates to diocesan conventions in the 1920s. At those conventions women helped elect delegates to the House of Deputies, from which women were barred until the 1970.[31] Missionary Bishop Anson Graves opened parish offices and his diocesan meetings in Nebraska to women in the early 1890s, but missionary district women had limited rights in the rest of the church.[32] The situation was even more complex in Rhode

Island, where vestries formed under a state act of incorporation. In 1912 the Rhode Island legislature changed the law so women could be members of a corporation. Two years later, a diocesan committee surveyed parishes and found that women voted in thirty-six parishes, did not vote in eleven, held office in twenty-two, were ineligible for office in nineteen. As a result, the diocese voted in 1915 that women had "perfect equality with men" in parish and diocesan governance.[33] Even so, women were slow to hold parish offices until after 1950, although they served at the diocesan level.

Women's receiving voting rights in male-dominated structures reinforced the view that the male organizations were "the parish" or "the church." Because women theoretically had a voice, meetings could make a claim to being generic despite the inequities of power built into the structures. Women continued to exercise leadership through their separate groups, but the extension of the parish franchise to women changed the relationship of the vestry to the guilds and of the parish annual meeting to the women's annual meeting. In parishes such as All Saints in Northfield, where the men and women had held simultaneous annual meeting in separate rooms—the men holding the "parish" meeting and the women the annual women's meeting—the franchise meant that women's groups had to change their annual meeting time to allow women to be present at the parish meeting.[34] It also meant that women began to present reports at the annual meeting, thus symbolically accepting the role of a committee of the parish rather than a coordinate governing body with its own unique concerns.

At first, other than the inconvenience of changing their annual meeting, women's groups at the parish level continued their traditional activities. They may have viewed the extension of the vote as a source of additional power that would ensure that projects dear to women's hearts would receive the attention of the entire parish. Women collectively were still powerful, and vestries and clergy ignored or irritated the women at their peril. Vestries appointed committees that included representatives of women's groups. Relations between guild and vestry often resembled diplomatic negotiations with ambassadors invited to formally address each other's meetings or small committees charged to present their group's views at the other's meetings.[35] At the diocesan level some dioceses treated the separate women's groups as separate entities. The Diocese of Olympia in the state of Washington, for example, voted in 1921 to give the Women's Auxiliary a vote and number of seats at its convention equal to those of the parishes.[36]

It is possible to interpret the extension of the parish franchise as recognition of women's importance in parish life. Active parish membership included many more women than men, and vestries often had to struggle to fill vacancies. In 1913, for example, All Saints Parish in Northfield could not find a treasurer. The vestry then tapped Lucille Haber, the treasurer of the guild. Because she could not legally serve on the vestry, Haber prepared financial reports and sent them to meetings with her husband, who did serve on the vestry. A number of Rhode Island congregations had the same trouble and chose the same solution at the turn of the century.[37]

Similarly, parish meetings could be tiny without women. At one early-twentieth-century meeting in Northfield only eight ballots were cast by the men present.[38] *The Churchman* in an article noting the beneficial effects of women's participation in diocesan meetings in Maryland and Washington, D.C., described an annual parish meeting before the inclusion of women this way: "In other years it was the custom for the vestry, with the possible addition of half a dozen faithful parishioners, to meet in the church, go through the form of electing themselves, and then proceeding to the business of the year."[39]

Apparently, despite the opening of the franchise to women, in some places few women made use of the opportunity until the 1920s. Most continued to see their guilds as the female structures within the parish. Interpretation of the canon defining a member in good standing as a contributing member of the congregation may also have barred women who did not make pledges separate from those of their husbands. This was certainly the case in Northfield, where the rector in 1919 described his parish as having forty noncontributing members, including the "wife where husband makes pledge for the family."[40] A similar comment appears in the brief history of St. Andrew's Episcopal Church in Port Angeles, Washington. Parish records for 1914 "show 75 members, 75 in the ladies guild, and 60 Sunday School members." The guild thus appears separate from "members."[41] In fact, the extension of the vote may have been an attempt to prevent women from becoming too independent of other parish structures and to reassert the primacy of the parish meeting.

By 1900 men were clearly bothered by women's control over parish life. The national church sponsored and encouraged activities designed to make room for men within the parishes. Graves had found to his chagrin in Nebraska that women outnumbered men about two to one at his convocations, a reflection of their dominance in the mission communities that elected delegates to the convocations.[42] The founding of boys' choirs not only provided community for young men but excluded women from a traditional area of control: worship music. The formation of chapters of the Brotherhood of St. Andrew provided men with a service and social organization within the parish. Churches opened new programs aimed at boys: military drill teams, sports teams, guilds for acolytes.[43] Many of these groups had only a short life in any given parish, but their existence or potential existence helped to bolster the vestry's image as an umbrella organization for the entire parish. In this model, men's and women's groups provided parallel opportunities under the watchful guidance of the parish meeting and vestry. This is in contrast to a parallel model where guilds and vestry acted independently to provide different aspects of congregational life. Such concerns about the feminization of American culture were not limited to churches. Turn-of-the-century colleges, for example, were also worried about the impact of coeducation upon men and took a number of steps to encourage male participation in education and the liberal arts.[44]

From the 1920s on there were strong integrative forces in American society that would increasingly make the separate women's church organizations an anomaly.[45] Social and economic factors would also slowly erode the power of women within their separate parish organizations. By the time of the depression women's fund-raising efforts began to fall behind the sums raised by the vestry through pledges. Women's traditional means of fund-raising were beginning to be out of step with the industrialized economy of the United States. "Homemade" became a stigma rather than a measure of pride, thus reducing the desirability of goods offered at bazaars. Young women found secular organizations at schools and in the community competing for their time with church activities. No longer was the choir rehearsal or the church social the highpoint of social life for young people. An ice cream social was tame entertainment compared to the movies. By the 1940s married women were beginning to enter the work force in substantial numbers, thus preventing these women from attending traditional daytime guild meetings.[46]

The rejection by the national church of the parallel church model at the end of World War I also forced women to work for inclusion in male structures within the national and diocesan hierarchies. In 1949 three dioceses and a missionary district elected women as delegates to the House of Deputies, forcing that body to meet the issues of women's exclusion head-on. For nearly two decades, the national church would study and stall before admitting women in 1967.[47] What many scholars may be unaware of is that part of this stalling may have reflected the wishes of large numbers of women whose parish experiences still led them to think in terms of separate parallel churches. Consider the reaction of members of All Saints Guild, the older women's guild, in 1951 when surveyed by their southern Minnesota Women's Auxiliary about admission of women to the General Convention's House of Deputies. The minutes tersely record, "Concensus of opinion was that as Ladies Auxiliary meets at the same time and doing missionary work—seems unnecessary for them to concern themselves with the House of Deputies—in charge of men."[48]

Younger women, however, were less sure of that separate tradition. Although All Saints Guild members such as Lucille Haber had experience stretching back to 1900, when the guilds clearly operated as independent coordinate groups with the vestry, the women who had reached adulthood after 1930 were used to participating the parish meetings as well as the guild. They more readily accepted the idea of the guild as a subordinate group within the parish and expected full citizenship in the "real" parish, that is, seats on the vestry and so on. This younger generation readily accepted "Episcopal Church Women" (ECW) as a replacement for the time-honored title "Women's Auxiliary" as the name of the women's group. The tradition of power and separate activity at the parish level for them was not strong enough to overcome the stigma of marginality evident in the word *Auxiliary*.[49]

Changes in women's lives and attitudes also undermined the separate tradition of the guilds after World War II. Throughout the 1950s and 1960s a growing number of married women joined the paid work force. At first the women's groups adapted by expanding programs into the evening. Employed women, however, carried double burdens of work at home and on the job. Many found that church work had to be a lower priority in their lives. They had less time for the community-building, social activities of the guilds. Shifts in attitudes in the 1960s provided little support for women's parish activities, and encouraged younger women and women with less and less discretionary time to choose not to work with the guilds. The social activities of the guilds seemed out of date, part of the formalism that many younger women rejected in society at large. The 1960s also emphasized male values and culture. The emphasis in civil rights and in the early stages of the revived women's movement was on inclusion in the areas controlled by the white-male power elites. Women's work in the parish was domestic, and domesticity was out of style. Housework, including church housework, was simply a set of dirty tasks relegated to women while males made the "big" decisions.[50] These attitudes were clearly articulated by some of the women interviewed by Joanna Gillespie and others for this volume.

The decline of women's networks and the emphasis on equity and male values helped to remove the last barriers to women's service on vestries. As long as women could not serve on vestries, women viewed their own organizations as the appropriate way to exercise church leadership. As long as women's ministries and networks flourished, women might choose to work through traditional organizations and rarely seek vestry service, even when it was possible for them to serve. Despite all the pressures, women's guilds in the 1950s and early 1960s had continued to provide needed parish support. Local parishes continued to house two sets of institutions. The experiences of Rhode Island, where women had long held the right to sit on vestries, and Minnesota, where women could not serve on vestries until the mid–1960s, are instructive. A Rhode Island parish (Church of the Ascension) first elected women as wardens in 1920, but women did not serve as vestry members until the 1950s or 1960s in most parishes. In 1952, for example, Kitty Sherman announced at the annual meeting that it was time for a woman to serve on the vestry of St. Mary's Parish, Portsmouth, Rhode Island. She nominated (and the congregation promptly elected) Norma Copeland, who was president of the Holy Cross Guild. In Minnesota, on the other hand, where women could not serve, the vestries experimented with creating parish councils where ECW officers met with wardens, or with offering the guild officers honorary seats on the vestry. As it became possible for women to serve on the vestry, the first women elected were usually guild or ECW officers.[51]

That ECW and guild officers served as the first women on vestries should not be surprising. They were, after all the proven and trusted leaders of the women in the parish. The election of officers of the guild to the vestry in many parishes carried an implication that these women represented the women's organizations on the vestry.[52] Such representation has several implications. At one level, it is an admission of the continuing strength of the women's parallel church. At the same time, representation subordinated these independent groups to the official hierarchy, and provided a way to merge two institutions into one. From a third perspective, comments and press releases surrounding the election of the first woman to a vestry suggest that women were at last admitted to the "real" circles of power, and that this might change church policy. The *Northfield News,* for example, headlined its coverage of the 1965 All Saints Parish annual meeting "ALL SAINTS PARISH ELECTS WOMAN MEMBER OF VESTRY." The article suggested that the election of Margaret "Peg" Langworthy was expected to influence the way the parish's delegates would vote at the diocesan convention.[53]

The inclusion of women on the vestry exacerbated existing leadership problems for women's groups. Women who served on both the vestry and as officers of the women's groups found that they had less time to devote to women's ministries. There were also fewer women willing to pick up women's traditional tasks.[54] Vestry service attracted some younger women who bypassed any service with women's groups. In earlier generations such women's skills might have gone into guild work.

When the General Convention voted to admit women in 1967, the image of parallel churches seemed doomed. The ECW discontinued its national meetings. At the diocesan level many organizations followed suit. Local ECW chapters, already under stress because they could not count on the full support of a younger generation, often found it difficult to hold meetings or choose officers. Many ECW chapters went dormant. In Iowa the diocesan ECW was terminated because it was expected "that women would be fully incorporated in the life of the church and not need their own organization."[55] Congregations soon learned how much they missed the work of women through their separate organizations. These guilds, even as they had been struggling for survival, continued to pour money into church projects and buildings. They continued to be essential to the maintenance of church programs (such as care of the altar and linens), outreach (who would take care of the food shelf?), and choirs (who else would sew new robes?). The women's groups continued to serve as the center of parish social activity, including suppers following annual meetings. The churches had tried to drop the separate ministries without inventing new structures to pick up the essential housekeeping, community-fostering, mission, and fund-raising duties long considered "women's work." Men began "helping" with some of the activities, and some parishes replaced traditional women's events with all-parish events, but not all the pieces were replaced.[56] Thus, by 1985 women at national and local levels began reversing the process. The ECW met again in the Triennial.

But the church could not turn back the clock. It was impossible to reinvent separate spheres. The ideology and social networks that had reinforced women's separate sphere could no longer provide support for a parallel church. Women at the parish level and elsewhere tried to split their time between their separate organizations, in which women's networks and organization still gave them a power base different from that of men, and the vestry. The national church, however, has not come to terms with women's ministries, nor truly validated them. Hence, it cannot evaluate what parts of the women's activities should be incorporated into the ministries of the current church. For example, women clergy serve in a variety of nontraditional ministries that build upon laywomen's ministries in social service and missions. National studies of women in ministry interpreted this as marginalization of the women rather than enrichment of the church.[57]

In fact, efforts at integration seem to be leading toward the refeminization of the parish. Small parishes and dioceses with many missions are leading the way in this trend. Nationwide in 1987 women held between 20 and 30 percent of leadership positions once open only to men, but in smaller parishes and dioceses the proportion ran as high as 40 percent. The diocesan level seemed more open to women than the national church, especially when reviewing lay positions. Requirements reserving some committee spaces for clergy mean that until there are as many female clergy as male, some committees will continue to have male majorities. The study also noted that women had lower participation rates in areas where there was a strong ECW. We need to explore more thoroughly which is the cause and which the effect. Are the women's groups strong because there are still barriers to women's participation in traditionally male areas, or is women's participation less in these areas because they see women's organizations as viable sources of power and leadership?[58]

A case study of one of the dioceses with large numbers of small congregations will help to illustrate the extent of refeminization of the local parish. The Episcopal Diocese of Minnesota has approximately 131 congregations, many in mission status or sharing clergy. A survey of the data from parish officer reports indicates that half the parishes had one woman serving as warden. An additional eleven parishes had all female wardens. More women than men held regular vestry seats in the diocese. For fifty-three congregations, women constituted a clear majority of vestry members, and forty-three more vestries were evenly divided between men and women. Women held all the regular vestry seats in six congregations. Consider that in addition to these traditionally male offices, women continue to hold positions of leadership in traditionally female areas; for example, 91 percent of the reported Sunday school directors and 65 percent of the music directors were women. The total effect is that women in small parishes may hold an absolute majority of all leadership positions.[59]

It is possible to construct a feminization score by awarding points for each position controlled by women. Such a scale provides a rough transferable measure of the extent to which women have moved into leadership areas traditionally reserved for men. Possible scores ranged from 0 (no office controlled by women) to 10 (all offices including the priest and an assistant were female). The average for Minnesota parishes was 2.53, with the actual range from 0 to 7. Thirty parishes scored 4 or over on this scale.[60] It was not possible to factor other parish leadership positions into this tally because the diocese does not have complete records on the leadership of parish groups. What it is safe to say is that women hold a majority of these offices, too, especially since local guilds remain among the most visible groups within parishes.

At the higher levels of church governance, however, men have retained a majority of power and of offices. See Mary Donovan's discussion in this volume for the ways the policy of inclusion resulted in exclusion for women at the national level. Thus, ironically, the asymmetrical nature of today's church structures may actually manifest itself as a return to the nineteenth-century division of power between men and women. Men control the upper levels of the hierarchy, and women the parish. In more ways than one, the church may have come full circle.

Notes

1. Joan R. Gundersen, "Parallel Churches? Women and the Episcopal Church, 1850–1980," *Mid-America* 69 (April-July 1987): 88–97.

2. Elizabeth Howell Verdesi, *In But Still Out: Women in the Church* (Philadelphia: Westminster Press, 1976); Theressa Hoover, *With Unveiled Face: Centennial Reflections of Women and Men in the Church* (New York: Women's Division, General Board of Global Ministries, United Methodist Church, 1983); Virginia Lieson Brereton and Christa Ressmeyer Klein, "American Women in Ministry: A History of Protestant Beginning Points," in *Women in American Religion,* ed. Janet Wilson James (Philadelphia: University of Pennsylvania Press, 1980), pp. 172–184.

3. The term "womens [sic] church" appears in the correspondence of Mrs. H. C. O'Ferrall to the Reverend George Tanner, 20 November 1888, Diocese of Minnesota Papers, Box 2, Minnesota Historical Society.

4. Frederick Mills, *Bishops by Ballot: An Eighteenth-Century Ecclesiastical Revolution* (New York: Oxford University Press, 1978).

5. Joan R. Gundersen, "The Non-Institutional Church: The Religious Roles of Women in Eighteenth Century Virginia," *Historical Magazine* of the Protestant Episcopal Church 52 (1982): 350.

6. Anne M. Boylan, "Evangelical Womanhood in the Nineteenth Century: The Role of Women in Sunday Schools," *Feminist Studies* 4 (October 1976): 62–80.

7. Mary Ryan, *The Cradle of the Middle Class: The Family in Oneida County, New York, 1780–1865* (Cambridge: Cambridge University Press, 1981); Jane Hunter, *The Gospel of Gentility: American Women Missionaries in Turn-of-the-Century China* (New Haven: Yale University Press, 1984); Joan R. Gundersen, "The Parish as a Female Institution: The Experience of All Saints Episcopal Church in Frontier Minnesota," *Church History* 55 (September 1986): 307–322; Susanne Lebsock, *The Free Women of Petersburg: Status and Culture in a Southern Town, 1784–1860* (New York: Norton, 1984), pp. 195–236; Nancy Hewitt, *Women's Activism and Social Change: Rochester, New York, 1822–1872* (Ithaca: Cornell University Press, 1984), pp. 40–101; Mary Donovan, *A Different Call: Women's Ministries in the Episcopal Church, 1850–1920* (Wilton, Conn.: Morehouse-Barlow, 1986). Mary Donovan sees the Women's Auxiliary as calling forth the local activity, but the activity clearly predates and extends beyond the interests of the auxiliary.

8. Frederick Deane Goodwin Diary, May 16, 1836, manuscript collections, Virginia Historical Society.

9. Margaret J. Gillespie, "In the Beginning: Women as Founders of Parishes," in *Remembering Our Sisters: The Rhode Island Herstory Project,* Susan Hagood Lee, ed. (Rhode Island: private printing, 1987), pp. 67–68.

10. Joanne M. Scallon, ed., *More Than 100 Years of Ministry: The Episcopal Church in Western Washington* (Seattle: Diocese of Olympia, 1988), pp. 28, 32, 35, 45, 57, 67, 69, 82, 84, 108, 111; Gundersen, "The Parish as a Female Institution," pp. 310–312; Julie Roy Jeffrey, *Frontier Women: The Trans-Mississippi West, 1840–1880* (New York: Hill and Wang, 1979), pp. 98–99.

11. Joan R. Gundersen, *Before the World Confessed: All Saints Parish, Northfield, and the Community 1858–1980* (Northfield, Minn: Northfield Historical Society, 1987), pp. 51–65; Scallon, *More than 100 Years;* "Episcopal Church Women Convention," *Faribault Republican,* 14 October 1981, supplement.

12. See, for example, Rima Schulz, *The Church and the City: A Social History of 150 Years at St. James, Chicago* (Chicago: Cathedral of St. James, 1986), pp. 105–157; see also the chapters in this volume by Rima Schulz and Elizabeth Turner for the experience of women in larger, wealthier congregations. Trinity Parish, New York City, had an all-male corporation that controlled the assets and endowments that supported several chapels, a settlement house, and numerous other socially active projects. Women worked in these and formed auxiliaries to raise discretionary funds for particular projects. For example, Trinity ran a summer program on Long Island for poor children. The property was in the hands of the corporation. The auxiliary furnished the summer home, hired the matrons, and oversaw the management.

Charles Thorley Bridgeman, "The History of Trinity Mission House, 1876–1956" (typescript: New York, 1957), Trinity Church Archives; and Minute Book, The Women's Auxiliary, Seaside Home, Trinity Church Archives.

13. *Year Book and Register of the Parish of Trinity Church, in the City of New York, A.D. 1878* (New York: Styles & Cash, 1878), p. 77.

14. Bettie Lu Thorn, *1973–1983, An Historical Update Marking the 60th Anniversary, St Luke's Episcopal Church* (San Diego: St. Luke's Parish, 1983), [15] (unnumbered pages).

15. Secretary's Book, Ladies Social Circle, All Saints Parish, Northfield, 1858–1863. Joseph Kett, *Rites of Passage: Adolescence in America, 1790 to the Present* (New York: Basic Books, 1977), p. 192; Lewis E. Atherton, *Main Street on the Middle Border* (Bloomington: Indiana University Press, 1954).

16. Ladies of the Sewing Circle of Grace Church Parish and Their Associate Members to Mrs. H. Derby, November 11, 1887, Gray Family Papers, Section 21, Virginia Historical Society.

17. "Mom's Column," *Northfield News*, 23 July 1964, p. 3A; interview with Margaret Starks, 17 June 1983, Northfield, Minnesota. See the Chapters by Irene Q. Brown and Joanna B. Gillespie in this volume for evidence from the Lilly Project interviews.

18. Committee for the Full Participation of Women in the Church, *Reaching Toward Wholeness: The Participation of Women in the Episcopal Church* (New York: Prepared for . . . 69th General Convention of the Episcopal Church, July 1988), p. 45.

19. Richard Upjohn, *Upjohn's Rural Architecture: Designs, Working Drawings, and Specifications for a Wooden Church and other Rural Structures* (New York: Putnam Press, 1852); Loren N. Horton, "The Architectural Background of Trinity Episcopal Church," *Annals of Iowa* 43 (July 1977): 539–548; James L. McAllister, Jr., "Architecture and Change in the Diocese of Virginia," *Historical Magazine* of the Protestant Episcopal Church 45 (September 1977): 297–323; Joan R. Gundersen, "Rural Gothic: Episcopal Churches on the Minnesota Frontier," *Minnesota History* 50 (Fall 1987): 258–268.

20. All Saints Parish, for example, added guild rooms in the 1890s and a new kitchen in the 1920s. In the 1950s it expanded the nonworship part of the church by building a basement under the church for use as Sunday school and guild facilities. Trinity Church, Escondido, California, followed another typical pattern. The parish acquired its first hall in 1905 by converting its old church to that use after building a new church. The parish constructed a building designed for parish activities in the 1930s. Gundersen, *Before the World*, pp. 125–139; Margaret Dove, *Trinity Parish, 1889–1982* (Escondido, Calif.: Trinity Episcopal Church, 1982), pp. 3, 48. For women's role in ritual, see Brian Heeney, *The Women's Movement in the Church of England, 1850–1930* (Oxford: Clarendon Press, 1988), p. 63.

21. Bishop Henry Whipple used the "daughters of the church" imagery in a number of his public statements. The term "Mother" appears in the letter of

Jane E. Harris to the Reverend F. M. Garland, as she is describing her memories of parish life during the Civil War. *Journal of the Tenth Annual Convention of the Diocese of Minnesota* (12–13 June 1867): p. 15; Jane E. Harris to F. M. Garland, April 28, 1917, All Saints Parish Archives.

22. Susan H. Lee, " 'Liberal and Persevering': Women Organizing for Mission and Nurture," in *Remembering Our Sisters: The Rhode Island Herstory Project*, ed. Lee (private printing, 1987), p. 29.

23. Donovan, *A Different Call;* Thomas J. Williams, The Beginnings of Anglican Sisterhoods, *Historical Magazine* of the Protestant Episcopal Church 16 (December 1947): 350–72; Sister Mary Theodora, C.S.M., "The Foundation of the Sisterhood of St. Mary," *Historical Magazine* of the Protestant Episcopal Church 14 (March 1945): 38–52.

24. Mary Donovan has covered the failure of the national church to incorporate the Women's Auxiliary as a coordinate body with power to select members to serve on national church committees when the national church restructured in this period. What I find interesting is that this model was presumed as a given by the women who proposed changes to the national church. What they found, however, was that the males of the General Convention had a different model in mind. Donovan, *A Different Call.*

25. Mrs. H. C. O'Ferrall to George Tanner, 20 November 1888, Diocese of Minnesota Papers, Box 2, Minnesota Historical Society.

26. Susan Hagood Lee, " 'An Equal Plane with Men,' " in *Remembering Our Sisters: The Rhode Island Herstory Project*, ed. Lee (private printing, 1987), p. 69; Sandra R. Boyd, "Women in the Church, 1870–1920: The Episcopal Church in Nebraska as Case Study" (unpublished paper provided by the author, unpaged). Cited hereafter as "Nebraska."

27. Lucille Haber served for one year as treasurer of All Saints Parish in 1913. She was the treasurer of All Saints Guild. In 1988–89 the author served as treasurer of both All Saints Parish and the ECW.

28. The official history of the Diocese of Minnesota notes Smysers' work but not her license. The issuing of the license was itself irregular since the national church had not yet opened licensed lay ministry to women. George Tanner, *Fifty Years of Church Work in the Diocese of Minnesota, 1857–1907* (St. Paul: Diocese of Minnesota, 1909), p. 471. For Smyser's license, see *Minnesota Missionary* 14 (August 1890): 82; Gillespie, "In the Beginning," p. 67.

29. The development of parallel churches followed by an effort to reassert control over these women's groups is not unique to the Episcopal Church. Sweet noted a similar trend in his study of evangelical clergy wives, and Theressa Hoover commented on it in her study of Presbyterian women. Leonard Sweet, *The Minister's Wife: Her Role in Nineteenth-Century American Evangelicalism* (Philadelphia: Temple University Press, 1983), pp. 233–36; Hoover, *With Unveiled Face,* pp. 16–20. Virginia Brereton and Christa Klein also recognize the parallel or shadow structure. Their study refers to the years 1861–1925 as

"Women Alongside the Churches." See Brereton and Klein, "American Women in Ministry, p. 174. See also Jackson W. Carroll, Barbara Hargrove, Adair T. Lummis, *Women of the Cloth: A New Opportunity for the Churches* (San Francisco: Harper and Row, 1981), p. 41. Where I differ with these studies is that I see the attempts to gain control as being incomplete at the parish level, and argue that there were strong survivals of this women's power in the Episcopal Church as late as 1970.

30. Lee, "Equal Plane," p. 69.

31. *Minnesota Missionary and Church Record* 20 (May–June 1896): 27; Salome Breck, "The Church's Women: Their Changing Structure," *The Living Church* 19 (1 September 1985): 3.

32. Graves may have been influenced by his early ministry in Northfield, Minnesota, where women were very powerful. For his Nebraska experience see Boyd, "Nebraska," (unpublished paper provided by the author).

33. Lee, "Equal Plane," pp. 69–70. The fact that women used the suffrage in only half the parishes where they had it suggests the strength of the parallel church paradigm. Women saw themselves as acting through their guilds and men as acting through the corporation.

34. *Northfield News,* 8 April 1899, p. 4, and 18 April 1903, p. 4. The parish franchise came at widely different times to women in different dioceses. The dioceses of Washington, D.C. and Maryland, for example, gave women the parish vote about twenty years after women in Minnesota received it. *The Churchman* (1923): 77. In the missionary diocese of the Platte, women served on vestries after 1891 and had the franchise. Boyd, "Nebraska."

35. For examples of these relations see Gundersen, *Before the World;* and Rima Schulz's chapter in this volume.

36. Scallon, *More Than 100 Years,* p. 132.

37. Gundersen, *Before the World;* Lee, "Equal Plane," p. 69.

38. Gundersen, *Before the World.*

39. "Women Stimulate Parish Meetings, *Churchman* (1923): 77.

40. Parish Study, July 1919, Treasurer's Book, Vestry Records, All Saints Parish, p. 33.

41. What is intriguing about this statement is the possibility that the seventy-five members and the seventy-five guild members are one and the same. If so, it is a totally female parish. If the comment is taken to separate membership from guild membership, then the idea of parallel structures is evident, with women's membership represented through the guild figures. Scallon, *More Than 100 Years,* p. 75.

42. Boyd, "Nebraska."

43. Kett, *Rites of Passage,* pp. 173–211.

44. Frederick Rudolph, *A History of American Higher Education* (New York: Vintage Books, 1962), pp. 323–325; Charlotte Conable, *Women at Cornell: The Myth of Equal Education* (Ithaca: Cornell University Press, 1977); Helen Horowitz, *Alma Mater: Design and Experience in Women's Colleges from Their*

Beginnings to the 1930s (New York: Alfred A. Knopf, 1984); Barbara Solomon, *In the Company of Educated Women: A History of Women and Higher Education in America* (New Haven: Yale University Press, 1985).

45. For a discussion of these forces see Nancy Cott, *The Grounding of Modern Feminism* (New Haven: Yale University Press, 1987), pp. 85–114, 145–174.

46. William Chafe, *The American Woman: Her Changing Social, Economic and Political Roles, 1920–1970* (New York: Oxford University Press, 1972).

47. Breck, "Church's Women," p. 9.

48. Minutes, 14 February 1951, All Saints Guild, All Saints Parish, Northfield, Minnesota.

49. Raymond Albright, *A History of the Protestant Episcopal Church* (New York, 1964), p. 357; Brereton and Klein, "American Women in Ministry," p. 186.

50. For the social and attitudinal changes, see Sara Evans, *Born for Liberty* (New York: Free Press, 1989), pp. 263–314. Evans does not discuss religion in this section except in terms of ordination, but she provides a good overview of other areas of society and the women's movement. Evan's choice to discuss only ordination is itself an indication of the emphasis on inclusion. Her book, an overview of women's history in the United States, drops all discussion of women's religious lives after 1830 and the formation of women's church groups. It does not pick them up again until the 1970s. For denigration of housework see the classic essay by Pat Mainardi, "The Politics of Housework" in Leslie Tanner, *Voices from Women's Liberation*, (New York: Signet Books, 1970), pp. 336–342.

51. Gertrude K. C. Miller, "Norma Coggeshall Copeland," in *Remembering Our Sisters: The Rhode Island Herstory Project*, ed. Susan Hagood Lee (private printing, 1987), pp. 85–87; Lee, "Equal Plane," Ibid., p. 72; and Dorothy R. Belden, "Mary Gallagher Annin Durfee," ibid., p. 80; Minutes, All Saints Parish Vestry, 12 October 1955, and 8 June 1960; interviews with members of All Saints Parish; Minutes, 13 January 1965, Annual Meeting, All Saints Parish, Northfield. The experiences of parishes in the Diocese of Olympia and in the San Diego area seem similar. Scallon, *More Than 100 Years*, p. 90; Dove, *Trinity Parish*, p. 70.

52. During my service on the All Saints vestry from 1977 to 1985, nominating committees always checked to be sure that at least one of the guild officers was on the vestry.

53. *Northfield News*, 21 January 1965, p. 4b.

54. Committee for the Full Participation of Women in the Church, *Reaching toward Wholeness*, pp. 38–39.

55. See the histories of guilds in the Diocese of Olympia, for example, St. Paul's Mission in Mt. Vernon and Christ Episcopal Church in Blaine, in Scallon, *More than 100 Years*, pp. 69, 33; and in Northfield, Minnesota in Gundersen, "Parallel Churches," p. 96. For Iowa, see the Committee for the Full Participation of Women in the Church, *Reaching toward Wholeness*, p. 69.

56. For example, St. Michael's and All Angels in South Bend, Indiana, replaced its traditional bazaar with a parish fair co-chaired by a man and a woman. This occurred while I was a member of the parish in the years 1969–1974.

57. The furor surrounding Barbara Harris's election as bishop illustrates the point. One complaint raised was that she had never served as rector of a parish. Harris had instead worked with prisoners and in other social service ministries. The recent study by the Committee for the Full Participation of Women in the Church, *Reaching Toward Wholeness*, pp. 36–45, shows the same bias. The study discusses the fact that a disproportionate number of women priests serve in small parishes as a sign of lower status. The report also measures leadership only in terms of holding office in formerly male-only positions. The report from the Diocese of Maine as a part of the 1988 study notes that the survey defined leadership in a narrow way:

"It should be recognized that there are other commissions and committees in the diocesan structure in Maine, and in other dioceses, where women could have leadership roles. It appears that in the preparation of the Survey instrument these ministries were not considered as significant. The Survey also did not recognize nonstipendary ministries as a vital part of the institutional church. (p. 76)

An exception to this emphasis on male models is the affirming study of women in the priesthood by Mary Donovan, *Women Priests in the Episcopal Church* (Cincinnati: Forward Movement, 1988).

58. Committee for the Full Participation of Women, *Reaching Toward Wholeness*, pp. 6–26.

59. Parish Officer Notebook, Diocese of Minnesota. I wish to thank the diocese for opening its current records to me.

60. The actual points assigned were 1 for each woman as a warden; 1 point for a vestry evenly divided between men and women (this included awarding 1 point when a vestry had an odd number of seats and the men's and women's totals were within 1 seat of each other), 2 points for a vestry wherein women outnumbered men by at least 2; 3 points for a woman as clergy-in-charge; 2 points for an assistant minister; and 1 point if the treasurer was a woman. All Saints Parish, which was used as an example throughout this chapter, was typical of the diocese. Its score was a 3.

4

Beyond the Parallel Church: Strategies of Separatism and Integration in the Governing Councils of the Episcopal Church

Mary Sudman Donovan

The Episcopal Church, through most of its history, operated with two separate definitions of church membership: one for men and another for women. Until 1970 membership for women did not include participation in the church's political life. Though Episcopalians prided themselves on having a polity that was both traditional and democratic, they were generally blind to the crucial error in the church's claim to be democratic: the exclusion of women members from its political processes. At baptism, women were welcomed as equal members of Christ's kingdom and urged to work and pray and give for the spread of that kingdom, but their voices were not heard in the assemblies that discussed the means of spreading that kingdom, nor were their votes counted when leadership for the earthly church was being chosen. In most dioceses, prior to the 1950s, women were not allowed to serve on parish vestries nor to represent the parish at diocesan functions.[1]

Symbolic of this exclusion was the fact that women were barred from serving as deputies to the General Convention, the church's central governing body composed of bishops, priests, and laymen representing each diocese. Though political efforts to include women in the General Convention began as early as 1916, the campaign intensified after World War II. At every meeting of the General Convention from 1946 until 1964, the motion to allow women to serve as deputies was defeated by the all-male body.[2] Between conventions, the administrative authority in the church rested in the Executive Council. The size of this body varied over the years; in 1964 it consisted of thirty-six men and six women.[3]

Not until 1967 did the General Convention finally approve a resolution that would allow women to serve as deputies to that body. However, because the measure required a constitutional change, it did not take effect until it was overwhelmingly ratified at the beginning of the 1970 General Convention. Twenty-nine previously elected women deputies were officially seated. With that vote, the constitutional barriers to women's participation in the church's political life were eliminated, but the larger task of removing the barriers of custom and tradition remained. This chapter will explore the efforts of the General Division of Women's Work (GDWW) to integrate women into the church's organizational structures. At the outset, I must note that the Episcopal Churchwomen's activities during the 1970s were intricately linked to the drive for the ordination of women to the priesthood, and the two campaigns intersected in many and complex ways. However, because other chapters in this volume deal with women's ordination, this chapter will focus on the move for lay participation.

The Episcopal Churchwomen

Though theoretically every Episcopal woman was a member of the Episcopal Churchwomen (ECW), in most parishes probably less than half of the women were actually involved in ECW activities. Representatives from parish groups met each year in a diocesan convention, and that body, in turn, selected delegates to the Triennial Meeting of the women of the church, which was held in conjunction with the General Convention.[4]

An administrative reorganization in 1958 had changed the name from Woman's Auxiliary to the Board of Missions of the Domestic and Foreign Missionary Society of the Protestant Episcopal Church to General Division of Women's Work of the National Council (GDWW). Local and diocesan groups were called the Episcopal Churchwomen (ECW). Administration was the responsibility of three national staff officers: an executive director and two associate secretaries (for supply work and for the United Thank Offering). The former Woman's Auxiliary staff—secretaries for education, Christian social relations, and personnel—were transferred to the corresponding departments of the National Council (personnel went to the Home Department) but continued to meet with the GDWW. The division was governed by a council of twenty women—eight elected by Triennial, one representative of each province, and four individuals representing, respectively, the Church Periodical Club, the Daughters of the King, the Episcopal Service for Youth, and the Girls' Friendly Society. The GDWW became one of the church's most active bodies. Generally, the women who were elected had served as officers in both their local and diocesan ECWs and could draw upon a wide range of organizational experience. They met for at least two days four times a year, and assumed responsibility for specific program areas during the interim, maintaining close communication with the GDWW national staff.[5]

Crucial to this discussion is an understanding of the ECW financial structure. The Woman's Auxiliary was founded in 1871 as a money-raising arm of the Board of Missions, and as such did not control its own funds. The national secretary and later other staff were provided by the board, and the women's financial contributions went directly into the board's general fund, over which the women had no control. Even after the extensive reorganization of the church's national administration in 1919, salaries and program expenses for women's work came from the national church budget. Earlier, however, in 1889, the women had established one separate fund, the United Offering (later called the United Thank Offering, UTO), which they controlled. By the 1960s, women were raising over a million dollars annually for the UTO—a significant source of income for the church's missionary program. Each Triennial Meeting decided how the offering raised in the previous triennium would be spent, carefully considering requests for work in all parts of the world. The one constant priority was support for women church workers—underwriting their training, salary, pensions, and insurance.[6]

The evolution of the professional woman church worker was a direct consequence of this fund-raising. The Episcopal Churchwomen recruited such women and established and funded the necessary training schools.[7] Graduates of the schools entered a variety of occupations: missionary activity, teaching, nursing, institutional administration, religious education, parish visiting, and college chaplaincy. Some, but by no means all, of the graduates entered the order of deaconess; others entered Episcopal sisterhoods; most worked as lay professionals. Salaries for most of these workers came from the United Thank Offering. The crucial factor was that the entire program for women church workers was con-

ceived, developed, supported, and maintained by the women of the
church. Diocesan and national church structures (aside from the GDWW)
had almost nothing to do with the recruitment and training of the women
workers, though they depended heavily upon the workers' dedication
and expertise.

The Parallel Church

Thus, by 1960, as Joan Gundersen demonstrates in the previous chapter,
Episcopal women, barred from participation in the church's political
structure and from the ecclesiastical roles of deacon, priest, and bishop,
had organized for themselves a parallel structure. At the local level,
women were members of the parish Episcopal Churchwomen (ECW). In
most parishes, certain functions were generally the private preserve of
the churchwomen: Christian education, care of the altar and liturgical
vestments, the parish's social events, and most of the outreach work:
tutoring, parish visiting, corresponding with and supplying domestic and
overseas missionaries, sewing garments or collecting clothing or food
for the needy, and supporting such community projects as the Red Cross,
mental health clinics, or peace societies. Though most parish women
were only vaguely aware of the national ECW, that organization *set the
standard expectations for churchwomen's roles.* In parish after parish,
women filled their UTO boxes, joined with other denominations for a
yearly World Day of Prayer service, and studied "missions in Japan"
or "the plight of the migrant worker," with no conception of the vast
international organizational networks that were shaping these programs.[8]

This "parallel church" for women developed a strong life of its own,
though most women viewed their work within it as their basic Christian
commitment. Weekly church attendance was a given, but women also
followed a pattern of daily prayer and Bible study, often guided by the
"Forward Day by Day" devotional pamphlet. Weekly Bible study
groups, midweek eucharists, and Advent and Lenten Quiet Days as well
as diocesan ECW retreats marked the ecclesiastical year, a spiritual discipline far more rigorous than that practiced by the average layman. A
network of parish, diocesan, and national "devotional chairmen" generated the resources and publicity for these events, making them available even to the women not actively involved in ECW activities.

Similarly, the "parallel church" had its own financial network. The annual pledge to the parish church was a commitment for both women and men, but women were encouraged to establish a pattern of daily giving—coins dropped into the UTO blue box in thanksgiving for God's many blessings. Much of the focus of the parish ECW was upon fundraising; the women generally produced one large event each year—a bazaar, smorgasbord, fair, musicale—that raised a substantial sum of money to be used either for an extrabudgetary allocation to the parish or for outreach—gifts to a host of social service agencies or organizations, often with loose or no connections to the Episcopal Church. Men often assisted in these productions, but they were generally there at the women's request. It was an unstated assumption that the money the women raised was to be given away. Although vestrymen often objected to designating even a tithe of the parish's income to work outside the local parish, churchwomen deliberated about the justification for withholding a tithe of their income to support their own ECW.

Diocesan and national structures for Episcopal Churchwomen paralleled those of the wider church: the women assembled for the ECW Meetings during the Diocesan Conventions and held their national Triennial Meeting in conjunction with the General Convention. Women who felt called to ministry became professional church workers, assisted primarily by women volunteers: church school teachers, youth leaders, and guild officers. Even in the national headquarters, the women's national staff replicated that of the church as a whole, with secretaries for Christian education, home and overseas mission, personnel, and Christian social relations working with the director of the General Division of Women's Work.

The framework and fabric of Episcopal women's activity bore a strong resemblance to patterns prevailing in the general culture. As other chapters in this volume suggest, nineteenth-century commercial and industrial growth intensified the sexual division of labor, fostering the separation of men's and women's social and economic spheres of endeavor. White middle-class women (and these are generally the women who emerged through the labyrinth of the ECW) increasingly adopted the life of domesticity, cultivating and defending a shared morality and ethos. Creating female networks of kin and friendship, they developed a separate world insulated from the ways of their menfolk. They, as well as their men, enjoyed the satisfaction of a refuge from the apparent chaos of economic transition. The great majority of women were not interested in the push for equality and admission into public activity launched by the suffragists. By the twentieth century, indeed, the female world of "rituals and relationships" had formulated the essential strategy for "the creation of a separate, public female sphere [that] helped mobilize women and gained political leverage in the larger society." A separatist political strategy, often unconscious, permitted women to move from the world of personal networks to construct mechanisms for "female institution building," which carried them into the new century and made them a genuine force in the wider society.[9] The ECW clung to this familiar structure well into the post–World War II era—longer than many other public organizations. The structure worked for these women. It gave them a presence and authority in the corridors of male power that was otherwise denied them.

By the late 1960s several factors underscored the need for a change in the status of the Episcopal Church's women. Certainly foremost among these was the growing sense of professionalism among women church workers, trained women who for decades had labored alongside the clergy, carrying the major burden for the social work of the church with scant visibility and even less prestige or economic security. The simultaneous impacts of the civil rights movement and the feminist movement helped these women find their voice and raise the conscience of the voluntary women's structure that supported them. Furthermore, the structure of voluntary women's labor, whether fund-raising or providing administrative direction, could no longer be taken for granted as churchwomen, like middle-class women throughout society, entered the paid labor force in increasing numbers. The mechanisms of the larger church were also in transition. Financial crisis produced a massive retrenchment in the national church staff. Coincidentally, the church awakened to the potentiality of lay ministry, whose value was now acclaimed as the presence of salaried administrators dwindled. The catalyst of the civil rights movement brought all these developments into high visibility.

Impact of the Civil Rights Movement

The most dramatic symbol of the confrontation between the civil rights movement and the Episcopal Church was the 1967 General Convention, which met in September, just after the long, hot summer of racial confrontation in such cities as Detroit, Los Angeles, and Newark. Presiding Bishop John E. Hines, after touring the devastated areas and meeting with black and white leaders, came to the convention determined to focus the attention of the church upon the problems of poverty and injustice in America. He persuaded the Program and Budget Committee to completely rewrite its proposals the week before the convention. Then, in a dramatic opening address, Hines challenged the Episcopal representatives to direct the church's attention and resources to healing the social divisions so evident in the past summer's violence. As a part of this challenge, he called for the creation of an urban crisis fund dedicated to enabling oppressed people to build better lives, and he asked the deputies to revamp their own priorities in order to support that fund.[10]

First to respond to the presiding bishop's call were the Episcopal Churchwomen. The United Thank Offering committee had come to the Triennial Meeting with a proposed list of missionary and educational projects to be funded by the $4,900,000 offering. But after a presentation by Hines, careful committee work, and an intensive debate in open plenary, the ECW voted to change from a triennial to an annual system of allocating funds and pledged $3 million to the Urban Crisis Fund. News of this dramatic gift quickly reached the House of Deputies, challenging the male deputies to respond with equal dedication. The Reverend Bennett J. Sims said:

> I don't know that the men could have responded as those women did in six days. . . . They were the first to act on John Hines' daring challenge to put the Episcopal Church on the urban firing line with nine million unattached dollars for the poor during the next three years. They reshuffled their whole UTO procedure and committed two and a half million dollars of their five million total to the Presiding Bishop's call. They may have made it virtually impossible for the Deputies and Bishops to do anything but follow suit.[11]

However, Hines had called for more than a financial response. His emphasis was upon self-determination—the need of minority groups to have a part in the decision-making process, particularly when the decisions directly affected their lives. But his focus on the question of adequate representation for minorities in church councils also highlighted the fact of women's absence from those councils. When the General Convention and the Executive Council were subjected to such scrutiny, it became evident that although blacks were underrepresented on these bodies, women were totally excluded from the convention and drastically underrepresented on the council. While preaching self-determination to others, convention deputies could not with impunity continue to exclude women. On September 19, 1967, the convention approved the necessary constitutional changes to allow women to serve as deputies, subject to ratification by the 1970 convention.[12]

Thus, the official exclusion of women from the House of Deputies came to an end, but the process of integrating women effectively into the policy-making councils of the church had just begun. There were two important aspects to this process: opening the church's employment system to professional women church workers, and integrating women into the church's political councils on the local, diocesan, and national levels. Though both areas interacted, let us look first at the changed status of professional women workers.

Professional Development of Women Workers

Professional development was the mandate of the Association of Professional Women Church Workers (APW). Organized in 1952 by women employed by national or diocesan offices and parish directors of religious education, the association worked to develop professional standards in both performance and training, insure adequate salaries and benefits, recruit women church workers and provide opportunities for further study, spiritual refreshment, and fellowship. As the major lobbying group for professional women workers, the APW usually scheduled triennial meetings that coincided with the General Convention. By providing resource leaders for Triennial, the APW strengthened its ties with the General Division of Women's Work, enhancing the bonds between the professional workers and the ECW leaders.[13]

The chief problem the APW faced was that except for deaconesses (included in the canons since 1889), women church workers had no defined status within the Episcopal Church. Though many of these workers had trained at the same schools and shared a high sense of professional identity, they found it difficult to communicate that identity to the church at large. In the 1960s the APW formulated a canon on professional women church workers (Canon 52) that was adopted by the General Convention in 1964. That canon set educational requirements and provided that such workers be registered with their bishops. The convention appointed the Joint Commission on Women Church Workers: three bishops, three priests, and six women experienced as volunteers and professionals. The commission's successful recommendation established a pension plan for lay employees through the Church Life Insurance Company, available to dioceses and parishes.[14]

The absence of accurate information about professional church workers hampered the effectiveness of both the APW and the joint commission. In 1964 Betsy Rodenmayer, newly appointed to the national

Division of Christian Ministries and a former member of the St. Margaret's House faculty, surveyed the Christian educators currently employed by the church.[15] Of the workers who responded, just over half (53 percent) had received more than three months' training; and less than half of that group had graduated from Windham or St. Margaret's House. Many others had degrees from nondenominational seminaries and a few had studied at Episcopal seminaries. The average salary for the seminary or training-school graduates was in the $4,500–5,000 range, with 32 percent earning less than $4,000, at a time when the median salary for Episcopal clergymen was $8,256. Particularly disturbing was the fact that although most women who added comments said they would choose the same profession again, very few said that they encouraged others to become Christian educators. Among the frustrating aspects of the job were "lack of understanding of Christian Education on the part of the clergy, lack of staff support, lack of dignity of a professionally trained person, long hours, poor salary, and the church's treatment of women."[16]

The impact of this report, coupled with new admission policies on the part of six of the eleven Episcopal seminaries permitting the matriculation of women students, led to a reassessment of the need for separate training schools. Faced with rising costs and falling enrollments, the boards of the two remaining training schools for women—Windham House in New York City and St. Margaret's House in Berkeley, California—decided to close those institutions. St. Margaret's House graduated its last class in the spring of 1966, and Windham House closed in June 1967.[17] The final statement issued by the Windham House board reflected the ideology that governed the dismantling of the "parallel church": "Our identity as an institution has been with women and women's work. In this identity we have served a purpose. *We are willing to lose our identity as an institution* with the hope that the service of women in the Church may be more fully accepted in the totality of the lay ministry."[18] The Windham House property was eventually sold, with the proceeds designated for lay ministry programs.

After the 1967 General Convention, the Joint Commission on Women Church Workers turned its attention to the order of deaconesses, an order that had existed since 1889 in the Episcopal Church but had been kept canonically separate from the male order of deacons. Because the 1968 Lambeth Conference—the worldwide assemblage of Anglican bishops—had approved the inclusion of women in the diaconate, the joint commission urged that the General Convention pass the proposed canon "On Women in the Diaconate." The canon provided for the

142   HISTORICAL PERSPECTIVES

ordering as deacons of those women who fulfilled the conditions previously required for male deacons, and granted women deacons equal
access to pension protection. Existing women deaconesses were retro-
actively admitted to the diaconate. Another recommendation made several changes in the canons, replacing the word "laymen" with "lay
persons." Both recommendations were approved by the convention.
Thus, the Episcopal Church's first order of ministry, the diaconate, was
opened to women; the deaconesses who had quietly agitated for years
against the anomaly of their position in the church had finally gained
acceptance as equal members of that order. Its mandate accomplished,
the joint commission requested its own dissolution, with further over-
sight to be left to the Board for Theological Education (BTE). To provide
continuity, former commission member Marion Kelleran was appointed
to the BTE.[19]

While the status of professional women workers was being redefined
by legislation, a significant revision was also being made in the hiring
practices at the national office. At the insistence of Vice-President War-
ren H. Turner, Jr., all national staff positions were evaluated and salaries
assigned on the basis of the level of responsibility, thereby eliminating
the flagrant gender inequities that women staff members had experienced previously.[20]

Thus, by 1970 the status of the church's professional women workers
had decidedly changed. Canon law recognized the profession. Women
were eligible for all staff positions open to laity, with salaries assigned
in accordance with responsibility, not gender. Professional workers in
parishes and dioceses were eligible for the national pension plan, and
pressure was applied to employers to enroll them. The diaconate included former deaconesses and was a new career option for women,
and the representation of women on the Board for Theological Education as well as the expanded function of the Board for Deployment
of Clergy offered an ostensible measure of protection to those deacons
who were women.[21] Most of the church's seminaries admitted women.
The professional women workers had good reason to believe that they
had effectively moved into the Episcopal Church's administrative mainstream. However, these improvements in their status had the ancillary
effect of highlighting the church's segregated priesthood. The same General Convention (1970) that approved the acceptance of women as deacons also discussed a resolution to "affirm that women are eligible to
seek and accept ordering to the diaconate and to the priesthood and to
be ordained and consecrated to the episcopate." Though the resolution
was narrowly defeated in the clerical order, it set the stage for the next

six years' campaign for women's ordination.[22] The resolution was defeated a second time at the 1973 General Convention. Nevertheless, in a dramatic action designed to challenge the church's conscience, eleven women deacons presented themselves for ordination to the priesthood in Philadelphia in 1974 and were ordained by three bishops who claimed the authority to act "in obedience to the Spirit." Four women were ordained the following year in Washington, D.C. Finally, in 1976 the General Convention authorized the ordination of women to the priesthood and the episcopate. It is against this backdrop that the move to dismantle the parallel ECW structure must be viewed.[23]

The Episcopal Churchwomen

Concurrent with the changes in the status of professional women workers was a substantial reshaping of the organizational life of the Episcopal Churchwomen. By the late sixties, frustrated by declining interest and attendance in local ECW groups and inspired by new concepts of lay ministry that were just beginning to be explored in the United States, ECW leaders began to question the effectiveness of the present organizational structure.

Interest in lay ministry stemmed from the experience of churches in Europe during World War II. Christians there had made two important discoveries. First, that faith, to be effective, had to be practiced within all areas of life—at work, in school, and within the political community. Second, that the church could function in these areas quite effectively even without clerical leadership. This rediscovery of the ministry of the laity and the focus on the world as the arena for Christian action was reinforced after the war by several European-based renewal efforts: the Church in World Movement in the Netherlands; the founding of evangelical academies such as Bad Boll in Germany; and the Ecumenical Institute opened in Switzerland by the World Council of Churches. The First Assembly of the World Council of Churches, held in 1948, established the Department on the Laity, defining its concern in a report entitled "The Significance of the Laity in the Church."[24]

The movement made little headway in the United States at first because in the postwar boom churches were growing in attendance and membership, and large numbers of men were entering the seminaries as candidates for holy orders. It was "business as usual" for the Episcopal Church, a church that depended heavily upon clerical leadership. Not until about fifteen years after the war, when the religious optimism of the postwar era began to fade, did Americans begin to listen to what their European brothers and sisters were saying.

In 1960 Peter Day published a book for Episcopalians that began with the intriguing sentence, "If you are a member of the Christian Church, you are a saint."[25] *Saints on Main Street* formulated an ideology of lay ministry based upon the Bible and the *Book of Common Prayer*. His book electrified the Episcopal Church. Parishes began to rethink both their mission and the means they used to accomplish that mission. They were guided by a vision articulated by the founder of Parishfield, the Reverend Francis O. Ayres:

> Laity includes men, women, boys and girls, young men and young women.
> . . . The church, along with the culture of which it is too much a part, tends to fragment people into various and conflicting groups—men, women, youth, old age, married, unmarried, clergy, lay. The church needs to recover a sense of its wholeness, of being the people of God in which there is neither Jew nor Greek, neither slave nor free, neither male nor female—in other words, neither basic nor primary distinctions.[26]

This emphasis on a unified ministry of the laity led to a broad range of experimentation in parish structures: vestries were opened to include women and youth; male-female committees did the work of the Altar Guild or the Every Member Canvas; joint task forces examined community problems. And in many cases, the old structures, including the Episcopal Churchwomen, were simply abandoned. Parishes also tried to shift their focus from internal matters to the world at their doorsteps. The different gender expectations under which churchwomen had operated for so many years enabled them to accept the shift in focus far more readily than did their male counterparts. Women claimed the image of lay ministry—men and women working together in areas of social need—not realizing that they had internalized a commitment to social activism while the men in their parishes had had little experience or interest in such action. So they willingly abandoned their ECW structures to continue that same ministry in a new form.

Cognizant of the growing number of such changes on the local level, the 1964 Triennial Meeting called for a "critical analysis of the organizational structure of Episcopal Churchwomen at every level." Responding to that mandate, the General Division of Women's Work surveyed diocesan ECW presidents to determine the extent of local and diocesan restructuring. Eighty-six of 103 diocesan presidents responded. Their answers revealed that extensive experimentation with new structures was already taking place. In Central New York, the diocesan

Departments of Christian education, Christian social relations, laity, Episcopal churchwomen, and stewardship were consolidated into one department of men and women; and the diocese assumed the financial responsibility for women's representation at the Triennial Meeting and the Provincial Synod. In West Texas, the diocesan (though not necessarily the local) ECW structure was dissolved and the diocesan Lay Activities Committee appointed in its place. The Episcopal Churchwomen of Idaho voted to disband their organization, and the Convocation of the Missionary District of Idaho agreed to send delegates to the triennial and provincial ECW meetings. Symbolizing Idaho's support for a gender inclusive Triennial, the convocation elected the Reverend William Spofford, Jr., as a Triennial delegate. In Maryland, members of the ECW Board were appointed to the diocesan departments and divisions, not to represent the "woman's point of view" but as full working members of the committees. Though the women also continued to meet together periodically as the "Women's Committee of the Diocese," the meetings were seen as temporary until the restructuring was completed.[27]

Local churchwomen's groups were also changing. Over forty diocesan presidents reported changes in the parish structure, and others indicated that local groups were seeking new organizational models. Often the ECW activities had been enlarged to include the participation of men. Many presidents reported canonical changes to allow women to serve on vestries, as deputies to diocesan conventions, or as members of diocesan councils and committees. A number also stressed that women had taken a fresh look at their financial participation, generally integrating their giving with that of the diocese.[28]

Confronted with the immense changes already taking place, the GDWW believed that national reorganization was necessary. Because the Executive Council was also reshaping its structure, the GDWW leaders realized that their changes had to be incorporated into the new council structure. They were also hopeful that the proposed constitutional change to allow women to serve as deputies to the General Convention would be passed in 1967 (which it was), and knew such a move would also have organizational implications. Hence, the GDWW board asked the 1967 Triennial for freedom to make whatever structural changes seemed necessary during the next triennium. The Triennial agreed, giving the GDWW the authority to amend or totally suspend the Triennial Meeting bylaws, subject to written approval by two-thirds of the GDWW board members and a majority of the diocesan ECW boards.[29]

Together the Structure Committee of the Executive Council and the GDWW formalized reorganization plans, which took effect after the 1970

General Convention. They dissolved the General Division of Women's Work and replaced its board with the appointive Standing Committee on Lay Ministries. The separate office for women's work was discontinued and its staff members reassigned to other offices. To administer the United Thank Offering, a new committee was created, made up of one representative elected by each province, two members of the present GDWW board, and two members of the proposed Lay Ministries Committee. Thus, the UTO Committee became the only national body with representatives chosen by women. The completed plan was sent to all diocesan ECW boards for approval. By December 1, 1968, a majority of those boards had approved the measure (the vote was 74 in favor, 5 opposed). The bylaws suspended and the GDWW dismissed, Episcopal Churchwomen now had no organized structure to represent them at the national level.[30]

The most crucial aspect of the new system was the change in the position of the "women's desk" within the church's national office. The General Division of Women's Work had been an independent office, with its executive officer, Frances M. Young, responsible directly to the presiding bishop. The division made up its own budget, which Young then submitted to the Program and Budget Committee of the General Convention. Because she was head of an administrative division, Young took part in the subsequent discussions on budgetary allocations, so that the national budget was always formed with the active involvement of the GDWW. However, once that division was disbanded and the staff members transferred to other offices, budgetary and administrative decisions had to be made within those offices where women staff members were, once again, in the minority. As co-ordinator of lay ministries, Young was transferred to the Program Office, and Alice Emery, UTO coordinator, was transferred to the National and World Mission Office. The placement of the UTO in the Mission Office was particularly significant, for there the financial needs of specific missionary programs rather than the women's spending preferences gradually took over the allocation of funds. Thus the "integration" of women into the national administrative structure resulted in not only the demotion of women officers to subordinate staff positions but also the complete dissolution of women's separate power base.[31]

Sweeping though these changes were, they were accomplished with a remarkable amount of unanimity on the part of the GDWW board. This was primarily due to a general feeling on the part of women leaders that it was a time for new beginnings, a time when the church could, and must, experiment with new forms of organization to allow "self-determination" and "participation" for all church members. Presiding Bishop John Hines had sounded the clarion call at Seattle when he challenged the 1967 General Convention to find new ways to deal with the nation's problems, and many of the church's leaders responded to that call with enthusiasm and excitement. That convention had taken the first step to include churchwomen as deputies; the Executive Council it elected was genuinely interested in building inclusionary structures. To capitalize on this interest, the GDWW requested, and received, a major block of time on the Executive Council agenda for consideration of the changing position of women within the church. At the September 1968 meeting, the council heard extensive presentations by several women. Former Triennial Chairwoman Theodora Sorg stated the central problem:

> As long as I have worked in the Church, I have heard women saying that their work should be done as part of the work of the whole church, not separately. . . . Women have been urged by their leadership to plan their programs jointly with men in dioceses and parishes. . . . Nevertheless, it takes two to tango. It is difficult to be part of anything that is not interested, or even aware, that one is part of it.[32]

The council responded with lively discussion and finally created an ad hoc committee to chart the integration of women into the total life, planning, and work of the church. It also pledged to include the subject on the agenda of the Special Convention of 1969.[33] The Special Convention exemplified the spirit of new possibilities in its very organization; women, youth, and ethnic minorities were to be included in every diocesan delegation and discussion group. The Triennial leaders who voted to disband the ECW as a representative organization saw the Special Convention as a model for the future—an assembly in which all the church's people had substantial representation.

Unfortunately, the spirit of optimism that emanated from the 1967 General Convention quickly dissipated in the wrangling over the administration of the General Convention Special Program (GCSP). Taking seriously its mandate to "empower the powerless," the GCSP office granted funds to some groups whose political agendas were at odds with those of many Episcopal Church leaders, at times without the consent of the diocesan bishops involved. In the barrage of negative publicity that surrounded these procedures, some Episcopalians responded by reducing their pledges to the church. Dioceses, feeling the financial pinch, refused to fill their national church quotas. The 1969 Special Convention itself, instead of being the forum where *all* voices of the church were heard and *all* issues considered, was polarized when black leaders seized control of the podium and demanded a "reparations payment" of $200,000 to fund a Black Economic Development Conference. In the resulting uproar, women's issues were relegated to the sidelines.

The next year Episcopalians looked to the regularly scheduled General Convention to restore a sense of order to church deliberations. At its opening session that convention ratified the constitutional amendment allowing women deputies, and twenty-eight women took their seats. In addition, the convention repeated the previous convention's format with work groups that included convention deputies, and Triennial and youth delegates to discuss and formulate legislation. This gave the women present a sense of involvement with the issues even though voting on the legislation was reserved to the duly elected deputies. Those deputies did revise the canons, eliminating the six seats on Executive Council that were reserved for women nominated by the Triennial Meeting and opening all the lay seats to women. Women were to take their place as equal citizens in the church's structure. When the final ballots were counted for Executive Council, however, only four women were elected, along with twenty-six men. The previous system had reserved six seats for women; the new procedure produced the unexpected, indeed unfortunate, result that women's representation was actually reduced rather than enlarged.[34]

In its separate meeting, the 1970 Triennial ratified the proposal to transfer the General Division of Women's Work's responsibilities to the new Standing Committee on Lay Ministries and approved guidelines for that committee.[35] In so doing, the delegates dismantled the political structure that represented Episcopal Churchwomen in the national church and vowed that women would be represented, as men were, by the General Convention and Executive Council. The suspension of the bylaws was continued and the Triennial adjourned without elections—for there were no representative posts to fill. The Triennial delegates did, however, retain two uniquely important prerogatives: control over the United Thank Offering—the historic trump card of Episcopal women—and the right to meet again as a body during the next General Convention. However, even the means of choosing representatives for the UTO Committee was no longer totally controlled by women because committee members were chosen by the provinces. Several provinces (One, Five, Six, and Eight) no longer had provincial ECWS, and others (Two, Three, and Four) elected the UTO representative by ballot in the provincial assembly made up of women and men.[36] Though there seemed to be a tacit agreement that only women would be chosen as members of the UTO Committee, women had seen other such agreements violated. As for the future of the Triennial Meeting itself, suggestions ranged from abandoning the meeting altogether to enlarging it to include men as well as women, making it a lay assembly focused on program and perhaps held apart from the General Convention. After considerable debate, the 1970 Triennial requested that the Committee on Lay Ministries, in collaboration with diocesan and provincial ECWs, plan another Triennial Meeting to be held in conjunction with the 1973 General Convention. The women's consistent refusal to either disband Triennial or open it to male delegates testified to the persistent attraction of the separatist strategy and belief in its strength.[37]

Thus, by the end of the 1970 General Convention, women were ready to move into all areas of the Episcopal Church as enfranchised laity. They could serve on vestries, and be elected deputies to diocesan and general conventions in all but three dioceses.[38] Responding to this new openness, the women had dismantled their own parallel structure. They gave up their separate elected representatives, the General Division of Women's Work, and determined to work through the church's elected representatives, the Executive Council. Through the Committee on Lay Ministries, they expanded their vision of ministry and their expertise in communication and Christian education to include laymen also.

It is important to note that the decision to dismantle the parallel structure and work within an integrated system was not made by a few, select individuals. The process had extended over six years and had provided for an extensive response from diocesan and national leaders. Many dioceses and individual parishes had moved ahead to dissolve their own structures and institute new forms of cooperative organization before the national decision had been reached. Though there were a few dissenting voices, they rarely attracted much support.

The decisions were not made naively. National leaders, particularly, were aware of what the cost might be. This fact is amply demonstrated in the minutes of the 1970 Triennial Meeting Planning Committee. The women's sophisticated understanding of the implications of their decisions surfaced often in their discussions. One member asked, "Is part of the problem analagous to that of the blacks? Once women see themselves being integrated—but on a very small scale—they realize that they might exercise more power by staying separate." Another observed, "We must face the fact that once we dissolve as a women's committee and become integrated, our ability to make any decisions, including financial, vanishes."[39] These were thoughtful women with long experience in, and extensive knowledge of, ecclesiastical politics who, with an acute appreciation for the difficulties ahead, were nevertheless willing to support the move to dismantle the structure. Unfortunately, what they failed to do was install a mechanism to protect women's representation on a proportional basis, one that would claim at least the authority they had enjoyed as a separate hierarchy. By dismantling the structure, these women unwittingly removed themselves from the national arena where decisions were made.

Executive Council Program Advisory Committee on Lay Ministry

The new Committee on Lay Ministries, in which the women's hopes were invested, was hampered by ill-defined membership, gender differences over the scope of lay ministry, and an unmanageable work load. Initially, membership was recruited from the Executive Council, which allowed its members to choose their own committee assignments.[40] The Lay Ministries Committee ended up with three bishops, one clergyman, and one layman—no women.[41] Women leaders were devastated. One former activist on the General Division of Women's Work complained, "Frankly I don't know whether to laugh or cry when I read the names of some of the Council members on COLM [Committee on Lay Ministries]. All great men with special talents, I know, but it's hardly the way we saw it. . . . What happened to the 'Oscar Carr' type of layman we dreamed about?"[42] In a half-hearted effort to mute this outcome, the names of a number of women were hastily appended to the list, and Alice Emery (UTO coordinator) was assigned as staff, along with Frances Young, the lay ministries coordinator.[43]

The fact that men did not share the vision of lay ministry that women held soon became evident. When Theodora Sorg, who had served in many ECW positions including that of Triennial presiding officer, verbalized her hope that the Lay Ministries Committee would "find ways to get off the see-saw and into a rowboat where, as men and women of the Church, we can learn to pull together," she epitomized the hopes of many women for the new structure.[44] But most laymen were content to continue the ministries they had always held: serving as ushers and vestrymen, as church treasurers, or occasionally, as church school teachers. They were not interested in developing a new understanding of lay ministry. This split even divided the committee itself. Responding to a call from committee members for a longer meeting in which some of the theoretical issues of lay ministry could be explored, the staff arranged for a two-day session with Mark Gibbs, a leading theoretician in lay ministry. Almost all the women, but only one man, attended the session.[45]

In addition, the areas of responsibility for the new committee were far too broad. Essentially, it was assumed that the group would oversee the general areas formerly covered by the GDWW as well as develop a stirring new program of recruitment, training, and support of lay ministry—all this on a yearly budget of $5,000. Among the immediate issues that came within the committee's purview were planning the next Triennial Meeting; deciding upon the future of Windham House; establishing a data bank on lay professionals in the Church Deployment Office; preparing a booklet on the ordination of women; and setting guidelines for membership on decision-making bodies of the church.[46] These were simply too many programs to be managed by a small committee meeting only four times a year. Under the previous system, most of the women who had served on the General Division of Women's Work had been unemployed and had considered the GDWW their primary volunteer effort. They gave long hours and concentrated attention to the work. In contrast, the majority of the lay committee members were employed full-time and had other volunteer responsibilities as members of the Executive Council. Furthermore, they had no specified constituency back home to whom they were responsible and from whom they might receive either assistance or criticism. Once the connection with diocesan and provincial ECWS was broken, there was no group demanding accountability from the committee members.

Compounding the difficulty of establishing an effective lay ministries committee was the fact that the next six years were a period of extensive administrative change in the Episcopal Church's national office. Widespread public disapproval of programs funded by the General Convention Special Program led to a precipitous decline in giving to the national church. The budgetary shortfall made staff cuts necessary; in December 1970 half the national staff members found their positions terminated.[47] Work loads and administrative responsibilities were adjusted and reassigned, but the next three years were chaotic for those who survived the cuts. In the midst of that adjustment, frustrated by his own inability to communicate to the church his vision of social responsibility, Presiding Bishop John E. Hines resigned, and the House of Bishops elected John M. Allin to that position in 1973. Allin was a conservative, deeply suspicious of Hines's social action programs.

He installed several new staff members and began to redirect national church priorities. The growing dissension over women's ordination also added to the divisive atmosphere, making it difficult to reach consensus on any issue.

As early as 1972, some of the weaknesses of the Lay Ministries Committee were evident. One laywomen wrote to Frances Young:

> I am more and more concerned that the Church and the Women as a whole are not with us, nor ready for the united plan. But I suppose they never will be ready if we don't push-pull-cajole-browbeat them into it. I guess my fear is that if we really insist upon a men-women group before the men are fully "with it," that it will die of its own weight just as the Laymen's Committee did several years ago, and we'd be left with nothing.[48]

Louise McQuiston wrote, "The ECW in Alabama no doubt is different in many respects from the country at large. Mainly, the majority of the women here still feel a real need and purpose in a separate organization for women."[49]

The effectiveness of the Lay Ministries Committee was questioned. "I don't believe we'll get far with lay ministry until we turn it over to the laity," said Cynthia Wedel, an Episcopal laywoman who was then serving as president of the National Council of Churches. She called for a wholly new committee consisting only of laity.[50] Of a meeting of the Maine ECW, Mary Flagg reported: "We were all agreed that the leadership [Executive Council] should *lead* more daringly and pick up the pace a little! There are more people 'out there' who really are way ahead of the hierarchy in their willingness to experiment and change."[51] Finally, in 1972, frustrated in dealing with an unsettled bureaucracy and convinced that women's concerns were simply not being heard, Frances Young resigned as lay ministries coordinator, took early retirement from the national staff, and moved to Hong Kong, where she served as consultant in religious education for the Diocese of Hong Kong and Macao.[52] To replace Young, the council chose a layman, Barry Menuez; Olive Mae Mulica became the staff person for women in that section. The Lay Ministry Program Group continued to function until 1976, when it was subsumed in the Ministry Council with ten major affiliates, eight of which dealt primarily with ordained ministry.[53] Though various other committees or task forces on lay ministry were established in subsequent years, they never accomplished the massive transformation that women leaders had envisioned. Without a strong organizational link with the local parish such as that the ECW had provided for the GDWW, the lay ministries program failed.

The Effects of Dismantling the Parallel Structure

The question remains, what was the effect of dismantling the women's parallel political structure? Did that action accelerate or retard the integration of women into the church's political life? Obviously, the answer is complex.

One aspect of the change was positive. The separate system through which women were recruited, educated, and employed as professional church workers was eliminated. National staff officers' salaries were set regardless of gender, and women became eligible for the church-sponsored pension funds. These national changes inspired similar changes in some local and diocesan employment practices. Women already employed in diocesan and national staff positions reaped the benefits of these changes; generally their salaries increased dramatically when they were placed on the same scale as male employees, and their pensions provided an economic security unknown to earlier women missionary workers.[54] The chief detrimental effect for professional women workers was the loss of positions reserved exclusively for women. Theoretically, under open employment practices, the best person got the job; practically, a church with an all-male ecclesiastical hierarchy was ill-equipped to evaluate the skills that professional women church workers offered. Without positions reserved for women, employment opportunities for professional women church workers declined.

Unquestionably, the most significant change for women workers was the admission of women to theological seminaries. Though many of the first women students entered seminaries with the intention of pursuing careers in Christian education or church-related social work, once there, they began to question a gender-segregated priesthood. Women students at the theological seminaries were among the earliest and the most dedicated advocates of women's ordination, and much of the effectiveness of that movement must be attributed to their work. By closing the separate training schools for women church workers, the Episcopal Churchwomen accelerated the move of women students into theological seminaries, thereby hastening the move toward women's ordination.

Financially, the dissolution of the General Division of Women's Work was a disaster for women's work. The operating costs of the General

Division—salaries for at least three staff officers, office and operating expenses, expenses for GDWW board meetings, and the cost of preparing for Triennial Meetings—had been included in the national church budget. With the transfer of staff positions to other offices, budget items specifically for women's work disappeared. The Executive Council authorized the use of funds from the Wright legacy, bequeathed to the church specifically for the work of the Women's Auxiliary, for the expenses of UTO Committee meetings so that committee would be able to meet quarterly.[55] The Lay Ministries Committee assumed financial responsibility for planning the 1973 Triennial Meeting, but informed the 1976 Triennial Planning Committee that it would have to find its own funds. An emergency appeal to diocesan ECWs raised $50,000 for the meeting.[56] But from that time to the present, each committee planning Triennial has had to wrestle first with financial provisions. The national church was willing to allow its women to continue to meet in a separate group if they so desired; it was not willing to continue to fund such meeting as a part of the ongoing program of the church.

Even without the national ECW structure, the United Thank Offering grew each triennium: the women had $4 million to distribute in 1970; over $5 million in 1979. But the determination to use that money to promote women's missionary work had disappeared. UTO funds were no longer used primarily for the salaries of professional women workers. Continued were a small fund for women missionaries' incidental expenses ($200 per missionary) and a $3,500 annual grant to the deaconesses' retirement fund (which supported women set apart as deaconesses before 1970). The percentage of the offering used for scholarships for religious workers decreased each triennium, and the scholarships were awarded to men as well as women students. Overwhelmingly, the offering was used to support missionary work at home and abroad, particularly to encourage new forms of missionary outreach and social service.[57] One important exception to this policy, however, was a grant for an "enabler" who, "working with seminary students, faculty and alumni, will assist in defining and clarifying goals for women as they assume new roles in the church."[58] That grant went to the Reverend Suzanne Hiatt, a deacon whose work with seminary students and faculty eventually resulted in the organization of the Episcopal Women's Caucus (EWC), a key strategy group for the women's ordination movement.

As the political agenda of the EWC became apparent, opponents of women's ordination mounted a campaign of vitriolic letters and negative publicity against the UTO Committee for its support of a "lobbying organization." Though committee members were careful to point out that the funds were used for counseling women seminary students and not for lobbying, they firmly supported the grant. UTO Coordinator Alice Emery gathered and distributed a packet of letters from seminary deans praising Hiatt's effectiveness and the need for the work she was doing.[59] Though the grant to Hiatt was clearly an exception to the UTO committee's general tendency to avoid grants focused specifically on women, it was a significant exception and played a crucial role in the subsequent move to women's ordination. The furor caused by the negative publicity about the grant forced many women leaders to come to terms with their own feelings about women's ordination. As Edna Goss, former GDWW board member from Kansas, wrote, "Believe me, I do not have strong feelings one way or the other regarding [women's] ordination; only when I hear someone speak against it."[60]

In retrospect, the most questionable component in the drive to dismantle the parallel women's structure was the suspension of the Triennial Meeting bylaws, which eliminated that group's authority to represent the church's women in any national forum. Perhaps the leaders should have listened more carefully to the arguments being used to support continuing the Triennial Meeting. The following statements indicate the general tenor of the remarks:

> We need and want representation in the decision-making bodies of our Church, but we also need and want the fuller participation which . . . has allowed us to feel a part of the mainstream, and has given us a channel through which to express our thinking and our needs.[61] (ECW Executive Board, Diocese of San Joaquin)

> If—at a challenging and crucial period when every alert person is being bombarded with a diversity of facts, opinions and actions—there should be a deprivation of opportunity for the Episcopal Churchwomen to meet together for exchange, evaluation and reenforcement of constructive ideas and procedures which the Triennial Meeting has heretofore afforded, it would be a highly detrimental disservice to the work of the Church.[62] (ECW Executive Board, Diocese of Massachusetts)

> We Episcopal Churchwomen of the Diocese of Washington [D.C.] are members of the Diocesan Council, sit on every Diocesan Department and our counsel is welcomed by the Bishop, the Staff and the men of the Diocese. But we still maintain our vitally active women's groups to help accomplish every goal of the Diocesan program. Thus we feel the same should be true in our National organization.[63]

Indeed we want to be part of the decision making bodies from the parishes
on up, but we know this, at best, would involve only a very small percentage of the women. Where then do all the rest of the women look for
help and guidance?[64] (Ann Pettingill, ECW president, Diocese of Newark)

The counterargument was that it was necessary to dissolve the General
Division of Women's Work in order to free women to move into positions of responsibility in the national church. In the decade between
1970 and 1980, most of the women who served as deputies to the General
Convention or were elected to the Executive Council had come up
through the ranks as ECW officers and delegates to Triennial.[65] They
brought a wealth of experience in parliamentary procedure and knowledge of national church programs gained through ECW work. Some of
those women may well not have moved into the House of Deputies,
had the GDWW structure continued. With its dissolution, the women who
would have formed the GDWW board instead were serving on the Executive Council or on the standing committees of the General Convention. In those positions, they pressed for women's inclusion in national
church programs and added a woman's perspective to the discussion of
current issues. These gender-integrated committees did indeed better
represent the total Episcopal population.

As women sought to become responsible members of such national
groups, however, they came face to face with the crucial reality of the
distribution of power within the Episcopal Church. Because the committees generally required equal numbers of bishops, priests, and laity,
women (barred from the first two categories) were always in a small
minority. Hence, their ability to determine policy was severely limited.
The marginalization that talented women leaders experienced on such
national committees, particularly in contrast to the power they had held
in the GDWW, forced them to recognize the political ramifications of the
church's all-male ecclesiastical hierarchy. Women's ordination became
important, not just for the women who sought clerical status but for all
women who sought to make their voices heard in a church controlled
by men. "The more I think about the way the Church is run by men,
the more I think we need some lobbying for women. . . . I am even more
enthusiastic about the ordination of women than I was," wrote Frances
Young in 1973, after three years with the new system.[66] As long as
women were isolated in their parallel structure, they had been able to
avoid the reality of patriarchial power by organizing specific programs
within a limited realm of action. By giving up the protection of the
parallel structure and plunging into the political life of a church con-

trolled by a clerical hierarchy, Episcopal churchwomen found themselves confronted with a series of issues they had scarcely imagined. In confronting those issues, they moved to a position of support for the ordination of women.

Thus, the transition from separatism to integration had two important effects on the subsequent history of the Episcopal Church. The experience accelerated the move of ECW leadership into the pro-women's-ordination camp, lending the weight of their "respectability" to the cause. No longer could the call for women's ordination be considered the lonely cry of a few radical feminists. The strong ECW support moved the issue from a fringe to a centrist position, and was a major factor in the passage of the women's ordination bill in 1976. Concurrently, however, the failure of the Lay Ministries Committee had taught the women the folly of abandoning their separate power base without sufficient safeguards to insure that another network would take its place. By 1979 women leaders were seeking new ways to reconstruct their female power base. Since that time, though they have continued to move into positions of authority within the national church hierarchy, Episcopal women have also built a variety of task-oriented women's networks and have reorganized the Episcopal Churchwomen into a form similar to that which prevailed before 1967. A strategy of separatism continues to hold authority for the women of the Episcopal Church.

Notes

1. From 1955 to 1967 the number of dioceses that allowed women to serve on vestries went from 39 (of 101 dioceses) to 77; those that allowed women to serve as delegates to diocesan convention went from 41 to 77. General Division of Women's Work, *Responding to Change* (New York: Executive Council of the Episcopal Church, 1967), p. 6.

2. In 1946 Mrs. Randall Dyer, representing the Diocese of Missouri, was seated as a full-fledged deputy based on Judge Augustus M. Hand's ruling that the word *layman* was an all-inclusive term. The 1949 General Convention, by a 321–242 vote, refused to seat four duly elected women deputies, making official the literal interpretation of the word *layman*. General Convention of the Protestant Episcopal Church, *Journal of the General Convention* (hereinafter cited as *Convention Journal*) (1946): 102; *The Living Church* (15 September 1946): 6; Frances M. Young, *What Ever Happened to Good Old "Women's Work"?* (New York: Episcopal Women's History Project, 1986), p. 3; Mary S. Donovan, *A Different Call: Women's Ministries in the Episcopal Church, 1850–1920* (Wilton, Conn.: Morehouse-Barlow, 1986), pp. 162–166.

3. Membership on the Executive Council (earlier known as the National

Council) was specified in the national canons. The 1964 canons provided that the General Convention would elect three bishops, three presbyters, and five laymen to six-year terms (to join an equal number of men elected the previous convention); each province would elect one representative; and six women would be nominated by the Triennial Meeting and confirmed by the General Convention to serve three-year terms. Also included on the council were the presiding bishop, two vice-presidents, a secretary, and a treasurer. Canon 4, Section 2 (a), *Constitution and Canons of the Episcopal Church* (1964). Women were first elected to the Executive Council in 1934. From that year until 1964, the number of women members was four rather than six. Changes in the canons over time are reviewed in Edwin Augustine White and Jackson A. Dykman, *Annotated Constitution and Canons*, 2 vols. (New York: Seabury Press, 1981), 2:243–274.

4. General histories of the Episcopal Churchwomen include Anne Bass Fulk, *A Short History of the Triennial Meetings of the Women of the Episcopal Church* (Little Rock: Democrat Printing and Lithographing Co., 1985); Avis E. Harvey, *Every Three Years: The Triennial Meetings, 1874–1967* (New York: Executive Council of the Protestant Episcopal Church, 1967); Margaret Marston Sherman, *True to Their Heritage: A Brief History of the Woman's Auxiliary, 1871–1958* (New York: National Council, 1958).

5. General Division of Women's Work, *Changing Patterns* (New York: National Council, 1961), pp. 1–5.

6. Frances M. Young, *Thankfulness Unites: The History of the United Thank Offering* (Cincinnati: Forward Movement, 1979).

7. Over the years, schools were established in Berkeley, Chicago, Minneapolis, New York City, Philadelphia, and Raleigh. By 1960 only Windham House in New York City and St. Margaret's House in Berkeley remained in operation. Donovan, *A Different Call*, pp. 115–117, 172; Johanna K. Mott and Frances M. Sydnor, *A History of Windham House, 1928–1967*, (New York: Executive Council of the Episcopal Church, 1967); "St. Margaret's: Graduate School for Women," special edition of *The Witness*, 1 October 1959.

8. National women leaders recognized the divisive potential of a separate women's structure and repeatedly stressed that the General Division of Women's Work was simply one aspect of the church's overall program. As Frances M. Young, its executive director from 1960 to 1970, wrote, "We were always intersecting with the Church, and working hard all the time to make more intersecting. That was the goal of the Woman's Auxiliary, and of the GDWW." Frances M. Young to author, 28 January 1990, in the author's possession. Though the women staff officers worked toward inclusion, I suspect that the men who served on the national staff did not share the same understanding. Studies on theological education rarely mentioned women; "stewardship" was approached as an exclusively masculine preserve. "Metabaghdad" conferences, for example, were developed in the early 1960s as a model for assessing urban ministries. The instructional materials for these conferences made no mention that women

should be included in the conferences or on the design teams; promotional materials were almost devoid of photographs of women or of study documents that focused on women (e.g., incidence of poverty among families with female heads of households). See promotional materials in the Department of Christian Social Relations Records, 1925–1973, Record Group 151, Archives of the Episcopal Church, Austin, Texas. (Archives of the Episcopal Church, Austin, Texas, hereinafter cited as AEC.)

9. Estelle Freedman, "Separatism as a Strategy: Female Institution Building and American Feminism, 1870–1930," *Feminist Studies* 5 (Fall 1979): 513, 515.

10. David E. Sumner, *The Episcopal Church's History, 1945–1985* (Wilton, Conn.: Morehouse-Barlow, 1987), pp. 46–59.

11. Bennett J. Sims, "Confession of a former parish minister at convention" (typescript), 1967, Record Group 152–1–21, AEC. Though the women did fund the proposed list of grants for the first year, they immediately donated the $300,000 reserved for emergencies to the Urban Crisis Fund and pledged the remainder from the next two years' income. Aileen Rucker, interview by author, 7 January 1989, pp 41–45, Episcopal Women's Oral History Collection, AEC. Though many church publications identify women almost exclusively by their husband's names, I have chosen in this paper to identify women by their given names wherever possible.

12. *Convention Journal,* 1967, p. 168.

13. Frances M. Young, Virginia M. Harbour, Marjorie G. Mitchell, and Betsy Rodenmayer, "A History of Workers in Christian Education in the Episcopal Church in the USA" (typescript) April 1966, pp. 5–6, 11–12, RG 152–1–4, AEC.

14. Mrs. Francis O. Clarkson, an ECW leader from North Carolina; Cornelia Marshall of Washington, a former church worker; and Helen Loring, GDWW board member from Massachusetts, served on the commission with consultants Betsy Rodenmayer, Aileen Rucker, and Deaconess Ruth Johnson. The joint commission's 1967 report discovered that only about one-third of dioceses were certifying Women Church Workers as provided by Canon 52, and that even fewer dioceses provided pensions, annuities, or medical insurance for such workers. Ibid., p. 10; *Convention Journal,* 1964, pp. xviii, 250; 1967, pp. 96, 454, 35.1–3.

15. A total of 525 women were included in the study; 73 percent of the women and 82 percent of their employers responded. Betsy Rodenmayer, "Report on Study on Training and Employment of Women in Professional Positions in the Church" (typescript), October 1965, RG 111–2–22, AEC.

16. Ibid; "Report of the Executive Council on Clergy Salaries", *Convention Journal,* 1967, p. 14.5.

17. St. Margaret's House became the Berkeley Center for Human Interaction of the Graduate Theological Union. Since Windham House's program was controlled by its board, but its facilities were owned by the Executive Council of the Episcopal Church, the board terminated the program on June 30, 1967, and left financial arrangements to the Executive Council. The dates seminaries ad-

mitted women to the bachelor of divinity programs varied: Berkeley Divinity School, 1937; Episcopal Theological School, 1958; Virginia Theological Seminary, 1963; Church Divinity School of the Pacific, 1964; Episcopal Theological Seminary of the Southwest, 1967; Nashotah House, 1967; and Sewanee, Seabury Western, and General Theological Seminary, 1971. Sumner, *History,* pp. 17–18; General Convention, *Green Book* (New York: Executive Council, 1967), Appendix 21; General Division, *Responding* (New York: Executive Council of the Episcopal Church, 1967), pp. 32–33: Rodenmayer, "Study on Training," p. 4.

18. Board of Windham House, "Recommendations," 8 March 1966, quoted in Mott and Sydnor, *Windham House,* p. 16 (emphasis added).

19. *Convention Journal,* 1970, pp. 242, 249, 270, 355, 769–770.

20. Interview of Frances M. Young by author, 12 December 1989.

21. Barbara C. Harris from Philadelphia (later the first woman bishop) and Charity Waymouth from Maine were appointed to the Board for Deployment of Clergy. *Convention Journal,* 1970, p. 4.

22. The vote was clerical—yes 49 1/4, no 28 3/4, divided 21; lay—yes 49 1/4, no 28 3/4, divided 13. According to General Convention rules, divided votes are counted with the negative votes and a bill must pass in both orders. *Convention Journal,* 1970, pp. 160–161, 175.

23. Mary S. Donovan, *Women Priests in the Episcopal Church* (Cincinnati: Forward Movement, 1988), pp. 7–14; Carter Heyward, *A Priest Forever* (San Francisco: Harper & Row, 1976); Suzanne R. Hiatt, "How We Brought the Good News from Graymoor to Minneapolis: An Episcopal Paradigm," *Journal of Ecumenical Studies* 20 (Fall 1983): 576–584; Heather Ann Huyck, "To Celebrate a Whole Priesthood: The History of Women's Ordination in the Episcopal Church" (Ph.D. diss., University of Minnesota, 1981).

24. Francis O. Ayres, *The Ministry of the Laity,* (Philadelphia: Westminister Press, 1962), pp. 13–15.

25. Peter Day, *Saints on Main Street* (Greenwich, Conn.: Seabury Press, 1960).

26. Ayres, *Ministry,* p. 21.

27. General Division of Women's Work, "Critical Analysis" and "Full Participation" as reported by diocesan ECW presidents (typescript), 1966, RG 152–1–10, AEC.

28. Ibid.

29. General Division, *Responding,* pp. 3–6. The amendment was approved by a vote of 387 to 29. Minutes of the Triennial Meeting of the Women of the Protestant Episcopal Church in the United States of America (hereinafter cited as Triennial Minutes), 1967, pp. 23–24. See also Resolutions Seven and Eight, "On the Restructure of the General Division" and "Redefinition of Representation to Triennial Meeting," in General Division of Women's Work, *New Directions, New Climate* (New York: Executive Council of the Episcopal Church, 1970), pp. 42–42.

30. The GDWW board functioned as the transitional body (called Committee

for Women) until the 1970 General Convention ratified these changes. General Division of Women's Work, *New Directions,* pp. 3–19.

31. Before the 1969 change, the administrative structure of the national office consisted of six major departments (Christian Education, Christian Social Relations, Home, Overseas, Communications, and Finance) and three general divisions (Women's Work, Laymen's Work, and Research and Field Study). Department and division heads were responsible directly to the Executive Council and to the presiding bishop. Frances M. Young, interview by author, 12 December 1989; "The Executive Council," in *The Episcopal Church Annual* (New York: Morehouse-Barlow Co., 1968), pp. 28–30; Resolution adopted by Executive Council, 21 May 1969, Subject: United Thank Offering Committee, RG 161–2–4, AEC.

32. Presentation by the Committee for Women to the Executive Council, 25 September 1968, RG 176–2–18, AEC.

33. Presenters included Frances M. Young on women's contributions to church life; Caroline Bird, author of *Born Female,* on the changing reality of women's lives in contemporary society; and Theodora Sorg, presiding officer of the 1964 Triennial, on ways integrate women's work into the church's total program. General Division, *New Directions,* pp. 8–13.

34. Lueta Bailey, Martha Wilson, Jean Jackson, and Marion Kelleran were elected. The number of women serving on the Executive Council remained at four until 1979, when ten women and thirty-two men were elected. Subsequent council membership: 1982, 8 women, 30 men; 1985, 12 women, 26 men; 1988, 13 women, 24 men. *Convention Journal,* 1970–1988.

35. Triennial Minutes, 1970, pp. 50–54. Discussion of the guidelines revealed that many women were reluctant to relinquish elected representation on the committee, but the final vote endorsed the guidelines as presented, with the provision that the Lay Ministries Committee was responsible to the Executive Council, not the Episcopal Churchwomen. See also Fulk, *Triennial Meetings,* pp. 34–36.

36. Minutes of United Thank Offering Committee, 23–24 November 1970, RG 130–7–47, AEC; Triennial Minutes, 1970, pp. 36–39.

37. Theodora Sorg, "Time of Testing and Transition", *The Episcopalian* 135 (December 1970): 28–31; Triennial Minutes, 1970, pp. 42–47 and Appendix.

38. By 1970 only the dioceses of Dallas, Northwest Texas, and South Carolina did not permit women to serve as deputies to diocesan conventions, and South Carolina had completed the first step in erasing its prohibition. "Women's Rights in the Church: A Quiet Revolution Almost Concluded," *The Episcopalian* 135 (October 1970): 40.

39. Membership included Peg Ewell (South Florida), 1970 Triennial presiding officer as well as cochair of the General Convention Agenda Committee; Frances Young, Aileen Rucker, and Olive Mae Mulica of the national staff; Dorothy Higley (Central New York), former GDWW chairman and current Executive Council member; Elizabeth Battle (Indianapolis), 1967 UTO committee chair;

Edna Goss (Kansas), GDWW board member; Mary Durham (Michigan), president of both diocesan and provincial ECWS, and GDWW and Executive Council member; and Marion Kelleran, professor of pastoral theology at Virginia Theological Seminary. Triennial Planning Committee, Minutes, 14 March 1970, p. 3; 16–17 May 1970, p. 3, RG 161–1–31, AEC.

40. The Lay Ministries Committee guidelines approved by the 1970 Triennial were revised later by the Executive Council. Originally, the committee was to include four members of the 1967–1970 Committee for Women, four members of the 1969–1970 Special Committee on Lay Ministries, four members at large selected to assure broad representation of the church, and at least two members of the Executive Council. The revision changed the committee from standing to advisory, with primary membership from the Executive Council. Committee for Women and Special Committee on Lay Ministries, Minutes of Joint Subcommittee, 25–26 July 1970, 2, RG 161–2–4, AEC. The official name was Executive Council Program Advisory Committee on Lay Ministries (hereinafter referred to as Lay Ministries Committee).

41. The Executive Council members of the committee were Bishops Wilburn C. Campbell, Archie H. Crowley, and Philip F. McNairy; the Reverend Dillard Robinson; and Dupuy Bateman. Minutes of the Program Advisory Committee on Lay Ministries (16–17 February 1971), RG 176–2–19, AEC.

42. Oscar Carr was a layman from Mississippi whose witness to the Christian's responsibility to work for racial justice won wide acclaim at the 1969 General Convention. Edna Goss to Alice [Emery] and Fran [Young], 30 January 1971, RG 213–1–12, AEC.

43. The additional members were Virginia Culley, Nancy Lea, Margaret Raney, and Ellie Wiener from the Committee for Women; Dr. Wilber Katz, Eleanor Lewis, and Charity Waymouth from the Special Committee on Lay Ministries. Minutes of the Executive Council Program Advisory Committee on Lay Ministries, 15–16 February 1971, RG 176–2–19, AEC.

44. Report of the Ad Hoc Committee on the Laity of the Executive Council, May 1969, 10, RG 161–2–4, AEC.

45. Mark Gibbs was the associate secretary of the Association of Lay Centres in Europe. Mark Gibbs and T. Ralph Morton, *God's Frozen People* (Philadelphia: Westminster Press, 1964); Executive Council Program Advisory Committee on Lay Ministries, Minutes, 19–20 April 1972, RG 176–2–19, AEC.

46. Executive Council Program Advisory Committee on Lay Ministries, 15–16 February, 18 May, 27–18 September, 1971, RG 176–2–9, AEC.

47. Young, *What Ever Happened?* p. 18.

48. Keith to Frances Young, 28 August 1972, RG 153–1–5, AEC.

49. Louise McQuiston to Frances Young, 22 September 1972, RG 153–1–5, AEC.

50. Cynthia C. Wedel, "Some Reflections on Lay Ministry in the Episcopal Church," 18 September 1972, RG 161–2–4, AEC.

51. Mary Flagg to Frances Young, 13 September 1972, RG 153–1–5, AEC.

52. Frances Young, interview by Joanna B. Gillespie, 9 October 1986, pp. 124–131, Episcopal Women's Oral History Collection, AEC.

53. Council for Development of Ministry, Report, *Convention Journal,* 1976, AA–59–65.

54. Unfortunately, these economic changes were not retroactive; women who had already retired continue to this day to receive meager pensions based on the small salaries they received during their working years, supplemented in cases of known need by bonuses granted at the discretion of the national missions office. Helen Turnbull and Marcella Pambrum, interviews by the author, 20 October 1989.

55. The Executive Council resolution, ratified by the Committee for Women at its final meeting in October 1970, provided that the annual income would be reserved for the expenses of the UTO committee and the expenses of next Triennial Meeting. Emilie G. Wright left the bequest in 1951. In 1970 the assigned value was $595,927.51 *Trust Funds,* 1967 (New York: Domestic and Foreign Missionary Society, 1967), p. 49; ibid., 1985, p. 50; Triennial Minutes, 1970, p. 54.

56. Fulk, *Triennial Meetings,* p. 37.

57. See pamphlets issued yearly, "United Thank Offering Grants" (New York: Executive Council of the Episcopal Church), AEC.

58. "United Thank Offering Grants, 1971" (New York: Executive Council of the Episcopal Church, 1971).

59. United Thank Offering Committee, Minutes, 13–24 March 1972; Alice Emery "To Whom it May Concern," 15 June 1972; "U.T.O.—For Lobby Funds," *American Church News,* Ascension, 1972, RG 130–8–3, 5, AEC.

60. Edna Goss to Alice Emery, 22 October 1972, AEC RG 213–1–12.

61. Ellen Onstad to Frances Young, 17 November 1969; Onstad to "All Diocesan ECW Presidents," 20 November 1969, notebook in the possession of Marjorie L. Christie, Franklin Lakes, New Jersey.

62. Marjorie Nichols to Frances Young, 21 January 1970, ibid.

63. Judy Whitlock to Frances Young, 5 March 1970, ibid.

64. Ann Pettingill to Members of the ECW Executive Board, 4 December 1969, ibid.

65. I have identified as former diocesan or national ECW officers all except four of the seventeen women who served on the Executive Council between 1970 and 1980, and all except six of the twenty-nine women deputies elected to the 1970 General Convention. The lack of identification does not necessarily mean that the woman had no ECW background; only one woman, Jean Jackson, who served both as a deputy and on executive council has been definitely identified as having held no previous ECW diocesan or national post. I am grateful to the 1991 National Board of the Episcopal Church Women for assistance in these identifications.

66. Frances Young to Alice Emery, 28 June 1973, RG 213–1–31, AEC.

II

CONTEMPORARY VOICES

The essays in this section seek to provide a perspective that historians often assert they honor but rarely attain: the perspective of the "ordinary" person. Feminist scholarship's insistence that women's experience be a focus of historical inquiry is one reason for including these essays. Another is the need for students of American church life to examine more attentively the religious and experiential realities of the people in the pews. And most of these, now as in centuries past, are women.

"Gender and Generations in Congregations" is based upon the questionnaire and interview responses of hundreds of Episcopal women in four quite different parishes. Joanna B. Gillespie, the historian who directed this innovative investigation, finds that women's sense of themselves, their God, and their church often varies by generation as different life issues and experiences shape their religious identities. The many voices that speak from this essay offer beautiful glimpses into the inner realities that scholars intuitively know are indispensable to religious institutions but that are so rarely open to view.

Three other distinct voices are given opportunity to speak in the other essays included here. Marjorie N. Farmer writes out of her experience as an African American woman, blending her own story with the written and oral history of African American Episcopalians in Philadelphia as sources of reflection upon the distinctive issues facing her church and community. Irene Q. Brown brings to voice Mrs. Margaret Langlois, a working-class white woman deeply attached to the Episcopal Church, though now, in her seventies, unsettled by the changes it has undergone in recent years. Sandra Hughes Boyd's autobiographical account of her own journey toward priesthood discloses the personal impact of the changes in women's lives and in the church during the past generation.

This medley of unique voices is far less representative of the diversity of Episcopal women than it should be, of course. Even so, it furnishes insights into several worlds in transition and provides a composite portrait of many quite different women as they seek to find and express the spiritual truths of their lives.

5

Gender and Generations in Congregations

Joanna B. Gillespie

Although all women in contemporary America have experienced profound change in the last half of this century, little inquiry has focused on women associated with mainstream churches. This research was designed to elicit the perception of the "woman in the pew." We aimed to gauge her responses to changes in women's role and possibilities in the institution by comparing age groups within a given congregation. We chose a generational approach as the means of producing a visible intersection of personal change with institutional change.

The institutions through which we contacted our informants, their local parish churches, have also changed considerably in the present century. The most visible and profound changes—altered ritual and practices in the 1960s, and the opening of ordained leadership to women in the 1970s—took place in the worship life of those churches. Both of the primary worship manuals, the two books used at every service, were revised: the *Book of Common Prayer* (1978), and the *Hymnal* (1987). Laywomen have experienced revisions incorporating theological change that altered the mores, the conduct, the order of the liturgy, and the language of worship itself.

But in a sacramental church, the most earthshaking change was the entry of women into the ordained clerical role and its central act of worship, the celebration of the eucharist. What does it mean for women to receive the bread and wine from the hand of a woman for the first time? How do laywomen now think about leadership? Whom do they see as capable of being leaders, within their congregation? What effect does a changed image of religious authority have on other relationships and symbols? During our research in congregations (1989), the consecration of the first woman bishop in the Episcopal Church heightened awareness of this dramatic change.

A third element of change, growing out of the secular women's movement, rearranged the entire set of assumptions about women's service activities: "volunteering," a woman's offering of her personal efforts, and money, to and through her congregation. Laywomen have always been the majority of attendants at worship, and down through history have carried out the bulk of the congregation's "hands-on" service work. Changed attitudes about paid employment outside the home had a major impact on the relatively privileged American women likely to be found in Episcopal, Presbyterian, and other mainline Protestant churches. Once careers or paid jobs became a standard possibility for the white, well-educated, middle-class Episcopal laywoman, her view of what it meant to belong to a church was profoundly altered. African-American Episcopal churchwomen, in contrast, have always juggled church work and paid work. Because of this paradigm shift affecting the laywoman's time, "traditional churchwomen's work," as it was known, has disappeared from many congregations, or is being restructured.

We pursued women's self-perception in response to these changes by tracing four strands or currents of thought: their relationship with their particular congregation; their attitudes toward work, both paid employment and volunteer; the place of family in their identity; and their inner life. To capture the generational dimension of these themes, we arbitrarily set chronological boundaries for generations: a younger generation, women aged forty and under; a bridge generation, women between forty-one and sixty years old; and an older generation, women over sixty-one. By asking all ages the same questions and comparing their responses generationally, we took a vertical "boring" through the three simultaneous layers of a given congregation—exposing a slice of living history, so to speak. As a second stage of the inquiry, that baseline information was amplified through structured interviews with a sample of fifteen women from each of the four congregations. We chose not to focus on women unrelated to an ordinary church because we wanted to see what impact an externally heightened consciousness of gender had exercised on the average woman in an ongoing congregation. Many of our assumptions took a different twist than we expected, among them the degree to which women would be critical of the institutional church. What we found was a surprising loyalty, a commitment to self-realization within the institution, a variety of feminist self-awareness and self-direction seemingly determined to find "things needful" for survival and meaning *within* a patriarchal religious structure. Women have assimilated an enormous amount of change, not always consciously, while the congregational structure itself had changed somewhat.

The approach we chose—to work through a congregation as the basic unit for our study—meant that the women we contacted were not those who had become completely disillusioned and "left the church." They were not the rebels and world-changers who created newspaper headlines in the 1960s and 1970s. Even if many had dropped out of church for a time, they were back in by 1989, to the degree that their names appear on a congregation's membership list and they were willing to take the time to complete our questionnaire. Thus, women who had become totally disaffected from the church eluded our study. The women we reached defined themselves as having a need for the institutional dimension of faith. They identified their spiritual hunger and the ways they found to fulfill it within their churches. In each of the four congregations there were a few women who linked activism in secular political or civic causes with their religious commitment; though only a yeasty fraction of their congregations, these were known and valued by their fellow parishioners for their stance and causes.

To allow for maximum regional diversity in a small-scale study, our research locations—four midsize, "typical" (predominantly white middle-class) Episcopal churches—were as geographically widespread as possible. We chose what would be considered the average rather than the unusual congregation: not too experimental but having some experience with women as ordained leaders; not just in cities but not tiny isolated congregations; not rich and prosperous but also not "missions" or financially assisted congregations in ethnic-minority neighborhoods.[1] Each of these congregations had a few ethnic minority members: African American, Hispanic, or Asian.

Our congregations, their names and particulars changed for purposes of anonymity, included:

1. *Grace Church,* a traditional New England congregation with an average Sunday attendance of 200 (from a much larger communicant list) in an industrialized river city;

2. *Church of the Advent,* a New-South, Old-South amalgam with Anglo-

Catholic worship, drawing about 135 worshippers of racially and economically diverse backgrounds on an average Sunday, in a partially reclaimed
inner-city area near a state university;

3. *Church of the Redeemer,* a progressive and cohesive congregation
averaging about 135 on a Sunday morning, on the edge of a small, rail-
crossroads city on the Great Plains; and

4. *Church of the Nativity,* also about the same size as Redeemer, a
"family" church in dynamics as well as in metaphor, located in the gen-
trifying neighborhood of a Pacific Coast city.

Each of the congregations had some recent history in common, a link
we discovered only after we had begun visiting them in 1988–1989. Each
was enjoying a kind of renaissance, an upsurge of young families seeking
a church identity. "It felt like coming home when I transferred here,"
sighed a woman in her midthirties. After the "church-vacuum" of early
adulthood, new members brought a palpable vitality with them. Several
were horrified that they'd been raised in "the classic Episcopal pattern
that says, 'Hang in till you get the membership card,' and then forget
it."

Another segment consisted of women raised in other churches who
had been thrown into religious confusion by various changes, and later
chose the Episcopal Church. One young woman in Nativity Northwest,
tracing her twenty-year lapse from the Roman Catholicism of her childhood, remembered the post–Vatican II period as sudden and disorient-
ing: "Folk masses. No Latin. No more . . . holy cards. All my rituals
were leaving me. . . . [The folksong] 'Michael Row the Boat Ashore'
simply wasn't doing it for me." Still another pattern was exemplified by
the young single professional who considered "leaving church" a natural
part of growing up and putting away childish things. "College for me
was all very intellectualized and principled," she explained. "I studied
quantitative psychology and became a behaviorist. . . . I just sort of cut
out all religious and faith questions." In her twenties concerns about
ultimate meaning and religious identity were easy to shelve.

All the young women with whom we spoke had recently "returned"
to serious church participation, determined to have a church belonging
as well as direct connection with God for themselves once again. They
viewed it as self-realization—their application of the self-awareness and
self-determination they had absorbed during the growing-up years. They
were not angry or dissatisfied at what they found; they were still discovering and assimilating this new dimension of their lives. The magnet
drawing a young office manager back, after the standard drift away
during college, was inclusiveness—discovering a congregation that, un-

like church in her childhood, welcomed "all sorts and conditions" of people. "[We have] a real diverse bunch of people here . . . not just married people with kids. *Anybody's* welcome here, regardless of sexual preference, or gender, or income level, or anything." Beneath this rationale for a revitalized interest in church, however, was a deep longing for the sacred and for institutional stability in their adult lives. "It's the structure that I really wanted," one young mother acknowledged. Differing from the *Newsweek* explanation of young families' religiosity in the 1980s—for the sake of the children—these young women sought out congregational membership for personal, including feminist, self-fulfillment.[2] They had responded to the ideal of female autonomy by choosing, rather than rejecting, a religious identity. They were there "as my own person," to use their words—a very different phenomenon from nostalgic reenactment of "a family reason." Though many linked religious rediscovery with the responsibilities of parenthood, the commitment was their own rather than their responsibility to a family unit.

Each of the four research congregations currently enjoyed male (and some female) clerical leadership of the type that encapsulated the changes in the late-twentieth-century Episcopal Church. Each church prided itself on women's recent, more visible participation in worship leadership and on governing boards or vestries; each was conscious of needing to adjust meeting times (some had already made changes) because of women's employment. The rectors in each were credited with helping the congregations change, with "dragging us in[to] the present," as a young New England woman said. "The rector *should* be the pathbreaker, pushing us, pulling us along into the future."[3] The four rectors were men in midcareer, established for approximately five years in the present congregation. In two cases ordained women served on the staff as associates; in the other two cases, the congregation had had some experience with ordained women.

All four congregations had also suffered severe numerical decline in the previous decades. The "bad times" were variously ascribed to "flaky clerical leadership in the sixties, you know, real out-of-control liberal," or "a few old families maintaining a stranglehold on the parish so that newcomers were discouraged," or to the general disillusion with institutions that was the mood of the 1960s. Among older parishioners, the reawakened religiosity of young families was welcome, if accompanied by certain regrets that had to be muffled. A woman in her seventies confided: "I can't quite get used to . . . taking the children up to the altar. . . . they take communion, and they come back from the altar [elaborate chewing motion] like that. [Children of all ages, from infancy up, now receive the eucharist after being instructed; confirmation is no longer the gatekeeping rite of passage.] I think that just isn't right. And . . . when they have the Peace [a ritual during eucharist, following confession and absolution, when the celebrant says, "The Peace of the Lord be always with you," and worshippers turn to share God's forgiveness with one another, saying, "And also with you"], people actually move out of their pews . . . and shake hands, and hug each other! [In some congregations, the exchange becomes a break in the formality of the worship.] I just don't do it. I just stand there. One of our rectors said to me, 'Oh Mrs. Smith, you'll get used to it,' but I just don't think I ever will."

A more comfortable adjustment to changes in the congregation came from a bridge-generation college professor who, as a member of the choir, had a ringside place in the choir stall from which to watch all ages of parishioners come forward to communion. "I love seeing all the little kids coming up, especially at Easter with their bonnets on. . . . It connects you to the generations coming." But a woman of the same generation said, "Sometimes, when all those kids are making a fuss, it's okay—but sometimes it bothers me terribly." A remarkably articulate woman of sixty-nine put the most positive reading on the newcomers. "For a long time it seemed we had an older church and a younger church, with very little in the middle. . . . Now we have thirty- and forty-year-olds, and . . . you can just feel people [reaching] out to one another." She perceived the rebirth as "almost a revival." Differing responses to congregational rejuvenation illustrate the "intrinsic generational strain toward adjustment" that occurs, almost unnoticed, in any institution. Each generation must endure a process of accommodation, in order to coexist with other age groups and eventually achieve a kind of harmony, or at least balance.[4]

Research Design

We distributed survey questionnaires to all women on the membership roster in three congregations. In our pilot congregation, Grace New England, we instead distributed questionnaires to a randomly selected sample of one-third of the women on the parish list. In all, we obtained 269 completed surveys.

For background, we also mailed questionnaires to approximately thirty-five "designated leaders" in each congregation; these were men and women heading organizations or committees, who were viewed as opinion shapers among the members. Their names were selected, in each church, by a female lay volunteer-coordinator who coordinated our project in her congregation, and the clergy. In practice the designated leaders were all current and some past elected officials, plus those on the cutting edge of appointed leadership, such as, head of the Christian Education Committee or leader of youth work. We received seventy-three completed leader surveys from the four parishes, 66 percent from men and 34 percent from women leaders.

We interviewed six of the designated-leader group in each congregation: the clergy; one of the wardens (the two elected "trustees" of the congregation); the lay head of youth work; the lay chair of the Christian Education Commission; the president of a traditional "women's organization," such as the ECW or Altar Guild; and at least one retired vestry member (male). To get a sense of congregational ethos and "personality," we also reviewed the church's print materials (Sunday programs, displays on bulletin boards in the parish hall, newsletters); studied community census data on population change and other churches within the area; attended Sunday services more than once, and Lenten suppers or parish picnics; and visited stores or neighbors in the immediate vicinity of the church, for casual observations about the congregation.

When the questionnaires from the four locations had been compiled, names of women in each congregation who had indicated a willingness to be interviewed were placed in a hat and randomly drawn, five from each of the three "generations." We completed a total of sixty interviews, twenty in each of the age groups (fifteen from each parish), as well as the twenty-four background interviews, of men and women, from the four congregations.

Generations in Congregations

The lens of generation we applied was not so much in reference to an interval of time as an "energy field" or framework for remembering "crucial things"—a system of reference that illuminates a sense of collective identification.[5] In the present century, when the "social effects of generation" are multiple and complex, generations clearly demonstrate change in the mores and assumptions brought to their congregational identity.[6] Factors that had contributed to these differing worldviews became visible.[7]

What we call "generation" has three distinct components: women's actual chronological *age; period,* the factor that cuts across all generations (for example, the Vietnam War), what goes on that they all experience and respond to; and *cohort,* the term for a group that has lived through definitive historical experiences together, and therefore is likely to share overlapping generalizations about their era (for example, the Great Depression cohort). Each of these women defined her "life course" by at least some experiences similar to others in her age cohort. Key words were a signal of cohort assumptions. Because they had a common location in the sweep of history, they had been exposed to the same spirit of the times, at the same stages of life, and to similar social-structural constraints. For many of the older women in the four parishes, a cohort-forming experience was likely to be the Great Depression; for the middle-aged generation it was the civil rights movement and the emergence of the contemporary women's movement. The women forty and under had participated in, resisted, or at least registered the upheavals surrounding the Vietnam War.

Understanding the cohort dimension of an individual woman's responses helped us see that religious change is not imposed by outside forces. It is rather an internal absorption of some new outlook or rationalization. For example, these women's comments about employment outside the home (or not) were not in response to an external mandate that "forced" them to leave their homes and go out to jobs. They reflected simply the "countless separate decisions of individual women," each decision made within the woman's own circumstance and ethos. Decisions, reactions, plans were her "own" choice, made within the context of externally changed perception of the economic needs of self or family, and drives toward self-expression or -fulfillment.[8] Cohorts reflect each generation's commonsense or "folklore" views about the particular segment of history they remember. Cohort differences help explain why one generation's meanings are so hard, if not impossible, for other generations to comprehend.[9]

The three following sections trace some of the overarching themes that characterize the three generations of women in this study.

Older Generation

Congregational change itself was the focus of the older generation's point of view in this study. On her questionnaire, one older woman spelled out the sense of displacement she and others of her cohort now experience in church. In response to the question *What changes in your religious life have been most frustrating?* she listed and numbered:

1. "The use of 'table' instead of altar." (In her church, as in many since the 1960s, the priest now officiates at the eucharist facing the congregation instead of the altar; a table placed in front of the altar fixed against the east wall creates direct eye contact with the worshippers, in contrast with the earlier practice of having the priest's back to the congregation.)

2. "[I] object to the laity doing work the priest is paid to." (She reflects the increased participation of laymen and -women in the worship service itself. Women as well as men now act as chalice bearers, offering communicants the cup of wine after the priest has placed the host or bread in their hands. A second change is the use of lay readers, a member coming to the lectern from the congregation to read aloud a scripture lesson. A third but less publicly visible change to which she refers might well be lay visitors or "lay eucharistic ministers" who do much of the parish calling. They take the consecrated wine and bread after the church services to the ill or shut-ins, formerly the exclusive purview of the clergy.)

3. "[I] object to the church being used for all city and social events." (An exclusive territory, her "holy space," has been invaded by a wider constituency. Many churches or their facilities are used for special-interest group meetings, such as Narcotics Anonymous, Amnesty International, or day care programs.)

4. "Need for clergy to promote more 'in reach.' " (Her parish is very involved in "outreach"—social ministry programs for the needy.)

We could hardly have received a more cogent summary of her generation's angst. It has some nostalgia for a style of clergy leadership that included routine pastoral calls in the homes of all parishioners, especially lifelong members. They recall a childhood in which clerical visits to their parents were an honored prerequisite of parish membership; a venerable woman in a congregation could anticipate at least an occasional moment when the personification of her religious community was present in her own territory, and she would have his full attention. Since the 1950s, a more corporate style of parish administration has emerged. Regular calling in homes, if still practiced, is now often carried out by lay visitors. Ordained leaders concentrate mostly on "crisis" visits—when a person is dying, in trouble emotionally, or in the hospital.

Other older women regretted other changes, for example, the "loss of poetry in the language of the Prayer Book." Women who once knew the services and the Elizabethan-language prayers by heart find themselves off balance. Habits of worship established over a lifetime of Sundays are swept away—fewer "Thee's and Thou's," "too many choices" or options in a given order of worship. "Too much announcing of page numbers" reinforces awareness that they have lost an instinctive sense of location. "I spend half the time [in the service] finding my place, and when I finally get there, they've gone on to something else," was one poignant comment.

The older-women cohort shares two sets of painful memories that have an impact on their response to current changes. The major one relates to the church itself, the "bad times" in their congregations during "the crazy sixties," when, for example, Grace New England was "down to less than thirty people in church on a Sunday," or when one church had a dishonest rector whose bookkeeping took the parish to the financial brink. A second and prior experience, for women seventy and over, is the Great Depression. One woman, seventy-five, proudly recalled that it was her mother who found work with the WPA and held the family together, after her father lost his job. "She was the strong person of the family who, through sheer determination and without a feeling at all of being embarrassed, went out to work." A farmwoman near eighty said her only "real tragedy" was caused by the Depression. "I graduated from high school in '29 . . . [and] didn't get to go to college. And you couldn't even *buy* a job, they were so few."

Even with that backdrop for their young adult years, the pain over the 1960s congregational decline in numbers and status was uppermost in their consciousness; it seemed to temper their response to change. The prevailing tone in interviews was thanksgiving for the hope represented by the new young families. They also felt free to express delight in the fellowship and religiously sustaining company of one another, an indirect benefit from the women's movement; they had not been raised to credit the company of women. Citing her pleasure in the gatherings of her Circle—a subgroup of the once-ubiquitous form of women's organization known by the rubric Episcopal Churchwomen (hereafter ECW)—one woman reported gleefully: "In my car, at the November meeting, I had a 92-year-old, an 87-year old, an 85-year-old, a 77-year-old, and I was the baby at 74! Oh, well, we do have one young woman, about in her 40s. . . . My . . . does *she* have a lot of mothers!" If some felt free to resist change in the privacy of written responses to an anonymous questionnaire, strong self-censorship prevailed in face-to-face exchange; most of them seemed to feel that "too much" change was better than institutional lifelessness.

Of course no "generation" is uniform in response to change, especially to change in the deeply personal act of worship. Some older-generation women are more likely to be comfortable with women's new part in leadership than others. One, sixty-one, employed as a doctor's assistant, rejoiced in having found her own "ministry" (a word the older members of her cohort never apply to their own work) as a lay distributor of the chalice and participant in healing services: "[The laying on of hands in prayer is] a complete outpouring of unconditional, perfect Love.... You can feel it. It's draining, in a way, and yet fulfilling. ... In healing, *we* are healed." Another, seventy-four, was dismayed by the reaction of a friend to her congregation's hiring an ordained woman. "That woman's so against women, it's just terrible. I don't understand that a woman could feel that way against themselves! I don't think Jesus would feel that way at all, you know. ... " A retired businesswoman located her disapproval of women priests in a generalized protest about the range of upheavals since the 1960s: "I sometimes think you reach a stage in your life where you have changed as much as you're willing to.... [P]erhaps I've reached that age . . . where . . . I'm just not willing to compromise any further." Her concluding hope was "not too much more change" in her lifetime, lest "I can't tolerate it."

Overall, the older generation displayed a very game spirit. A wife, seventy-four, of a retired navy captain, was very "realistic about things" in the congregation. Some contemporaries "want it the way it's always been, but you have to go with the flow. You just can't have it like it was in 1925, for heaven's sake!" For the most part, this generation tolerates or welcomes the higher level of noise accompanying the influx of new life in their congregations, a greater informality of decorum, and alterations in the order of worship. Most of the women we interviewed were remarkably accepting of the larger issue, the changed visibility of women. (Undoubtedly this was a factor in their willingness to be interviewed.) One, seventy-five, a retired office worker, enthusiastically remarked, "I believe in the place of women in the church as a concept! [In women's] participation in all the forms of religious life, from doing dishes in the kitchen to being bishop, the highest calling! All the way through, all the way through!" Another, also seventy-five, more cautiously perceived "little *advantage* to having women in clerical roles," but defended it in distinctly contemporary language: "because women *should* be liberated." The coolest response to an ordained woman was expressed by a former teacher of nineteenth-century English literature, nearing ninety: "I've had little contact with her, actually.... She seems—what should I say?—adequate."

The vast majority of the older cohort gave some rhetorical assent to the principle of ordaining women (only eleven in the sample of eighty-seven older women openly opposed it, in the questionnaire). However, language changes were easier to resist, especially the use of less hierarchical, exclusively masculine language about God as a step toward inclusive language (or supplemental liturgies).[10] Assimilating change through the eye was one thing, through the ear and the mouth much harder. When the phrase "Inclusive Language" on the questionnaire was not forthrightly rejected, objections could be buried in the "No Opinion" option. Or they were selective. "I like traditional things in general, although of course I don't mind some change—but not the Lord's Prayer," warned a former visiting nurse, seventy-eight, in her interview. Another, seventy-two, proudly supported other changes, involving herself in lay reading, chalice bearing, and serving on the vestry. But changing the language was, in her view, a passing and unworthy fad, designed only "to meet some strongly-held [feminist] feelings." Most of this generation used some standard or traditional religious vocabulary in their written responses to the questionnaire, but when they spoke they used distinctly "everyday" language rather than "church words."

Insofar as older-generation women are able to assimilate change in their congregation—both from the external society, and within the internal, liturgical life of their church—they are cherished and respected by fellow parishioners and clergy. Our summary impression is that this generation of churchwomen wants to find, and to a remarkable degree has succeeded in finding, ways to live with the changes, no matter how hard. They are determined to remain part of "their" church.

Younger Generation

The younger generation was preoccupied with reconnecting or rediscovering the institutional church. If it was critical at all, it was impatient with "tradition."[11] Criticism of the church reflects the new women's consciousness. A storeowner, forty, with children in high school and college, recalled her confirmation class as totally superficial and sexist. "We were told not to wear nail polish or jewelry or *any* make-up for the big day of Confirmation. No adornment," she recalled. "Do you think the *boys* got any special instructions like that?" An unmarried businesswoman, thirty-five, in a large city, stumbled into the change about women. "I didn't go to church from age 20 on—Vietnam made it impossible—till I walked in the door here, about eight years ago." When a childhood habit of churchgoing resurfaced, she followed a sudden impulse. "I put on a dress, walked in here, knelt down to say my prayers, and—and they'd changed the Prayer Book on me. I was appalled!" (laughter). She continued: "No kidding, I was really horrified. And then—the lay reader was a SHE—wearing little red half-glasses, and long earrings with little balls on the end!" About halfway through the service, she began to relax, saying to herself: "THIS IS GREAT! Look what they've done to my church!" Even women clergy were a shock, though welcome. Asked about that, she said in her gentle drawl, "It's about damn time."

Though aware of the struggles preoccupying their congregations in the previous decades, they are absorbed with other concerns: the process of sorting out their own identities, juggling time pressures and multiple role demands. Having reclaimed their link with a church, they now search for their own niche in it. The 1960s had left its mark on them. A young physician from Advent South wept as she recalled antiwar demonstrations at her college. To her they were not exhilarating but confusing and fearsome: "It was absolutely traumatic for my psyche. I became nearly mute for awhile." Another young businesswoman reported total disinvolvement in the same phenomenon: "I don't even remember Kent State. Only later I thought: Hey, wait a minute—they were shooting *kids* over this." The women forty and under with whom we spoke were not celebratory about their generation's impact on institutions and "tradition." Though as a cohort they had participated in it more or less, its primary impact was reflected in the career choices they were able to take for granted.

Many were eager for their "new" congregation to be "on the move," a reflection of their own self-understanding. "[The present rector] has really gotten this church out of the stupor it was in for years and years. . . . He encourages children [to be] in the church [during the adult service]. 'I don't care if there is noise,' he will say, 'we're going to get some life going on in here,' " one reported approvingly. But change itself is not an unqualified good for all members of any generation. A professional musician admitted she had considered and discarded the idea of becoming a priest "because . . . I'm afraid women in the church have not meant such positive things to me. . . . They weren't *ever* given any real authority." In her eyes, women's new possibilities within the church were not substantive, only superficial.

For the younger generation, the idea of "traditional churchwomen's work" has come full circle. An automatic association of women with bake sales and sewing circles, the "location" the professional musician had in mind when she spoke of women as having "no real authority" in the congregation, has changed. Its demise is bemoaned by the older generation and viewed with relief (and guilt) by the bridge generation, while a surprising number of the young express nostalgia for it. They have no experience of being limited to that arena merely by virtue of being female. At the very time in their lives when they are not free to

participate in that "traditional" form of good works, they romanticize
its historic image. A medical technician commented, "I think [ECW cir-
cles] would be great—though instead of just women, couldn't it be
everybody's activity? My husband likes to make things, too." Some
want to reclaim it entirely, including handwork-and-devotional meetings
in one another's homes: "It would be fun to go to other people's homes,
do crossstitch, and . . . get to know people better, like you do in their
own surroundings." But some are still suspicious of the words "churchwomen's work"—and, by implication, the traditional view of women's
"place" in the congregation. The professional musician traced her neg-
ativity from childhood, when "all a lay woman could be was Altar Guild,
a Sunday school teacher or flower arranger. . . . " She had absorbed
powerful condescension toward those tasks. She had been taught that
such "unimportant" work made the church too "social, not really godly
. . . just another excuse for a social gathering." Even now, when the
formal organizational framework no longer existed, she feared the
"woman's work" image. "I still have those feelings, and they keep me
distant. I don't want to get into that stuff."

But in larger terms, the women forty and under want to be fed by,
and conform to, their institution. They have rejoined a church because
they need a religious connection—for themselves and, for those with
young children, for their families. "I think it's important for children
to *grow up* in the church, not just get confirmed, married and buried
in it; I want them growing up in a Christian community," one young
mother said. They worry not about the church itself but about the
maelstrom of demands in which they feel enmeshed—family, church,
career, community involvement, self-identity. "I just want two hours a
week, to do whatever I want to," lamented a mother of preschool
children. "So far, I'm about seventeen weeks behind."

Today's young-generation churchwomen in our four congregations
reflect their middle-class, relatively privileged "baby boom" childhood.[12]
They have never questioned their right to make their own decisions.
Surfeited with stuffed animals as little girls, they became big girls at a
time when barriers to all-male occupations had crumbled. They could
choose to be anything for which they could afford to study. Even those
from economically limited homes remember always knowing they would
manage their own actions. Not surprisingly, this cohort of women maintains deliberate control over the ways they relate to their church, in
terms of volunteer time. They exercise a right of "bestowing" their time
and effort in the congregation that is literally unimaginable to the older
generation.

Older-generation women assumed that they were actively responsible for maintaining the church building, its programs, and its activities. They were taught to be unquestioningly content with remaining in the background. The younger generation brings a need for self-fulfillment—a more individualistic evaluation of religious expression and meaning— to its relationship with a congregation. Between them are women in the bridge generation. They were the ones who actually lived out the rupture in self-definition and organizational structure during the 1960s and 1970s.

Bridge Generation

Congregational change consciously intermixed with the changes in their nonchurch lives, and self-perception is still a central issue for churchwomen in the middle (forty-one to sixty years of age); theirs is the most problematic and complex of the three generations. An aphorism pegs the bridge years as "the old age of youth and the youth of old age."[13] Those at the upper end of the cohort literally lived in (white middleclass) total domesticity in the Cold War era. They were raised to exalt family, suburb, and church as their contribution to defense against world communism. They found themselves confronting ideas from the women's movement that led them to reject the "feminine mystique." Many dated their life-changing experiences from the civil rights movement. The younger end of the cohort struggled with the drug, anti-institutionalism, and media culture during parenthood.[14] Only a few who had had Episcopal childhoods commented on any need for "conversion" to the changes in worship. "I love the new hymnal and . . . the new rituals," a lawyer, forty-four, said, "even though I knew the old Prayer Book by heart." She had attended an Episcopal school with daily chapel. "But I even like the modern version of the Lord's Prayer now— in spite of the fact that it feels like it was written by a committee!"

The most striking characteristic of the bridge generation is its enjoyment of having escaped (not its word) from the home. Even if the jobs they now hold are not professional, even if their entry into the paid work force was occasioned by financial necessity, they *like* "being out of the house." They are excited about new possibilities, "experiencing growth," as career volunteers, for example, in gerontology or literacy programs, or in paid jobs as professors, business executives, real estate agents, members of city councils, or secretaries.

When the older women of this cohort married after World War II, they expected to find their fulfillment in the domestic circle. Church was part of that sphere. Coming from comfortable upper-working-class or affluent middle-class circumstances, many of them were proud that they, unlike their depression-era mothers, would never *need* to earn a living. Husbands would and should support them. They felt relieved at not having to "choose" a career. But after release from that mind-set by the women's movement, they are grateful for a less static and (as they now see it) restrictive definition of their "place." When the world of study or employment opened to them, all their relationships were subject to new scrutiny. "All of a sudden, you look at your husband and say, 'Hey! you're not the person I married!' " One middle-aged woman's return to finish a college degree was exhilarating and affirming. "It was the best thing I ever did, and I went at it gung ho. . . . I sat in classes with kids right out of high school, the age of my own daughters." The age difference? "I was always the oldest person in the class." To her surprise, "the kids looked at me as [just] another student, not automatically . . . as a mother."

A New England office manager, employing one of her cohort's key words, "communication," reflected on that new perspective. "Strains with my husband came, I think, from the fact that for years and years I was not very communicative about things that bothered me." A former nurse who always supposed her twenty-five-year marriage was satisfactory, blamed lack of communication for her divorce. "No one ever said anything—he would never talk at all, even when I confronted him!" She found, after recovering, that getting a job and being on her own was liberating. "Returning to work was pure joy. . . . You need to be needed." Now in her late fifties, she is an aide in a special-education kindergarten where she finds great self-fulfillment. "Nurturing is just one of my ministries," she said contentedly.

Jobs became central to bridge women after the children were grown, if only to contribute to the family retirement fund: "I work as a Kelly temporary because it gives me more freedom to take off and travel with my husband," reported another woman near sixty. A woman just turned fifty, on the other hand, having worked to help with children's college tuition, now values her leisure specifically because it affords her the luxury of time to pursue a variety of spiritual interests: "I have the opportunity to *wonder*. When I commuted back and forth, . . . and realized what you have to do—put in forty hours a week, and study, and try to keep a house, and try to be a wife—women who have all that just don't have the opportunity."

How much the world changed, for this generation, is summarized in one teacher's dream of "quitting work" and volunteering in different parts of the world, "maybe something on the order of the Peace Corps."

She was thrilled by the racial upheaval that horrified her parents in the small southern city where she grew up. Now she rejoices in being able to spend a summer vacation studying and living in countries with predominantly black populations. "I was called a nigger-lover in high school, because I took seriously the Methodist 'all God's children' teaching of my youth. Now, on islands that are 85 percent black, I'm allowed to associate with people!" She is determinedly "not a typical Southerner—I like my [Massachusetts-born] husband because he doesn't try to tell me how to live my life, to be an ornament." Her brother's standard of college achievement—"a grade of C is plenty good enough for a girl"—had spurred her emancipation. Also independent religiously, she enjoys "a great deal of excitement about life, and I think that's from God. I have a hard time praying to God in church and [using] traditional prayers, but I'm very aware of God in my life as Love, a force of Love, Energy, Work, and Harmony." She enjoys being on the periphery of her parish because of her many civic and "cause" activities, but she has no intention of relinquishing it entirely.

Meanwhile, the churches to which bridge women belonged began opening new possibilities in congregation to women. Many we interviewed in this cohort had chosen to take advantage of them. "This parish respects you as a person with your specific gifts, not [looking at] whether you are male or female in a certain job," a businesswoman announced. A bookkeeper, forty-seven, who admitted being far less involved now than "when my children were young," was really "very proud of a church that accepts as much change as this one has." A nurse, forty-four, asked to become the first woman in her congregation to take a new role, had "prayed about whether I should be a lay reader." Was that really something women were supposed to do? "The feeling I got from the other lay readers was: 'We don't *want* a woman.' And it hasn't ever been easy for me, being up in front of people. . . . But God has proved to me that I could do it, and not pass out!" Now enjoying the new role, one of several women in it, she is thankful for the spiritual expansion it has given her. "If folks come up and the communion rail and go to the other side, where there's a man chalice bearer, I think to myself, 'Hey, the Love's over here too, guys; but—if you want to go over there, well, okay.' " Another woman neatly delimited the parameters of this particular change, for the bridge generation: "When I see a woman in a job that has traditionally been male, I don't say 'Ooooh-eee, we've got a *woman* up there now!' Nor do I question whether she should be there or not. It's just becoming normal, for people over forty-five."

Some of the bridge generation, while rejoicing in a new sense of possibilities, nonetheless have some ambivalence about women in formerly-all-male positions in the congregation. For example, ushering: "Aren't women taking absolutely *every* job away from men?" a loyal wife in her late fifties wondered. A different awareness of gender anxiety in her congregation was expressed by a former junior warden, just turned fifty: "Do only those women who make it in the business world stand a chance of getting elected to the vestry? Is that the only thing that qualifies a woman for leadership? Do we really have only 'business-men'—male or female—running our church?" She had been radicalized when her parish elected as warden a young man "who's never done anything, except usher." Her candidate was a competent, highly qual-ified woman who should have won, hands down. But she realized that the woman was, in a sense, "invisible—she's always out of sight, teach-ing Sunday school, when Coffee Hour's going on. And—she's not a man."

These middle-aged, middle-class women view Sunday morning church time as their time and space for solitude and spiritual self-nurture, jus-tifiably earned. This cohort expressed great awareness of its own spiritual needs. When asked on the survey to *rank the importance of various parts of the worship service,* their primary choice differed from both the younger and the older generations. Although all three indicated "Re-ceiving the sacrament" as first choice, for bridge women "Internal in-dividual devotion" was second. This contrasted with the younger and older women's emphasis on corporateness, "Sense of participating with others." Bridge-generation women come to church with a sigh of relief, and immerse themselves in private introspective communication with God. They feel they have earned it. A research scientist said, intensely, "I just can't *wait* to get on my knees every Sunday, for my time before the service! I have a long *list* of things to pray for. And it keeps getting longer. Whatever has been going on, good or bad, I *need* that peace."

The generational perspective in congregations is a way of contex-tualizing the oppositions that inevitably arise within a given body of worshippers. In spite of a shared belief and ritual, human beings have distinctive opinions about what is central to them in congregational expression. The older generation's devotion to an institution that is changing beneath them forces them to cope with and address change itself—one explanation for the mingled serenity and frustration in their words. The younger women struggle to find their own identity and place in a relatively new identity, church membership. And the bridge-generation women literally incarnate both the process and results of change, institutional and societal.

An experiential, "environmental" lens such as generation offers women new ways to think about themselves and the organizations to which they give allegiance. Any institution dependent on the interaction between structure and individuals could benefit from a generational perspective. But the environmental hermeneutic of "generation" seems particularly apt for present-day Episcopal congregations. Over the course of time, Episcopalian polity, "the *via media*," has pursued melioration—the absorption of conflicting points of view. Institutionally, it has not found a means of using disagreement. "Change" in local congregations is often by accretion, unacknowledged until it is suddenly a *fait accompli*. Then it is legitimated historically. It becomes "something we've *always* done this way," although "always" means only a year or two.[15] Generations offer a way of contextualizing disagreements and avoiding factionalism.

These three generations of women-in-the-pew are located somewhere between the poles of traditionalism and modernism. The younger two generations embody the late-twentieth-century tension, for educated women, between feminist self-realization and femininity. Further, their religious "home" is a church (denomination), itself gradually evolving in the direction of more diversity and pluralism. The stuffy *Life With Father* image of early-twentieth-century Episcopalianism is out of date. So is former awe of priestly authority and church demeanor. With an increasingly "immigrant" (rather than birthright) membership, these congregations now have more pluralistic views of authority; they live with more liturgical choices, and operate internally along more democratic lines. Together, these women and congregations are edging the organizational framework in which they intersect toward more equality, collegiality, and spirituality. Within it women are carving out "their own" space and place, as they have historically.[16]

Four dimensions of women's self-definition are particularly relevant in a study of mainline Protestant women and change: family, paid work, church, and inner life.

Family

Our women respondents, reflecting both the family and the church cultures in which they are located, are less likely to be single and divorced than the national average, and more likely to be married, remarried, or widowed. Respondents from Advent South, the urban inner-city Anglo-Catholic parish (itself atypical, in its geographic context) were closest to the national average of single and divorced women in the general population; both Grace New England and Redeemer Plains were well below it. The bridge generation in all four churches was below the national average in its proportion of divorced and widowed women.[17]

Perhaps, then, it is not surprising to find that this sample of women, when faced with a questionnaire list of choices under *Conflicting Time Demands,* selected "family" as their "highest priority." Similarly, the most popular choice under *Personal Goals* was "quality of family life." The phrase "quality of family life," one we would change in a succeeding survey, seemed to tap a deep psychic core. The interviews revealed "family" as more than an idealized Norman Rockwell togetherness around the backyard barbecue, or a stair-step group of relatives sitting in the pew on Christmas Eve. "Quality of family life" was apparently the most comprehensive, even implicitly religious, choice among the goals we gave them to rank. These were:

My own personal development
My own physical health
Quality of family life
Community outreach and social concern
My local parish (growth and support)
Global concerns (e.g.peace, environment)
My own spiritual growth

What surprised us was the relative lack of emphasis on "personal development." Perhaps in their socioeconomic class the younger and bridge cohorts could take for granted a level of occupational satisfaction and had little need to choose it. Perhaps also the fact that the questionnaire was "about church" heightened the religious dimension of family symbolism. On the other hand, responsibility for and care of one's relatives is clearly a profound aspect of female identity for this group of church-affiliated women across the generations. For them, a choice other than "family" would be the aberration. A large number of the women interviewed testified to strong emotional and spiritual bonds with their grandmothers.

Not only was "family" important as a topic, it was a major image for interpreting the way a congregation should function. The term "family" seemed to imply a "home-centered belief system," intertwined with religion. It implied emotional content that could not have been cast in explicitly spiritual vocabulary without making them uncomfortable.[18] Describing her congregation with this metaphor, a young public-relations writer said, "I love the verse of [the hymn] "Land of Rest" that says 'Together met, together bound, / We'll go our separate ways,'—because I need a family that isn't family." A divorced landscape architect told us: "I felt I could just bring my children to the church building and turn them loose, and say, 'You're *home.*' "

Participation in the congregation was valued by some for its enhancement of family life. A young mother, married to the church organist and choir director, reported: "For us, church is literally our social life—and [as for] volunteer life, church is it; most of our recreation is church events or with church friends." She explained, "You know, relatives and friends—just about all of our close friends are from here. People we socialize with are either from here, or other churches." Even conversation was largely about religion, she reflected: "We talk a lot about church—what goes on here, family, bringing up our kids with Christian values, expecting them to behave in a moral way." Another young mother of two beamed with the pleasure of "really *reading* the hymns as I sing them," and listening to the sermons. She appreciated the way the clergy helped "relate the Bible, and world things, into the context of your life." For her, family and faith are one: "I like when the four of us go up the steps to communion together. . . . I always feel I'd like to be looking down at us [from the balcony] then, when we're here together as a family." A fusion of family and church identity pained a divorced grandmother who felt its exclusionary impact. "Even today, this church is no place for a divorced woman." Although people in her congregation had been lifelong friends, "The emphasis here is so much on families, it makes the single woman very hard-pressed indeed. . . . We want and need different things."

Among the younger generation, particularly, the topic of family revealed many complexities. These women try to keep family at the center of their lives, at the same time they wrestle with self-fulfillment through work. The costs to themselves were couched in terms of family. Defending her part-time job as an evening waitress to help meet the house payments, a young mother complained: "People have the nerve to ask me, 'Who's home with your kids now?' [Customers] try to lay a guilt trip on me about leaving the children, even when my husband's home with them." Another young mother from the same New England congregation, combining college with child rearing, felt devalued for an opposite choice: "It isn't so important to me to have a career—there's one waiting at home for me, with two kids . . . but nowadays, a lot of women don't see that as worthy . . . and I guess *I* have to grapple with whether I do."

Two young southern women expressed a more subtle anxiety related to "family" symbolism. Because their careers demanded they exhibit self-determination and authority, they looked to religion for affirmation of a feminine valuation of relationships. They resented the mind-set exalting career over family as the "only fulfillment" for intelligent women. In their region of the country, where white middle-class femininity has been more narrowly defined, they were made to feel that they must deny aspects of themselves in order to "pass" as professional. A pediatrician, mother of two young children, agonized over unstoppable tears as she labored to save a dying infant. "I've had to spend my entire professional life trying to keep from crying in front of other doctors!" A young therapist recalled a supervisor who "looked very forbidding when I filled up with tears. She actually said to me: 'Professionals are supposed to be strong!' I just always kept getting the message that I was too emotional." The strain of conforming to organizational mores of emotional detachment deepened their spiritual need for church "family."[19]

The older generation reflects the significance of "family" in a different way. Living alone is the norm for many, surrounded by the family in photographs. Their social-class background enables and encourages their independence. More than half reside in a "retirement home" or small apartment. Their emotional language is about family, not themselves. Introductory conversation locates them within a kinship network, despite the actualities. "Oh, I see my family when they have time for me," said one active eighty-year-old philosophically. "My daughter is very busy. I talk with her on the phone." Their concern is retaining genuine connections with family relationships—to be agreeable enough that children and grandchildren will want to visit them.[20] An eighty-year-old grandmother from Redeemer Plains rehearsed her end of an important conversation. "Somebody sits down next to you on the sofa, he's about fourteen or sixteen years old, and he says, 'Granny, what's life all about?' . . . and I say 'Love.' How else can you put it in a nutshell, at a moment's notice? And you may not get another crack at it."

"Family" imagery legitimized a ministry of hospitality for several lively older-generation women. One, seventy-five, explained: "I used to volunteer out at the big mental hospital. But now I am, well, we used to call it the social relations chairman—when we had a guild. I'm the one that calls on people who are Episcopalians in the nursing homes." She also arranges hospitality or food for the funerals of church members. The practical expression of "family" as the model for church relationships means that a number of older women actively create surrogate family within the church-fellowship groups. "I can't imagine waking up and not having anything you are really heading for," said a retired visiting nurse, seventy-eight. "I spend at least one day a week at this 'drop-in place' for many of us [a gift workshop in a church-owned building.] . . . We've become a group that's gotten quite attached to each other. . . . We're very supportive. . . . It's really the big thing on which I spend time." The gift workshop of which she spoke serves the older women of her congregation as a club, a prayer group, a workplace, a reason for getting out of bed each morning, a common bond, and— younger women would call it, as older women do not—a sisterhood, in a deeply religious sense. The handmade items they fashion—Christmas tree ornaments, toys, alphabet charts—are produced around a big table in an extraordinarily humane assembly line. One person cuts the elephant, the next glues on the eyes, the next sews on a tail. What they share, as they work together, eat their sandwiches, and drink their cups of tea, is family, literally and figuratively: the latest pictures of kin, and problems with family. The workshop talks about the congregation as "family"—their financial responsibility for it, their family functions for each other. "At least three people who had mental upsets are very benefited from coming in and working with us, just being with real-live people, and forgetting [their troubles.] . . . The average age [here] is in the 70s." (Question from interviewer: What aspect of belonging to this church is most important to you?) "This group—[both] because of friendship, and because of the work."

One congregation particularly cultivated the ethos of "family." A retired schoolteacher who had recently completed a master's degree in pastoral care, sixty-nine, reported that in a "weekly group discussion some of us have formed . . . to springboard ideas off one another," the conversation turned to "just how filled with love this church is." Special attention is given to anyone who is sick. "Gwen was saying how surprised she was; she wasn't really sick, all she had was a viral infection. There was a knock on the door, and [there were] flowers from our Circle," a gift usual "only when somebody's in the hospital or something. But, out of the blue, Gwen got this lift," because people here are "such caring folks." Another grandmother, seventy-four, in the same congregation, said simply, "This is where all my friends are. I have no family here, you know, and we have to depend on other people . . . so this really is our family."

Grandparents, actual or surrogate, see church as a place to help out as extended family. "Because their parents sing in the choir, these [two children] came running up to sit with me after Sunday school last week. They call me the Doughnut Lady because I often help at coffee hour."

The children sat quietly, writing their names and drawing pictures. Her reward came when "Mary got tired and curled up in my lap, with her thumb. . . . It made the service very special to me."

"Family" was also significant in terms of denominational membership—a salient issue for all mainline Protestant churches in the late twentieth century. In response to survey questions *How long have you been a member of this church, and of this denomination?* and *What attracted you to this church, and this denomination?* both generation and location counted. Among the younger women in Grace New England and Nativity Northwest, family was the primary source of affiliation: "born into it," "raised in it," "parents converted before I was born," or the rationale for personal choice, "I looked for a family feeling." However, in Advent South, the parish characterized by the highest amount of ideological conviction, ("choice" as the reason for membership), family was less relevant than a program of religious activism. Two-thirds of its younger generation offered reasons for joining such as "This is the kind of church that lives the Gospel, not just talks about it." Family was the main rationale of the bridge generation only in Grace New England. In the older cohort of Nativity Northwest, where the phrase "cradle Episcopalian" was more than mere jargon, "family" was the primary rationale and "choice" scarcely mentioned.

Less than half our sample were "born into" the Episcopal Church. In the two parishes celebrating "choice"—Advent South and Redeemer Plains—membership in both denomination and congregation was "newer" than in the other two. Obviously family was less important for them than the distinctive qualities of their congregations relative to other available religious choices. In Advent South, a clear outreach ministry to a diverse urban population including retarded adults living in a parish-sponsored group home, homosexuals, and racial minorities, seized women's idealism. One young businesswoman explained, "This is the most community-involved church I've ever been to; here in slumland, it's obvious that [this is] a church that finally takes the word of Jesus literally." Women from this congregation told us they drove past several other Episcopal churches in order to belong to Advent.

Redeemer Plains, the other ideological-choice congregation, was a church of refuge. Many of its women had landed there out of a sea of fundamentalist or authoritarian congregations. "I actually went church shopping . . . for the place I could feel the most spiritual connection and acceptance. [This church] gave me the most individual space for self definition," a young executive said. She had settled on Redeemer because "it really allows the *spirituality* of religion to come through; you can talk about it if you want, or you don't have to. Nobody preaches it down your throat." In these two congregations, younger and bridge generation women found personal affinity more important than loyalty to the religion of one's biological family.

Family serves as a source of both continuity and change for Episcopalian women. They see it as giving a larger meaning to their religious participation. All three generations of women entwine female self-fulfillment with a relational spirituality. Perhaps that is one reason many of their religious reflections are often subsumed under, and expressed in the imagery of, family.

Work

Women in the four research congregations are involved in two kinds of work: the unpaid labors assumed to accompany church membership, volunteering in church or community; and paid employment outside the home. The relationship of age cohort to both is immediately apparent. Looking first at women's paid work, we can speculate that greater numbers of women who identify themselves as Episcopalians are now employed outside the home, than ever before. However, no quantitative data exists to confirm that. Our demographics show that two of our four congregations, Grace New England and Redeemer Plains, have women in paid employment in proportions similar to the national trend.[21] The importance of region is confounded, however, because Advent South— a location that might lead us to assume fewer Episcopal women in paid jobs—is an anomaly. The proportion of women in careers or outside employment in that context is the highest among our four congregations. (Possible factors explaining that circumstance are that its female members have the highest level of educational degrees in our study, its location near a state university campus, and the highest percentage of single women. It is also Anglo-Catholic in theology and worship, and politically liberal in a conservative setting.)

Beyond the percentages of women employed in paid jobs—43 percent of this sample of Episcopalian women are actually employed (83 percent of the younger, 78 percent of the bridge, and 14 percent of the older generations)—we were interested in women's reasons for being employed. Though "financial necessity" is a factor, particularly among the younger generation, changed assumptions about self-worth and achievement in the world of employment were influential among the younger and bridge generations. National census figures indicate that the largest increase within the past decade in numbers of women employed and income growth, in fact, appears among the middle-aged group.[22]

Generation shaped the *reasons for being employed outside the home.* Only the younger women selected an answer implying egalitarianism: "Want to carry my share of the financial burden." Quintessential career-versus-children arguments surfaced only in New England. Several younger women felt beleaguered. "I'm taking three and a half credits at college, have kids, and 'do I work?' What more do they want? I don't want to be disloyal to women who are working . . . but I wish they could respect *my* decision." Pragmatically, she added: "I'm home in the afternoon, so where do all the kids play, whose mothers work?" The evening waitress, thirty, viewed the "real emotional trauma. . . . [of] day care . . . from five-thirty in the morning until five-thirty at night" as a terrible waste, producing "a real women-against-women thing" within the faith community. Evangelical or charismatic Christians were outspoken in their criticism of "working mothers," with no allowance for need or special circumstances. She sighed. "Women go to work and feel guilty— and they feel guilty if they're not working," was her existential summary.

More than half the older generation had formerly been employed. The few (14 percent) still employed listed a functional reason: "Financial necessity." Women of the bridge generation, having absorbed the greatest change in attitude about women's employment, were past the child rearing time conflicts of the younger generation. Their reasons for working emphasized the pleasure it represented. Their major choice among the questionnaire options was "I enjoy paid work more than being at home."

The bridge generation in Redeemer Plains offered the most interesting responses. Perhaps related to their social and geographic location, ideas from the secular women's movement were very evident. Their reasons for working were expressed in terms of self-fulfillment, even if it was a necessity for those who were divorced or facing a husband's business troubles. The women in this congregation represented the elite in their city; the primary option they checked was ideological: "I want to use my education in a meaningful job." They are women who have the psychic—if not the actual—luxury of choice. In comparison with women in the surrounding churches, the educational level of Redeemer Plains women, and their mandate for self-fulfillment required paid recognition outside the home. Only one younger woman in that congregation announced she would choose to stay at home even when the children were all in school, because she "was fulfilled" by gardening and house-renovation.

When women ranked personal goals, generation was again significant: "personal development" was important to the younger women across the sample (second after "quality of family life," discussed above). But it was not the choice of a single older woman in any of the four congregations, a clear example of cohort effect. Self-fulfillment was not part of their vocabulary, when they were young. In response to the statement "When conflicting time demands require setting priorities" the options were

Paid work
Immediate family and homemaking
Church activities
Relatives
Other volunteer/community activities
Personal development, hobbies, activities
Friends
Recreation

The first choice of the younger and bridge generations in all four congregations was "Immediate family," the second being responsibility to "paid work." For the older generation, however, "church" was second. Other goals important to them, but ignored by the two younger cohorts, were "physical health" and "spiritual growth," an awareness of chronology. But one who had just turned eighty said vigorously in her interview: "John and I, we paint our own house, and do all our own yard work. . . . I'm not just going to sit down and die!"

The benchmark of generational difference among churchwomen, however, is their differing perspective on the other kind of work, volunteering. Service work for the young, either through their church or in the community, differs in complex ways from that of the older generation. Grandmother's model called for "fitting in wherever needed." One older woman wrote on the questionnaire, "I am one of a small group who is called on whenever a specific need arises." Another wrote, "When a job needs doing, you just fall to and do it." The older cohort prided itself on versatility, and on shouldering major (fund-raising) roles for the physical upkeep of the buildings. And they cherished their ability to do this from the background (a stance Margaret Miles's chapter identifies as "privileged subordination"). Their mode and self-image were articulated by an older woman, nearing eighty, from Redeemer, Plains, who still "helped out in the office" when the church secretary was swamped: "But I hide it a little bit. I don't want anyone to think I'm overdoing anything. . . . I don't want them to think 'She's taking over!' I try to stay in the background." In contrast, the younger women talk of needing to find "my own" area for serving; they must look for what will be self-fulfilling as "my ministry." They strive to find a particular gift of time or talent to offer—nothing that could be taken for granted, something that will give them a satisfying place in the larger body. Women between forty and sixty are, once again, somewhere in the middle.

The best statement of this change in mind-set came from one of the bridge generation, forty-nine. "Women of this church—maybe all churches—really hold the church together." She is now completing teacher certification and will soon be employed full-time. "Believe it or not, they're the organizers. . . . In the past it was the woman's group that [raised] all the money to do things." She saw changes in the present congregation as totally related to women. "Now the women my age and younger are all working. It's changing the support of the lay people. Now there's more of a choice. [Women will say] 'I intend to do *some* lay activity,' rather than 'It's my *responsibility* to be making pies so we can be buying curtains for the basement.' "

One probation supervisor, thirty-seven, with two children, depreciated her volunteering; she said it was currently "as little as possible." She had done "the usual"—teaching Sunday school, organizing coffee hours. She had even donated "real fine, fancy mending for the Altar Guild, you know, with little teeny tiny stitches. I'm the kind who automatically cleans up after a reception or coffee hour. I'm just a big Martha" [the biblical woman who busied herself fixing the meal rather than sitting at Jesus' feet with her sister Mary], she concluded. In denigrating her contributions, she reflected the dismissive attitude of the larger church toward "women's work." The young owner of her own public-relations firm, thirty-six, expressed a more conscious and feminist view. "It's not just what you *get* but also what you *give*, . . . by your faith, by being here." She had a unique volunteer role, using her business skills; she designed an annual fund-raising Christmas card for the community feeding program housed in her parish hall.

This individualist mode of service work, even within one's own congregation, was the popular choice of the younger generation in response to the question *What is your greatest concern about the future of your particular congregation?* The majority checked an individual, not an institutional, statement, the most personal option among seven choices: "I'll *find ways* to participate, in spite of the time constraints in my life" (emphasis added). The principal of a high school for disturbed adolescents who called herself "a born feminist—I grew up with no preconceived notions of what I couldn't do," had decided to join the Altar Guild because it was important to her to "do something with women" in her church. A young African-American professional, employed full-time in a state agency and "just reclaiming my body" after nursing her second child, said: "I haven't decided yet what I'll do in this church; it might be lay-reading, it might be a prayer group. All I know is, I need some *Jane*-[pseudonym]*time* in my religion!" Her rare, precious time for religious participation must meet her spiritual needs, not just fill a slot in some organization. For the younger generation, volunteer work is as deliberate a choice as paid work.

Church

Both interviews and surveys elicited a variety of ways in which a woman related to her congregation. We hoped to learn if the three generations had differing views of what it meant to belong to a church. We expected to find generational differences in language but the differences related to church organizations were more distinctive.

Significantly, women in the older and bridge generations associated the idea of "church," first and foremost, with activities and products. For the older cohort, the nearly unanimous rationale for centering their lives in church was action. Being "active," *doing* something, was evidence to themselves that they were worthy members. Their standard exacts a painful toll when the physical disability of aging sets in. These were the daughters of mothers who found great fulfillment in the late-nineteenth-century women's club movement, and its high-minded ideals of self-education and service. Women's clubs then were filled with churchwomen; the memberships often overlapped. Our older cohort understandably viewed "traditional women's church work" as *the* valid expression of Christian commitment. A retired bookkeeper, seventy-two, had "always done a lot of volunteer work, in the schools and especially in the church, until my children were grown." Her "good example" was "my own mother [and her friends, who] always did a great deal of this."

Unlike family symbolism, with its many religious nuances, "traditional women's work" evoked two opposing images simultaneously: humble and exalted. Traditional tasks took place in the background (kitchen and handwork), but women had accomplished wonders in that offstage location up to the 1950s. Pride in both location and work, however, had become tarnished by an increasingly dismissive evaluation. In their youth and middle age, they had enlisted as the congregation's foot soldiers; they provided the many hands and funds that kept a religious organization running. (Irene Brown's chapter in this volume tells a poignant story of one older woman's present-day adaptation of this identity.)

In the older generation's earlier years, weekday "work" beyond home and family was largely confined to one or another aspect of Christian discipleship in church-sponsored programs and organizations. Even some women in the bridge generation remembered and were grateful for that earlier training. A computer manager in her forties traced her administrative skills to "traditional churchwomen's work": "Where I grew up there were lots of women's circles; the women ran this and the women did that—because—they were home and had the time." From catering wedding receptions to running the thrift shop, women became skilled in practical administration. "The Junior Circle that did the men's breakfast," a service carried out by teenage girls themselves, was the place where this speaker had gotten her start. "Do you know, I could manage a kitchen with thirty people in it! I grew up in that tradition." One of her peers, a businesswoman and member of the local city government, had less positive associations: "The women I'm involved with spend more time out in the working world. I don't find women's circles real fulfilling. Give me a good Bible study or something, but not sewing circles."

Handwork and food preparation, the locale of early administrative experience for older women, became code in the 1970s for the "mindless" and unrewarded aspects of "traditional women's work." Another of the bridge generation demonstrated how important it had become to choose the kind of church work that was personally fulfilling for her: "I feel better about myself when I'm in my own situation" [being a lay reader at services], totally disengaged from what the older women in her parish were doing "up there in their gift workshop." She said, "They seem to enjoy it, and certainly it seems to do a lot of good for the parish. But it's not something I'd take time for. Nor, at this point, would I have any interest."

What had gotten lost, between the older women's equating "traditional women's work" with "belonging to a church" and the bridge generation's flight from it, was the theological vision that formerly empowered kitchen work and handcrafts. Earlier churchwomen, imaginatively involved in the late-nineteenth-century missionary enterprise, knew it supported the Lord's work in far-flung and exotic foreign or urban mission fields; fund-raising formed a tangible, as well as spiritual, connection for them. They built schools, hospitals, orphanages, and training programs—women's purview in the denomination—with their church suppers, bazaars, and "egg money." A larger, numinous meaning hallowed the mundane "church work," ennobling and justifying "their jobs." The tasks themselves pointed beyond themselves, and allowed women to transcend everyday circumstance. As they perceived it, those tasks were their witness in a grand arena—"throughout all the generations" (Ephesians 3:21).

Church-belonging was defined, in their minds and symbol systems, by activities rather than by internal, private spiritual experience. The older women in our sample did not associate "church" with words about prayer and interior life, only with "women's work." And volunteering outside the church was not a substitute for such church work but an addition to it, for that generation. One retired professional woman in her late seventies had obviously struggled to have her extra-church volunteering count as Christian service. She stated her credo almost belligerently: "For me, community work is really church work. . . . All I've done for the community, and in the community, I've really done for the church." In earlier days, her attitude was questioned, though today's younger and bridge generations understand and share it. Counting all one's "good works" as meeting the Christian obligation is a view that has expanded into the churches since the mid-twentieth century.[23] Bridge-generation women, shaped by the mandate of action as part of church membership, have taken their "action" into religious leadership: lay reading, lay visiting, eucharistic ministry. They disdain the traditional fund-raising but invest equal time and energy in "higher" activity that is more directly related to pastoral and worship tasks. For the younger women today, there is no separation between religious or handwork contributions. They view all their activities, including attendance at church itself, as part of their volunteering, a personal investment of choice and time.

The significance of time in a culture of choice contributes to altering and broadening the purview of what is now considered volunteer. The women we interviewed have more choices than most, and the major way they express choice religiously is allocating their time. Thus, going to church itself has become a "voluntary" task, a decision equated in some ways with other types of volunteering, like visiting aged relatives or helping at the blood bank. Attending church on a Sunday represents a conscious choice among competing time demands. Religion, "a private thing for my husband and me," led a young new mother to explain her regular Sunday worship on purely personal grounds: "When someone says, 'Are you going to go to church Sunday?' it's not 'Am I?' it's 'I *need* to.' " A bridge woman said, "If—Sundays, we don't come, I really feel guilty; I miss it"; an older woman said, more explicitly, "I have to be here. If I don't come every Sunday, I get off track."

The evolutionary stages in the meaning of "traditional women's work" were reflected by a just-retired school teacher. In her young adult life she had been president of the women's group and "very, very active . . . but—talk about change! Now women participate in everything but the men's choir—and men participate in everything except the Altar Guild. We don't even have a women's group as such, anymore." Though another older woman, seventy, enthusiastically supported women in new worship roles, the interview theme on which she lavished pleasurable detail was women's handmade products. They were evidence, to her, of the companionship and creativity associated with their production. A "coffee hour flea market" each Sunday, after church, was selling "the most adorable baby-like running suits . . . and a crocheted laprobe, and embroidered dishtowels . . . homemade bread and cookies, orange marmalade. . . . All those Scots-background Episcopalians just seem to love orange marmalade! . . . And our most beautiful knitter makes the most darling sweaters." Her enthusiasm was directed to the self-giving that enhanced the products rather than their financial value. In this case, however, they were also buying a new roof for the parish house.

Each of the four parishes we studied said it no longer has a traditional churchwomen's organization. In that assertion, they typify a significant proportion of Episcopal congregations after the 1970s—and identify a sharp break with their own history. Churchwomen's associations were an omnipresent feature of congregational life from the early nineteenth century onward (for example, the Ladies' Circle of Industry, 1831–1941, at Immanuel Church, Bellows Falls, Vermont).[24] The story of such organizational flourishing, and the way in which women administered parish-, diocesan-, and national-level organizations, is told in Mary S. Donovan's *A Different Call: Women's Organizations in the Episcopal Church, 1850–1920* (Wilton, Conn.: Morehouse-Barlow, 1987). Several chapters in this volume (by Gunderson, Donovan, Turner, and Brown) extend that narrative into the contemporary era. In the early twentieth century, churchwomen's joint labor and cash contributions merited their own office in the national denominational headquarters in New York City. Until the demise of the Women's Desk in 1967 (see Donovan chapter, this volume), it functioned as an extensive communications network—today we might even call it a form of continuing education— that gave Episcopal women across the nation a programmatic linkage around study themes and outreach tasks.

Some of the women in two of our four congregations triumphantly announced that they had specifically "voted out the ECW" (the women's organization) within the past two decades; for them this was a forward-looking step. Having not participated in that decision because she'd gone back to work and wasn't present for the decision, one older woman reflected on that "progressive" step ruefully: "When I was young, we really *worked*... [through] guilds and women's money-makers, [like] covered dish suppers." Recalling women's pride in being "the backbone of the church" then, she remembered a guilty sense of relief when she "had to go back to work" after a divorce; a job gave her a "good excuse to drop out since I couldn't go to afternoon meetings." She felt almost as if she had graduated from one level of church identity to another: "My children grew up, so I didn't have to do that anymore." But later she was "shocked when I found that the guilds and the women's groups had dissolved." Differentiating between the spiritual and the practical, as she had been taught, but reluctant to surrender a sense of their interrelationship, this retired teacher commented, "I can't say we had any great religious experiences in those guilds, but the fellowship" had built real community. It was the great leveler and connector, where "someone that you just nodded to in church" worked "side by side with you" in the kitchen. "We often, us old ones, talk about those days [when] we all felt we were putting our talents to work for something bigger, you know."

By the late 1960s that type of organization seemed out of tune with the times. Gender-segregated church work was passé for enlightened Episcopal women; the modern goal was to break down the barriers between men's and women's organizations, not perpetuate them. True progress would result in an inclusive volunteer pool of "lay ministers," male and female.[25] Calling *all* volunteer tasks—leading worship and programs, building maintenance, fund-raising, and missionary outreach—by the gender-neutral appellation "lay ministries" was both an attempt to bestow dignity on lesser-status tasks, women's backstage work, and, conversely, an avenue allowing women to enter the higher-status (formerly all-male) roles within the parish, such as serving on vestries and policy committees, including worship and finance. A major factor motivating the "enlightened" mind-set (obliterating gender-specific roles) was the *type* of work associated exclusively with women. They believed the church valued them for "nothing but raising money that *they* [men] spend!" In terms of representation at the national denomination meeting, the General Convention, their outrage was justified; women were not seated as deputies until 1970.[26] But a second

factor was gathering momentum, among women themselves, for changing the canons to ordain women (see Donovan chapter, this volume).
Both factors rendered kitchen work colorless and of secondary appeal
in congregations. Also, within their own organizations, women were
consciously absorbing the societal trend toward the use of "experts."
The ECW wanted "professional" leadership for its all-women gatherings:
"We only invited women as speakers who were really trained, and out
there doing something!" An all-volunteer cadre of women undermined
its own validity by cultivating "specialization" and invoking more secular
standards of "authority" for women who addressed their meetings.

In an institution that based itself so heavily in "tradition," the abrupt
dismantling of a national churchwomen's network seemed, to some, like
cutting out its own heart. The split among Episcopal churchwomen, and
generations, still festers in the consciousness of parishes like Advent or
Nativity. One woman recalled the 1970s, with mixed despair and excitement, as a time "when any laywoman worth her salt was going off
to seminary." Women had begun to be admitted for graduate work at
theological seminaries in the late fifties and early sixties, another step
toward professionalizing the laity. Ordination—the usual goal of seminary education—was, however, still out of the question.[27] The churchwomen who felt uncomfortable with, or theologically and psychically
confused by, women's sacramental leadership found themselves edged
out of the mainstream, sometimes embittered. At the practical level,
congregations floundered over who was responsible for such formerly-
taken-for-granted women's work as coffee hours. "Modern" women in
the parishes were happy to vote out the ECW and take off their aprons;
but "traditional" women felt demoted and betrayed. Many of the latter
turned their energies into resisting further change, specifically the canonical change that would legitimate the ordaining of women.

One former president of her parish's ECW spoke for the revolution
experienced by the bridge generation. She is now deeply involved in
training for the new (to Episcopalians, though not to those in the Roman
Catholic monastic tradition) function of spiritual director. "We used to
put on elegant teas, very Anglican things, and we had all this God-talk
that didn't take a lot of intelligence or depth." Retrospectively, it seemed
to her that the churchwomen's organization had little more importance
than "one of many clubs women could belong to." In light of today's
emphasis on and seeking for spirituality, she believes, "only a nucleus
here [would like to be] still caught up in that." The women who interest
her in the congregation are really "ahead of the game, not wasting their

time on the artificial." Her "new" standard for what is artificial and what is real is literally unthinkable for most of the older generation. The age-old dilemma of women's integration into or separatism within the Episcopal church, nationally and locally, was resolved for her. At the leadership level (national, perhaps diocesan, and in some more sophisticated congregations) integrating women into all aspects of the life of the parish was the goal—but women who weren't leaders found the organization that had validated their "work" excluded.

Two of the four parishes in our study (Grace New England and Nativity Northwest) have a segment of older women who still grieve over this particular change. Their actual "work" within parish and community organizations, however, goes right on and is substantial, both in terms of money earned and parish functions. As one of them said, *"We're* the only ones around during the day to do anything!" They feel ambivalently overneeded ("There aren't enough of us left to do the work that used to be done by the women") and rejected ("We expected to be able to turn over this work to the younger women but they're all working! Besides, they're not interested"). Their volunteer labor is still essential to the life of the parish, but its significance is tarnished because they have been robbed of the honor of handing on "their work" to the next generation.

In the worship aspect of church, the role of lay reader, open to women since the 1970s, has given them public association with the authority of the Word, and a visible location (formerly filled only by men) within the worship service. At the junior level, girls can now be acolytes, cross- and candlebearers at the head of the liturgical procession. (Several of the younger women we interviewed shared their adolescent outrage at having been excluded from the acolytes' guild "when my brother could be in it"; they could not remember having wanted to be a priest, however, because that remained beyond their imagination.) The one visible "uniformed" role open to women in the worship aspect had been, as far back as the early 1800s, singing in the choir. Being in the choir set them apart from the rest of the congregation, provided an esthetic worship experience, and legitimated the expression of religious emotion. Membership in the Altar Guild related women to worship in yet another way: as caretakers of the Holy Table that is focal point of the eucharist. Up to the late 1970s it offered women the closest proximity to priest-controlled sacred things that could be allowed. Our three generations of churchwomen thought the Altar Guild had "always been" gender segregated.[28] Few of these women were aware that altar work had been

provided by sacristans (by definition, male) until the beginning of the
twentieth century; overnight it had become the "territory" of women
when laymen were no longer interested in that role.

So although each of our four parishes would say they no longer have
any "real" women's organizations, three still have an Altar Guild
"manned" solely by women. (Advent South is the exception; it has male
sacristans as part of its Altar Guild.) The work done by women in Altar
Guilds is exempt from the current negativism about traditional women's
work, even if the tasks themselves would otherwise be derogated as
"women's work." Altar Guild women set the table (arrange the chalice,
paten, and altar vessels), open the large Service Book (to the proper
pages, for the celebrant of that liturgy), decorate the altar (with the
appropriate seasonal hangings and flowers), and do the cleanup (bleach-
ing out spots of spilled wine, vacuuming up bread crumbs, washing and
polishing the vessels). One older-generation representative, who began
her active churchwork in a Junior Altar Guild and has continued through
her adult life, explained it as an act of private worship, spiritually nurturing and esthetically satisfying. "There's something deeply endearing
about caring for the Lord's vessels." Acknowledging that women primarily devote this "very special attention to [a major] function of the
church," and do it "almost invisibly," she tried to find words for its
meaning: "You give this gift in a very secret way; that makes it so
precious and so deep."

Thus, even today Altar Guild volunteering escapes the opprobrium
of other "women's work." Rather than its private aspects, valued by
the woman above, the young feminist administrator chose it for its
communal nurture, the "camaraderie of other women." Altar Guild
work also implies an emblematic "team" relationship with the authoritative leaders of worship, though few clergy have altered their evaluation of women's "background work" enough to acknowledge it. But
this volunteer relationship with one's church falls more into the category
of piety and worship than cooking a parish supper; this type of "serving"
is legitimated by its holy function. Altar Guild women deny subordination by hallowing it (see the Miles chapter, this volume).

One older woman, farm-born and -raised, spoke fervently about the
rewards of her thirty years "on the altar." She had always found great
satisfaction in making things "pretty" and "shiny." "Sometimes, when
I'm alone in the church, and just polishing the brass till it glows, and
I'm praying . . ." Her voice broke and her eyes filled with tears. She
added, almost in surprise, "That's when I know He's there." After a
silence, I said, "It's lovely to hear you say that." She spoke thoughtfully,

"Never said it before. No one ever asked me before." When asked what it is about "altar work" that transforms it into a kind of worship for her, she responded, with deep emotion: "I was doing it for Him, and for our priest, and for our people . . . I just always felt that it was *one* thing I could do for my religion, that I loved."

All three generations in all four locations indicated on the questionnaires that their "*primary religious activity*" was "worship." Commitment to regular Sunday attendance is its own statement. The question *What is your congregation's attitude toward traditional women's work such as fundraising and church suppers?* elicited a range of answers, however, showing the effects of both generation and geography. All three generations in Redeemer Plains objected more strongly to "traditional women's work" than did women in the other parishes. Plains women were separating themselves from a regional stereotype that viewed women as persons who do (only) handwork, kitchen work, cleaning, and coffee hours. All three generations also registered satisfaction and pleasure in a congregation that encouraged their intellectual activity—"using your own mind." As several of them commented, "This church *expects* you to do your own thinking." Obviously, reaction against the constrictions they knew, or had fled from in surrounding churches, was key in their response to women's relegation to the kitchen.

Women (and congregational opinion leaders, male as well as female) were asked on the questionnaire to *locate themselves and their congregation* on a *continuum*, a scale from 1 to 7, in terms of *traditional to modern attitudes toward gender*. Geography emerged as the most significant factor in this item. Only in Nativity Northwest was age and generation more significant. Advent South women who viewed their parish as the most modern—"on the cutting edge of change"—were especially gratified by the contrast between their unusual congregation and other Episcopal churches in the same city. "Modernity" for them meant inclusiveness, active engagement in social ministries, and a climate that supported women's self-assignment.

A majority of the women in all four parishes agreed with the following questionnaire statements: "*Men and women share equally in leadership positions*" in their congregations; "*Open disagreement on policy issues within the parish is acceptable*"; and "*Women are free to join any activity in which they are interested.*" They also agreed that "*the rector was key in parish decisions and direction,*" though the younger generation was more skeptical of that organizational truism. Between two-thirds and three-quarters of the women in the sample felt that "*their congregation's worship challenges its members to express their religious beliefs in daily life,"* a positive view of their religious practice and its impact on their weekday tasks. In this sense, "church" in their identity was considerably more than an isolated Sunday morning activity.

Asked *"What is your greatest hope for the future of this congregation?"* generation was the telling factor. Younger women expressed determination to *"find ways* to participate" that could meet their needs for self-realization and congregational participation; bridge women hoped for *"closer spiritual community"*; older women hoped for both earthly nurture and ecclesiastical survival: *"closer community"* and *"that the parish will grow"* numerically.

Inner Life

Women's responses to questions about their interior life demonstrated unanimity in the highest-ranked selections, and then clear cohort effects. First choices under *"your primary faith activity,"* the "parts of the worship service they found most nurturing," and motivation to pray (*"I turn to God most often for . . ."*) were remarkably similar across the generations and across all four parishes: "Regular worship" was the major faith activity, "receiving the eucharist" the most meaningful aspect of worship, and "gratitude for blessings" the primary reason for praying.

After those uniform first choices, however, second choices followed generational lines. The younger women chose the "sense of participating with others," reflecting their recent rediscovery of corporate worship; the bridge generation selected "internal individual devotion." Few older-generation women thought "listening to the sermon" was very important. One related her present stage of spiritual development to the physical debilities of age. She had previously been blessed with good health—"I liked to hike, to ski; I was always involved . . . if they needed someone to serve church dinners." Then she developed severe arthritis. "It has been really something to come to terms with . . . be at peace with." At first, "[as] with every loss," she battled it by saying, *"Yes I can*—do this or that!" Her new learning was acceptance and transformation: "Hey, I can't do *this,* but there are many, many things I *can* do, and be joyful about." The work with troubled children for which she had trained turned out to be too demanding physically, "but at least I can still pass out God's love [as a nursing-home visitor]."

The younger women in all four parishes disagreed with the statement *"My spirituality is private and not generally talked about with others,"* as did about half the bridge cohort. In all four parishes, the generational divide between the two younger generations and the older one was sharply visible on the issue of privacy and spirituality. In Grace New England, all women above sixty approved that statement. In the other three parishes, nearly two-thirds of the older generation agreed. Guardedness about religious conversation reflects cohort differences in the nature of women's formative experience about what is "public" and what is not. Older women viewed religious membership as activity; one's interior life was no one else's business.

A two-part narrative question—*What changes in your religious life have been most gratifying? and most frustrating?*—asked women to state religious issues into their own words. The older generation named as frustrations their increasing physical limitations: "I can't kneel anymore"; "Loss of energy and the health that I had five years ago keep me from enjoying my church." A woman from Advent South wrote, in very contemporary language: "I need a support group to help me cope with depression." Other frustrations addressed changes in worship. One woman wrote bluntly, "I hate the Exchange of the Peace." Physical contact in the liturgy—a transgression of personal privacy—was a desecration of sacred time and space. Other changed etiquette was also bothersome to them: "Clapping in church offends me." Another listed "not enough quiet and mystery in the service anymore." One cryptic response cited "man-made rules." Another specified "women clergy."

Older women's gratifications, in contrast, focused on their new understanding of time and spiritual serenity: time enough for "participating in the pastoral care of others," for "a surrender of self to God's care," for being "more at home in the church than ever before." Even in her eighties, one woman found spiritual gratification in a new realization of her own voice (at least in the privacy of a written questionnaire), an image more typical of the bridge or younger generations. "I'm able to speak more about my real feelings than ever before," she wrote. Another, nearing seventy, wrote of the "privileges" she found in retirement: "Time with friends, time to give of yourself, time to appreciate a lot of the good things in life." She connected age with discovering a deep need "to be at peace, where I am" and to realize that "what God means for me to do is just to show love to other people." Another older woman, eighty-two, described God's vividly sustaining presence during a household accident. While alone in her house, making the bed, she had fallen "and hurt my back. I didn't know what to do." She wondered if she could get to the phone, or if she could even stand up: "I'd heard the bone crunch." Cautiously, she tried one foot, "and it worked, and I said 'Thank you, God.' " Confiding that she talked to God more or less continuously, "just casually, you know—don't even know whether He has time to hear it all—I got up on the other foot, and *it* worked. So again I said, 'Thank you, God.' " She was finally able to reach the telephone. "Things just kind of took care of themselves, after that."

The younger generation's frustrations were focused on themselves and their inability to attain the spiritual depth and clarity they want, and on the big issues of their time. "What is God's role in AIDS? Had a friend die of it last year." "Desire for material security interferes." "My worldliness, selfishness, and laziness seem to be stronger than the truth of Christ." One written cry from the heart longed for more genuine religious connection with fellow parishioners: "We never really discuss our faith, Jesus Christ, God in our lives. This is true of every Episcopal Church I've ever attended." Others wrote about how hard they found it to live faithfully: "Unable to have a constant spiritual connection"; "How to find ways to incorporate faith and Christ in my daily life." Religious symbolism evoked the loneliness of one who is out of tune with her clergy leader: "I feel without a shepherd, since I don't like my rector."

Among the younger women, gratifications centered around the maturation in thought and experience that accompanies "independence," the first real autonomy of adulthood. For many, it was associated with worshipping on one's own, or becoming a parent. One woman wrote exuberantly, "It's great to be here out of choice, not others' expectations!" Another wrote: "Church feels like a family." A third observed, "I'm now more open to others [and am] incorporating religion into all my daily life." The joys of leaving behind the alienation of youth were acknowledged: "I'm finally comfortable with the language of belief." Another said, in her interview, "I've decided to 'go public' with my faith, for the first time. Like wearing a cross to the office, or reading the Bible with a friend at lunchtime. I wouldn't have done before."

In each of the congregations, a few among the younger and the bridge generations (but none of the older women) used the phrase "having a personal relationship with Jesus Christ" to epitomize gratifying religious change. (The older-generation women were distinctly uncomfortable with evangelistic language.) Relationships were primary for the younger generation: relationships with family, God, and Jesus, and being part of a larger entity, a congregation. These "old-fashioned" experiences were their religiously "fulfilling" discoveries.

A young, single career woman, in her interview, realized that she wanted her congregation to be her "counterculture," because of "what it's like to be a seeker after Christ among the yuppies." She was dismayed at the "shallow, self-centered pressures on you" from people who have been "raised in privilege and religious arrogance." Valiantly struggling to "make my life work" and to "be a good person," the "world outside the church" had exposed her to brutal realities, including attempted rape by a professional colleague. She wept at the many aspects of the "world around you" that are "so cruel and destructive," and she yearned "toward justice and truth, racial harmony and a more open, honest world."

Another younger woman located her spiritual security in the feminine dimensions of God: "Subconsciously, having a female priest here made it safer," she explained. She acknowledged confusing "the person, Mary, the mother of Jesus" and "the spirit, Mary, the feminine part of God." She expressed "real conflicts [feelings of fear and distaste] about the bleeding Son, the body, and the cross." On the other hand, she cherished "a cheap piece of religious art that had hung on my grandmother's living room wall." It visualized for her "the two aspects of God—the demanding, legalistic, conditional-love God," and that "unconditional, nurturing, 'I'm going to take care of you whether you ask me to or not' God." This maternal "ikon" conveyed symbolic and actual spiritual power: "It's there, in that picture, for me."

The bridge generation's response to the questionnaire was more beleaguered about choices and time constraints than the older generation's, and more institutionally critical than the younger one's. About half their frustrations were directed at the church itself: "awareness of bureaucracy in church groups"; "organized religion frustrates me"; and, identifying a lack of trust in the congregation—"we really have nothing more than nodding acquaintance, here." One wrote that she was struggling to understand "what it means to try to love as part of a community." Another wrote that she waged "a continual struggle [within her congregation] to explain my view of Jesus as a feminist." She also felt there was "too much busy-work" in the congregation, which "interferes with spiritual growth"; she felt that "changes toward modernization are very, very slow." Organizational frustrations are fresh and pointed for this generation. "Women have been exploited and used in this church," one wrote. Another felt that ethical-political issues now in open church discussion, including sermons, seemed intrusive: "Too much talk about abortion, homosexuality, women clergy and the new prayer book." Personal spiritual frustrations included "an inability to open up and get close to others," the "realization that Altar Guild work is not as important in value [in the eyes of this

congregation] as a regular job outside my home," and the fear that
in her congregation "caring and love are only rhetoric here; doing
your own thing is everything."

A bridge woman, a professional musician aged forty-two and a former
Methodist, spoke of her religious hegira with equal amounts of frustration and gratification. "I was a twenty-year dropout, not away from
religion, but away from church." She equated it with "a real 1960s
experience." "You know, more and more doubts about the creed—'I
believe in eternal life.' Well, do I?" She remembers when, "in college,
the 'God is Dead' issue of *Time* came out" and she felt completely
turned off. "Gradually, I found a returning of a church-like interest
within my own personal framework [a liberal social consciousness,
among other things], a place for at least the *thought* of once again
attending church." She had been sustained by private religious practices,
and had always been able to "reach out, in times of crisis, and get help.
I started rediscovering the Bible ten years ago." What finally drew her
back into active affiliation with a congregation? "Obviously there was
Something there—I needed to know more about what it was that was
reaching out, and finding me."

The gratifications for the bridge group are grounded in its more confident grasp of perspectives on self and spirituality. Some middle-agers
listed new experience of special gifts: the "gift of tongues," "a meaningful prayer life," "an increase of faith and valuing of Christ's teachings." One bridge woman wrote: "Bible reading makes more sense."
A few were frustrated by their congregation's negative view of the ecumenical Bible study group that had been religiously significant for them.
One younger member (forty-four) of the bridge generation spent much
of her interview explaining how, through this group, she had connected
with the Bible for the first time. It made "the difference between night
and day" in her life. Four others had also benefited from the same
Neighborhood Bible Study Fellowship, in their own locale. "That's why
people call it a conversion experience, even though it isn't anything like
St. Paul," one of them explained. Serving as parish organist in her
adolescence, this woman in her early forties was one who, growing up,
was just "always at church." She knew now that "in spite of hearing
the liturgy and the words so many times, I'd never really paid attention
to them." The absence of real soul-sharing in her congregation was
literally starving her: "Episcopalians mostly have very secular conversations . . . about their kids or something . . . never about a problem, or
bringing God into it." However, she had no plans to find another church
or a different denomination. "It's my church, and I'm not feeling like

I'm supposed to leave. God has given me places to serve, and . . . my quiet place, kind of behind the scenes, is very meaningful to me." Somewhat cautiously, another of this generation wrote on the questionnaire: "It's easier to live with doubt now." Returning to the church brought another woman a new "depth of appreciation for the movement of the liturgical seasons."

The satisfaction mentioned most often by the bridge generation was the major step of being able to exercise religious leadership. One who had come to maturity at the height of the secular women's movement wrote that for her, religious gratification meant she was now "free from 'crutch' highs like conferences and seminars." Finally, there was the sense of deep religious groundedness: "making Episcopal practices my own," "less separation between life and religion," and the "comradeship of a small prayer group."

One bridge woman articulated the sense of continuity she experienced in worship and the liturgy: "I would like [the next generation] to be able to experience that link with history that is within our church." Maintaining that there was "no substitute for its sense of tradition," she waxed lyrical about "the ties—through worship, through prayers, the music, the language, the gestures, the vestments, the windows, the architecture—going back through generations and generations. I can actually touch someone who had a deep faith way back then, by repeating the same words they said." Middle age permitted these women to look back on the life-giving quality of their worship habits, internal and communal.

From the perspective of the institutional church, the absence of theological vocabulary in the interviews is a concern. "It is as though [these] women [had been] unaffected by the evangelical, the Anglo-Catholic, the liberal, the Social Gospel, the existential, and the Jungian movements that have profoundly reshaped the Episcopal Church . . . in its history," one seminary professor noted in puzzlement.[29] Even though we wanted their "personal" experience, we assumed some code words of religious jargon would have been absorbed because of their faithful attendance at church.

But the women whose words, tears, and experience form the substance of this research do not talk stereotypically about their inner lives and faith. At first glance, the interview transcripts appear totally mundane because they have no "church words" such as *salvation* or *discipleship*. On paper, unaccompanied by facial expression and the language of the eyes, the spirituality they express appears to be wordless. In contrast, their words about denomination, and the meaning they find in church membership, were unrestrained. Our challenge was to discern what language—or nonlanguage—they did employ about concerns of the spirit and their inner lives.[30]

Women's verbal inhibition about the essence of religious affiliation—the spiritual—was labeled, by some of them, as a denominational poverty of rhetoric. The young woman who saw Episcopalians as uncomfortable with anything but "secular conversation" evoked the current WASP stereotype captured by dramatist A. R. Gurney.[31] An older woman, a retired teacher, went further, offering a theological explanation (in effect) of her refusal to use theological terms. She saw the language of theology as little more than verbal gymnastics, a stumbling block to "real religion." "What's in the Bible is what's important," she argued. "Who said what, when, with history, with theology, and needing to know all that—it's all just background; it has nothing to do with religion!"

Another interpretation of the avoidance of theological terms by twentieth-century laity is that laypeople have learned to associate theology with the intellect, whereas religious experience is personal and emotional. One young clergywoman explained that opposition. "Laywomen have been taught, at least non-verbally, in a clerical church, that you're supposed to *separate* emotion and intellect. And that one is more important, higher, than the other. They have come to think that theology belongs to the world of mind, which is more important, and that their emotions must be kept out of it—so they don't feel any identification with theological words." She thought a moment, then asked: "But how about the statement '*I believe in God?*' That's not an intellectual statement! It's an emotional one."[32] The women in this study spoke as if "churchy" words did not belong to them but were a speciality out of reach for the average layperson. Very few cited a scriptural image; those who did used the familiar reference to women known for their differing responses to Jesus, the sisters Martha and Mary. There was no reference to the Social Gospel movement of the early twentieth century, even in the congregation clearly involved in its late-twentieth-century version. Apparently, if these intelligent women thought in those categories at all, they censored their own use of it; *theology* and *ecclesiology* were terms for a sermon, not their own lives. Avoidance of *salvation* and *born again,* specifically, may be more simply explained by associations in the popular mind with evangelical or television preachers. When these women thought about personal, profound experience of the holy, it could not be sullied or cheapened by words they viewed as inappropriate.

Conscious self-limitation to "ordinary words" in talking about transcendant experience was singled out in *Habits of the Heart* as a characteristic of contemporary American mainline Protestant culture. The authors found that twentieth-century Protestants had lost, or rejected, the "second language" that once was used to express deepest longing and commitments—the religious self.[33] Response to an item on the questionnaire provides an interpretive clue. Asked to rank the spiritual "tools" they use in their private religious life, very few in the four congregations named Bible reading or scripture as one of their important sources of spiritual nurture. (Many did list the use of devotional and other religious self-help literature.) Those involved in ecumenical Bible study outside their own parishes were the primary ones to identify scripture as part of their ongoing spiritual discipline between Sundays. Because the source of a "second language" has historically been scripture, the paucity of "religious" vocabulary has a certain logic. Nevertheless these women maintain a deep commitment to the religious institution of the local congregation. How is it possible, without the appurtenance of a theological vocabulary? From the research point of view, can we discern spiritual experience if the external sign of language is absent?

Throughout history, women have learned to "layer" workaday activity with levels of meaning, allowing themselves to find and express spiritual issues and insight in the quotidian dimensions of life (see the Brown chapter, this volume). In this regard mainline Protestant churchwomen made of their church lives both more and less than it appeared externally; they "used" their church work in the same psychic and spiritual manner, and for some of the same reasons, as African Americans "used" religion—for survival, and as a subversion that created space for their own type of fulfillment.[34] This helps explain nostalgia for "the good old days" of women's church work. Working together with their hands, for example, conveyed to women a larger religious significance: the numinous dimension of concrete experience, religiously motivated and dedicated. Kitchen work or needlework can carry a layer of meaning that honors community and personal dedication at the same time it runs a soup kitchen or a successful bazaar. Similarly, women's unexpressive language about "family" gave no audible signal of its layers of religious and spiritual meaning. The language of the eyes, and the tears evoked, did. Our conclusion is that women's expression of "theology," far from being absent, is indeed a spirituality expressible only in relational terms. These women see themselves as "doing" theology (insofar as they connect their own actions with a type of thought usually associated with clergy) in terms of service or "giving," in terms of spiritual relationships, and in deep bonds of identity with the faith and narrative of their congregation.

Intergenerational Perceptions

The interviews provided illustrations of intergenerational stereotypes, some oblique and others obvious, as well as cross-generational bridge building. Even the process of the interview contributed; some interactions confirm the speaker's dismay, others were an occasion for insight and sympathy. A commonsense perspective from a younger woman was the occasion for self-enlightenment. "The old way is truly breaking down—men doing some things, women doing other things," she began. And then sighed, "But *real* slowly. Oh, women had their guilds and their little bake sales, but . . . Today, ask one of the older women to be a lay reader, and she'll say, almost scandalized, 'Oh no, *I* could never do that!' " She deplored older women's inability to seize the new opportunities. "They just can't see themselves doing *that*, any more than I . . . " She stopped. She had recalled that in her childhood, "I didn't use to be able to see myself as an acolyte, because it was something only boys could aspire to. I couldn't even think it, it just seemed so impossible!" She had stumbled over a link with the older generation that had not occurred to her before. Realizing the generational parameters of her own imagination suddenly illuminated the phenomenon she was describing.

Being part of a congregation was credited by another in the younger generation as having given her permission to "discover" the older generation. A mother's death became a religiously transforming experience for her, a first real appreciation of cross-generational friendship. "My whole life has just drastically changed," she said, "thanks to help from an older woman in the parish who just seemed to know how difficult mother's dying would be for me." The youngest daughter of a divorced parent, she found her mother's illness "very scary, 'cause I always thought she'd live forever. Of course that [made] it easier for me to live forever, too." [The friend] "gave me the 'Jesus prayer' and taught me how to use it, to see me through. It was all new to me, the prayers, and this caring from church people." Another young woman was forced to become more empathetic with older women through painful awareness that "people here think I'm too permissive, that I let my kids run around too much." Formerly impatient with the way the older members seemed to dominate her congregation—"remodeling the nursery was always *second* on the list"—she learned to hear them. "The older members are truly uncomfortable with the kids zipping in and out. They don't want to fall and hurt themselves." Surrendering her defensiveness, she acknowledged, "Kids can be pretty unnerving, if you're not used to them."

The bridge-generation view of the older generation was sometimes impatient: "Old people grumble [about inclusive language] because they have to change the way their mouth works around it," a feminist surmised, unsympathetically. Some who pioneered the breaking of gender barriers had smarted under the disapproval of older women: "I remember when I was the first woman usher. . . . Oh, I tell you, that was so—a woman looked at me like I was about to . . . !" But such intragender antagonism is a thing of the past, she admitted: "Today, no one bats an eyelash [at women ushers] anymore!" Another woman, fifty, was sure it was only older members in the congregation who had greeted the announcement in church that a woman bishop had been elected with "a loud gasp": "I think there are probably a lot of them who thought it was wrong, judging from the gasp. But . . . change always comes hard." Another bridge woman cited the anomaly of being in the middle: "One of the problems in the church, to me, has been age exclusiveness. You're either in your sixties, and active, say, in the gift workshop, or maybe you're in the nursery . . . but nothing counts, in between."

A more patient view of older women's seeming intractibility came from a member of the bridge generation who taught a class of mentally retarded adults in Sunday school. "I have sympathy for people who've grown up a certain way, and who are still complaining about the new hymnal or the new prayer book—how many years later is it, now?" But she could empathize with "someone who'd done this a certain way for seventy years." Adjustment is difficult. "It's got to be hard, you know." But experience was the great eye-opener: "Once you *see* that it can be done another way, and the walls are still standing—that God didn't strike the church down"—even the most inflexible elders were able, finally, to accept change. At the other end of the spectrum, a bridge-generation woman reflected only satisfaction in her parish, generationally, in terms of gender and social outreach. "With our Jubilee dinners [for the homeless]," she began her list, "and the adult education programs, and Sunday school, and the coffee hours, it seems this is a real parish family. I think we've got a nice balance of all ages, and of both men and women."

A member of the older generation, reflecting on her own age group, said: "Maybe I don't give them enough credit . . . change does make a difference, to them. But—they've sure been good about it; they keep their mouths shut, you know, at least to the degree we've gone, anyway." Warming to her theme, she offered what she saw as an improvement, or change, in both decorum and dress: "I feel like we're a lot more caring for the outside world [than in the old days.] Not that women sit around, and make bandages and that kind of thing, anymore. Visitors really used to think Episcopalians weren't friendly and warm." She smiled about the in-house Episcopal self-mockery, "God's frozen people." "But that's kind of gone out, along with wearing hats." The metaphors were more descriptive, perhaps, than she imagined.

In two of the parishes the gap between generations was pronounced. The one expression of generational rejection came from a New England older woman: "There's quite a few young people in the church; it really bothers me. . . . Where are they now?" Younger and bridge women's lack of participation at a fund-raising dinner the older women had put on was disillusioning. "The people in the parish don't seem to get behind a lot of the things they [we older women] do." With the new energy in the congregation, from "all these young people," she couldn't help but wonder: "Where the heck are they? I guess women are active [she meant the older ones] because we've always been that way." Her generational blinders could not let her see other styles of participation and church participation than the traditional model. She uttered the timeless observation, "It's a changing population, I guess, and that changes everything," as if hoping to derive comfort from it. Countering that gloom, the breezy eighty-year-old in Redeemer Plains bubbled with enthusiasm about the younger generation: "These young women, they're marvelous. I'm always thrilled to be asked to show the Altar Guild girls how to do something. They're just all so wonderful, and do such a good job—and of course, I love to keep my hand in."

A thoughtful summary of generations in her congregation came from a retired bookkeeper, an older woman still involved in lay leadership. "The older women, here in particular [in their gift workshop], find that the church offers them a great deal; they are really fortunate, they have opportunities to do a lot of things." If some of them complain, she surmised, it was probably because they feel asked to do too much, to carry more responsibility than their generation should. "And sometimes I think they might be, for their age; but in this day when so many women are working, those of us who are *not,* just have to carry a little heavier load, in some ways." She had a very generous view of the bridge generation: "And those women who are working now [the ones we might have expected, before, to take more active part in church functions], they do take part, they help in various ways—they make sandwiches and drop them off on their way to work, et cetera." And she understood the different pace of life for the younger generation: "It's not their fault that there are just too many other activities for their youngsters, other than church, these days."

The generational shift in attitudes about volunteer work and time commitments implies a question about organizational maintenance. In particular it worries the older women. When the present generation of younger women is the generation of older women in the congregation, will it take up the tasks of institutional maintenance? Habits of involvement in "little" tasks—mending the carpet, mailing out the bulletins, cleaning the restrooms for a busy Sunday—are not being formed. One male congregational leader spoke about a potential long-term result of the new self-assigned volunteering: "You can always get plenty of volunteers for a one-shot task, like moving the Christian education equipment from one building to the new room. People are willing to sign up for a particular job, but consistent help, over the long haul will be another story." A female congregational leader in her fifties understood perfectly: "Today's young women want to *do* what we used to call 'mission.' They want to actually go out and engage in hands-on work, at soup kitchens or at the women's shelter; what they *don't* want is to join a women's organization that studies *about* mission." A bridge-generation woman thanked us for the research project in her congregation, because "at least we now have a name for our disagreements—generation—and it gives us a way to move! We haven't known how to think about it, before."

Reflection

The three generations of women in these four congregations have made substantial moves toward new dimensions of leadership for and by women, particularly in their appreciation of ordained women. Women in the younger generation have turned their need for self-fulfillment into building a solid relationship with a church; they develop a strong religious identity, and are signs of hope to their congregations. It is clear, however, that a major pattern through which women formerly received religious legitimation—"traditional churchwomen's work"—has been undermined by the changes in the latter part of the twentieth century. The Episcopal Church as an institution is under stress. The changes that have been incorporated may be the source of new vitality for the twenty-first century, or the first cracks in the foundation of a structure about to disintegrate.

The differences in what men and women seek through a church affiliation—not a specific question in this study—could undoubtedly be documented to show that men, more than women, go to church to find a rule for how to live. Whether or not that is the case, the women here are clearly going to church in order to be fed, not to receive rules. Both the middle-aged and younger women have explicitly stated that they don't need an additional place, or organization, in which to be "active" in the earlier pattern; their complex late-twentieth-century lives need, and they have the personal authority to seek, substantive spiritual nurture from their religious affiliation. They also expect it to challenge or goad their earthly consciousness. In this era of choice, it matters to these women that a congregation to which they give their allegiance has a sense of mission and social outreach.

Self-help or special interest groups, the extrachurch component of most contemporary congregations—Al-Anon, Alcoholics Anonymous, Episcopal Peace Fellowship, Order of St. Luke's, and other "support groups"—were taken for granted by the women we interviewed. A few women from each of the congregations had reached beyond the walls of the parish for a special interest group proffering spiritual nurture: interdenominational Bible study, charismatic prayer groups, the Curcillo or other spiritual-renewal retreats, study groups, feminist spirituality workshops, New Age seminars. Some had initiated their own support groups: for women going through divorce, for discussing feminist concerns, or for spiritual sharing.

Also, in each of the four parishes there were a few women whose religious commitment was focused on local or national political issues, such as nuclear disarmament and peace, the environment, and world hunger. Some translated their understanding of discipleship into overt (financial and information-diffusing) support for causes such as peace in Central America or antinuclear groups. These women defined "Christian commitment and ministry" in broad social terms, considering their volunteer work and financial contributions to causes beyond the local congregation an equally legitimate expression of faith. This diversity of interest and fulfillment was expected and accepted in the four congregations, even if, from an organizational point of view, it diffused the energy and charitable resources of the congregation.

One question on the survey asked, *Beyond the parish, which of the following presents the most important opportunity for women to expand their ministries and develop leadership?* The overwhelming first choice (58 percent) was "Involvement with social issues in the community"; the second (41 percent) was "Encouraging women to translate Christian belief in specific ways into their lives at home and out in the world." On the other hand, the option of women's increased activity in denominational organizations, beyond the local parish or diocesan level, received a paltry number of checks. Less than 5 percent of the 269 Episcopalian women responding to this study located any potential for the kind of self-development they sought within their own denominational hierarchy—surely a serious disengagement from the denomination's national institution and identity.

Dimensions of church participation (particularly among the younger and bridge women) reflect the psychological and religious messages they have absorbed: that they must be participatory rather than passive; that they must make their own decisions rather than unintentionally falling into a pattern or an organization; and that they themselves bestow the burden of "authority" to whatever it is that "speaks to their lives." In cases where loyalty is weaker, spiritual isolation and congregational apathy have fueled the discontent. A disjunction between a young mother's struggle to pay the bills and feeling trapped by the care of a toddler, and her own religious quest, created this poignant observation. "Spiritual things have become a luxury, almost"; she felt alone in a world that recognizes only material achievement. "It's hard to find people to relate to, in my age group, who are interested more in spiritual things, and less in materialistic things." A feeling of being overwhelmed in a consumer-driven society led her to search for others who truly value the spiritual things in life, but "that's not in the mainstream of the Episcopal Church." Against all her upbringing, education, and mind-set, the support and feeding she found was among "people involved with Eastern religions."

Ours is an age and culture that encourages experimenting with— "trying on"—varieties of religious authority. In this study, many of the younger generation had experimented with various churches as well as other non-Christian forms of religion and worship. The young journalist quoted earlier for her intergenerational insight was one who had searched for the "right" congregation until she found it. The derogation of choice—testing religious authority, particularly among women—is a rhetorical convention in religious magazines. "Church shopping" has been a pejorative label.

One male commentator recently compared "trying on" religious affiliations with testing different kinds of perfume. He suggested that its reason for being was because "brand loyalty is weak." The endemic quality of religious experimenting is so pervasive, he wrote, that in "a support group of two dozen young [female] urbanites," each could have the "spiritual perfume of choice, her celebrity-endorsed religious beguilement." The options represented in the group included channeling, Rolfing, Zen, macrobiotics, crystals, humanistic Judaism, astrology, and even Sheilaism (the self-defined individualist "sect" of the *Habits of the Heart* narcissist). He quoted the only Episcopalian in the group, an ordained priest, as saying to him, "I'm the only one who comes from, and in a way represents, what the polls say is the faith of 80 percent of the American people. But *I'm* the one regarded as eccentric, in that circle."[35]

Some of the women in our study would compare themselves with that "eccentric" Episcopalian. Their contemporaries seek religious certainty in fundamentalist or charismatic congregations. They have friends for whom religious authority is no longer located in any specific ritual or institution. Their present faith and the church to which they belong are under pressure. Yet surprisingly, and against all rational explanation, their denominational loyalty is extraordinarily high.

Perhaps *the* great untapped resource for renewal in congregations is the endlessly questing heart of its generations of women. In many locations women have yet to be perceived as a genuine part of "the whole church"—by leaders either in their own congregations or at the national organizational level. But the women-in-the-pew in our study are increasingly less willing to accept beliefs and practices on prescription. They are finding and creating their own space within the institution. Our research uncovered amazing pockets of devotion and spiritual depth among women in all three generations. Regardless of the care with which they avoid standard theological language, or in what seemingly trite images they convey their religious questions, a common denominator is their belief and commitment amidst earthquakes of social and ecclesiastical change. Despite the lack of nourishment and welcome from the denominational leadership during first half of this century, these women's piety and loyalty to their brand of church persists. That alone, if identified and nurtured, is the ground from which new forms of spiritual power can emerge. Somehow the national church has hardly begun to tap this dormant resource in local congregations. The major future task for women clergy in a "mainstream" church may be just that.

Acknowledgments

I am grateful to Ann Swidler of the University of California, Berkeley, for suggesting the lens of generations as our organizing concept, and for her generous help at each stage of research and writing. I am also grateful to Catherine M. Prelinger for her determination to include an empirical component in the overall project. A colleague whose insight and collaboration has been irreplaceable is Rima L. Schultz (her chapter in this volume).

Others whose efforts were indispensable are Nancy Van Scoyoc, Washington, D.C., for the design of the original process of parish survey questionnaire and interview outline; Paula Nesbitt, Iliff Theological Seminary, Denver; for statistics and sociological analysis; and Joseph Serdakowsky, Brown University, for computer design and analysis. I also thank two colleagues whose sensitivity and skill assisted in the interviewing: Margaret Woolverton, Center Sandwich, N.H., and Margaret Rubel, East Greenwich, R.I.

Notes

1. Each type of ethnic minority congregation would be poorly served by inclusion in a survey focused on the "typical" Episcopalian (primarily white) congregation. Official church records do not register the racial identity of members; estimates of ethnic minority percentages of the total membership, based on the known number of congregations of a given minority, are only suggestive. Out of a total membership of 2.5 million, 4–5 percent are African Americans, .6 percent are of Asian ancestry (the fastest growing membership), .8 percent are Native Americans, and 1 percent are of Hispanic background. There is no way to count or even estimate individuals of ethnic-minority background who are members of predominantly "white" congregations.

2. *Newsweek,* 17 December 1990, cover story, "And the Children Shall Lead Them."

3. Peter Drucker, *The New Realities* (New York: Harper & Row, 1989), describing the "knowledge society," suggests that churches are the institution of change. In the face of rootlessness, dissolution of the traditional family, and small-town horizons, religion is the sphere where individuals gain self-mastery through serving, and discover bonds of community.

4. Matilda White Riley, "Aging, Social Change and Ideas," *Daedalus* (Fall 1978):39–52, 45.

5. Annie Kriegel, "Generational Difference: The History of an Idea," *Daedalus* (Fall 1978):23–38, 29.

6. Douglas Alan Walrath, *Frameworks: Patterns of Living and Believing Today* (Philadelphia: Pilgrim Press, 1987), characterized religious generational mind-sets: the older generation, Strivers, shaped by World War II and the depression, are committed to hard work, institutions and struggle; Challengers are his middle generation, shaped by the influence of the civil rights movement and the Vietnam War; and the younger generation, Calculators, were socialized in the mid-1970s and 1980s.

7. Kriegel, "Generational Difference," pp. 23–24.

8. Riley, "Aging, Social Change and Ideas," p. 46.

9. Ibid., p. 44.

10. The term "inclusive language" was current during the interviews, but has been supplanted by the less antagonizing term "supplemental liturgies."

11. See Pamela W. Darling, " 'Tradition' vs. Women: Conflict and Change in the Episcopal Church 1870–1990" (Ph.D. diss., General Theological Seminary, 1991), for analysis of the legislative manipulation of "tradition" to exclude women's participation.

12. Elaine Tyler May, *Homeward Bound: American Families in the Cold War Era* (New York: Basic Books, 1988).

13. Riley, "Aging, Social Change and Ideas," p. 43.

14. May, *Homeward Bound.*

15. See Joanna B. Gillespie, "What We Taught: Christian Education in the American Episcopal Church, 1920–80," *Historical Magazine (Episcopal Church)* 56 (March 1987):45–85, about resistance to, and then validation of, the Seabury Series in the 1960s, a new curriculum for Episcopal Sunday schools.

16. Mary S. Donovan, *A Different Call: Women's Ministries in the Episcopal Church, 1850–1920* (Wilton, Conn.: Morehouse-Barlow, 1986; Darling, " 'Tradition' vs. Women."

17. *Statistical Abstract of the United States,* 1989 #49 (U.S. Bureau of the Census, Current Population Reports, series P–20, #423) and earlier reports.

18. Kathryn Allan Rabuzzi, *The Sacred and the Feminine: Toward a Theology of Housework* (New York: Seabury Press, 1982), p. 81.

19. Carol Gilligan, *In A Different Voice,* Cambridge, Mass., Harvard University Press, 1982; Karen Offen, "Defining Feminism: A Comparative Historical Approach," *SIGNS* 14 (1988):119–157.

20. Andrew J. Cherlin and Frank F. Furstenberg, Jr., *The New American Grandparent* (New York: Basic Books, 1986).

21. *Statistical Abstract of the United States* 1989 #621 (U.S. Bureau of Labor Statistics), *Employment and Earnings* monthly; *Monthly Labor Review,* September 1987.

22. *Statistical Abstract of the United States* 1989 #715 (U.S. Bureau of the Census, *Current Population Reports,* series P–60, #161).

23. Robert Wuthnow and Virginia A. Hodgkinson, eds., *Faith and Philanthropy in America* (San Francisco: Jossey-Bass, 1990), p. 112.

24. Sandra Hughes Boyd, ed., *Cultivating Our Roots: A Guide to Gathering Church Women's History* (New York: Episcopal Women's History Project, 1984), p. 19.

25. Frances M. Young, *Whatever Happened to Good Old Women's Work?* (New York: Episcopal Women's History Project, 1985).

26. Darling, " 'Tradition' vs. Women," p. 225.

27. J. B. Gillespie, oral histories of Frances M. Young and Helen Turnbull, Archives of the Episcopal Church, Austin, Texas.

28. Barbara Gent and Betty Sturges, *The Altar Guild Book, a History and Practical Handbook.* (Wilton, Conn.: Morehouse-Barlow, 1982).

29. Seminaries are concerned at the avoidance of the language that is their currency. This questioner is a church historian and longtime advocate of women's full participation in the church. Personal communication, Dr. Frank Sugeno, Episcopal Theological Seminary of the Southwest, Austin, Texas, 6 June 1990.

30. Robert Darnton, *The Great Cat Massacre* (New York: Random House, 1985), suggests that in analyzing historical documents, "Where we cannot get a proverb, or a joke . . . we know we are onto something. By picking at the document where it is most opaque, we may be able *to unravel a system of meaning*" (emphasis added), p. 5.

31. A. R. Gurney, Jr., depicting mid-twentieth-century WASP families in *The Dining Room* (1982), *The Middle Ages* (1985), and *The Cocktail Hour* (1989).

32. The Reverend Susan Lee, comment, Episcopal Tri-History Conference, Los Angeles, June 1991. Also the Reverend Loren Mead, Alban Institute, Washington, D.C., substantiating the same phenomenon in parishes during the 1970s, personal communication, July 1991.

33. Robert N. Bellah, Richard Madsen, William M. Sullivan, Ann Swidler, and Steven M. Tipton, *Habits of the Heart: Individualism and Commitment in American Life* (Berkeley: University of California Press, 1985), p. 8.

34. I am grateful to Rima Schultz for this observation, and for corroborating these findings with the same survey. She tabulated responses from 406 Episcopal women in the Diocese of Chicago during 1989–1990, with very similar findings. Four percent of her younger and bridge-generation respondents were African-American; 8 percent, older generation.

35. Martin Marty, "M.E.M.O.," *Christian Century,* 18 October 1989, p. 943.

6

Different Voices:
African American
Women in the Episcopal Church

Marjorie Nichols Farmer

Black people must tell their own story.
Myrtle Gordon, "Black Women's Agenda"

The story of twentieth century women in the Episcopal Church as reviewed in other chapters in this volume is, quite appropriately, a generally Anglocentric account. We are, after all, an English church, a member of the worldwide Anglican communion. This chapter will offer a counterpoint: the story of the women of what has been called "the invisible church,"[1] almost unseen in our "official" histories, and generally unmarked in the prevailing perception of who Episcopalians are. Though black Episcopalians fully share the traditions and the liturgy of the Episcopal Church, we bring to that heritage a very different social history. My task is to report that difference: its roots in our common history, its impact on the life of this church, and its influence in shaping the future of the Anglican faith community.

A Philadelphia Story

Philadelphia, a city that has been described as having "more Episcopalians per capita than any other city,"[2] has been the setting for many of the crucial events in Episcopal church history. Its name (literally translated from the Greek "brotherly-sisterly love") serves, too, as a useful metaphor for the building of a new community of faith and fellowship.

Philadelphia is the home of "Historic St. Thomas' Church," the first African Episcopal church, founded in 1792. The social process that led to this event defined the clear and continuing division in the African American church community between those who chose to separate entirely from the white church—Richard Allen and his associates who organized the African Methodist Episcopal (AME) Church, and those who chose to remain within the Anglican fold as the congregation of St. Thomas Church, the first of many separate African (later "black") Episcopal congregations in this country. These two separations mark the special character of black Episcopalians, defining their unique role in "the healing of the nations," both within the broader black faith community and within the Episcopal Church and throughout worldwide Anglicanism.[3]

Another significant Philadelphia connection is the "irregular" ordination of eleven women priests, which took place in 1974 (two years before the national church voted to make the ordination of women to the priesthood canonically possible) in the Church of the Advocate, where Paul Washington, a distinguished advocate for social justice, was rector of the predominantly black congregation in a predominantly black neighborhood.[4] Barbara Harris, who as crucifer led the procession at the ordination service, was serving as interim rector of the Church of the Advocate in 1988 when she was elected suffragan bishop of the Diocese of Massachusetts, the first woman bishop in the history of the worldwide Anglican communion. Washington was the preacher at her consecration in Boston the next year in a service that was for many "a day when the angels sang." For many others throughout the world, the day was a sign of a deeply troubling rift in the community of faith.

In October 1989 the House of Bishops met in Philadelphia's Christ Church, marking the bicentennial celebration of the first meeting of American Episcopal bishops in the same place. High on their agenda was discussion of a report prepared by an international panel on "ways to preserve unity within the Anglican Communion in the face of disagreements"[5] growing out of both events—the ordination of women as priests and the consecration of a woman as bishop. The *Christian Science Monitor*, commenting on the accord reached in this conference, observed that "Anglicanism has long been distinguished by its ability to harbor Christians with very different beliefs."[6] It was this unity in diversity that the House of Bishops celebrated. And it is this unity in diversity on which this chapter reports—the *via media*, the "middle way," by which Episcopalians are defined.

Two more recent Philadelphia events serve further to center the focus of this essay: the 1990 conference of the Union of Black Episcopalians, and the planning under way in 1991 for the 1992 bicentennial of the founding of St. Thomas Church, a celebration to be shared by the Episcopal Church throughout the country.[7]

This chapter, then, is the story of our separateness and of our journey toward reconciliation, and of the special role played by black women in their ministries, lay and ordained, throughout this history. And it is "a Phil-adelphia story," a story of "how we Christians love one another" across all the differences that divide us.

Different Priorities: The Black Women's Agenda

> I am because we are.
>> John S. Mbiti, *African Religions and Philosophy*

The strong, though deeply threatened, sense of community that marks the African religious experience is what we heard in the voices of spokeswomen for the Black Women's Task Force at the Third National Conference of the Episcopal Church Task Force on Women, held in Indianapolis in November 1981. The conference sought to examine "the tension between racism and feminism," a tension that the task force perceived as a "major block for women, the church and society in general." Four major papers from that conference were published in 1982 as a "Black Women's Agenda."[8]

Deborah Hines, who served later as a president of the Union of Black Episcopalians, said, "Black women's goals and agenda are very different from those of white women [because of] the concerns we have for our children and our men, . . . who are psychologically defeated by still not having equal access to jobs or equal pay." Citing the disproportionate numbers of black men in military service and in prison, Hines declared, "Our agenda involves maintaining, strengthening and uplifting our race, our families, our culture and heritage, our men and ourselves."[9]

Myrtle Gordon, an Atlanta educator, emphasizing the importance of our telling our own story, and speaking in our own voices, said that we need to talk about the real strengths of black family life, and to remember that the civil rights leadership of the 1960s was centered in the black church.[10]

Mattie Hopkins, a teacher in Chicago's public schools, expressed concern about the disparity between the educational achievements of black men and black women. "Over the years a larger percentage of black women graduate from high schools and colleges than do black men. Why indeed should black women feel competitive with their men?"[11]

Barbara Harris echoed this common theme. "Our concern is for the wellbeing of black men, our black children, and our black church." For this reason, Harris believes, inclusive language, a major concern of the feminist movement in the church, is not likely to be so important for black women:

> Black people don't have any problems relating to "God the Father or to his Son. Jesus Christ is not, to us, just heir or firstborn. He is the role model we have to hold up in the community that needs strong male images. We need the maleness of Christ. A hymn like "Rise up, O men of God" is a challenge for our brothers to come and join us in the struggle.[12]

How does the black women's agenda differ from that of our white sisters?

> Our agenda in the black church is to build strong congregations that are not only centers of worship, but centers of nurture, centers of guidance, centers of leadership development, resources for survival and models of the extended family. We have a parenting function and responsibility, a pastoral care function and responsibility, and [a responsibility for] the preaching of the good news to the poor, in tangible forms. So do you. But we come at it with different priorities, born out of different needs and different experiences.[13]

The black women's agenda in the church is, then, an agenda that grows out of our history, and that therefore necessarily focuses first on the need for honoring the family and working for the health of the whole community. Concerns for women's access to particular roles and ministries are important only in relation to the primary agenda.

In a paper presented to the Conference on Afro-Anglicanism held in Barbados in June 1985, Harris affirmed the ministries, lay and ordained, of African Anglican women: "So great a cloud of witnesses should be utilized to the fullest potential of their human as well as their traditional financial resources for the building up of the kingdom." But their ministries must be their own, for "while their Anglican heritage has given them the melody of their song, their black religious experience, which cuts across denominational lines, has given them the lyrics and the courage to sing it."[14]

The Black Women's Task Force continues to serve in an advisory capacity to the national Episcopal Church women's desk, defining its role in this summary statement: "We must be prepared to fight for the survival of the part of ourselves that is *women* and that *whole* of ourselves that is a *Black Person*: The total race—men, women and children— must survive, if any of us are to survive. We need strong Black male and female images and success to motivate our young people, if we wish to reach our potential as people *also* chosen of God and made in his Almighty Image."[15]

Different Experience: A Separate Church History

In their 1787 separation from "the white church" and their 1792 separation from "the black church," African-American Episcopalians set out on a separate journey, as *ecclesia,* a people called out to do a special ministry, and prepared, through their history, to serve a unique reconciling role in the church and the society.

At a time (1787) when "no church edifice could be found through the whole country, owned and controlled exclusively by persons of color,"[16] St. George's Methodist Church in Philadelphia was a welcoming center of worship for freedmen living in the city. Richard Allen and Absalom Jones, both itinerant preachers in the Methodist style, had attracted large numbers of "the colored population" to that ministry, so many that separate seating had been provided for them. One Sunday morning, at a time when the house of worship was full to overflowing, Jones and Allen were interrupted at prayer and asked to move to the separate section for colored worshippers. They left the church with their friends, and gathered later to form the Free African Society. "A moral earthquake had awakened the slumber of ages."[17] The society was founded on April 12, 1787, "without regard to religious tenets . . . in order to support one another in sickness" and for the benefit of widows and children.[18] In 1789 Allen separated from the Society and with some associates succeeded in establishing the Bethel African Methodist Episcopal Church. In 1792 Jones led the organization of the St. Thomas African Protestant Episcopal Church.[19]

So the separate journey of black Episcopalians was begun. Separate *from* the black church community, separate *within* the Episcopal community, yet deeply connected to both.

Lydia Wright discusses, in a Forward Movement monograph, some characteristics of the separate black churches:

> 85% of Black Christians are Baptist or Methodist. Episcopalians share ... 14% with Presbyterian, Lutheran, Congregational, Roman Catholic Churches and smaller groups. Black Methodists and Baptists have adopted Christianity to serve pressing earthly needs. Their churches through the years have fulfilled important community roles. They are sanctuaries and tactical headquarters for the poor and oppressed. They are the primary means of communication between black leaders and the black masses. They are the primary spawning ground for militant black leaders. They are the most successful voter registration centers. They are the primary means of attracting members to the NAACP. One fourth of all the presidents of the NAACP chapters have been ministers. They are the most successful organizers of boycotts of products, buses, schools and services. Because of successes in these roles, black Methodists and Baptists are sometimes referred to as the "visible" black church and black Episcopalians as the "invisible" black church.[20]

Different Experiences: A Separate Women's Program

> I used to come across the phrase "church work among Negroes,"
> and my thought ... was that this was a curious thing.
> Joyce M. Howard, "The Church's Work among Negroes" (1982)

One of the nearly one hundred women "leaders, organizers"—many from clergy families, many holding college degrees—who were trained in the period from 1928 to the mid-1950s for lay ministries was Fannie Jeffrey, who served as a field secretary (1940–1948) for the national church. Jeffrey wrote that "the National Church was conscious of its separateness—of its black and white church ... and so my job was not to be an integrator but to work in separate situations, being the liaison between the White side and the Black side."[21]

Of the women, most of whom were trained at the Bishop Tucker School in Raleigh, North Carolina, Joyce M. Howard said in 1982, "They did much in the way of quietly and persistently working to break down the wall of brazen racism within the church that exhibited itself in such ways as segregated seating in conferences and meetings held in churches. . . . " Their work covered a wide range of church and community services in missions, churches, diocesan offices, colleges, correctional institutions, recreation centers, migrant workers' communities, and a Navajo reservation. They were social workers, teachers, religious education directors, and catechists. And they worked often under "oppressive conditions" marked by the "racism that existed throughout the society." Howard summed up the impact of their ministry: "To me, it means that the church will grow into unity in most every way."[22]

The voices of nearly seventy of these women are heard in Howard's collection of letters and interviews.[23] One woman, Wilhelmina Wynn, says of her training experience at the Bishop Tuttle School, "What we became for having lived and learned there is more important [than the physical changes in the building in which they studied]. Wherever Tuttle trained people are, it is certain that they still work and give in the tradition of Tuttle School."[24] One of Wynn's classmates was Ollie Carden, who grew up in the House of the Holy Child, a residence for "colored Episcopal girls" in Philadelphia, and was educated in St. Augustine's College and Morgan State College. What Carden became was demonstrated at the 1990 reunion of the decidedly interracial, intercultural, intergenerational group of nearly fifty former pupils from her thirty years as a kindergarten teacher in Philadelphia. As they appreciatively recalled the lessons Carden had taught them through seeds to be planted and dolls to be cherished, she reminded them that we may be "all different on the outside, but inside we're all alike."[25] The gratitude expressed at the reunion is testimony to "what she became" through her Tuttle School training—an effective witness for reconciliation.

Different Traditions: Diversity within the African Anglican Community of Women

Sensitive to the cultural differences that pervade and permeate countries, particularly in Africa and the Caribbean, I refrain from proposing any absolute model for enabling the full ministry of Black women—ordained and lay—in the loosely bound communion called Anglicanism.

Barbara Harris, *"Cloud of Witnesses"*

The Church of St. Matthias in the West Oak Lane section of Philadelphia provides a remarkable microcosm of Anglican churchwomen in a tiny (thirty-fifty average Sunday attendance) congregation. Many adult communicants are fairly recent immigrants from Caribbean and South American nations; others are indigenous to the United States, though most of these have a Caribbean connection in their family history. Nations represented include Haiti, Jamaica, Trinidad, Guyana, and Barbados.

What follows in the next several paragraphs is based on a series of focused conversations with several St. Matthias women in an informal (church picnic) setting in July 1989, along with conversations with two other African American Episcopal women, one a recent convert from the AME tradition, the other a priest, a lifelong Episcopalian. Conversations were directed to these issues: (1) reasons for choosing or remaining in the Episcopal Church; (2) opinion of recent liturgical changes; (3) interest in the church beyond the parish; and (4) the ordination of women.

Two women—mother and daughter—of the Haitian family offered significantly diverse experiences and perceptions. Marie Casimir, who grew up in Haiti and came to the United States in the early 1970s with no command of the English language, found in the Episcopal church here an important connection to the Anglican tradition she'd left behind. She noted these major differences: "More music (especially tambourines) in Haiti; more incense, more services of worship. There was a 6 o'clock mass twice a week; in Advent and Lent the worship day began with prayers at 4 A.M." Although she is comfortable with women as priests, Casimir believes that it is important to encourage the participation of men in the church. Her husband, Jean, is one of the very few strong male leaders in this congregation.

Casimir's daughter Elsie, a dental school student who came to the United States in her preteen years, also with no command of English, is a faithful member of St. Matthias, having led a weekly prayer group throughout the year. She is also an active, devoted member of the Church of the New Covenant, a flourishing, exciting, independent congregation with strong, effective Caribbean leadership.[26] On her summer break from studies, she was leading New Covenant teenagers in Bible study and Christian "rap." Elsie said her "focus is on God," more than on any particular faith community. During her undergraduate years at Beaver College, she found spiritual nurture in a Christian group on campus that was led by a student in nearby Westminster Seminary, a strongly fundamentalist and evangelical school. She described members of that group as "more interested in seeking answers to questions about God ("how as a creature of God you fit into his Kingdom"). She contrasted this questioning spirit with worship in the Episcopal Church ("just going to church" as a religious activity, a duty, with "a lot of stuff not really understood"). In the New Covenant community, on the other hand, Elsie spoke of "the teachings" as central to the worship experience. Like other informants, Elsie expressed no interest in the institutional Episcopal Church beyond her own congregation, though she attended a convention once and found it "interesting."

Three other women—Millicent Hinds (Trinidad), Mildred Perry (Barbados), and Claudina Carey (Guyana)—are also lifelong Anglicans. All agreed that they find a woman priest "easier to talk to." One expressed the opinion that "some men feel threatened by women priests."

Two converts to the Episcopal Church are included in the sample: Ernestine Motley, a member of the St. Matthias congregation who grew up in the Baptist Church, and Margaret Higginbotham, a visitor, who grew up in an AME Church in a small town in western Pennsylvania. Motley likes the liturgy, especially "the communion, kneeling at the altar." She feels that the congregational experience is "warm—like finding a family you had lost." Higginbotham finds that the "ritual—gestures, movements, symbols"—because it separates corporate worship from the everyday ("something you don't do all the time"), gives a sense of being "closer to the spiritual realm." The "sense of order makes me feel more religious." She "needs that help," though she is sensitive to the fact that this worship style sometimes makes her physician-husband uncomfortable. It's important to both of them, she said, "not to be false," to really understand the meaning of liturgical actions. Higginbotham is impressed generally with the importance of study and discussion in the Episcopal Church. In her congregation, the large, flourishing Church of the Good Shepherd in Los Angeles, she is glad to find "intelligent people who can sit down and communicate with you." There are for her no significant theological differences between AME and Episcopal faith communities; the major difference is in worship style. She finds women in the Episcopal Church "more supportive, less competitive" with one another and with men. "We must support our men," she adds emphatically. As for women clergy, Higginbotham sees this change as part of the broader fight for liberation in all parts of society, "not as a big difference," or as a separate characteristic of church life.

Sadie Mitchell, a lifelong member of St. Thomas and a priest serving as an assistant at St. Luke's, believes that the impact of recent liturgical changes and a recent influx of converts from other denominations have led people to question "why things are being done," to "want to know the meaning behind" liturgical action, shaking up "cradle Episcopalians," who, with generations of the tradition behind them, have "a tendency to become complacent." Confirmation classes she believes, invite the use of reason. Asked about congregational interest in *Lift Every Voice*, a supplemental Episcopal hymnal of worship music in the black church tradition, Mitchell pointed out a significant difference between its use in St. Thomas ("a lot") and in St. Luke's ("occasional, mostly at the offertory"). Very few people in either parish are much interested in diocesan affairs, although in both churches interest is encouraged by the clergy. Commitment is primarily parochial. Interestingly, as a continuing legacy of its shared historic roots with the AME Church, St. Thomas has more direct involvement with the black church community than does St. Luke's, a congregation that has been identified as a black parish for less than twenty years.[27] "Women's issues" are distinctly unimportant to these women. The consecration of Barbara Harris was of great interest to them only "because they know her," not because of the historic issues involved. Both congregations were well represented at the service in Boston.

Though none of the women interviewed consider recent changes in the liturgy or in the role of women especially significant in their worship experience, all are sensitive to the different liturgical and worship interests of their men, and concerned about the effects of this difference on the life of the church and on their family lives. Casimir and Higginbotham, for example, reported diametrically opposite experiences of the importance of theological study and discussion in the Episcopal Church. Fresh understandings of our similarities and differences continuously grow out of such dialogue across the cultural diversities within the community of black Episcopal women.

Episcopal Women of the Past, a recent publication of the Episcopal Churchwomen of the Diocese of Pennsylvania, provides brief biographical sketches of sixty-nine women whose gifts for ministry helped shape the lives of our congregations in this century.[28] Twelve are black women; three have Caribbean ties; four are wives of priests; six are professional teachers or social workers; six are noted for fund-raising; eight are leaders of parish ECW groups, seven have given significant leadership diocesan and broader church levels; eight have had significant public recognition for their community leadership and service; and four are associated with St. Thomas Church, continuing that congregation's tradition of leadership in this faith community. They are, indeed, broadly representative of black Philadelphia women in the Episcopal Church; their ministries are generally similar to those of white women in this diocese and in the church everywhere. We are far more alike, after all, than we are different.

Toward Reconciliation: The Pathfinders

I speak for my race and my people—the human race and just people.
Pauli Murray, *Dark Testament*

Possibly because most of the first group of women to enter the priesthood were, like Pauli Murray, coming from careers in other fields and from significant experiences as active laywomen, there is a keen awareness among women priests of the priesthood of all believers, and a deep awareness of our continuing connectedness to one another's ministries.[29] So it is appropriate for us to hear the voices of three ordained women who have been models, mentors, encouragers for countless others, lay and ordained, serving as exemplars of the ministry to which we are each differently called.

Pauli Murray, the first African American woman ordained to the priesthood, wrote of her first celebration of the eucharist in the North Carolina chapel where her grandmother had been baptized as a slave child:

> Whatever future ministry I might have as a priest, it was given to me that day to be a symbol of healing. All the strands of my life came together. Descendant of slave and of slave owner, I had already been called poet, lawyer, teacher, and friend. Now I was empowered to minister the sacrament of One in whom there is no north nor south, no black nor white, no male or female—only the spirit of love and reconciliation drawing us all toward the goal of human wholeness.[30]

Of that mixed heritage, Murray said in her family memoir, "I had to recognize that my grandmother's story was a human story as old as the Biblical narrative of Abraham, his bondwoman Hagar, and their son Ishmael; and that it pointed up the complex interrelationships within slavery that defied monolithical classification." Her grandmother, Murray believed, saw her own life "as a symbol of the possibility of reconciliation between races and classes."

Nan Arrington Peete, Canon to the Ordinary in the Diocese of Atlanta, carried the ministry of reconciliation forward in somewhat different terms. She brought to her new work significant experience in the corporate world as a management consultant, and in her first parish served a middle-class congregation in Indianapolis, where she encouraged development of a refuge for the homeless. Speaking at the 1988 Lambeth Conference of bishops from the worldwide Anglican communion, Peete observed, "Today we celebrate the life and witness of Mary Magdalene, the first one to whom the Risen Christ had chosen to be revealed, and who was charged to go and tell the others. The least expected one was the chosen one to the disbelief of the other disciples. In the fullness of time Mary had seen the Lord."[31]

This theme of the fulfillment of God's purpose in bringing together what has seemed irremediably separate is repeated in what Peete had to say of the service of consecration for Barbara Harris: "We rejoice because the possibilities and opportunities we had once thought closed, God has now opened. Barbara's consecration has made it possible that everybody's gifts can be used to their fullest."[32] Peete's own ministry has remained significantly directed toward the oppressed and the marginal in the society.

In a conversation about women in ministry, Barbara Harris noted many connections between her own ministry and those of her sisters in the faith.[33] Like Peete, she had a successful career in corporate management, and she has a distinguished record of ministry to the hungry and the incarcerated. "Pauli Murray," she said, "was partly responsible for my pursuing ordination. Her advice to me was, 'Get yourself in a seminary.' " Thus, Harris's journey toward ordination found her well prepared for her role as guide, mentor, and encourager for others—men and women, lay and ordained. As she responded to the invitation of the Diocese of Massachusetts to the ministry of bishop, Harris reminded members of the diocesan convention that "our walk together must begin venturing out on that broad platform of faith. Although we may not see clearly the full pathway that lies before us, we know that the God who chooses the foolish things of the world to confound the wise and the weak things of the world to confound the mighty has brought us safe thus far, and we trust our God for the next step of the journey."[34]

The next step of the journey was, for Harris and for the church, the day of Shalom—some have called it "another Pentecost"—in Boston: on February 11, 1989, she was consecrated Suffragan Bishop of Massachusetts. Peete wrote of this event:

> The ends of the world have met. In July of 1988 the *London Times* ran a picture of Barbara greeting Li Tim-Oi. The caption read, 'The Rev. Barbara Harris, who wants to be the first woman bishop, meets the first woman priest.' What a wonderfully prophetic picture to open the Lambeth Conference! Then on February 11, 1989, Li Tim-Oi came to participate

in Barbara's consecration and I watched them exchange greetings during the Peace. For me, this meeting of these two women, so small in stature but so large in spiritual presence, was one of those once in a lifetime, moving moments. It took place quietly and in a simple embrace that brought tears to the eyes. The word was made flesh.[35]

And what did Li Tim-Oi, understand this event to mean?

I, a Chinese woman, was ordained the first Anglican woman priest and now Harris, a Black woman, is consecrated as the first woman bishop. To me, this certainly has great significance, since the Anglican Communion was predominantly in the hands of the White race in the past. This evolution helps the Anglican Communion play an increasing role as peacemaker in a multi-racial society. And it cannot be denied that racial peacemaking is particularly important as the 21st century is fast approaching. This connection immediately calls to mind what St Paul said: "For Christ Himself has brought us peace by making Jews and Gentiles one people. With His own body He broke down the wall that separated them and kept them enemies."[36]

In that service not only was the congregation "truly a gathering of the Church Catholic," with many people from various parts of the country representing different ethnic backgrounds and different cultures,[37] but the liturgy was also intentionally planned to speak of and to the whole world. After a musical prelude in the classic European and Anglican traditions, a Chinese choir and an AME choir were followed by the Schola Cantorum singing Anglican chant. The Gospel was read in Spanish as well as in English. The new bishop's vestments were made of Italian silk and Ghanaian kente; symbols were embroidered in Greek and Ashanti. Alla Renee Bozarth wrote of this entire experience, "It's Pentecost again."[38]

Many of the congregation heard their own voices in the service with new clarity, as they recognized fragments of their own heritage in the words and the music of worship. "Each of us, carrying out faithfully our own ministries wherever God calls us, can own this new perception of our special place in God's wholeness and love. We can know that that place begins where we are being our own best selves, made in God's image—women, men, Asian, Hispanic, European, African, American—each part of the divine self expression."[39]

Toward the Kingdom . . . Already but Not Yet . . .

In June 1990 the Union of Black Episcopalians (UBE) met in Philadelphia, with a commitment to work toward increasing the number of blacks both in ministry generally and in positions of authority and power. Further, the Union was determined to build up the diminishing population of young black Episcopalians. This was the first truly intergenerational conference of the UBE; the young delegates sat with the main conference rather than in the traditional separate meeting room. The title of the conference, "Do the Right Thing: The Challenge for the Church in the 90's," recognized the centrality of the youthful presence. And the conference took seriously the comments of a sixteen-year-old representative from Connecticut who attributed the prevalence of black crime against blacks to a lack of self-esteem rooted in young people's ignorance of African American history. The conference concluded with the election of Judith Conley, a former youth adviser, as president.

Black women at work in the church continue to seek new ways of developing ministry that reaches effectively into the lives of young people. Sadie Mitchell is convener of the Black Clericus, an informal association of black clergy in the Diocese of Pennsylvania, whose members have undertaken a proactive course of recruiting, encouraging, and supporting young African American candidates for ordained ministry. Mary Adebonojo, a former youth ministry coordinator for the diocese, represented women clergy of the diocese in the 1991 ordination of the first women priests in the diocese of Mityana, Uganda, Africa.

In 1992 the nationwide celebration of two hundred years of the black presence in the Episcopal Church will culminate in a November Service at St. Thomas Church, Philadelphia, with Archbishop Desmond Tutu of South Africa as a special guest.

In this fragmentary and partial account, told in the voices of some of the women whose story it is,[40] Philadelphia—word and city—has served as paradigm for the whole ministry of twentieth-century African American women in the Episcopal Church. Other voices[41] will be heard as we continue our journey, with our sisters and brothers of every race and nation, in the ministry of God's reconciling love: that all may be one.

Acknowledgment

The author is deeply grateful to her informants and to the countless others whose story this is. Special thanks to the Reverend Van S. Bird, Philadelphia priest and sociologist, for his thoughtful review and helpful comments.

Notes

1. Lydia Wright, *The Black Experience in the Episcopal Church* (Cincinnati: Forward Movement, 1986), pp. 8, 9.

2. Kit and Frederica Konolige, *The Power of Their Glory* (New York: Wyden Books, 1978), especially p. 372.

3. Note, also, plans for the bicentennial celebration of Historic St. Thomas Episcopal Church in Philadelphia: "To educate the wider Episcopal Church about the historical witness of the African-American Episcopal Church." Frances I. Clark and Arthur K. Sudler, chairpersons, memorandum, 22 April 1991.

4. See on this, Mary S. Donovan, *Women Priests in the Episcopal Church* (Cincinnati: Forward Movement, 1988), p. 7.

5. Michael D. Schaeffer, "Episcopal Bishops Meet to Talk of Unity," *Philadelphia Inquirer,* 23 September 1989. See also Richard H. Schmidt, "Bishops Pull Together on Episcopal Visitors Plan," in *Episcopalian* (Diocese of Pennsylvania) 154 (November 1989): 1ff.

6. Lawrence J. Goodrich, "Pact Smooths over Controversy," *Christian Science Monitor,* 6 October 1989.

7. Clark and Sudler, memorandum.

8. Deborah Hines and Barbara Harris in separate conversations—21 August 1989 and 13 December 1988, respectively—identified this document as key to understanding the position of black women on feminist issues. Myrtle Gordon, "Black Women's Agenda: Part 1," and "Black Women's Agenda: Part 2," *Witness* 65 (February and March 1982).

9. Hines, quoted in Gordon, "Black Women's Agenda: Part 1," pp. 5–8.

10. Ibid., pp. 8–9.

11. Mattie Hopkins, quoted in Gordon, "Black Women's Agenda: Part 2," p. 16.

12. Harris, quoted ibid., p. 18. It is important to note in this connection that Harris has been widely honored for her contributions to the general women's movement. For example, the Lucretia Mott Award of Women's Way, Philadelphia, recognized her effective "opposition to racism and her struggle for the advancement of women" (15 May 1989).

13. Ibid.

14. Barbara Harris, "Cloud of Witnesses" (Paper presented at Conference on Afro-Anglicanism, Barbados, June 1985,) p. 14.

15. "The Black Women's Task Force of the Episcopal Church," brochure, n.d.

16. William Douglas, *Annals of the First African Church in the United States of America—The African Episcopal Church of St Thomas* (Philadelphia: King & Baird, 1862), p. 2.

17. Ibid. p. 11.

18. Ibid. p. 15.

African American Women in the Episcopal Church

237

19. Ibid. p. 23.

20. Wright, *The Black Experience in the Episcopal Church,* especially, pp. 7, 8.

21. Jeffrey, quoted in Joyce M. Howard, "The Church's Work among Negroes" (Paper delivered at the Episcopal Women's History Project, Austin, Texas, 1–3 June 1982), p. 43.

22. Ibid. p. 46.

23. Joyce M. Howard, "A Wonderful Purpose—An Account of Black Women Working in the Episcopal Church" (unpublished paper, 1989).

24. Ibid., p. 138.

25. Ibid., p. 56; "A Teacher's Love," *Leader,* (Philadelphia), 18 July 1990; "Planting the Seeds—," *Philadelphia Inquirer,* 17 May 1990.

26. See on multiple church memberships, Kortright Davis, *Emancipation Still Comin': Explorations in Caribbean Emancipatory Theology* (Maryknoll, N.Y.: Orbis Books, 1989), p. 52.

27. St. Luke's Church, where the Reverend Sadie S. Mitchell serves as assistant to the rector, the Reverend Canon Charles Poindexter, is among the largest, most affluent congregations in the diocese. A relative newcomer to the black church community, St. Luke's—like St. Matthias—is a congregation that gradually replaced a white congregation as the community changed. Kimberly Turner, "Black Ministries in the Diocese of Pennsylvania" (brochure, 1990), identifies 19 congregations of the 181 in the diocese as black ministries. Of these 8 are missions, 11 are independent, 7 are served by white clergy, 2 are served by women priests.

28. Episcopal Churchwomen of the Diocese of Philadelphia, *Episcopal Women of the Past* (1986), shows Mary Harbison Logan as exemplifying the clergy connection among women church workers: her husband, John; sons John, Jr., and Thomas; and grandson, Thomas, Jr., have together given well over one hundred years to priestly ministry.

29. Pauli Murray, *Song in a Weary Throat* (New York: Harper & Row, 1987), p. 435. Like Harris (*n. 12 supra*), Murray was active in the national movement for women's rights; in 1966 she worked with Betty Friedan and others to organize the National Organization for Women (NOW).

30. Pauli Murray, *Proud Shoes* (New York: Harper & Row, 1956), pp. xv, xvii. "There was a self-imposed silence about the past" (p. ixn). In Philadelphia the Sarah-Hagar theme was explored in a series of 1990 sessions of Women Interacting, an informal group of white and black women, lay and ordained, convened by Jerrie Bartlett and with a leadership team that included, along with other white women, several black women active in diocesan ministries.

31. Nan Arrington Peete, "In the Fullness of Time" (Paper delivered at the Lambeth conference, 22 July 1988).

32. Nan Arrington Peete, "The Ends of the World Have Met," *Witness* 72 (April 1989): 26. The entire issue is devoted to papers on the ordination of Barbara Harris as bishop.

33. Barbara Harris, 13 December 1988.

34. Barbara Harris, remarks to Diocesan Committee, Diocese of Massachusetts, 4 November 1988.

35. Peete, "The Ends of the World Have Met," p. 26.

36. "Li Tim-Oi on Barbara Harris," *Witness* 72 (April 1989): 7.

37. Peete, "The Ends of the World Have Met," p. 27.

38. Alla Bozarth, "Pentecost Again," *Witness* 72 (April 1989): 24.

39. Marjorie Farmer, "Spirited, Happy-go-lucky Barbara . . . ," *Witness* 72 (April 1989): 5.

40. Conversations with many women other than those named, among them Elizabeth Forrester and Karey Smith, the first two black women to serve as presidents of the Episcopal Church Women in the Diocese of Pennsylvania; Jane Cosby, a former president of the Philadelphia Chapter of UBE and a member of the bishop's staff; and especially all the women of St. Matthias Church have helped provide the information and understandings that have shaped this chapter. Verna Dozier, a widely respected Washington, D.C., educator and leader among lay ministers, adds the promise of reconciliation across the newer barrier of age ("Saying 'Yes' in a 'No' World," *Witness* 75 [May 1990]: 8, 9.

41. Out of the more than 15,000 clergy listed in *Episcopal Clerical Directory 1991, The Directory of Black Clergy in the Episcopal Church 1990* identifies 494 black persons. Of these, 22 are bishops, including 1 woman; 439 are priests, including 30 women; 33 are deacons, including 15 women. Of 26 postulants and candidates for ordination, 6 are women. The appointed staff at the Episcopal Church Center includes 23 black church professionals, 13 of whom are women. Of the 20 black diocesan executives throughout the country, 6 are women. Resources for further inquiry include *Linkage,* a newsletter of the Office of Black Ministries, and *Jubilee—Social Concerns and the Episcopal Church.* Both are available through the Office for Black Ministries in the Episcopal Church Center. The *U.B.E. News* is available through the Office of the Treasurer, Box #87, Lawrenceville, VA 23868–0087.

7

Women's Works of Devotion: Feasts, Fairs, and Festivities

Irene Q. Brown

Interviewer: When do you feel nearest to God? What do you experience, what do you feel?

A: Well, I'm probably happiest when I think I've done something *genuine* for another person. It doesn't have to be that I've said something about God, but just that I feel like it was God who helped me. But it *always* concerns a relation to another person. I can get one of these lightning-fast certainties that it was God, it was God's happiness and God's love and all that. . . .

Interviewer: What's your picture of God's kingdom?

A: . . . when people live in love without broken relations to one another.

For another person in the same congregation God's kingdom

is here, in this world everyday. We see it in our relations with others. I can tell you two situations where I'm especially aware of God's kingdom. First, in church almost every Sunday. And second, when I talk to people in day-to-day situations and I feel we really reach one another. When that happens I feel there's been contact and learning, some kind of progress. You experience God's kingdom when you help another person or are helped by another person, when you give another person what they most need, whether that's a word about God or a pair of shoes.[1]

These interview segments come from an anthropological study of a Lutheran Pietist congregation in modern-day Stockholm. They are the words of two women who will help us to understand an important aspect of the religious life of an older Episcopal woman from New England. She no longer goes to church every Sunday, but she has made a major commitment to the church's soup kitchen, which I view as a significant expression of her spirituality.

I

Concentrating on commitment and spirituality, the anthropologist Peter Stromberg did not consider the significance that gender might play in shaping either. In particular, he explored how believers experienced grace—what he calls commitment—individually, in a way that also affirmed group solidarity. He found commitment and community are both built on a shared but not identically experienced body of beliefs or symbols. Therefore, community does not rest on consensus and orthodoxy but always on an authentic relationship between individuals in community. In modern-day Sweden the Pietist tradition allows for this resolution of individualism and communitarianism through this process of individual commitment. In Stromberg's view, however, this resolution also has implications for churches and other committed groups elsewhere. I believe it has particularly important implications for appreciating women's spirituality and participation in church life.

Stromberg's insightful and subtle work is especially important for illuminating the perennial feminization-of-piety issue. Christianity and other forces have traditionally fostered female cultural preferences for thinking and acting in relational terms.[2] Women's piety may therefore rest, more easily than does men's, on the transformational power of commitment. If that is true, then we need to look at women's ways of expressing commitment by interpreting what they actually do in churches as part of their spirituality.

If sociality and grace/commitment are interpreted by believers as manifestations of salvation, as Stromberg argues, then how women contribute to sociality deserves close attention.[3] This chapter can only begin such an exploration. It does so mainly by listening to one cradle Episcopalian's account of how she contributed to the life of her church through what we have come to call "traditional" female church work. More than a decade ago, two scholars concluded, "New forms of theory are needed to account for middle class church participation." They particularly urged "greater attention [be paid] to motivations generated by church life itself, both doctrinal and social, than has been true in the past."[4] Stromberg's theory, taken together with a closer look especially at what women actually do in churches and why they do it, may contribute to such an effort, especially if it is sensitive to individual voices.

In his recent assessment of scholarly work on religious change, Wade Clark Roof expressed frustration at the difficulty of tracing such change, much less interpreting its meaning. To be sure, the use of survey techniques has heightened our appreciation of the social characteristics of church-oriented religion, but these techniques have also decided limitations. "The religious impulses most important in personal and social experience are often beyond the grasp of institutional indicators and standard survey items."[5] One solution, not without its own dilemmas, in his view, is the biographical approach, including a focus on the life-cycle pattern among churched and unchurched.

> There is a need for intensive individual life histories and the events surrounding individual decisions to drop out of, or return to, the churches. . . . Despite its limitations . . . , biographical analysis can reveal important insights into the interrelation of religious and secular themes, and *especially as these interact with age and gender experiences, indeed it may be the only way to explore the subtle shifts of religious meaning and belonging as they relate to personal identities and distinctive experiences* [emphasis added].[6]

This chapter explores some of the subtle shifts of meaning and belonging expressed by one informant who reflects on her long life in the Episcopal Church. The interview centered especially on her participation in "traditional woman's church work." It revealed a surprising degree of ambivalence—not so much about such work but about the meaning of belonging to her church. Both church and society have markedly changed since she first became a member in the 1920s. Rather than documenting the reality of this change, we hope the interview will allow us to assess more fully what meaning change had for our Episcopalian.

Following our informant's words and thoughts about her work, in a biographical framework, we are sensitized to the meanings she attaches to her actions.[7] Her sense of loss is connected with the labor she performed in her church, and therefore with her gender. And this was a significant loss. The work of her hands belonged to her practices of commitment, and, I argue, to her devotional life. In still another way her experience of change was connected to her gender. Many changes in her church involved efforts to include women more fully in the life of the church. Thus, at one level, her account becomes sadly ironic. At a deeper level, however, it reveals once again, how subtly gender colors experience.

Survey techniques and statistical analysis, although they may well confirm its existence, appear particularly inadequate to capture the subtleties of female religiosity.[8] Studies show women are more churched, and perhaps more pious than men, and have been so in the American Northeast since the day of Cotton Mather. But one looks in vain for a thorough examination of this phenomenon in the publications of the society devoted to the scientific study of religion, for example. We still have much to learn about the meaning of holiness and the sacred in the lives of women, both past and present. One reason may be that women have continued to perform certain service functions in the family and in society, which makes it more difficult to separate their lives as neatly into public and private roles as one can men's.

A significant part of our informant's religious commitment occurred at the intersection of the sacred and mundane world, what I am calling the world of feasts, festivities, and bazaars of women's traditional church work. These activities held much significance for her, even if she did not or could not express their value in so many words, perhaps even to herself. Thus, as the church changed, the loss of those half-known, half-felt meanings could not be acknowledged. Nor could she readily shift from the church of her childhood, youth, and years of maturity—spent largely in a separated, gendered church life—to the new life of a more homogeneous, gender-inclusive institution. Powerful but unacknowledged associations to old ways still remained. Her familiar world had been disrupted, without any explicit process that might have helped her to recognize how she needed to disengage in order to make new commitments to new ways.

Hans Mol has suggested that the process of sacralization and commitment also requires desacralization, decommitment. As an example, he used the marriage rite in which the bride leaves her family of origin to join the family "she is now forming with her new husband."[9] Interestingly, he sees her decommitment from her family but does not consider the possibility that the bridegroom has a similar experience. Female decommitment is exaggerated and becomes too distinctively a female phenomenon. But this does not deny the validity of exploring the process of decommitment, or even desacralization, as it affects either sex.

Ties may well have different meanings, and involve different myths and denials, for women than they do for men. Men are encouraged to form "new families" in such a way that their breaking a tie with kin is denied altogether. For women, by contrast, the shift from new to old may be less dramatic, and more subtle than Mols suggests. Female decommitment may always be incomplete; old ties may remain not only latent but real, especially because they are linked to family identity and early childhood, years in which personal identity itself took shape. This process of decommitment and commitment has significance for any church, I submit, that seeks to move into a new age with congregations of many women from different generations, some with ties to past church lives that they treasure in ways hitherto hidden to others, if not themselves.

One way we can begin to trace these ties and associations, commitments and decommitments, is to ask more about them. In our case, a striking feature of our informant's life is that she experienced a significant degree of alienation from her lifelong church at the same time that she was widowed. How that personal crisis confounded her associational life cannot be fully explored, but it surely raised her expectations about the need for belonging. That conflation of crises made any move in the direction of decommitment problematic, I suspect, without some special response from her religious community. Quite likely, moreover, such an institutional response was wanting, in part, because we do not appreciate the role of decommitment in women.

Too preoccupied with attachments when it comes to the female gender, our culture and to some extent even recent feminists have tended to undervalue the need for separation. This can even have consequences for churches, where women are often a majority. In the case of our informant, at least, her recommitment and reattachment to a changed but still-loved church has remained partial. Is she only partially committed now because she could not attach herself fully to the new church she found too alien? Or was she unable to detach herself satisfactorily from what she saw as the old?

From Robert Wuthnow we know that surveys between 1972 and 1984 show Episcopalians, along with Presbyterians and Jews, as unusual in having a majority of feminist women, and a higher proportion of educated women than did most other denominations.[10] Our informant, however, was neither a feminist nor a highly educated woman. As a lifelong employed woman, however, she had much in common with feminists and with formally educated women. As we shall see, she is not completely forthright about her views. The word *feminism* does not appear in the interview, nor does *liberal* or *conservative*. But it is clear she is speaking about changes that she has experienced in her church.

Wuthnow noted two features in the surveys of American churches in the 1970s and 1980s. First, feminism was one of the issues that separated liberals from conservatives. Second, education was not a force for overcoming prejudices between them. Quite the opposite: conservative college graduates held more antiliberal views than did conservatives without a college education. "And among liberals—perhaps because they tend to be better educated than conservatives—this tendency [to be intolerant] was even stronger." Surveys revealed that the division between liberals and conservatives within the same denomination was so strong that they held higher negative images and feelings about each other than they did about those belonging to other denominations (p. 219).

Wuthnow found that prejudices against others did not diminish among church members with more education. Nor did proximity, family relationships, or friendship make a difference. Only one rarely practiced method, involving the heart and, perhaps significantly, the divine, transformed attitudes. According to his analysis of survey data, people's negative impressions of one another declined only if the type of contact involved

> intimate communications, for example, in prayer fellowship. Unfortunately, however, these kinds of settings were not the most common sources of contact. Instead, each group was most likely to have had contact with the other "among friends or neighbors," "among family or relatives," "at work," or "in a former church." All of these settings resulted in higher than average levels of negative stereotyping. (p. 217)

In these seldom-applied methods involving intimacy, we may indeed be seeing the results of commitment or grace, as Stromberg uses those terms. In any case, this evidence is suggestive for exploring more closely what else, apart from prayer fellowship, might constitute intimate communication in churches.

In my view women's traditional church work, the practice of working together for a common good—namely, the welfare of the godly and loving community—is precisely such an arena of church activity involving such intimate communication. We will see traces of this meaning as our informant speaks of her church work. We learn, sometimes by indirection and never as completely as we might wish, how that work exemplified and to some degree still does, a habit and practice of commitment to a beloved institution of a lifetime. What follows is an exploration of religious practices that are part of a long tradition of female piety that we are beginning to understand more fully at the same time that women's institutional role in churches is also gaining authority. This bodes well for the future of mainline churches.

II

We'll begin with a look at the life of a woman in her mid-seventies who has been actively involved in a soup kitchen ever since it was established by her Episcopal church eight years ago. She also continues to make items for the Christmas bazaar. Apart from this church work, however, she is now strangely distanced from the church of her childhood, youth, and mature years. In her lifetime not only the United States but also her church changed markedly, and so of course did her own life and some of her expectations about it. She knows that, too. In speaking of those years past, she avoids nostalgia, catching herself momentarily, so that in the end she gives an account that is remarkably dry and matter of fact. She is, after all, speaking with a total stranger, and she is remembering deeply felt times.[11]

Our talk skirts around some of those times. Although eager for the sake of this project, I find I cannot ask her every question, especially not some about her faith, about the times and the way she prayed. Held back by my own reserve, I realize some questions cannot be asked by a stranger.[12] Questions about her devotions seem too intrusive; they touch on intimacies more private than some family matters might be.

So in the end this interview becomes an exploration of the traces of the life of a woman who was significantly committed to her church. It did not yield the full path. Others are needed for that research, probably those who already have the trust of such women as Mrs. Langlois, not researchers who appear for a lengthy interview only to disappear again. And yet such traces of a committed life that has not flourished as completely as one might expect offer enough to explore the spiritual and not only the communal and financial dimension of women's handwork in the life of the church.

A project concerned with Episcopal women needs to try to understand the ambivalence that a lifelong Episcopalian like Mrs. Langlois has reached in her old age. Is it a coincidence that she still contributes to the Christmas bazaar, or that she has joined the soup kitchen more recently, while in other ways removing herself from the church that once occupied much more of her life? Soup kitchens are an example of special purpose groups that, as Robert Wuthnow has noted, have proliferated in recent years and act as intermediaries between church and sect.[13]

What attracted Mrs. Langlois to such an intermediary group, while the larger church community failed to do so?

Our congregational survey asked women about their participation in "'traditional women's work'—fund-raising through crafts, bazaars, or dinners." In three of the four parishes, it was still a significant activity for 20 percent to 30 percent of the women, who saw it as a way to build community, and who appreciated its financial contribution. Others were forthright in their near-scorn for such work, some explicitly contrasting it with Bible reading and Bible study. Joanna B. Gillespie's chapter explains more fully how the parishes differ on their mixture of regard and disregard for this traditional women's work. One parish stands out in having a truly unique group of elderly craftswomen, another for experimenting with a new group of mothers who meet on Friday evenings to talk, and, interestingly, to sew. The very range of opinion about such church work is itself revealing. In an age when choices and pluralism are otherwise so highly appreciated, such church work appears meaningless, even oppressive, to some, while it is welcomed by others. What such a range of views just among women church members might mean for individual congregations is worth pondering.

In this chapter I want to explore the possibility that this traditionally feminized activity not only has significance for the social and financial well-being of the church but also is an expression of female spirituality. Our survey did not invite women to tell us whether this work had spiritual significance for them. Indeed, one might well ask whether many could have admitted to such a significance on a questionnaire. To the extent that it exists, I suspect, the spiritual meaning of such church work is quite well hidden beneath consciousness, even as it is felt. To acknowledge such feelings, to articulate them, is itself a novel process that requires care.

Our cultural conditioning as women is powerful. The idea that this kind of carefully wrought work of our fingers and hands, sometimes performed around the edges of other activities, could have religious meaning might even strike some as a profanity. They may be persuaded that there is a wide gap between the work of nimble fingers and the devotional life. But why does the church bazaar continue to thrive in this postindustrial consumer society? Is it only the thrill of finding a bargain and the chance to raise money that underlie these ritual events associated with Christmas? Or is it not part of a counterculture that uses the "second language of habits of commitment and tradition," as examined in the study *Habits of the Heart?*[14] That counterculture rejects the commercialized holiday spirit and yearns for the genuine article, the authentic gift, freely given, primarily by women, mostly purchased by women, only to be given in turn to other women.[15] If the fuller meaning of this exchange of giving that has partially incorporated the cash nexus were more fully explored by the artisans and the community, what might *be* the consequences for the church and for the women involved in that newly validated handwork? To begin to answer these questions, let us turn now more closely to the life of Mrs. Langlois as she has revealed parts of it to this interviewer.

Her interview points to a longing for belonging and community that is also connected with her sense of self. Following in the interpretive line of the anthropologist Peter Stromberg, I argue that in her search for a Christian religious community, she is indeed seeking the experience of grace, what he alternately terms "moments of discovery," "the presence of God," or a "free gift." Stromberg the scholar prefers the neutral, "non-spiritual" synonym—commitment—to describe such experiences.[16] In speaking about her handwork, Mrs. Langlois is not simply looking for any association of craftspeople or even a fellowship of those who seek to help the needy. Her interview conveys a readiness for a renewed commitment to the church of her past or, more guardedly even, to the transformed church of her past. At some level her involvement with crafts has religious meaningfulness, as distinct from meaning, a distinction that Stromberg uses to convey a level of significance that is not readily articulated even to oneself, much less to others. "Grace is a possibility for commitment and transformation, for establishing a relation to the symbol that entails a highly personal meaningfulness for the believer . . . I do not say *meaning,* for such a relationship is not necessarily articulable, and it is certainly not significant mainly as a vehicle for communication to others" (p. 52).

The interview also conveys a reticence, for real and legitimate reasons, having to do with Mrs. Langlois's responsibilities as a caregiver, and with the limitations on her mobility she faces as an old single woman. Finally, she also projects a certain amount of diffidence, a reluctance to initiate, to ask for assistance, reflecting her ambivalence about the changes she knows and accepts about her church. Yet it is her willingness to work for the bazaar and the soup kitchen that stands as an open invitation to bring her into the community more fully again. That, I suggest, however, can happen only if the spiritual significance of her handwork is more fully recognized by the community she once joined so completely and for which she still yearns. Let us turn now to learn more about Mrs. Langlois, her work life, marriage, and church involvement. We will conclude by briefly considering the potential spiritual significance of women's handwork for the church today.

Margaret (Benton) Langlois has been a lifelong Episcopalian in her native place, a New England mill town, where she was born in 1914. This daughter of English immigrants was brought to the local Episcopal church nursery when she was two years old. A few years later she learned her catechism "a page at a time" and was confirmed at twelve. When seventeen or eighteen, she became a textile worker at the factory where her father had initially been employed. The company president, the superintendent, the chemist, and the foreman, she emphasizes in her interview, were all Episcopalians, as were other white-collar employees. As an Episcopal pieceworker on the floor, however, she was unusual.

A few years later, in 1938, she was again an unusual Episcopalian, though not the only one in the area, when she married a Roman Catholic from a French-Canadian family. Her husband supported her wish to raise their children in her faith. With the help of her rector, who to her surprise had some experience with such matters, and a Roman Catholic priest in a nearby community—not the local one—their carefully laid plans were realized. A Roman Catholic wedding did not mean their two children grew up Roman Catholic. She took them to her church; her husband went to his, down the street. She saw no reason that he should give up his faith for her sake, although he had offered to do so. One of the unusual features of this arrangement was that the French-Canadian grandparents would come to church events involving their granddaughter and grandson. For the grandmother, and kinkeeper, this must have been somewhat poignant. Earlier she had insisted the children, and especially her grandson, be raised Roman Catholic. But her son and daughter-in-law had defied her wish. "She gave up," said the daughter-in-law quite firmly, even now, years later. And so the grandparents came to the Episcopal programs, "even though few French Catholics even went *into* the Episcopal church."

Margaret Langlois worked for twenty-five years at the textile mill, in the years of the Depression, World War II, and the postwar boom, retiring in the mid-1950s, without a pension, at a time when her two children were teenagers. Her sister, who still lives downstairs with her now quite ailing husband, took care of Margaret's children while she worked. Moreover, her retirement was brief. A friend persuaded her to take a new job at a nearby motor factory. She stayed there for fifteen years before really retiring from paid employment, this time with a small pension. "The work was easy," she still remembers.

Those years of gainful employment, the busy years of her marriage and motherhood, were also busy years of church work. She served in the Altar Guild (twice as directrice), and raised money through the Service League. She recalls feeling such a sense of peace while performing her duties, even if it was not always convenient for her to be there. Handling the special treasures that people had given for use at the altar long ago, she felt, was a sacred trust. The donors "were looking down at you." Even now she still appreciated the rector's wife, who had told her "only certain people can do that work, . . . have a feeling for it. . . . I was very friendly with the rector and his wife, . . . she reminded me so much of my mother."

For years Margaret also helped with church suppers and contributed aprons, knickknacks, and Christmas decorations to the annual bazaar. "The church needs money; you help out . . . instead of giving money yourself. The Christmas bazaar raised $3,000!" Lots of people participate. There is much planning; she emphasizes that, takes pride in it. The things are handmade. "People really appreciate what they buy. They get more for their money." Only later in the conversation does she mention that she also personally valued the fact that for years the work of the bazaar was conducted in the homes of women who met together to do it.

At this point she is still preoccupied with the pleasure of doing a good job, serving the public in ways that lead to sales, and that even involve kin who share her values. A few years ago, she mentions, her niece who had brought her Methodist husband into the Episcopal Church, and who now lives in Arizona, had sent two new items that had been "hot sellers" from her bazaar; mother and aunt might want to copy them for their bazaar. Sitting in her sparklingly clean living room, with a partially completed sweater in her lap, she describes the items with delight, especially the little cotton handkerchief that had a dual, and I would emphasize a sacred, purpose. It could be a bonnet for a baby's baptism, or a daughter could use it at her wedding! Bazaars are by no means disappearing, she emphasizes. Quite the opposite; there is even much competition between them.

She still makes things for the bazaar, but the church, and even the work of the bazaar have changed, as have her private life and her involvement with the church. In these alterations one hears the echoes of developments that have touched the larger Episcopal Church as it moved into the latter half of the twentieth century.

Mrs. Langlois's husband died in 1977—"I was still working. I gave up the Altar Guild," she explains. "There was nothing to draw me to church. There are a lot of youth programs now," she adds. Transportation became difficult, and at her age she no longer walked so easily the considerable distance from her neighborhood, across the river, to the church. She also felt more and more strange in the church of her youth, where the choir and organ are in a different location in the sanctuary. She misses some of the old, familiar music. "Times have changed, I liked it better the other way; . . . the prayers have all changed. . . . I have to read the bulletin." Withdrawing more and more from the larger church, she continued to meet with other women in their homes, however, making things for the bazaar: "That was the only thing that attracted me."

But after four years of widowhood another activity also began to attract her. She and her sister were among the first church members to join the new soup kitchen that has become a thriving, major institution, now supported by several denominations and other civic organizations. She works there two days a week, clearly feels efficacious, and has gained some real insights into the lives of the people who come there for their meals, and into herself. "Until I came there I never knew the problems people have. . . . Some drink, some are retarded, others can't hold a job. People socialize there. It's like a second home to them. Their faces light up. . . . If you have a tendency to feel sorry for yourself [this experience at the kitchen] puts that into perspective. . . . You feel that you've done something."

She also goes to Sunday services at times, but her ambivalence to the church remains strong. Recently, a parishioner who wanted to be kind to newcomers welcomed her as one at the church door. She, a newcomer, she who had been a member for more than seventy years?

This well-intentioned greeting and its effect on her shows that in some ways, of course, she is a newcomer to a new church. Its membership is growing, new families have joined in the years when she has been largely absent from services. And yet it is also the same church she joined long ago. Are there ways in which her emotional and spiritual experience, which she only hints at between the lines of her interview, can be shared? Could it be validated by members of her church, so she could feel more integrated again, and so others, younger people as well as newcomers her own age, might share her devotion to her faith? Above all, can she be served by the church she loves? One senses at some level she dares not admit this need, even to herself.

In several ways she feels displaced by the facts of age, which make her more dependent than she likes to be. Her own continued devotion to her family—the sister, now frail, who had cared for her children, and her even more ailing brother-in-law, who both need her—poses a problem. She cannot be away from them too long. Even attending church becomes difficult: she can't go to church, come back, and prepare a meal. How she reconciles this with her days spent at the soup kitchen is not clear. Here we see some of the dilemmas posed by conflicting practices of commitment—those to family/kin, to the church, and to self—when she recognizes the consequence of aging. "Most of my [fellow church] members are *now* in the nursing home," and not nearby. She doesn't go out much in the evenings to such things as the festival potluck supper. "I could ask for a ride, but I don't. It's *me*. I do go babysitting, and so I could be out. [But] at night I'm tired. I love to *read*."

Where there is ambivalence about membership in a church that is no longer quite so familiar as in earlier days, any obstacles to feeling at home in her church assume still larger proportions. And yet these obstacles are not insurmountable by any means, for the wish for a vital connection is still quite strong—so much so that she has not joined the Baptist church that she attended on occasion with a friend, and where she comments on the warmth people express toward one another, something that is not so evident in her church. "I feel more at home there than in my own church." But it is significant she does not join the Baptists. However, she has joined an organization within her church that also extends beyond it, the soup kitchen. This decision and her continued work for the Christmas bazaar to my mind are significant indicators of her deep wish for a closer link with her church.

III

In this section I want to suggest the value of thinking about women's "traditional work" of bazaars and church suppers as a function of a special purpose group (SPG); to consider briefly how Stromberg's work on commitment may be especially significant for SPGs within churches that are very pluralistic in character; and finally, to return briefly to the discussion of decommitment and desacralization in women's piety. One of the many reasons for the dramatic expansion and flourishing of SPGs, according to Wuthnow, is that they offer individuals a chance to fulfill limited tasks in a limited time. Modern life makes great claims on people's time is the argument.[17] But if we look at women's work, even in the nineteenth century, it is not at all clear that they had so much leisure. Nor did Margaret Langlois in the next century, for that matter. Instead of leisure, nineteenth-century women had more discretionary time than did their predecessors in preindustrial society. Faced with more choices, nineteenth-century women learned to make more time by layering activities. In their activities they continually crossed boundaries between spiritual and ordinary work, between social life and leisure, even as they affirmed the existence of a hierarchy between spheres.[18]

Time management was not an invention of industrial capitalism but part of an old Christian tradition, in which the devotional life took precedence over other things. When the Reformation spiritualized the household, it reinforced and spiritualized the time management of housework. Much later this pattern of moral and spiritual economy was articulated in formal works of "domestic economy." Thus, one finds it being promoted by Catharine Beecher in her highly popular household management book, *A Treatise on Domestic Economy* (1841). This daughter of a famous Evangelical Congregationalist, by the way, became an Episcopalian later in life, joining the faith of her mother.

My point is that women's handwork on behalf of the church lends itself very well to a time-management approach and can fit into a pattern of devotions, which is also interspersed with daily life. Such work is slipped in between other jobs, as anyone who knits or sews knows. One can be employed in Christian usefulness while other, more earthly chores are also under way. Indeed, not only does handwork consciously prepared for the church have spiritual goals but the time spent in its production can be part of the devotional life. Joining a group dedicated to making such goods means joining a group that differs from a secular group. As a special purpose group within the church, its subtle dimensions of spirituality deserve exploration.

Wuthnow argued that SPGS underlie much of the vitality of the churches since World War II. Yet he also recognized they represented a potential problem. Their members might be more closely drawn to them than to the church itself. For this reason, it is interesting that Joanna B. Gillespie's survey of the four parishes (see chapter 5) attests the importance of women's regular church attendance and the value women attribute to private prayer. In *Habits of the Heart,* also, the authors point to the example of the thriving church of St. Stephen's in San Francisco, where participation in church services was seen as a major support for the work parishioners undertook, work that tended to fit more into the categories of SPGS.[19] *Habits of the Heart* regarded small towns as the place where the "second language of commitment" has survived more readily than in anonymous urban settings (p. 154). Yet Margaret Langlois, living in a small town and involved in the soup kitchen, is not reinforced by regular attendance at the church service. Her experience is more that of the urbanite who is not so fortunate as to belong to a St. Stephen's. In her case we find significant alienation, certainly ambiguity.

What has happened to her commitment? I believe that a vital link between her work in the church, as carried out in the SPG of the bazaar committee, and the larger church failed. Here is a woman who has been a church member for more than seventy years, but she has never been asked about those years of membership. The years of her widowhood coincided with years in which the church was changing, so it was hard for her to feel at home there, and she stopped going to Sunday services on a regular basis. The one remaining link was the bazaar committee, but it too changed, becoming less of a collective effort. No more meetings in one another's homes. Bazaar work can of course be done without access to other women's homes, but something important and spiritual is lost without that possibility of easy informality, without the rituals of refreshment that refresh not only body but soul.

Bazaar work can be done alone of course, or in the family, as part of the usual evening in front of the television. Even then it still has a spiritual component, since the goal of this work is the church. If productivity alone is the goal, even then, when conducted under the "ordinary" domestic circumances, I argue such work still has a spiritual dimension. But there is also no doubt that in ceasing to be a collective effort in the physical sense, gathering women or people across various differences together in the intimacy of their private world, this handwork loses much. Moreover, for those who have experienced it, like Mrs. Langlois, it is significant that the loss cannot be discussed or articulated. Most probably, this spiritual loss is only barely perceived, and thus contributes to a generalized sense that not all is well with the world.

Commitment, as Stromberg's Swedish study showed, was both a collective group experience and an individual one, linking the individual to the divine and the widely diverse members of the group to one another through variously experienced and yet shared symbols of community. One also senses in the recollections of Margaret Langlois, though she is not a Pietist, that her vague yearning for the church of her childhood and earlier life was shaped by such a lens of shared symbols. More recently, however, the scope of that lens contracted to a smaller set of shared values. She stood by and even withdrew from her church when it was changing and when she mourned the death of her husband. In fact, her spiritual needs may have been especially great, although she did not explicitly voice that, pointing rather to concrete reasons—primarily transportation problems—that made it hard to come to church regularly.

By removing herself from a scene of change, she did not participate in a formal act of letting go of the old, nor in another of accepting the new, reformed church. She avoided both desacralization and resacralization. Soon thereafter, even familiar practices of commitment in her smaller bazaar group changed, and with it an opportunity for spiritual renewal that might have helped bring her back to regular services. Only some years later, with the institution of the soup kitchen, did she renew her active ties to her church, and to this day that commitment remains the strongest link, one she shares with the relative who brings her.

As churches become larger, or more like train stations, with a constant flow of new populations, special purpose groups become more important as core groups that provide a sense of community, if not help shape the experience of grace. This is true for an individual like Margaret Langlois—old, more and more alone, easily overburdened with family cares for older dependents—who stops coming to the regular services. The same might be true for other populations like younger single mothers, who are also easily overburdened and isolated. In these situations SPGS are very valuable as mediating, smaller organizations, in which there can be face-to-face communication, and even perhaps a chance to bridge the gap between the domestic and the public.

The case of Mrs. Langlois and her commitment to the soup kitchen and to the bazaar suggests the value of fostering SPGS that connect with "traditional women's work." For many elderly women, this is a type of work in which they are skilled and take pride, and where they can feel and be useful. Such work can also bring individuals together across various differences. Margaret Langlois was quite conscious of how diverse the population of the soup kitchen was, both those who prepared the food and those who came to eat. She marveled about the early heroic days of the venture, taking delight in its success after its early improvisations. The very success of the soup kitchen has come to stand as a sign of grace or commitment to her, perhaps especially since she was one of the early participants in it and has seen it flourish. Another example of women's work that succeeded beyond very modest proportions is that of the Texas "Sewing Women." Their handwork is now scattered over the globe, quite literally becoming a testimonial to shared symbols across continents, symbols sewn on sacred vestments for all to behold.[20]

The Sewing Women of Texas lasted only while the generation of founders was well and able to carry on the project, however. The soup kitchen is a thriving concern with an institutional identity. Mrs. Langlois is clearly quite devoted to her responsibilities there. But one also senses something more could be done to pull her more fully back into the larger church. Here is a kindhearted woman with many burdens, often alone, who uses some of that time to make objects for the bazaar. But there is still a missing link. To flourish fully under modern conditions, even in smaller towns, the spiritual dimensions of women's traditional church work need special care and explicit attention. Otherwise such work resembles the kind of secular philanthropy that is readily seen as mere busywork, not touched by what Stromberg calls commitment.

Bazaar committees and analogous groups that foster the participation of women in traditional skills can help overcome varieties of contemporary isolation by also supporting the spiritual life that distinguishes church groups from pedestrian (or should we say truly worldly?) secular fund-raising activities. It requires the creation of another subgroup, another SPG. Its *special* purpose, precisely, would be to address the spiritual dimensions of handwork explicitly in such a way that the results of that work become part of the larger church community. Such a SPG could call upon those who have already spent years in this effort to articulate their thoughts and feelings about that work. Apart from strengthening the personal spiritual life of the participants and serving the financial needs and outreach role of churches, these women, skilled in a variety of now-diminishing domestic arts, can also play an important intergenerational role in their church. Those who sew, bake, or cook for the church, even if quite frail, could still be invited to come to Sunday School sessions on occasion. They could sew in the presence of the young. They might even teach them some skills, and also speak to the children about their lives and what their handwork has meant to them. Older children could videotape such a session for a later exchange with other congregations. Such Sunday School sessions could also be part of a conscious program celebrating and recognizing ethnic and cultural diversity in the church, and could even approach the more difficult subject of class stratification across that diversity. Meals, dress, and home furnishings are, after all, the most concrete, most treasured, and respected part of ethnic heritage.

The material culture of domesticity is part of everyone's history, linking generations across time, from cycles of birth to death, across the boundaries of the temporal and sacred, however inarticulated that may be. In this connection it is notable that the National Coalition of Ethnic Organizations of New York City launched the Citywide Ethnic Exchange Program in the summer of 1989. Its goal is to "pave the way to peace."

The first event involved two families who were planning to share a meal together: an immigrant Italian family of two parents and four children from Brooklyn's Bensonhurst neighborhood, and a black single mother with two children living in East Harlem.[21] The *New York Times* reporter describing the program noted, "The idea is to match New York families of strangers from disparate backgrounds, then give them free food, transportation and tickets to sports events." Then he quickly qualified this grand design with a "but." "But for these first families, it will just be dinner."

Just dinner? What is so mean and humble about a meal, prepared by some of the participants and eaten in one of their homes? Even if money were given for the purchasing of the food, to me it seems significant to avoid take-out food, or food consumed in a public space. Prepared according to the heritage or preferences of the families, a combined meal is transformed through the work of love and commitment. When eaten in a private home, the furnishings are a clue to the family's shared symbols of family culture. The meal can also become an occasion for sharing religious customs across difference as well, in a way that is difficult to do in public restaurant, no matter how fancy the food might be.

The work of loving hands in a setting that itself symbolizes the acceptance of the stranger into one's private, personal world, I suggest, only adds to the success of such a program, because it connects with deeply felt spiritual dimensions that link the family to the sacred, even in this, our very secular culture.[22] This dimension will be lost, I fear, with too much success, as long as that is measured by the availability of money that then allows families to meet primarily in public, commercial spaces. From the newspaper account it appears that this peacemaking program was not linked to a particular church, although the families at the first meal were both Roman Catholic, and they were even prepared to welcome the visit of their archbishop who supported the initiative. Such a program appears particularly promising for churches already committed to transcending, if not reversing, the powerful tendency to further class stratification in which congregations themselves participate.

More openly than other institutions, churches can base such a peacemaking program on the spiritualized household by making explicit and ritualizing how the "work" of domesticity enriches private and public, material and spiritual life. Sunday School programs, church suppers, and moveable feasts held in private homes are all part of practices of commitment to community and communion that help overcome the very real alienation and separation, both voluntary and circumstantial, that our society fosters in countless ways. Margaret Langlois's life in a small town and the new experiment of New York City both suggest the value of SPGS that are alert to particular needs of individuals. But equally important, SPGS can also embrace the variety of talents alive in their midst but that need special efforts of encouragement. There are those who are less mobile, not necessarily the elderly alone, but people of either sex who want to make a contribution with their hands and hearts. Handicapped younger church members, invalids, shut-ins are also possible recruits for such Christian usefulness.

As a committed community touched by grace, the church is different from a secular voluntary association. Expectations of a personal link, of the human-heart touch, if not the divine, are greater; at the same time disappointment is also greater when that touch is missing. Those who miss it may not necessarily complain but may grieve in silence. Here the potential of SPGS is great.

Devoted to the performance of specialized tasks, special purpose groups can link together parts of the church membership that are in danger of becoming marginal. Such groups not only perform a socially and spiritually rewarding and invigorating role in the lives of individuals but can also act as a means for confronting the realities of institutional change. Here the work of disengagement from the old and renewed engagement to the new may succeed more readily than in the larger church services. In such settings the silence of the parishioner who longs for bygone practices of pastoral care can be broken. Longings and disappointments can be expressed, or at least hinted at, generating a response and acknowledgment in the sensitive reformers who are helping to shape the new church that is coming to be, a church, after all, where women have a new kind of authority.

The case of Mrs. Langlois suggests that not all women are entirely comfortable with this emerging reality, especially not older women for whom the church represents familiar associations, linked with family and personal identity. At least in the case of our cradle Episcopalian Mrs. Langlois, one senses a still persistent unease with this new reality. Moreover, even scholars may not yet understand fully how this transition from old to new is being negotiated. In a recent review of current work on the relationship between family and religion, Barbara Hargrove has argued we still have much to learn about the subtle transformation of church and personal life in denominations where women clergy are now fully in evidence.

Although the attitude of some women to their careers as clergy seems dissimilar to that of men, there are as yet few studies taking those differences seriously enough to suggest that the change in gender of church leadership might affect the style of church activity or programs.

Yet it is here we may find the cutting edge of research in this area, for it is here that gender role research meets research on the family in relation to religion.[23]

That cutting edge of research, I suggest, will advance more quickly if we come to understand not only women clergy and their difficult journey toward full acceptance and authentic authority in a church that includes resistance but the behavior and expectations of the female parishioners who in some ways also resist the changes. At one level, moreover—in their reluctance to let go of a particular kind of Christian usefulness, that involving the work of their hands—I suggest that their resistance may indeed be part of the very same impulse that has brought their sisters into the clergy. Both are seeking a more authentic female form of holiness in the church. Hargrove's point may be especially apt here. We still have few studies that take gender differences in the clergy seriously enough "to suggest that the change . . . might affect the style of church activity or programs." It may not all be the fault of studies. It could also be the result of partial change. As the feminine assumes more authority in the church, female leadership also becomes fully authentic and effects further change, not only in *style* but, more significantly, in the *substance* of church activity and programs.

Concluding her review with a reference to William D'Antonio's 1979 presidential address to the Society for the Scientific Study of Religion, Hargrove comments that he urged his colleagues to reconsider the full role religion plays in rapidly changing modern societies. It functions not only as a means of social control and in a conservative fashion, he argued, but also as a means of social support, grounded in such family values as love. Citing as evidence the opinions of his university students, whose sex was not given, D'Antonio noted that they identified the fundamental problem of the human condition as "how to love." There is of course something exquisite about this learning experience in which the academy learns, or perhaps relearns from its own students about a basic Christian doctrine. Hargrove goes on to give more examples of how what one might call Carol Gilligan's voice of gender difference is bringing us to an awareness of "a new ethic of love."[24] But D'Antonio's admission and this small glimpse into the life of Margaret Benton Langlois also reinforce the need for some scholarly humility about the subtlety, hidden pains, and marginalization associated with religious change.

We have discovered an old woman, a lifelong wage earner, wife and mother, who never attended any university, and who fit neither into the cast of the typical Episcopalian nor fully into the church that was changing so much. If we are to understand the meaning of religious changes in the past two decades, we need to know more about individual experience, Roof reminds us. From the life of Mrs. Langlois, we can conclude that scholars, if not church reformers, may also need to relearn some old lessons. The daily life within the walls of one's domicile, where the remnants of a domestic culture of handwork still survive, almost like a counterculture to the consumer paradise, deserves more attention. It is part of the fabric from which not only the "ethic of love" but also the "theology" of love is woven. The material goods prepared largely by women for bazaars are offerings. They become spiritual goods for the larger community in their fullest expression only, however, when they are experienced as shared symbols of that community, "touched by grace," as Stromberg would have it.

In the nineteenth century and perhaps well into the twentieth still, that shared symbolic meaning was generally experienced, not simply understood, in the sense that Stromberg connects experience with action and with the body, not only with perception and the mind. The spiritual goods of handwork belonged prominently to the separate women's church that invented so many traditions of church life, and that bound family, not only women, to the church in multiple and gender-specific ties, as Joan Gundersen also shows in this volume. The revolution of the second wave of feminism, however, coming together with the advance of a more secular and more formally educated national civic culture, meant that the spiritual meanings, or more precisely in Stromberg's terms, the meaningfulness of these activities that so nearly resembled those of home and hearth, were lost to the younger generation of women. One even suspects they began to fade for many of their elders in the wake of the postwar consumer revolution that celebrated leisure more than industry.

Despite recent appearances, however, domesticity is not necessarily incompatible with feminism. The relationship between the two depends instead on larger cultural forces that shape expectations of what is useful and valuable. We cannot elaborate this complex subject here, except to allude to the background against which a woman like Mrs. Langlois, now in her seventies, has lived her life. Her widowhood coincided with the time when domestic virtues were not highly prized by the public culture that also helped to reshape the life of her church. On the other hand, this is not a permanent state of affairs. Feminist and female voices are being heard more fully in the life of the church. They alter the conditions of the church, giving rise to revisions of church life. If the life of Mrs. Langlois is not idiosyncratic but part of a more general cohort trend, then her experience can guide us to envision a new role for handwork of all kinds more explicitly treasured as a spiritual good of the church than has been true in recent years.

With the unprecedented "aging of America," if for no other reason, there needs to be a small group of people, sympathetic and knowledgable about handwork, who are also sensitive to the spiritual needs of church members interested and able to make items for a bazaar, even quite simple things. The production of handmade goods that are freely given to the church has special significance, as we have seen in the life of Mrs. Langlois. That also goes for church suppers to the community, where special care is given to making some favorite dishes. The bazaar and the supper become festivities of community that even extend beyond the church, to the degree that nonmembers join in. But the spiritual dimension of these feasts and festivities cannot be taken for granted in this age of spiritual illiteracy. Rather, that dimension needs to be openly acknowledged and nurtured, in young and old alike. It is after all, the work of love made by our bodies, frail and strong. Such work builds devotion and community among those who gather together, a devotion to a God who in turn sustains the community of believers.

Notes

1. Peter G. Stromberg, *Symbols of Community. The Cultural System of a Swedish Church* (Tucson: University of Arizona Press, 1986), pp. 94–95.
2. For a discussion of "relational feminism," see Karen Offen, "Defining Feminism: A Comparative Historical Approach," *Signs: Journal of Women in Culture and Society* 14 (1988): 119–157.
3. Stromberg: *Symbols of Community*, p. 97.
4. Dean R. Hoge, and Jackson W. Carroll, "Determinants of Commitment and Participation in Suburban Protestant Churches," *Journal of the Scientific Study of Religion*, 17 (1978): 124.
5. Wade Clark Roof, "The Study of Social Change in Religion," in *The Sacred in a Secular Age: Toward Revision in the Scientific Study of Religion*, ed. Philip E. Hammond (Berkeley: 1985), University of California Press, p. 76.
6. Roof, "Study of Social Change," p. 84.
7. For a discussion on the value of guided interviews in a biographical context, see Sarah H. Matthews, *Friendships through the Life Course*, Sage Library of Social Research, vol. 161 (Beverley Hills: Sage, 1986).
8. For recent surveys both in the United States and abroad, see Robert

Wuthnow, *The Restructuring of American Religion: Society and Faith since World War II* (Princeton: Princeton University Press, 1988), pp. 226–228.

9. Hans Mol, "New Perspectives from Cross-Cultural Studies," in *The Sacred in a Secular Age,* ed. Phillip E. Hammond (Berkeley: University of California Press, 1985), pp. 90–103, esp. 100.

10. Wuthnow, *Restructuring of American Religion,* pp. 228, 170.

11. Interview conducted by author; identity and place name shall remain confidential. I am most grateful for her thoughtful reflections. These interpretations are of course all mine, and she may not agree with them.

12. Stromberg's fine study of a congregation relied largely on indepth interviews conducted over an extended period of time by one of the male members of that congregation, under Stromberg's guidance. As Stromberg writes in his preface, his research brought him an "intellectual and *emotional* perspective on the members of Immanuel Church [emphasis added]." Had he also used a female research assistant, I wonder what more he would have discovered (*Symbols of Community*).

13. Wuthnow, *Restructuring of American Religion,* pp. 100–131.

14. Robert Bellah et al., *Habits of the Heart: Individualism and Commitment in American Life* (New York: Harper & Row, 1986).

15. On the importance of the gift in friendship, see Ronald A. Sharp, *Friendship and Literature* (Durham: Duke University Press, 1986). For spiritual dimensions of friendship, see Irene Quenzler Brown, "Death, Friendship and Female Identity during New England's Second Great Awakening," *Journal of Family History* 12 (1987): 367–387, and "Friendship and Spiritual Time in the Didactic Enlightenment," in *Autre temps, autre espace; an other time, an other space. Etudes sur l'Amerique preindustrielle,* ed. Elise Marienstras and Barbara Karsky (Nancy: Presses Universitaires de Nancy, 1986), pp. 111–127.

16. Stromberg, *Symbols of Community,* pp. 50–51.

17. Wuthnow, *Restructuring of American Religion,* pp. 124–125.

18. See Irene Quenzler Brown, "Leisure, Prayer and Inclusive Friendship, from Bunyan and Law to the Lowell Girls" (Paper presented at 1987 American Academy of Religion meeting, Boston).

19. Bellah et al., *Habits of the Heart,* pp. 239–240.

20. For an example of a highly skilled group of Dallas women who worked together weekly for more than twenty years, see Margaret M. Jacoby, "The Sewing Grandmothers," *Episcopal Women's History Project* 9, no. 2 (1989): 4–5. Growing out of a newly organized "Garden and Service Guild," the group sewed a wide range of vestments and other items used by churches in the United States, including Alaska, and by others from South America to the Philippines. For all its evident achievements, however, the group's weakness was its personal rather than institutional identity. In 1978 only two aging original members still survived, and at that point the group ceased to exist. No provisions for a continuous life seems to have been made, or at least to have succeeded during the lifetime of the founding members.

21. Douglas Martin, "A Road to Peace Is Being Paved with Pork Chops," *New York Times*, 26 July 1989.

22. Kathryn Allen Rabuzzi, *The Sacred and the Feminine: Toward a Theology of Housework* (New York: Seabury Press, 1982).

23. Barbara Hargrove, "Gender, the Family and the Sacred," in *The Sacred in a Secular Age,* ed. Phillip E. Hammond (Berkeley: University of California Press, 1985), p. 209.

24. Carol Gilligan, *In a Different Voice: Psychological Theory and Women's Development* (Cambridge: Harvard University Press, 1982); Hargrove, "Gender," pp. 209–210.

8

A Woman's Journey
toward Priesthood:
An Autobiographical Study
from the 1950s through
the 1980s

Sandra Hughes Boyd

A knowing chuckle and then applause ratified the question I posed to Theresa Kane during her appearance in Boston several years ago. She had been narrating recent events of the women's movement in the Roman Catholic Church but I wanted to hear her describe the historic confrontation with Pope John Paul II.[1] During the question-and-answer session following her talk, I asked: "As a historian seeking to discover how women themselves evaluate their participation in the church's life, I've been waiting a long time to ask: How did it *feel* to stand up to the Pope?"

My attempts to "tease out" of nineteenth-century women's accounts of their church work any depth of understanding about their religious vocational life-journeys often have been frustrating. For the most part, they described what they did or what others did. I want to know what they thought about what they did, how they felt about the choices they were making, about the ways they were able to live out those choices? I have often wished that I could transport myself back to the nineteenth century, seek out these women, and ask them these questions myself.

The task for our project collaboration has been to understand the experience of twentieth-century Episcopal women. We have—rightfully so—determined not to succumb to equating Episcopal women's experience with the ordained women's experience. For at least two reasons, however, an examination of the ordained Episcopal woman's experience can provide valuable data for our mission.

The first reason is that, for the most part and until recently in many places in the country, women's issues in the church have been identified with and symbolized by women's right to seek ordination to the priesthood. Although most of us have come to understand ordination to the priesthood as but one manifestation of the wide range of women's issues that are being raised in the contemporary church, its importance in the minds of others signifies the extent to which an examination of its dynamics may enlighten the entire field of women's concerns in the Episcopal Church.

The second reason is that most of us first-generation women who have been seeking to respond to what we believe to be God's call to priesthood have been afforded extraordinary opportunity for self-examination of our reasons and motives for doing so. This introspection has been externally motivated by the lengthy ordination selection process itself and internally motivated as we watched ourselves seeking to enter into territory previously occupied only by men.

We have been asked why we couldn't do what we wanted as lay women. Why should we seek ordination when there was no guarantee of a job and an oversupply of priests? What were we trying to prove, anyway? As we challenge patriarchal hierarchy at its roots, why would we want to be a part of that very hierarchy? We have asked ourselves: When I wear a clerical collar, what am I saying and to whom? Am I seeking a sense of authority? What does this collar contribute to my self-identity? Doesn't it separate me from the women who have been serving the church for generations and receiving precious little recognition for it?

As my contribution to our analysis of the experience of Episcopal women, I will seek to describe and analyze why I—as a woman—determined first of all to become an Episcopalian, and, second, sought to become a priest in the Episcopal Church. In this endeavor, my approach will be different from that of my colleagues. Beginning unapologetically with my own subjective experience, I will strive to provide an analysis of the factors that were involved in the decisions I made.

It might be helpful were I to distinguish between the factors of which I was conscious at the time these decisions were made and those of which I subsequently have become aware. I will not make such a separation. I am not at all sure that I would be able to do so, writing at a time years removed from many of the events. Second, space limitations prevent me from citing the myriad of ways in which I am indebted to others for insights that have contributed to the analysis I make here. The following, therefore, is made up of layers of awareness that have accumulated over the past thirty to forty years.

I acknowledge that this will be but one woman's story, but my hope is that what I have learned will help shed light on the experience of other Episcopal women of my generation, and that in smaller or larger ways my experience can be generalized and will make a contribution to Episcopal women's self-understanding—and to the church's understanding of us.

Cultural and Family Socialization as a Female

I am clearly a product of post–World War II socialization of females as wives, mothers, and homemakers. Although both my grandmother and mother experienced a certain amount of independence within the home during their respective spouse's absences during World War I and World War II, both were mothers of small children at the time. Neither worked outside the home during the war, or was forced to forfeit challenging and or relatively well-paid work when "the boys" returned home, but both certainly had to hew to the freshly and strongly articulated ideal of wifehood and motherhood during those postwar years.

That all of this took place in the conservative, small-town Middle West made its impact on me all the greater. I felt an enormous amount of pressure to conform to a standard in which girls were popular, cute and always had popular and cute boyfriends.

While internalizing the wife-and-mother socialization, I was at the same time somehow absorbing an intellectual curiosity, passion for justice, and broad-mindedness from my mother. That she, too, felt isolated while desperately trying to fit into this culture is illustrated by an event that took place one Christmas while she was serving as leader of my Girl Scout troop. Asked to suggest an appropriate gift that the troop might present to her, I blithely told them she liked books—philosophy books. She was mortified because she knew they would consider this odd and she wanted very much to feel accepted in the community.

From the time I was a young teenager, I worked part-time in the family business, an automobile dealership, where I performed a variety of clerical functions, from operating the switchboard and serving as cashier to record-keeping and accounting. The most important lesson I learned was the satisfaction that came from meeting the needs of our customers. In a small-town family enterprise in the post–World War II Middle West, the ethic I absorbed was that we were in business to meet two specific needs of our customers: acquiring vehicles and keeping them in good working condition. Our personal economic gain was not the ultimate goal of our enterprise.

My memory is that the entire family derived great satisfaction from our place in the community, which came from the visibility of the family business. In the late 1970s, it was sold, losing out to increasing competition from large-volume dealers and service departments. We were no longer able to afford to offer the personalized, careful service to our customers that had been the family hallmark for over sixty years.

In high school, along with many girls who would marry following graduation, I majored in home economics. At the same time, I took the requisite number of "college-prep" courses. I was neither intending to marry right out of high school nor to become a home economics teacher. And although I was expecting to go to college, I had no notion of pursuing a career of any kind other than being a well-educated wife and mother. There were no female models in my family for any profession other than teaching school while waiting to marry and have a family. All of which led to my selecting this odd combination of courses.

My acknowledged agenda for college was to meet my future husband, while the unspoken one was that he would be someone of proper parentage and class rank. Despite all this, I enjoyed my college career. I majored in economics—more suitable than a business degree for many reasons—and also took a fair number of English, philosophy, and religion courses. When I found myself a senior and not engaged to be or already married (as my mother had been), I was desperate. What was I to do with myself?

Had I been born only a few years later, there is a high probability that I would have gone into the family business. I had considerable practical experience there, had taken relevant college courses, and my personality was suited for it. During the next generation daughters began to follow their fathers into ownership and management of auto dealerships, but it never occurred to any of us that this might be an option for me.

I took the first job that came along after college, and was utterly miserable. Traveling around the Midwest to collect price information for the federal government's cost-of-living index, I worked alone, did not know anyone, and found it impossible to make new friends while living out of hotels. I desperately missed being in a classroom, but managed to persevere a year before I went back to school, enrolling in a graduate program in economics. I was totally unprepared for and uninterested in the abstract and theoretical approach to the study of economics I found there, and as a hedge, enrolled in library science courses.

I achieved two goals in graduate school. I met my husband-to-be—I was one of only three women in the economics program—and I earned a practical degree in a field certainly suitable for women. I went to work as a librarian while my husband finished his Ph.D. I was ecstatic when I became pregnant and was more disturbed about the other injustices I encountered at the company for which I worked than the fact that I was forced to quit my job when I began to be obviously "with child." Our two daughters were born in the mid-1960s while my husband engaged in university teaching and I in part-time and occasional library work.

Christianity and the Episcopal Church

My experience as a child with the church was closely tied to my attachment to my paternal grandparents, who lived nearby. With them I regularly attended services at our local Congregational church and went to their home for traditional Sunday dinner. I remember with great fondness those Sundays, for I had my grandparents' undivided attention, so very important for the oldest child in a family that was expanding to a total of seven members during those years.

I enjoyed Sunday School and although I cannot remember the content of the teaching, I do remember that my Sunday School teachers were kind and appeared to love their teaching. As I became eligible, I always joined the appropriate church choir, deriving great pleasure from participating in the worship service through its music.

Youth group was very important for me because church was a place where an effort was made to include awkward, unattractive, serious youngsters like me. One of the boys in the church youth group teased me by calling me "Pythag" (for "Pythagoras"), but in that setting the ethos and leadership kept most of the viciousness out of the teasing and provided a certain level of tolerance, for which I was exceedingly grateful.

Although it is true that on one visit to a regional youth conference,

I heard a woman minister preach, it was only years later that I remembered that event. My assumption at the time was that I would marry a minister.

As a teenager, I was also involved in other kinds of religious activities, even in semisecular and secular settings. In the local Masonic girls' organization Job's Daughters, I served as chaplain. The summer I was sixteen, I was the only female in a group of half a dozen teenagers who created, planned, and led worship services on behalf of our several hundred peers as we traveled by boat to Europe on an exchange program.

Although a devoted member of the Congregational Church, I was at the same time fascinated by the mystery of the Roman Catholic Church and apparently deep devotion of Roman Catholics. Anti-Catholicism was widespread in my small-town subculture, and I was not brave enough to challenge such assumptions to the extent of doing anything beyond admiring Catholicism from a distance. Although there were Roman Catholic children in the neighborhood, they attended Catholic school, removing them from many of our childhood play activities. None of them were among my closest friends.

This was not true of the Episcopal Church. Several of my friends were Episcopalians and I often attended church with them and their families. Midnight Christmas Eve services were particularly appealing, especially one at a local "high" church. I loved the beauty of the liturgy and the music and the church architecture. The eucharist was celebrated frequently, and fasting and kneeling were very meaningful to me.

Despite this, when one of my best Congregational friends converted to the Episcopal Church during high school, I was devastated. I remember crying throughout her confirmation service. I believed that she had deserted me and our family church, and I recognized that she had become a member of the church to which I was afraid to admit that I was very much attracted.

In college, away from home and on my own, I began to attend the early morning midweek eucharist held in the college chapel and presided over by an Episcopal priest who was also a member of the faculty. I faithfully attended these services, at which I was admitted to partake of the eucharist, not the usual practice in Episcopal churches of that era. There was a young man in the group, who after graduation went to seminary to prepare for ordination. Another college acquaintance became a Roman Catholic priest. I was intrigued by their career goals but cannot remember being envious—such a course was unthinkable for me.

When I was a senior, a number of intellectual and personal factors converged that made it possible for me to have the courage to make a considerable break from my family socialization. In an economics history course, we read the works of several authors that provided a description of and tools with which I began to analyze and critique the Midwestern small-town anti-intellectual subculture of the 1940s and 1950s in which I had grown up. R. H. Tawney's reworking of Weber's thesis on the relationship between Calvinism and what he called the "spirit of capitalism" helped me name and analyze the Puritan-Protestant work ethic.[2] Thorstein Veblen described "conspicuous consumption and waste" as symbols of competitive methods for enhancing individual prestige, which I had also seen in my home-town culture.[3] Vance O. Packard's exposé of the psychological aspects of advertising suggested not only a critique but a topic for my senior thesis: "A Study of the Moral Aspects of Persuasion in Advertising."[4]

Although I had become a member of what one scholar calls the "generations of students who were stimulated to think about the relationship between religion and economics,"[5] I had no idea of putting this to use in a career for myself. For me as a female, the family business was out of the question, and my socialization prevented me from considering further academic work in and of itself.

I greatly admired the Episcopal priest-professor and finally shifted from philosophy classes to his religion classes. Although I cannot remember the content of what he taught us, I was fascinated to see in him a model for the way that one could be both a serious scholar and an ordained priest of the church. Although I had no idea that I should or could find a find a professional place in any church, in the Episcopal Church I believed I might find a spiritual and intellectual home.

I made an appointment to see my priest-professor about the possibility of attending the Episcopal Church's "inquirer's classes." I told him of my anxiety about anticipated negative family reactions to any such move. Somewhat bewildered, his response was, "If you want to do it, why don't you do it?" I had sought out and been given the permission I needed, and I did it.

The inquirer's class leader was astute enough to make clear that by attending we were under no obligations until and unless we were ready to make a commitment. I was delighted with this and able thus to enjoy the course and free to make my own decision—on my own timetable— to be confirmed into the Episcopal Church. I fervently anticipated the event, which took place just before Christmas of 1960, and traveled home for the holidays to tell my family the news.

At the time I was a member of a college seminar focusing on issues of freedom and authority. When I informed the group that I had become an Episcopalian, I was instantly accused of being a social climber. This I hotly denied because I believed my hometown Congregational church to be of equal social status to the Episcopal church. Although this might not be strictly true—the local Episcopal church independently organized and ran our town's version of a debutante "coming out" every year—I believed I had made the correct choice.

I was also seeking a congenial church home that more nearly matched my emotional and intellectual needs. The beauty of the liturgy and music appealed to me very much. I needed to participate in a religious worship in which I could express with my body that which I was feeling in my heart. Kneeling, crossing myself, and moving forward to receive communion while kneeling at the altar rail were all physical expressions of worship.

I experienced this to be in stark contrast to the dry, spare, sermon- and pastor-centered worship style of the Congregational Church as I had known it. The centrality of the sermon in the Congregational Church worship and consequent focus on the person of the minister did not satisfy me. The pastoral prayers seemed to be centered more on furthering the congregation's enlightenment about what we should be believing than on giving voice to the "inarticulate groanings and seekings" of the worshippers. That the Congregational Church at that time commemorated the Lord's Supper only four times a year was the most serious example of its deficiency for me.

The use of the *Book of Common Prayer* and the structure of the Episcopal liturgy provided a certain freedom from focus on individual clergy. This is not to say that it was impossible for the priest to focus attention on himself, but the prayer book and liturgical structure made it less likely. I experienced a freedom to think my own thoughts and pray my own prayers, enhanced by the beauty of the music and architecture and liturgical arts.

Although I probably had a good grounding in the Christian faith from admired Sunday school and youth group leaders, the example of my Episcopal priest/professor in the college classroom and the inquirer's class experience taught me that to question and wrestle with faith questions was not only acceptable but invited and welcomed in the Episcopal Church. (Nearly all of the authors in one collection of essays by converts to the Anglican communion note the same experience of intellectual freedom and its importance to their decisions.)[6]

Although I did not admit this to myself at the time, I was also embracing the church of my mother and her family—and implicitly rejecting that of my father and his family. My mother, who had joined the Congregational Church when she married my father, quietly tried to soften the effects of his anger at my announcement that Christmas. I was warned by my father not to speak to anyone about this, especially my (presumably impressionable) younger brothers. My paternal grandmother admonished him for his attitude, pointing out to him that I was only being independent, which he himself had taught me to be. I now suspect that it was she and my mother who, in subtle ways, had been teaching me to be independent. I had occasionally attended the Episcopal church with my maternal grandmother. When she died suddenly less than a month after my confirmation, my mother sought and received my dad's permission to give me her prayer book, symbolizing that a certain level of unspoken tolerance had been achieved in the family.

Episcopal church services provided solace to me during the year after college when I traveled about the Middle West on my job. Although I made no attempt to join any of the various church groups and there was no pressure to do so, I regularly attended Sunday liturgy. The worship service was familiar and predictable and comforting. When I moved on to graduate school, I joined the Episcopal church on campus.

My second date with my husband-to-be was to invite him to attend church. Soon, both of us were deeply involved, participating in nearly all of the activities at one level or another. My fiancé found the Episcopal chaplain a helpful intellectual and spiritual guide, and his baptism and confirmation preceded our wedding, which was performed in my family's home by our chaplain-friend. By his pastoral sensitivity to the situation, our priest made a significant contribution to my father's acceptance of our choice of the Episcopal Church as our faith community.

The Episcopal Church indeed became an important community for my husband and me during our married life, as we moved from place to place in the Midwest and East. We always joined the choir, a community within the community of the parish, which we found eased entry into the parish's life. We were always eager participants in various activities and became personal friends of the parish clergy. Although we had many acquaintances from my husband's workplace and our neighborhood, our closest friends were from church.

Such was the case in the early 1970s when, in our reasonably staid suburban parish, several experiences formed the beginnings of what was to become an increasingly persuasive call for me to take some further action in response to my growing sense of Christian vocation. In January of 1972, the rector of the parish announced to the congregation that he had just attended the service of ordination of a woman to the diaconate. He didn't support this move, he said, but told us that women were now invited to become parish lay readers. At the door, as we shook hands, I heard myself submitting my application, the first woman to do so.

I attended Bible study classes led by the rector where we painstakingly worked our way through the book of Romans. In an evening study group, we read John A. T. Robinson's *Honest to God,*[7] through which I was introduced to Tillich's concept of God as "ground of being." This God was not remote, somewhere "up there." Nor was God "the old man in the sky" but immanent, sharing our pain, involved in everyday life. It was a transforming time for me. I was given the gift of articulation and affirmation for what I had long intuitively believed about God.

It is not surprising, in retrospect, that during that same spring I had a deeply spiritual experience. It is impossible to describe it other than to say that I became for a time profoundly aware of the love of God and experienced an intense joy in all of God's creation. At the same time, I was troubled by the experience because charismatic Christians appeared to seek out such events, glory in them, and judge others on the basis of whether they could claim to have been what they called "born again." A wise friend told me "In order to get their attention, God has to hit some people on the head pretty hard." This was, I was certain, the explanation for what I had experienced.

When I approached the rector about what I might *do* with all of this new knowledge and feeling, he reminded me that I had children to raise and a husband to take care of, and that I had probably better not think about doing *anything* with it. This certainly squared with his opinions and my socialization and I was not angry about this until years later. At the time I was unable to stop my reading or my spiritual quest.

Feminism and Christian Feminism

Despite all of this deeply felt spiritual experience and serious involvement in the church, it was within the secular culture that I first came to understand the importance of the challenges to the culture that women were raising. It was the time of the political campaigns to ratify the state Equal Rights Amendment in a number of states. My involvement came about almost by accident. Asked to be a last-minute substitute for a friend in giving a presentation on the Equal Rights Amendment, I was forced to acquaint myself with the issues. I had not been able to understand what all the excitement was about, but as a result of my study,

I became instantly incensed at the kinds of arguments that were posed against the ERA: that men and women would be forced to share bathrooms, for example. I thought such arguments to be absolutely ridiculous, that the justice of the matter was perfectly obvious.

At the same time, a church friend resigned her high-level position in retailing in order to attend seminary. Two years before, the church at its national convention had authorized women deaconesses to be recognized as deacons and other women to receive holy orders as deacons. I assumed that the church would carry through at its next General Convention by authorizing the ordination of women to the priesthood. In due course my friend would be ordained deacon and then priest. I watched her journey with great interest, not ready to acknowledge the extent to which I had a personal stake in her new career choice.

When the Episcopal Church, at its 1973 General Convention, rejected the ordination of women to the priesthood, I was devastated. Although I was not active in the church women's movement that gathered steam over the next few months, my name found its way into the informal network of persons who were concerned about women's issues. Through this network, I received a telephone call about the event to take place in Philadelphia on July 29, 1974: the ordination of a group of women to the priesthood by some retired and resigned bishops. The intent was to inform supporters around the country, not to make a major media event out of the occasion. I knew I had to be there.

A group of us borrowed a van to drive to Philadelphia. En route we emerged only shaken up following a triple spin on the wet, slippery Pennsylvania Turnpike and left unspoken the extent to which we believed this somehow confirmed the rightness not only of the event itself but also of our own participation in it. Public word of the ordination had leaked out and hundreds of people from around the country gathered at Philadelphia's Church of the Advocate that hot July day. Despite the considerable anxiety about the potential for violent reaction against this open challenge to the church's authority, it was a day of unforgettable joy and celebration.

We knew this was a historic event in the larger sense, but for many of us, it was an extraordinary acknowledgment of our own vocational calls. The women who were ordained to the priesthood that day had recognized and acknowledged their vocations without having any contemporary models. For the rest of us, those models now stood before us. These were *women* who were priests of the church! "Is *this* what I'm supposed to be doing?!" I asked God. And I had the terrifying recognition that the answer was: "Yes."

The Philadelphia traveling band formed the nucleus of a women's advocacy group in our home diocese following our return. I convened the group and wrote its newsletter, and when plans were hatched for a conference on women and religion the following spring, I was thoroughly involved. The keynote speaker was Suzanne Hiatt, one of the women who had been ordained in Philadelphia.

It had not been clear to me why the women felt that they must act "irregularly." Why couldn't they have waited for the church—in its own good time—to come around on the matter of women's ordination to the priesthood? I wondered. The answer to this was made clear in Sue Hiatt's presentation. She narrated the long history of women's struggle for recognition of their ministry in the Episcopal Church: the decades of waiting for the formal recognition of deaconess ministry, for the seating of women as deputies to national conventions, for appointment of women as lay readers and chalice bearers, and so on. It had become apparent to the women who were fully qualified and felt called to priesthood that the same thing would happen to them—that the church's own time was very protracted indeed. The women and their bishop colleagues had simply decided not to wait any longer.[8]

At the party concluding our conference, I introduced myself to Sue and asked for some private time with her. Her immediate response was "You want to go to seminary, don't you?" I hadn't realized it was that obvious. Later I broached the subject with my bishop and although he warned me there was no guarantee of a job when I finished, I received his approval to initiate the ordination process.

I had enrolled the previous fall in a master of arts program in religion at the University of Detroit. There I met several Roman Catholic sisters who were among the first to participate fully in the master of divinity program at SS. Cyril and Methodius Roman Catholic Seminary in nearby Orchard Lake. This seminary was on the forefront of Roman Catholic thought on a number of contemporary issues, most visibly represented by its dean, Anthony Kosnik, who was then in the process of editing a ground-breaking volume on Roman Catholic sexuality.[9] I applied to the Roman Catholic seminary and was accepted.

Later that summer, my husband received an offer to take a position with a firm in Cambridge, Massachusetts, whose offices were near Episcopal Divinity School, where Sue Hiatt was teaching. He accepted, I applied to the school, and early in the fall we moved our household to the Boston area. I was in my midthirties and our daughters were preteens. As we settled in New England that fall, the national church convention authorized the ordination of women to the priesthood.

Christian Feminist Woman Priest

Episcopal Divinity School, in its educational philosophy and academic curriculum, met my needs in ways I could not have foreseen. First of all, the major objective of all entering students was to formulate our seminary goals and outline the ways in which we would make use of the many program resources to meet these goals. This was done in the collegial context of a group of our peers, advised by a senior student and faculty member. Second-year students met in similar groups to formulate and report on results of projects designed by us to address particular issues of concern, as identified in our goals statements.

I was surprised and pleased both that the seminary would direct us to design educational work based on our own statement of goals and that it thereby valued the life experience of older students such as I. I could choose, for the most part, from courses taught either from a feminist perspective or from an open stance toward feminist issues. This meant, of course, extra work as I sought to understand the patriarchal context, undertake a feminist analysis, and outline the means by which our church and its theology and liturgy could be reconstructed based on that analysis. This is not to say that there was an absence of negative reaction to our feminist activism. There were angry responses to some papers I wrote and emotional confrontations on various theological assumptions that I was audacious enough to challenge. At the same time the feminist community—both faculty and students—provided enormous support and encouragement for these efforts.

I plunged in with energy and commitment and completed the final two years of my master of divinity program. In addition to course work, I did two units of fieldwork, wrote a thesis (which was optional), served as senior adviser to a first-year student group, and cotaught a women's ministry course. In preparation for ordination, I was obliged to retake one portion of my general ordination examinations because I unwisely had used as a resource the newly published and controversial collection of essays entitled *The Myth of God Incarnate*.[10] Its challenge to the traditional focus on the divinity of Christ at the expense of his humanity gave words to my own growing convictions but was not so appealing to my exam readers.

As I prepared to enter my final year of seminary, it became clear that parish positions for women were few and far between. One day I noticed that several members of the library staff were clergy. Would it be possible, I wondered, to combine my professional library skills and experience with ordained ministry? I approached the librarian with this question and together we designed a field education project exploring such a ministry. I worked directly with the student and faculty users of the library and at the end of the year, a permanent position as reference librarian was created for me. Because of my experience coteaching the women's ministry course, I was asked to repeat the course, becoming an adjunct member of the faculty. My parish placement was to be as part-time nonstipendiary deacon at a nearby parish.

For eight years, as deacon and then as priest, I continued in a pastiche of part-time ministries: seminary library work, seminary teaching/advising, parish work, researching and writing about women's issues in the church. As librarian, while I helped library users locate resources for their research, I also built the women's studies collection and, with a colleague, compiled and published a bibliography of works about women's religious history in the United States.[11]

As adjunct member of the faculty, I alternated between teaching the women's ministry course and serving as faculty adviser to the first- and second-year goal and project groups. Because I so thoroughly believe in the value of the educational process at EDS, I greatly appreciated the opportunity to participate in providing the context and support for students as they formulated goals and wrestled with crucial issues of concern to faith and ministry.

As member of the faculty, I participated in painful debates with colleagues about the continuing demands for inclusive language and creative liturgies in the seminary chapel worship. EDS had taken strong leadership in employing ordained women as faculty and in supporting feminist courses and scholarship, but challenges to the *Book of Common Prayer* were met, in some cases, by fierce resistance. That this should be the ground on which the major conflicts were waged is not surprising because the *Book of Common Prayer* is a principal symbol of the Anglican tradition. Neither was the issue in any way resolved by such debates. It remained a fact of considerable dismay to feminist students that the only area of study in which there were no regular women faculty was liturgical studies.

My part-time parish ministry included regular participation in the

worship at a nearby parish (where I was named priest associate), supply
work at several area parishes, and one two-year period as interim rector.
Serving in a liturgical leadership role in many parishes was both difficult
and satisfying in those early years. I was often the first woman whom
parishioners had experienced in this role. They did not usually tell me
this, but I was always aware that I was embodying an issue that previously
had been an abstract one. Although I found this emotionally and spiritually draining, I was buoyed by the fact that I was providing a model
for other females, young and old, of possibilities that may have never
occurred to them—as, indeed, it did not occur to me until I was nearing
middle age. In the role of ordained woman, I was concrete manifestation
of the inclusiveness of the Gospel of Jesus Christ, that within the community of Christian believers God can and does call females to ordained
leadership.

There were many factors that led to the dissolution of my marriage
in the early 1980s, but chief among them was the matter of a career for
me. We had agreed between us that I would have a career, but neither
one of us knew how that would actually work itself out. I had no models
in my family of women who were both wives/mothers and career women.
My husband's mother, although she had qualified as a medical doctor
at the age of twenty-one, practiced medicine only for a short period of
time during the World War II shortage of doctors. She chose instead
to remain at home, raising her family.

Toward the end of ten years at Episcopal Divinity School, I became
aware that I needed a new challenge. Having experienced both parish
and seminary ministry, I was certain that I wished to remain part of the
academic enterprise and I accepted a position as public services librarian
at Princeton Theological Seminary. In this position I was responsible
for the people who worked directly with the users of the library, as
distinguished from staff who are responsible for ordering and processing
library materials. The effects of my thoroughgoing socialization of the
value of service to others had never diminished, and in the large seminary
library I put this to work while I also developed management skills.

After four years in Princeton, I relocated to Denver, where I am
public services librarian at the Jesuit Regis University. In this setting,
I continue to work surrounded by books and people seeking information
by which to deepen their intellectual understanding of the Christian
faith. As one deeply committed to the importance of developing the
intellect's contribution to faith, in this role I can make accessible and
even intriguing the kinds of resources that will encourage rather than
stifle intellectual curiosity, and that will challenge rather than merely

confirm presuppositions. In this role I have significant opportunity to combine many skills in working with library staff and users, and with faculty preparing to teach these students.

An examination of my present career status brings to awareness several anomalies. The first of the two "professions" for which I have trained is a "female" profession and suffers from the lack of status that derives from that fact. This is particularly evident in the academic community, where librarians are usually seen not as educators but as mid-level administrators. Librarians have neither the prestige of classroom faculty nor the status of students (which students receive as "clients" of the institution). Librarians are often forced into a stance of passive service to the library's constituency rather than encouraged to engage in active participation in educational policy-making. As a female whose participation in the direct service of my family's business was valued but who was not expected to aspire to a policy-making role relative to that service, my sensitivity toward this anomaly is particularly high. Because I view myself as an educator and spend most of my working hours teaching users how to do research using facilities of the library, I experience a disjunction between how I view myself and how the institution views me. And because I do not exercise my profession as librarian from a stance of passive service, I am continually struggling to be allowed to participate fully in the educational enterprise.

The second anomaly is that the status of my second "profession" is declining. The most widely recognized (and bemoaned) cause is the decreasing influence on public life exercised by the clergy and the churches that they head. Related to this is a shift in the actual "job description" of clergy. Although many are still "in charge" of parishes, these congregations are declining in size and community influence. A smaller proportion of the clergyperson's time is spent on highly visible community leadership and a greater proportion is spent on what have been considered traditional "female" tasks: setting the table and feeding the family; looking after the family; tending the sick; counseling the distressed; seeing to the needs of the dying and the dead. It only exacerbates the negative aspects of these perceptions that the profession of the clergy is seen as being subjected to an "invasion" by women—persons who have been so thoroughly socialized to carry out these "female" functions, and who, for the most part, do them very well.

The third anomaly is that many of us in ordained ministry would prefer to participate in a team ministry rather exercising a solitary ministry. In this preferred setting, each member of the team would perform the functions in which she or he most excels, supported by the others and protected against isolation and burnout. What I and most of my sisters have found, however, is great difficulty in locating such a team ministry in which all members are equally willing to participate and cooperate in egalitarian team management. Our socialization, skills, and convictions are frustrated and we are significantly restricted in our professional options.

There are a number of paradoxes implied by or manifested in my autobiographical reflection as a female, as a Christian, as an Episcopalian, and as a woman engaged in professional ministry in the Christian church. The first is that although I rejected some aspects of my mid-twentieth-century, Middle-western, upper-middle-class socialization as female, I continue to see myself as a Middle-western, upper-middle-class woman, and remain very close to my family of origin, sharing many of its values.

A second paradox is that although my gender socialization led me into the stereotypically "female" profession of librarianship, it is one in which, as a female, I must continually battle for recognition and the opportunity to exercise my abilities to their fullest. At the same time I love working with books and with people, and continue to derive great satisfaction from the challenge of bringing them together in the service of intellectual wrestling with matters of faith.

Another paradox is related to my identity in the faith community. Although my family and cultural socialization made it impossible for me to see myself as an Episcopalian for so many years, I can no longer imagine myself as anything else. A certain degree of homogenization between denominations and the simple fact of the passage of years are partially responsible for this. But while it has been my participation in the community life of the Episcopal Church that has contributed the most to the development of my identification as an Episcopalian, it is also here that I have experienced the paradox of feeling both affirmed and rejected as female, as ordained woman, as "wise woman," and as feminist challenger of the faith.

It took even longer and it was a much tougher battle to visualize myself as a priest. The power of cultural socialization that I had to overcome was brought home to me one Halloween evening as I was walking past the church. Suddenly I thought: "Females are supposed to be *witches,* not *priests!*" At the same time, when I hear such things as the 1976 declaration from the Vatican that only males can be priests because Jesus was male,[12] I am sure not only that women can *be* priests but that I certainly *am* one.

Although it is within the faith community that my values have been shaped and where my commitments are so deeply shared, it is increasingly clear that this same institution—in which I trained for my second profession and in which I exercise both of my professions—is losing its voice and ability to be heard on issues of crucial importance to the modern world. As a leader of one of the constituencies that has been most vocal in its challenge to the faith community on these very issues, I could be justified joining others in saying, "We told you so." At the same time, I will not leave the faith community that, I believe, has been given by God a mandate to challenge the world on these very issues.

Another paradox, not unrelated to the above, has to do with my role as visible leader in an institution whose history, theology, symbology, and ecclesiology continue to oppress women. In this capacity, I participate in this oppression. And yet it is within this institution that I have experienced and been enabled to share in the most significant challenge to this oppression in which I can envision engaging.

The most vivid example of this powerful paradox is my participation as priest in the sacrament of the eucharist. Most of the language and symbology of that sacrament would lead one to the inevitable conclusion that the Christian God is one who chooses to sacrifice God's own offspring to the horrible death of crucifixion on a cross. Inevitably associated with that assertion is the belief that the sin of humanity is responsible for and even made necessary this ultimate sacrifice.

The paradox within the paradox is that it is in this very sacrament that I experience God in Jesus Christ embodying total acceptance and affirmation of human beings, sharing fully in all the joy and pain of human existence, thereby condemning all injustice and oppression. The outer paradox is that I continue to feel called to communicate this within a context that appears so often to contradict that very message.

Notes

1. M. Winiarski, "Theresa Kane Stance Wins Support, but Not in Rome," *National Catholic Reporter* 15 (19 October 1979): 1.

2. R. H. Tawney, *Religion and the Rise of Capitalism* (New York: New American Library, ca. 1926, 1958).

3. Thorstein Veblen, *The Theory of the Leisure Class,* rev. ed. (New York: New American Library, 1953).

4. Vance O. Packard, *Hidden Persuaders* (New York: McKay, 1957).

5. Lawrence Stone, "R. H. Tawney," in *International Encyclopedia of the Social Sciences,* vol. 15 (New York: Macmillan, 1968), p. 520.

6. Dewi Morgan, ed. *They Became Anglicans: The Story of Sixteen Converts*

and Why They Chose the Anglican Communion (New York: Morehouse-Barlow, 1960).

7. John A. T. Robinson, *Honest to God* (Philadelphia: Westminster Press, 1963).

8. Suzanne R. Hiatt, "How We Brought the Good News from Graymoor to Minneapolis: An Episcopal Paradigm," *Journal of Ecumenical Studies* 20 (Fall 1983): 576–584.

9. Anthony Kosnik, *Human Sexuality: New Directions in American Catholic Thought* (New York: Paulist Press, 1977).

10. John Hick, ed. *The Myth of God Incarnate* (Philadelphia: Westminster Press, 1977).

11. Dorothy C. Bass, and Sandra Hughes Boyd, *Women in American Religious History: An Annotated Bibliography and Guide to Sources* (Boston: G. K. Hall, 1986).

12. Leonard Swidler and Arlene Swidler, eds., *Women Priests: A Catholic Commentary on the Vatican Declaration* (New York: Paulist Press, 1977).

III

IMAGES OF A
NEW CHURCH

In the recent past, rapid change in gender relations and the emergence of an articulate feminism have transformed the context within which Episcopal women experience and express themselves religiously. Key episodes indicative of these shifts include the opening of Episcopal seminaries to women in the 1960s, the irregular ordination of women to the priesthood in 1974, and the consecration of the Reverend Barbara Harris as a bishop in 1989.

The controversy accompanying these and other changes has made it clear that such changes are important not only to ordained women but to the church as a whole. The theological debates, the unfamiliar images of authority, and the subtle adjustments of ethos that accompany the changing status of women in the church raise fundamental questions for ordained men and for laity of both sexes.

The three chapters in this section explore some of these questions. Catherine M. Prelinger's chapter on women priests shows that women's inclusion in the clergy challenges familiar patterns and also raises the question of whether women will reshape the priesthood or be reshaped by it in a masculine image. Constance H. Buchanan explores the powerful hold of that masculine image upon the self-perception of the Episcopal Church and challenges the church to undertake a thorough theological revaluation of what it means to be authentically and vitally human. In the final chapter, theologian Margaret R. Miles reflects upon the question of whether the church's historic and persistent subjection of women should lead women to abandon it.

Throughout this section, the androcentric character of the Episcopal Church as an institution is displayed and criticized. But the authors also hold out some hope that the theological, social, and ecclesiastical changes of this era may yet make the church a setting in which both women and men can participate in the fullness of their being.

9

Ordained Women in the Episcopal Church: Their Impact on the Work and Structure of the Clergy

Catherine M. Prelinger

The focus of our study is laywomen of the Episcopal Church. Nevertheless, so central to any consideration of the laity today is the response to women's ordination, it seems imperative to include an essay on the structure of the clerical profession. The issues raised during the ordination struggle, many of which have surfaced again in the discussion of women in the episcopacy, have mobilized laywomen. According to Princeton sociologist Robert Wuthnow, in contrast to other religious groups, feminists among Episcopalians are more likely to attend church than nonfeminist Episcopalians.[1] Never mind what he, or his source, the General Social Survey Cumulative File, mean by *feminist;* the perceived solidarity between feminist churchgoers and women priests is unmistakable. This chapter raises three principal issues: (1) lay response to the female priesthood, (2) the accomplishments women priests themselves think they are promoting, and (3) an analysis of the structure of the clergy as it exists today from a historical perspective. I feel that we need this critique not simply to understand the status of the women clergy but also to engage in the discourse concerning professionalism and the clergy, to which the Lilly Endowment has also contributed, notably in the work of Jackson Carroll.

From the oral segment of our investigation we collected many comments from laywomen about their experience with women clergy. A thirty-six year-old woman parishioner of the Church of the Nativity in the Northwest and former Navy medical technician, exclaimed, "I absolutely love it!" (female ordination). As a young girl, she had envied her brother's position as an altar boy and felt a profound hurt at her exclusion. Now, as she put it: "It is so refreshing to hear a woman speak. I thought, 'yeah, hello, we're human beings! God created us too.' It looked perfectly right to see her up there."[2] Another woman, aged sixty-nine, whom Joanna Gillespie interviewed, confessed: "Oh I wish they'd had them when I was young. I would have been a minister." Her comment is especially striking because, taken in conjunction with the sentiments of the woman above, it would suggest that support for ordained women is not confined exclusively at all to the young, presumably more "feminist" generation.[3] An interesting psychological insight came from a woman in the Deep South: "A woman priest makes submission in religion safer, somehow."[4] Mary Donovan, in her study of women priests, provides a number of additional examples of the esteem and appreciation women clergy have elicited from the laity. At the conclusion of her book she quotes a woman from Wyoming: "Knowing some clergywomen has reinforced for me the fact that God created male and female to be partners equally—not one subservient to the other." Another declared: "I have felt the deepest personal satisfaction and fulfillment in my own life in the Church to see women representing me and all women in the sacramental life of the Church. I did not know how much I had missed until I experienced the difference."[5]

The report of the Committee for the Full Participation of Women in the Church, released in July 1988, indicates that the more often congregations are exposed to women priests, the more likely they are to view ordained women favorably; many of those questioned believed that the deployment of women as interim ministers provides an ideal form of initial exposure.[6] Paula D. Nesbitt, author of "The Feminization of the American Clergy: Occupational Life Chances in the Ordained Ministry," a doctoral dissertation for the Department of Sociology at Harvard University, takes a somewhat less sanguine view. She divides the occupational possibilities within the Episcopal clergy into nine ascending levels of achievement. Within the first level, for instance, are deacons and various members of the parish staff; the third level includes assistant rectors; the fourth level, interims in charge, various chaplains, and others; in level six, rectors and heads of religious orders; and in level nine, diocesan bishops. Nesbitt then examines the sequential advance for women and men as they ascend the job scale. For male priests in every time cohort included, the modal title for the second job they hold is "rector"; for women, "assistant." One of the consequences this distribution of offices inflicts upon many parishes, in my opinion, is symbolic: the representation, at the sacred level, of women subordinate to men. Even as they reach their third through fifth job placements, the modal title for women is "interim"; men either remain rectors, the modal title, or move on up the hierarchy. Contrary to the report *Reaching toward Wholeness,* Nesbitt points out that women's exposure as interims generally does not lead to their reappointment as rectors: "The irony [is] that the replacement of interims overwhelmingly tends to be by *male* rectors."[7] Some dioceses—even relatively liberal ones—deliberately attempt to reduce the number of female and other ethnic and sexual minority candidates to the priesthood; one such diocese apparently required that the successful candidate be someone who, in its coded phrase, was acceptable anywhere.[8]

Clearly, not all of the response to the ordination of women has been positive, even on the part of the female laity. As one of the older women interviewed by Gillespie in the Great Plains region observed, "There is no advantage to having women in clerical roles so why should we do it?"[9] To cite an even more vehement laywoman in Wisconsin writing to *The Living Church:* "Let women be ordained into the holy priesthood, consecrated as bishops; even be Presiding Bishops. Let our precious Episcopal Church be run by women. It won't be long before men will no longer be the active participants Christ willed them to be."[10] However, women have indeed empowered men. In the *New York Times Magazine* column "About Men" of 3 April 1988, Dan Wakefield described as the best prayer he had heard by a layman, one offered by a young Ghanaian at the Men's Immigration and Naturalization Service Detention Center in Boston: "Dear God, we thank you for giving us this wonderful chance to study your Word—help us to understand, and give us much to put under our hat." Constance Hammond, an Episcopal graduate of Harvard Divinity School, was then minister to the detention center.[11]

Women clergy themselves comment in a variety of ways about the range of their work. Ann Coburn, for instance, a priest represented in Donovan's book on the female priesthood, sees herself particularly as a minister to women: "Women are awakening to the need to work on their spiritual life. They want to study the Bible and try to relate that to where they are. . . . They are dealing with the realities of women in this stage of society. How can you be a superwoman—have a family and work full time and be perfect in every way? I think there's a myth out there that women can somehow do that, and women put that myth on themselves."[12]

The Reverend Suzanne Hiatt, the woman who received a grant as an "enabler" from the United Thank Offering in 1971 and has been a mentor to women seminarians and ordinands ever since, believes that women clergy have the capacity to institute significant change in the church. She cites the change from competition to collaboration as the modus operandi at the Episcopal Divinity School (EDS), where she is a faculty member. EDS now has an 80 percent female student body. Members of the women faculty are trying to design the practice of pastoral counseling according to the psychotherapeutic models developed at the Stone Center at Wellesley College,[13] where there has been a shift in emphasis from "the psychology of the self to the psychology of relationship and connection."[14] EDS is affiliated with the Women's Theological Center (WTC) in Boston, an independent organization founded in response to the Vatican's 1976 declaration "which rejected the ordination on the grounds that woman did not bear a 'natural resemblance' to Christ." "WTC also leads students to experience women's collective experience, in an effort to challenge the dominant culture's ethos of individualism."[15] Another source of inspiration to this group of academic clerics has been feminist legal theory, which "encourages behavior that is caring about others' safety and responsive to others' needs or hurts, and that attends to human contexts and consequences," rather than the masculine voice of rights, autonomy, and abstraction.[16] Feminist faculty at EDS are committed to change at the structural as well as the substantive level of the Episcopal clergy, as witness their recent support of the Massachusetts Women's Caucus's successful efforts toward the election of a woman bishop.[17] Sue Hiatt believes that female ordination will have been in vain if women clergy are not committed to change.

Many women in the clergy, however, do not share these views. As one woman Mary Donovan interviewed reported: "I am a priest and never mind what sex I am; just let me get on with that ministry—doing what God has called me to do."[18] Others believe that the manifest power of their own authenticity will prevail in the contest with pettiness and bureaucracy.[19] It may not be possible, however, for women to continue to exercise effective ministries if the present ecclesiastical structure is not modified, for the present system tends to protect the route to leadership in a manner that will ultimately produce mediocrity. This is why we need to look at the clerical profession from the perspective of gender structure.

Modern professionalism as we know it today emerged during the second half of the nineteenth century. The impact of the culture of professionalism can scarcely be overstated. As Robert Wiebe suggested, the professional was at the core of the "new middle class in America," "responsible for integrating the 'island communities' of the late nineteenth century into a cohesive national society."[20] A person's profession became a principal source of social identity. There is general agreement among sociological writers about what constitutes a profession. Chief among its attributes are (1) a full-time commitment, distinguishing the professional from the amateur; (2) a body of theoretical knowledge transmitted by a training school; (3) a professional association that both protects the monopoly of the profession against intruders and enforces a code of ethics among its members; (4) autonomy against competing claims by bureaucracies, and (5) a commitment to service informed by a sense of vocation. As Joan Brumberg and Nancy Tomes pointed out in a brilliant essay a number of years ago in *Reviews of Books in American History,* standard histories of the professions fail to address the emergence of professional women because the women's professions apparently lacked the necessary expertise or autonomy to qualify; women in predominantly male professions were considered marginal. Hence, until quite recently, the whole area of women's professionalism has been viewed as an anomaly.[21]

The clerical profession, like other professions, assumed its modern form in the latter part of the nineteenth century. Previously, the clergyman had been primarily a learned gentleman and a local official, but, to quote Donald Scott's classic description:

> [B]y the 1850's, in institutional terms the clergy had become a profession, a coherent, self-conscious occupational body, organized and defined by a set of institutions which were outside lay or public control, which controlled the special learning needed to become a clergyman, and which possessed the power to determine who could enter the clerical ranks. . . . Responsible primarily to his profession rather than his community, the clergyman represented organized Christianity and articulated and defined God's word.[22]

The expertise specifically required for the clerical profession, however, has been a matter of some uncertainty, more so than, say, medicine, where training is pragmatic. In 1975 Peter Jarvis, a British sociologist, wrote "The Parish Ministry as a Semi-Profession" for the *Sociological*

Review; the literature on the utility of the professional model for the ministry has continued to be challenged down to the present, with, for instance, an article in *The Christian Century* of November 2, 1988, "The Pastor Is (Also) a Professional."[23]

At the beginning of the century a much greater sense of certainty characterized writing about the clergy. Here is what an Episcopal clergyman in Syracuse had to say:

> The first question to be settled to-day is not, "Do the young women like the young minister?" but this, "How do the young men like him?" "Has he the qualities which a man admires?" I am making a plea for scholarship. . . . [I]t is the question of the age. . . . [S]ervice will not do; social qualities aren't sufficient. . . . A parish grows today because the man who leads it is known to be a man of deep learning in the arts of life and whose ability is unquestioned by the men of the world. . . . The Church of the New Century must have strong men of the world to do her work. The weaklings can never do it.[24]

Here even scholarly expertise defers to masculinity.

Men were facilitated in the consolidation of the modern ministry by the simultaneous and reciprocal development of the deaconess order. Previously, the married clergy could delegate various recognizably gendered tasks to their wives, but the prestige and numerical frequency of clerical celibacy blocked this option for some and the multiple tasks designated as "women's work" in an industrializing society gradually overwhelmed the resources of the individual rector's wife. Orders of sisters also preceded the female diaconate, but these were few in number and they did not necessarily interact with the male clergy. Most orders were, in fact, independent foundations with no formal connection to the bureaucracy of the church. The General Convention of the Episcopal Church in 1889 passed a canon on deaconesses, giving sanction to an office that had been practiced unofficially for a number of decades. A training school was incorporated in New York in 1891. The canon provided that "women of devout character and approved fitness" could be set apart by a bishop for "the care of our Lord's poor and sick, the education of the young, the religious instruction of the neglected and the work of moral reform."[25] Brumberg and Tomes do not discuss the clergy in their formula but what they say about women professionals in general is equally applicable to deaconesses: "Women staked their professional claims in areas abandoned or unwanted by men. . . . [T]hey assumed care of the most unrewarding and disorderly of clienteles: the young, the poor, the immigrant, the intemperate, the sick."[26] The rise of the helping professions permitted the male-dominated professions to pursue the more orderly course characterized by scholarship and abstraction. The Reverend Sandra Hughes Boyd has written with verve about Deaconess Gore in the Diocese of Nebraska, where she conducted conscientious visits to isolated communities notwithstanding the complete absence of support or follow-up from her male superiors in Omaha.[27] This is not to say that women did not derive enormous satisfaction in their new situation, one that challenged them more fully than domesticity but at the same time did not violate any of their own deeply held convictions about what was appropriate. As late as 1923, Deaconess Helen Fuller wrote: "May we not well ask whether in our Church, at the present time, there is not great need for the employment of women in larger numbers in the lesser ministries to enable the clergy to devote more time to the administration of the Sacraments, to pastoral visiting and to preaching, that these things may be better done?"[28]

Long before the formal admission of women to the ordained priesthood in the Episcopal Church, the clergy was already a profession structured by gender. Although the deaconess movement contributed to the distinctive character of the male clerical profession, it was not the direct antecedent for the women's ordination movement. Most of the original female priests ascribe their own motivation to the secular movement for women's liberation. They do acknowledge in the experience of the historic deaconesses a usable past.

By late 1987, Mary Donovan reported there were over 1,200 women priests and deacons in the Episcopal Church. These included deacons ordained since 1970 and priests ordained since the passage of the canon allowing priesthood for women, which took effect January 1, 1977.[29] By action of the 1976 House of Bishops, the women who had been ordained priest before 1977, most notably those participating in the festive "irregular" ordination in Philadelphia on the Feast of SS. Mary and Martha, July 29, 1974,[30] were destigmatized and permitted to function as priests after "a public event . . . in which each woman was to appear with her bishop, except [that] the acknowledgement . . . was not to be a 'reordination.' "[31] The deployment office in 1988 registered the number of male clergy ordained since the end of 1976 at 1,929—a time frame obviously selected to permit comparisons with women clergy; previous to 1976 the Episcopal Church regularly ordained only men. There had been, in other words, since 1976 fewer than half as many ordained women as men, bringing the total proportion of women to approximately 11 percent of the entire clergy.[32]

Who are these women? To begin with, they are a contingent of highly educated people. The mean educational level at the time of ordination for a sample of 249 Episcopal women ordained until 1985 was calculated to be slightly higher than the master's degree.[33] In the *Episcopal Clerical Directory* for 1987, 68 percent of these women designated themselves as married; 31.7 percent listed themselves as single, widowed, or divorced.[34] Although nearly 75 percent did not indicate that they had had a previous occupation, the remaining 25 percent cited some prior occupational experience, the greatest number (thirty-one) having been professionals, such as professors and teachers, administrators, and managerial-level personnel of various kinds; the remainder worked in semiprofessional areas, clerical jobs, and religiously related positions. This last category comprised eighteen women functioning in such occupations as directors of religious education, choir directors, and editors of religious publications.[35]

Their training completed and having accepted the sacrament of ordination, these women hold what kinds of occupations within the Episcopal clergy? According to a report provided me by the Church Deployment Office of the Episcopal Church in 1988, 137—or 19 percent of all clergywomen—are either rectors or vicars in charge of individual parishes; vicars, who are restricted to missions and are not necessarily chosen by their parishioners but by the bishop alone, were not distinguished from rectors. Among the men, 893 hold these positions, about 46 percent of the total. Forty-six percent of the women and 36 percent of the men ordained since 1976 are assistants or associates. A total of 236, or 33 percent, of the women are in various specialized ministries; they serve in hospitals, prisons, and colleges, or as interim ministers. The comparable figures for men are 348, or 18 percent.[36] John Morgan, himself a priest and scholar writing in 1985, dealt with significantly fewer cases, but he also considered a wide range of factors, such as salary, housing provisions, and pension membership; he sent a questionnaire to 500 women priests, and on the basis of a response rate of 70 percent predicted that the Episcopal Church was engaged in creating a second-class priesthood.[37] However rewarding the unconventional ministries may be—and many clergywomen we have talked with find them profoundly rewarding[38]—they do not represent the commonly acknowledged route to authority in the church. Paula Nesbitt, writing in 1990, comments: "Though Episcopal women priests have moved upward in their careers, their attainment has tended to fall short of positions enabling them to exercise a significant degree of denominational influence and authority, especially when compared with the attainment levels of men within their cohort."[39]

H. Boone Porter, in what he intended as a conciliatory essay on the so-called disputed election of the suffragan bishop of Massachusetts, the Reverend Barbara Clementine Harris, faulted Harris for her lack of experience as rector of a parish.[40] This sounds very much like a catch-22. The ideology of calling and the rhetoric of servanthood are powerful inducements to women themselves, and the injunction to seek God in the faces of the poor undercuts the will to examine the special ministries by structural criteria. Women clergy often present themselves in the language of nurture and domesticity. Some, however—and I have in mind Rosanna Kazanjian, whose portrait appears in Donovan's book on women priests—caution about the dangers of duplicating "the cultural norms about women being nurturers." Her injunction to herself is "to be constantly intentional about my own creative role in shaping this community."[41] As I look at the public competencies and public attributes of the women clergy, particularly as they appear in the careers that many women left in order to enter the priesthood, I have a sense of unrecognized and underutilized resources.

Recently, there are some indications that women themselves are adopting a sense of futility with respect to competition for high status—or even middle-level—positions in the church hierarchy. To become a fully ordained priest in the Episcopal Church, one must first be accepted as a deacon. In the past the diaconate was almost exclusively a way station to the priesthood. In recent years, however, the "permanent diaconate" has grown conspicuously both in numbers and in the public deliberations of the church. To quote Nesbitt once again:

> For the 1985 cohort, the largest in number and ratio of female clergy, about one-third of all women were ordained only to the diaconate. This ratio, nearly double that of the 1980 cohort, was the highest of all female cohorts sampled. Women were significantly more likely to be permanent deacons in this cohort (1985), whereas the sex difference in earlier cohorts was not statistically significant. Thus, the permanent diaconate appears to be in the process of becoming disproportionately populated by women.[42]

A change of such dramatic magnitude suggests multicausality. Whether women have made the decision to foreclose their options in the clergy as a consequence of mutual and reciprocal discussion with their mentors, whether they have encountered insurmountable opposition from their bishops (this seems likely only in the few remaining dioceses where the ordination of women is prohibited),[43] or whether the reasons lie within the realm of personal preference, we cannot judge. I find it difficult not to surmise that women are, reluctantly perhaps, concluding that a prestigious future in the Episcopal Church is so unlikely that they should accept with what grace they may a less-high-profile post but one in which at least they will entertain fewer illusions and frustrations and one in which they may, if they are fortunate, also enjoy a greater modicum of control over their lives.

What I have found particularly distressing in the material I have reviewed is the suggestion not simply of status discrimination but also of psychobiological determinism. This would seem to be at least one explanation for the preponderance of women hospital chaplains; the presence of women, such as Nancy Chaffee, who are themselves handicapped in ministries for the handicapped[44]; and the deployment of black women as chaplains to prisons whose populations are predominantly black.[45] Barbara Harris's credentials in the public secular sphere, before her ordination, included management of the public relations department and a senior staff consultantcy at the corporate headquarters of the Sun Oil Company (Sunoco), and the presidency of Joseph V. Baker Associates, Inc., a national public relations firm in Philadelphia. While she was interim rector of Philadelphia's Church of the Advocate, she was executive director of the Episcopal Publishing Company.[46] Why wasn't she a good candidate for St. James Church in New York City, where white executives and publishers worship? Could color have been a factor?

Stereotypes in general have haunted the female priesthood. Older women, who in recent years have entered the clergy in large numbers, have been referred to as "housewives whose children are gone, divorcees, or women who've been working around the church so long they think they might as well run it."[47] As Nesbitt points out, such biases are not supported by evidence; they nonetheless permeate the attitudes of those influential in the placement of clergy.[48] Nonstipendiary clergy— more often but by no means exclusively women—are frequently resented by other members of the clergy: "they oughtn't to have the same privileges as parochial clergy."[49] Increasingly, the ratio of part-time positions within the Episcopal clergy has grown; the number of women, particularly at the lower job levels, have exceeded the number of men in part-time positions. And it has been statistically documented that marital status makes no significant difference for either women or men in the ranks of part-timers.[50] Yet the assumption is almost universal that women can afford part-time positions in the clergy because they are being supported by their husbands.

Inevitably, the issue of sexuality entered public discourse concurrently with the issue of women's ordination. Episcopalians in the United States might have been less overwhelmed by the intrusiveness of sexual concerns had they been familiar with the ordination debates in England after World War I, which followed on the heels of the suffrage debate. In 1920, when the Lambeth Conference decided to review the situation of " 'women and lay ministries,' " a distinguished female physician who was also an observant Anglican was invited to address the convention. She found no physical limitations that would prevent active roles for women in the clergy; after dismissing various alleged weaknesses in women as unfounded, she concluded that the reason for obstructing women's access to the priesthood was "a continuing, partly subconscious, belief in her 'ceremonial uncleanness', this supposed 'defilement'; superstitions about menstruation, she told the bishops, were of 'fundamental importance.' " Maude Royden, the most notorious champion of women's ordination in England at the time, wrote in a draft autobiography of the " 'singularly nauseous quality' of the opposition to women preachers, an unpleasantness 'which exceeded anything I had met with in the fight for the vote.' It was assumed, if not actually stated, that the presence of a woman in pulpit or chancel would 'result in the desecration of the Church', simply because of her sex and in spite of the highest spiritual qualities she might possess."[51]

I think we can assume that similar primitive sentiments unconsciously motivated—and still motivate—opposition to female ordination in the United States, although I don't remember such openness in the discussion. Certainly, there was derogatory speculation about the presence of pregnant women in the sanctuary. To my mind, the most ingenious rationale for sexual terror surrounding the anticipation of a eucharist celebrated by female ordinands was identified by Emily Hewitt and Suzanne Hiatt in their *Women Priests: Yes or No?*, published in 1973. They quoted an American psychiatrist and practicing Episcopalian who specialized in treating members of the Episcopal clergy. With respect to their fondness for vestments and ceremony, she had written:

> There is a definite insistence in our culture that the enjoyment of walking in the rustlings of silk and satins, lace petticoats, and magnificent cloth of gold, is an expression of femininity. The fact that men throughout the ages, throughout the world, have enjoyed these luxuries and considered them masculine, seems to have little weight in the argument. In our culture, a man in a cassock is wearing a skirt, and therefore is getting away with something which he could not do in civilian clothes. There is a certain pleasure in flaunting of a special privilege; there is a special conceit in doing what the ordinary man cannot do.[52]

Hewitt and Hiatt enlarged upon this intuition. Were a woman priest, particularly a cocelebrant, to break the bread, dispense the wine, then clean the sacred vessels after the communicants had received, the ceremony and its accoutrements might implicitly assume a gendered—in this case feminine—character, something that would never occur to either celebrant or lay person so long as the priests, performing the identical tasks, were male, functioning in sacred rather than secular spaces. Male priests would be cast in the clothes and functions of women when, in the company of women, their apparent similarity to women was made explicit—a severe taboo in twentieth-century Western culture.[53]

Churches such as the United Church of Christ or Presbyterian, where the pulpit rather than the sacraments is central to the role of the clergy, found it easier "to admit women to full liturgical participation" sooner because they were not inhibited by the kinds of magical implications embedded in the rituals of the more catholic churches, Hewitt and Hiatt believe.[54] A great deal of Margaret Miles's scholarship has been directed to the evil connotations of women in the sexual fantasies of men in the Judeo-Christian tradition. She describes her *Carnal Knowing: Female Nakedness and Religious Meaning in the Christian West* (Boston: Beacon Press, 1989) as a "discussion of the figuration of women's bodies as symbol of sin, sex and death in the textual and pictorial representational practices of the Christian West."[55]

Homosexuality also entered the domain of public scrutiny with the ordination of Episcopal women. In January 1977, when a great many women were either regularized in their previous ordinations or, for the first time, admitted legitimately into the order of priesthood, Ellen Barrett was ordained by Bishop Paul Moore at the Cathedral of St. John the Divine in New York. Previously Barrett had been active in the organization for gay Episcopalians, Integrity, and in August 1975 was elected as first copresident.[56] In 1972 Moore himself had refused to recognize Barrett as a candidate for the priesthood; she had also been rejected by the Diocese of Pennsylvania. In 1975, however, she reapplied to the Diocese of New York. Her record at General Theological Seminary was exemplary, she was highly regarded both academically and spiritually by the faculty, and Moore was convinced that her sense of vocation far outweighed her commitment to the "gay movement." She had, in fact, resigned her office in Integrity.[57] But Barrett certainly never denied her homosexuality. As Moore wrote to his fellow bishops: "Persons known, or virtually known, to be homosexual have been ordained for years. The only difference between such persons, whom many of us have ordained, and Ellen Barrett is her candor. Candor, or, if you will, honesty, is not a bar to ordination."[58] Along with lesbians, gay men are increasingly rejecting the hypocrisy of living a private life that contradicts public representations.[59] From the standpoint of women this was a fortunate outcome; the stereotypical assumption of woman's moral superiority is always suspect and generally demeaning to women.[60] The church, then and now, in its official stance has maintained the distinction between sexual orientation and practice or advocacy.[61] No true resolution between the official church and the conduct of various individual bishops on the issue of homosexual ordination has as yet been achieved.[62] To judge from the media, one might conclude that little else of importance was happening in the Episcopal Church. Nor is the debate an easy one to resolve. *Science Times,* a weekly section of the *New York Times,* reported that antigay stereotypes are harder to dislodge than any other, and the people who hold them "see hating gay men and lesbians as a litmus test for being a moral person."[63] Bishop Moore confirmed this observation in his copious quotations from correspondence received at the time of Barrett's ordination. In some instances, the level of abusiveness defies description.[64] Of forty-two bishops who wrote, only ten spoke positively. But among the ten, there were testimonials of enormous power and empathy. One wrote: "Not only do I entirely agree that some of our best priests are homosexual but in no way do I find homosexual orientation a bar to effective ministry. My mind goes back . . . when we were discussing this subject in the House and Ben Washburn rose to say that he wouldn't change one of his homosexual clergy for six 'normal' ones."[65]

Unfortunately, there seems to be little correspondence between commitment to professional performance and the prestige of the profession. In an article entitled "Mainline Protestant Ministers Turning from the Inner City," a reporter for the *New York Times* observed that in increasing numbers, the inner-city clergy were women and gay men.[66] But the tone here is at odds with that of Bishop Moore's correspondent: lost prestige is the implication. Informed theological educators as well as less-informed laypersons believe that the clergy no longer holds the prestige it once did. Reasons given are multiple. Certainly first among them is that the church no longer enjoys the status it held as recently as a generation ago.[67] In the Episcopal Church the pull of nostalgia is particularly great. Hewitt and Hiatt put it this way: "Episcopalians hear of the great Phillips Brooks and his illustrious contemporaries and are sad that the church no longer seems to produce such giants."[68] Most seminary administrators concede that the academic quality of their students is not what it used to be. (They also concede that their women students tend to be better than the men.) At universities such as Harvard and Yale, where the divinity school is only one among a number of graduate schools, its candidates alone are exempted from the Graduate Record Examinations (GRES). This is quite possibly not important in light of the kind of work ministers are subsequently called upon to do. A report to the House of Bishops from the Committee to Study the Proper Place of Women in the Ministry of the Church as long ago as 1966 called for the "development of new forms of ministry that permit greater flexibility and call for many more specialized skills than is the case when the ministry is limited largely to one priest in charge of one parish, a generalist rather than a specialist."[69] It may be equally unimportant that members of socially prominent families no longer tend to send their members into the Episcopal clergy.[70] The issue is a tricky one from many points of view, but it certainly does say something about prestige. With respect to prestige, it may be just as telling that none of the traditional professions command the respect they did until recently. In our society what young white males do is a good index of professional prestige. Yet even in the profession of medicine, the medical schools in 1988–1989 would have been unable to fill their entering classes had they taken every single male who applied. For the first time ever, white men made up less than half the first-year class.[71] As for the profession of the clergy, Paula Nesbitt has demonstrated that for the small number of males (probably white) who enter the clergy as young men with the highest possible educational credentials, the opportunity structure—the possibility of reaching high office and, with it, the accompanying prestige—has changed very little.[72] As to the more general case, even the most traditional of Episcopalians do not charge that the admission of women caused the decline in clerical prestige—this had already happened. Nor can it be truthfully argued that women have driven men out of the clergy. Nesbitt documents a 21 percent increase in the number of men entering the priesthood in 1985 over the two previous cohorts she studied—a 21 percent increase at just the moment the ratio of women was at its highest.[73] We are really returning here to where we started: in terms of prestige, the two-tiered clerical profession that John Morgan corroborated through his questionnaire—one, however, that although the second tier may be predominantly female, will include increasing numbers of men.

The Episcopal clergy is being restructured in another important way by the presence of women: demographically, it is growing more mature in years. A study by the Association of Theological Schools published in the spring of 1988 ascertained that in 1986, 39 percent of the Episcopal seminarians queried were over forty, 43 percent between 30 and 39. The seminaries represented were the Church Divinity School of the Pacific in Berkeley, EDS in Cambridge, and the University of the South School of Theology in Sewanee, Tennessee.[74] Episcopal mentors are discouraging even their male applicants from entering seminary immediately after college.[75] John Morgan's questionnaire documented the average for women at the time of ordination as 41.1 years.[76] In the fall of 1987 the average age of all entrants into the Pacific seminary was 40; of thirteen prospects for postulancy, twelve were women.[77] There have been some expressions of nostalgia in this connection. The Bishop of California, William Swing, for example, wrote an article for *The Living Church* in 1984 entitled "Where Have All the Young Men Gone?"[78] As he put it: "What is lost is the leadership of a group of priests who grew up in the church, who made youthful mistakes in the church, who learned from a lifetime of experience in the priesthood."

Although Swing regrets the impact of the new demographics on the clergy, others welcome its potential. The report "We Need People Who," which the Episcopal Board of Theological Education published in 1982, asks for flexibility in considering the credentials offered by second-career applicants.[79] And although Jackson Carroll does not explicitly allude to the implications of maturity for his own model of the ministry, I would suggest that this model might be most readily achieved within the context of the second career. Carroll's essay, "The Professional Model of Ministry—Is It Worth Saving?"[80] argues that whatever its limitations, the professional model remains the most reliable. The need for the full-time clerical leadership of many churches is likely to continue, and this, he argues, "implies a kind of professional leadership,"[81] particularly in churches populated by parishioners who either aspire to or are already defined by modern professionalism. There is general acceptance of the professions as the dominant model for the delivery of essential services. In fact, among less advantaged socioeconomic groups—Carroll designates minorities and women—aspiration to professional status continues, and disparagement of the professional model for the clergy by other professionals just as these groups are achieving this status can well be interpreted as sexist or racist.[82] An article in *Feminist Studies* a number of years ago was entitled "Women's Recent Progress in the Professions or, Women Get a Ticket to Ride after the Gravy Train Has Left the Station."[83] Carroll believes that one of the greatest virtues of the professional model is the emphasis on competence. At the same time he is not preoccupied with the skills or discrete roles in which the minister is engaged. He is not worried that although other professions are so structured that highest prestige ac-

300

IMAGES OF A NEW CHURCH

companies the most specialized expertise, for the clergy high attainment
is still associated with the parish rector whose skills are multiple, while
at the lowest end of the spectrum—the college, hospital, or prison
chaplaincy—the specialists are found.[84] He adopts the term "reflective
practitioner" to define what he thinks is desirable, and suggests that
seminaries could help students clarify their vision of God in such a way
that might give it relevance to the various concrete situations of ministerial practice. The sense of vocation and trustworthiness have been
generalized qualities of all of the professions—this is where the concept
of autonomy comes in. The professional is one who is not bound primarily by material standards or bureaucratic accountability. For the
priestly vocation, religious authenticity ideally informs practice and en-
ters into all the multiple dealings with the community demanded of the
minister. Carroll concludes his defense of professionalism by asking: "Is
it overly naive and optimistic to hope that clergy can model a union of
professional competence and authenticity that reflects calling in such a
way that other professionals (and non-professionals in the laity as well)
will be helped to recover their own sense of vocation and fiduciary
responsibility?"[85]

According to Owen Thomas, most of the women who come to EDS
are already members of the service professions. They look to ordination
and a vocation in the priesthood as a means of enhancement, not change.
It seems to me that this combination might precisely correspond to
Jackson Carroll's prescription. Many of the specific skills are already
available to these women. As mature candidates they can explore their
value systems in theological terms, nourish the authenticity he sees as
so essential, and bring this informed and inspired expertise to their new
vocation.

A Gallup poll, commissioned by the Episcopal Church, asked a representative sample of the "unchurched" under what circumstances they
would return to church. Some of the answers included:

If I can find a pastor or priest with whom I can openly express my spiritual
needs and religious doubts.
If I can find a church that is serious about working for a better society.
If I can find a church with good preaching.
If there is a crisis in my life and a church demonstrates a genuine interest in
me.[86]

Are these expectations really so hard to meet in the Episcopal Church?
With a devoted laity and the phalanx of dedicated women (and men)
in the clergy, a genuine renewal of fairness in access to positions of

authority, and a judicious exploitation of the resources readily available to us, it should be possible to make these reasonable hopes a reality.

Notes

Note: The notes to this chapter were edited by Sandra Hughes Boyd after the death of the author.

1. Robert Wuthnow, *The Restructuring of American Religion: Society and Faith since World War II* (Princeton: Princeton University Press, 1988), p. 229.

2. Joanna Gillespie oral transcript material, coded as #216–36.

3. This woman had grown up in Alaska. Gillespie oral transcript material, coded as #274–69. Rabbi Michael Goldberg of Atlanta, in a personal communication to Gillespie on 16 July, 1990, expressed his thrill at being present during a eucharist celebrated by an Episcopal woman priest; he said he felt as though he were present at the feeding of the world. There are, of course many dimensions to this reaction. The rabbi in question comes from a Jewish community that has not as yet empowered women for rabbinical roles. The Episcopal congregation he attended is distinguished for its unusually mixed ethnic composition. Finally, the rabbi's comment suggests one of the principal obstacles that women priests have encountered: the authority they exercise in the priesthood derives largely from their authority as women, the ostensibly natural authority of motherhood, not of the priesthood. This was an issue I raised in my paper, "The Contribution of Feminist Scholarship to the Study of American Religion," 11 April 1989, on a panel with the same title at a five-day conference sponsored by the Lilly Endowment in New Harmony, Indiana, for a variety of its project participants.

4. Gillespie oral transcript material, coded as #630–36, p. 28.

5. Mary S. Donovan, *Women Priests in the Episcopal Church: The Experience of the First Decade* (Cincinnati: Forward Movement, 1988), pp. 180, 178.

6. *Reaching toward Wholeness: The Participation of Women in the Episcopal Church* (New York: Prepared for . . . the 69th General Convention of the Episcopal Church, July 1988), pp. 16–17, 62.

7. Paula D. Nesbitt, "Feminization of American Clergy: Occupational Life Chances in the Ordained Ministry" (Ph.D. diss. Harvard University, 1990), chap. 5; quotation from p. 146, for which I am deeply grateful.

8. Personal communication to me by a male priest in that diocese at the Lilly Endowment-sponsored conference in Miami Beach, 26–28 February 1989, for researchers in mainstream Protestantism and those in the congregational study program. Outraged by this practice, he concluded by observing that "they seemed to be creating commercial airline pilots in a different uniform."

9. Gillespie's oral transcript material, coded as #418–75, p. 15.

10. Letter to the editor, *Living Church* (6 Nov. 1988): 7. More than a decade before this letter was written, in their book *Women Priests: Yes or No?* (New

York: Seabury Press, 1973), Emily C. Hewitt and Suzanne R. Hiatt anticipated this argument:

> Some people argue that for the good of the Episcopal Church we should not ordain women. They reason that the church is already a female-dominated institution. We should not drive out the few remaining members by allowing women to "take over." They suggest that all decision-making jobs in the church should be reserved for men. From their point of view the only way to keep men coming to church is to make them feel important. (p. 95)

Hewitt and Hiatt point out the insidious derogation of male integrity implied in this position. They also note another statistic leveled against increasing the number of clergy by admitting women: in 1970 there were 68 fewer parishes and 3,138 more clergy than there were in 1959 (p. 93). A serious surplus of clergy no longer seems to be the case. David E. Sumner, in *The Episcopal Church's History: 1945–1985* (Wilton, Conn.: Morehouse-Barlow, 1987), p. 96, asserts that in the 1980s the situation had been rectified in two important ways: there had been a significant addition of parishes and organized missions, and the number of clergy retiring each year had reached about 400 and the annual number of ordinations averaged only about 300.

11. Dan Wakefield, "About Men," *New York Times Magazine*, 3 April 1988, p. 16.

12. Donovan, *Women Priests*, p. 54.

13. See Donovan's chapter, "Beyond the Parallel Church? Strategies of Separatism and Integration in the Governing Councils of the Episcopal Church," in this volume, n. 57. Hiatt's comments are from personal discussion with me, 19 October 1988.

14. Christina Robb, "A Theory of Empathy," *Boston Globe Magazine*, 16 October 1988, p. 42.

15. Nancy D. Richardson, The Women's Theological Center: Learning and Acting for Justice," *Christian Century* 106 (1–8 February 1989): 132, 135.

16. Tamar Lewin, "Feminist Scholars Spurring a Rethinking of the Law," *New York Times*, 30 September 1988, p. B9. I am grateful to Fredrica Harris Thompsett for bringing to my attention this as well as the two previous articles.

17. "Women in the Episcopate: Reflections on the Election of a Suffragan Bishop in the Episcopal Diocese of Massachusetts," issued by the Educational Task Force, Massachusetts Chapter of the Episcopal Women's Caucus, 20 June 1988; kindness of F. Thompsett. Pamela W. Darling, " 'Tradition' vs. Women: Conflict and Change in the Episcopal Church, 1870–1990" (Th.D. diss. General Theological Seminary, 1991) describes the struggle for the election of the first woman bishop as the most recent among many challenges faced by women seeking mutuality and shared leadership in the Episcopal church.

18. Donovan, *Women Priests*, p. 168.

19. This is essentially the way I understood Barbara Lacerre, an Episcopal priest of great persuasiveness—indeed charisma—who was studying for an additional degree in ethics at the Yale Divinity School.

20. Quoted in Joan Jacobs Brumberg and Nancy Tomes, "Women in the Professions: A Research Agenda for American Historians," *Reviews in American History* (June 1982): 275.

21. Ibid., pp. 275–276.

22. Donald M. Scott, *From Office to Profession: The New England Ministry, 1750–1850* (Philadelphia: University of Pennsylvania Press, 1978), pp. 154–155.

23. Peter Jarvis, "The Parish Ministry as a Semi-Profession," *Sociological Review* 23 (November 1975): 911–922; Gaylord Noyce, The Pastor Is (Also) a Professional," *Christian Century* 105 (2 November 1988): 975–976.

24. George C. Richmond, "The Pulpit In the New Century," *The Churchman* 37 (24 January 1903): 127.

25. Mary Sudman Donovan, *Different Call: Women's Ministries in the Episcopal Church, 1850–1920* (Wilton, Conn.: Morehouse-Barlow, 1986), pp. 106, 96.

26. Brumberg and Tomes, "Women in the Professions," p. 287.

27. Sandra Hughes Boyd, "Women in Professional Church Work: The Episcopal Church in Nebraska as Case Study" (Paper read at the Sixth Berkshire Conference on the History of Women, Smith College, 2 June 1984).

28. Helen M. Fuller, *The Order of Deaconesses* (n.p.: Chicago Deaconess Chapter, 1923), p. 17.

29. *Women Priests,* p 15. By mid-1991, the official Episcopal News Service reported about 1,500 ordained women in its "Fact Sheet: the Ordination of Women to the Priesthood," issued 11 July, 1991. In December 1991 Mary Sudman Donovan reported the following updated figures on women clergy in the Episcopal Church:

A total of 1,822 ordained women (1,034 priests and 788 deacons) were registered with the Church Pension Fund as of November, 1991. The current number of Episcopal priests and deacons (active and retired) is 14,831, bringing the proportion of women to approximately 12 percent. Women make up an even higher percentage of the active clergy; 17 percent of the priests and deacons who are not receiving retirement pensions from the Church Pension Fund are women. A total of 3,970 clergy (including 13 women) were receiving retirement pensions as of November 30, 1991. The figures on women priests and deacons were assembled by the Right Reverend Alexander D. Stewart from the statistics sent to the Recorder of Ordinations for the Episcopal Church on November 7, 1991 and from Church Pension Fund records, Episcopal Church Center, New York City. The most recent figures available for the total number of Episcopal clergy are those for 1989 listed in the *Episcopal Church Annual, 1991* (Wilton, Conn.: Morehouse-Barlow, 1991), p. 13. That number does not include clergy in overseas dioceses (about 250) or bishops (about 300).

30. For a description of the "irregular" ordinations, see the fine account by the Reverend Alla Bozarth-Campbell, *Womanpriest: A Personal Odyssey* (New York: Paulist Press, 1978), pp. 101–143. Bozarth-Campbell, like many contemporary women priests, was married to an Episcopal priest whom she met in seminary. She describes with poignancy the terrible strain on their relationship when he decided to accept ordination during the period when women, notably

304   IMAGES OF A NEW CHURCH

his wife, were refused notwithstanding, in her case, much more extensive training (pp. 96–100). Other accounts are: Carter Heyward, *A Priest Forever: The Formation of a Woman and a Priest* (New York: Harper & Row, 1976); Suzanne R. Hiatt, "How We Brought the Good News from Graymoor to Minneapolis: An Episcopal Paradigm," *Journal of Ecumenical Studies* 20 (1983): 576–584; Norene Carter, "Entering the Sanctuary: The Struggle for Priesthood in the Contemporary Episcopalian . . . Experience," in *Women of Spirit: Female Leadership in the Jewish and Christian Traditions,* Rosemary Ruether and Eleanor McLaughlin, eds. (New York: Simon and Schuster, 1979), pp. 356–372; and Heather Huyck, "Indelible Change: Women Priests in the Episcopal Church," *Historical Magazine of the Protestant Episcopal Church* 51 (1982): 385–398.

    31. Donovan, *Women Priests,* p. 9. This decision reversed one taken the day before, 21 September 1976, by the House of Bishops at General Convention that spoke of a "conditional ordination." David Sumner, in *The Episcopal Church's History, 1945–1985,* describes the implications: "In effect, a second ordination would occur. Supporters of the irregularly ordained women were aghast . . . and raised questions of the women's subsequent actions and their sense of being priests" (p. 28). In addition to his good discussion of the irregular ordinations and the church's resolution of the resulting dissonance, Sumner offers a particularly vivid description of events preceding this event: the presentation before Bishop Paul Moore in December 1974 of five of the women who hoped that he would ordain them as deacons during the ceremony for male deacons at the Cathedral of St. John the Divine. When he refused, a third of the congregation walked out. The irregular ordinations and the immediate consequences are treated on pp. 19–30.

    Paul Moore, Jr., *Take a Bishop Like Me* (New York: Harper & Row, 1979), presents his equally moving account of the rejection of the women deacons, and goes on to describe the difficult deliberations among the bishops following the irregular ordinations and the dilemma among those who approved and those who condemned both the proceedings in general and Bishop Robert DeWitt as an officer of the church in whose former diocese the ceremony had taken place (pp. 1–3, 15–39).

    32. Tabulation of Annual Diocesan Reports for 1988, Office of Management Information Statistics, Episcopal Church Center, New York City (see n. 29 for updated statistics).

    33. Nesbitt, "Feminization," p. 115. The statistics were based on her computer study of women clergy registered, and cross-checked in the relevant years of the *Episcopal Church Annual,* the *Journal of General Convention,* and the *Episcopal Clerical Directory.* Her sample included all women ordained to the diaconate in 1985, 1980, 1975, and 1970 and subsequently ordained to the priesthood. It also included women ordained to the diaconate in 1971 who had completed seminary by June 1970 and who would therefore have qualified for ordination in 1970 had the 1967 General Convention permitted it. The mean figure is 5.2, based on the following values: 0 = no higher education listed; 1

= less than a bachelor's degree; 2 = bachelor's degree; 3 = bachelor's degree plus certificate; 4 = master's degree in field other than religion; 5 = master's degree in religious field, other than B.D. or M.Div.; 6 = Master of Divinity degree (three year program), including B.D. prior to 1975, the standard professional degree considered for ordination; 7 = two or more master's degrees; 8 = doctoral degree earned prior to a religious degree; 9 = Doctor of Ministry; 10 = Doctoral degree other than D.Min. earned following a religious degree; 11 = more than one doctoral degree.

34. Nesbitt, statistics from dissertation research database provided to me in printout dated February 1990, p. 10.

35. Ibid., pp. 10, 2.

36. Donovan, *Women Priests,* pp. 22–23.

37. John H. Morgan, *Women Priests: An Emerging Ministry in the Episcopal Church (1975–1985)* (Bristol, Ind.: privately published, 1985), pp. 23, 43, 77.

38. For examples, see the autobiographical chapter of the Reverend Marjorie N. Farmer in this volume and the chapter about the Reverend Nancy Chaffee in Donovan, *Women Priests,* pp. 45–51.

39. Nesbitt, "Feminization," p. 180.

40. H. Boone Porter, "Disputed Election" *Living Church* (13 November 1988): 8.

41. Donovan, *Women Priests,* p. 134.

42. Nesbitt, "Feminization," p. 108.

43. Mary S. Donovan reported in 1988 that five dioceses had not ordained women priests or deacons: Easton, Eau Claire, Fond du Lac, Quincy, and Springfield. Eleven other dioceses had women deacons but no women priests: Albany, Fort Worth, Georgia, Long Island, Louisiana, Nebraska, Northern Indiana, San Joaquin, Southwest Florida, Western Kansas, and Western Louisiana. *Women Priests,* pp. 24–25. By mid–1991 the Episcopal News Service reported that the number of dioceses which had bishops who did not ordain women to the priesthood numbered seven: Albany (whose bishop has, however, licensed a woman priest to serve in the diocese), Eau Claire, Fond du Lac, Fort Worth, Quincy, San Joaquin, and Springfield ("Fact Sheet: the Ordination of Women to the Priesthood," Episcopal News Service press release, 11 July 1991). Donovan reported in December 1991 that the diocese of Springfield has a new bishop who has stated publicly that he will ordain women.

44. Donovan, *Women Priests,* pp. 45–51.

45. Press release, "Biographical Sketch: Barbara C. Harris," from the Episcopal Church, at the time of Harris's consecration as bishop, 11 February 1989.

46. Ibid.

47. Nesbitt, "Feminization," p. 206.

48. Ibid.

49. Ibid., p. 209.

50. Ibid., p. 129.

51. Brian Heeney, *The Women's Movement in the Church of England, 1850–1930.* (Oxford: Clarendon Press, 1988), p. 25.

52. Margaretta K. Bowers, *Conflicts of the Clergy: A Psychodynamic Study with Case Histories* (New York: Thomas Nelson, 1964), p. 35, as quoted in Hewitt and Hiatt, *Women Priests,* p. 43. Hewitt and Hiatt were among the "Philadelphia eleven" ordained in the "irregular" ordinations 29 July 1974.

53. Hewitt and Hiatt., *Women Priests,* pp. 43–44; I have somewhat compounded their argument.

54. Ibid., p. 27. Jean Miller Schmidt, a faculty member of the Iliff School of Theology, in her comment at the conference of the authors of this anthology and other interested scholars held at Henry Chauncy Center, Princeton, N.J., 5 June 1990, made a similar point about the United Methodists. Because women "had the authority of the Holy Spirit to speak"—central to Methodist doctrine— it was easier for the church to assimilate them as full members of the clergy. The Methodists opened ordination to women in 1956. A position in almost diametric opposition to this one, and to that of Hewitt and Hiatt, can be argued with equal persuasiveness, and is, in fact, represented in this very volume in the chapter by Margaret Miles. Citing Owen Thomas, she points out that because Anglican theology has always been inclusive, held together by common liturgical and sacramental practice rather than by the Word, the Episcopal Church can be more open to feminist critique and revision. "Christian churches with a greater emphasis on confessional formulae, he says, find it more difficult to admit feminist revisions of the creeds than are seen as defining the character of these denominations." Miles herself finds that Episcopal "emphasis on practice—movement, posture, and gesture, reading and listening, eating and drinking—does facilitate women's participation, rendering the verbal content of worship less crucial" (see chapter 11, this volume). Both Miles and Thomas, however, were making their observations long after the institutionalization of women priests in the Episcopal church, and their comments embrace the laity as well as the clergy.
Krister Stendahl, commenting on the work of Elisabeth Schuessler-Fiorenza, a Roman Catholic, argued along somewhat similar lines at the December 1983 convention of the American Academy of Religion in Dallas. The centrality of the *ecclesia,* or religious community in Roman Catholicism, as opposed to the Word of God in Protestantism, accustomed her, he believes, to recognizing community as authentic religious experience, and hence her extraordinary sensitivity to the hitherto unseen discipleship of women during Jesus' lifetime and immediately thereafter.

55. Chapter 11, this volume, n. 16.

56. Sumner, *The Episcopal Church's History,* p. 64.

57. Moore, *Take a Bishop,* pp. 42–50, 64, 113. A news note in the September 1989 *Pacific Church News* reported that the Reverend Ellen Barrett celebrated the Friday eucharist and was given "a cordial and emphatic welcome by the Rev. Michael Merriman on behalf of Grace Cathedral." Barrett is here identified

as "the first openly lesbian person to be ordained by any mainline Christian church" (p. 1).

58. Quoted in Moore, *Take a Bishop,* p. 112.

59. Outspoken lesbian Carter Heyward, in her book *Touching Our Strength: The Erotic as Power and the Love of God* (San Francisco: Harper & Row, 1989), speaks for "an embodied—sensual—relational movement among men and women who experience our sexualities as a liberating resource" (p. 3). She identifies negative attitudes towards sexuality, whether homo- or hetero-, as unfortunate chapters in the Christian tradition. She does not reject the option of celibacy, provided it is chosen "in fidelity" rather than "in alienation" (p. 135). Heyward was one of the "Philadelphia eleven."

When Elizabeth Carl was ordained by Bishop Ronald Haines to the priesthood in the Diocese of Washington on 5 June 1991 she was acknowledged to have been for a number of years living openly in a loving and intimate relationship with another woman. The bishop asserted that "while the sexual orientation and lifestyle of a candidate for ordination warrant serious consideration, it is nevertheless my belief that they are not the only determinative factors" ("Struggling to Understand the Mysteries of Sexuality," *Episcopal Life* [July 1991]: 19)

60. I am grateful to Clarissa W. Atkinson for her insight into the early difference in female and male gay reaction to the ordination issue.

61. 1977 resolutions quoted in Moore, *Take a Bishop,* p. 168; see also *Time,* 13 November 1989, p. 89; *New York Times,* 12 February 1990, p. B6.

62. An equally thorny issue is that of formulating a church position on homosexual unions, an issue that will ultimately affect greater numbers of people than the ordination issue. Within certain rather circumscribed situations, various parishes have celebrated services of blessing for homosexual couples. The Diocese of Newark, under the leadership of Bishop John S. Spong, was the first to make the decision to bless homosexual unions (*New York Times,* 1 February 1988, p. B3). Spong is the bishop who ordained the gay priest who was subsequently dismissed amid controversy (ibid., 12 February 1990, pp. B1, 6). The difficulty of resolving the conflicts between official church statements and the conduct of individual bishops on issues of sexuality was vividly demonstrated at the 1991 General Convention when the House of Bishops voted to go into a rare executive session following a heated debate between two bishops over a human sexuality resolution. Presiding Bishop Edmond L. Browning noted that while he did not normally support executive sessions, he felt that bishops needed time alone to talk about "how we are going to share with one another, how we are going to debate with one another" ("Bishops Say Confidentiality Violated," *Episcopal Life: Convention Daily* [16 July 1991], p. 2; "House of Bishops Executive Session to Continue Sunday Morning Following Frank Exchanges," Episcopal News Service press release GC3–6, 13 July 1991).

63. Daniel Goleman, "Homophobia: Scientists Find Clues to Its Roots," *New York Times,* 10 July 1990, pp. C1, C11.

64. Moore, *Take a Bishop,* pp. 101–164. See, for instance, the letter quoted on p. 139: "You are a stupid ass—and your stupidity is only exceeded by the way you have vilified our beautiful church."

65. Quoted, ibid., p. 125.

66. Chris Hedges, "Mainline Protestant Ministers Turning from the Inner City," *New York Times,* 31 May 1990, pp. A1, B4.

67. The prestige of the Episcopal Church cannot be too badly affected, however, judging from Russell Baker's "Observer" in the *New York Times,* 27 June 1990, p. A23, shortly after public television had devoted four nights to reproducing Wagner's *Der Ring des Nibelungen.* In the column entitled "Fixing the 'Ring,' " Baker suggests: "Rewrite opening to eliminate the insensitive treatment of dwarfs embodied in the character of the dwarf Alberich. . . . Better make it clear, too, that he is an Episcopalian. . . . " There are nine suggestions in all, seven of which imply that Episcopalians are above any ethnic or social slur, the last being: "Change villainous Hagen's name to something that sounds more Episcopalian."

68. Hewitt and Hiatt, *Women Priests,* p. 29.

69. Quoted, ibid., p. 110.

70. Writers such as Robert C. Christopher, *Crashing the Gates: The De-WASPing of America's Power Elite* (New York: Simon & Schuster, 1989), assert that the WASP elite is a bygone in any event.

71. *New York Times,* 18 February 1990, p. A35.

72. Nesbitt, "Feminization," p. 206.

73. Ibid., p. 203.

74. Ellis L. Larsen and James M. Shopshire, "A Profile of Contemporary Seminarians," *Theological Education* 24 (Spring 1988): 100, 128.

75. Personal communication from Mary S. Donovan, whose husband is the Bishop of Arkansas.

76. Morgan, *Women Priests,* p. 14.

77. William E. Swing, "What Is Happening with Maleness?" *Living Church* (9 October 1988): 14.

78. *Living Church* (1 December 1984): 9. I am grateful to Joanna Gillespie for calling my attention to this piece. The subsequent quotation is from the same page.

79. Margaret Fletcher Clark, ed., *We Need People Who: An Exploration of Criteria for Ordained Ministries in the Episcopal Church* (A Report for the Board of Theological Education, September 1982), p. 69. I am grateful to Fredrica Thompsett for bringing this report to my attention.

80. Jackson W. Carroll, "The Professional Model of Ministry—Is It Worth Saving?" *Theological Education* 21 (Spring 1985): 7–48.

81. Ibid., p. 27.

82. Ibid., p. 28.

83. Michael J. Carter and Susan Bostego Carter, "Women's Progress in the Professions of, . . . " *Feminist Studies* 6 (Fall 1981): 477–504. Their argument is

somewhat different, and leans heavily on the Braverman analogy respecting the deskilling of occupations.

84. Sheila Briggs compared various professional models in a somewhat similar fashion in her response to the morning session of the workshop of authors of this volume held in Cincinnati, 27 December 1988.

85. Carroll, "The Professional Model of Ministry," p. 43.

86. Gallup Organization, *The Spiritual Health of the Episcopal Church* (Conducted for the Episcopal Church Center, July 1989), p. 17.

10

The Anthropology of Vitality and Decline: The Episcopal Church in a Changing Society

Constance H. Buchanan

Mainline Protestantism, widely understood to be the primary religious force shaping America's national identity and social values since the Pilgrims landed, is increasingly viewed as in decline. With it the Episcopal Church, long a flagship of the liberal Protestant establishment, is seen as in decline as well. It seems the center will not hold. This is one of the chief features of the landscape of American religion at the close of the twentieth century. Among North American Christians, the prominence of liberal mainline Protestantism is perceived as giving way in the face of the vitality of black Protestant groups, Roman Catholic Church membership, and the conservative evangelical churches especially.[1] The liberal religious establishment has been defined by scholars as at once a particular set of Protestant denominations and a personal network of leaders in American society connected with those denominations. It is this establishment that appears no longer to be in the position to direct American Protestantism as a whole and, as the dominant force in American religious life, to aspire as well to the exercise of broad cultural authority.[2]

Scholars, mainline religious leaders, and journalists alike tend to base their argument for decline on one major sign: the decreasing size of

Protestant denominations. The chief evidence for decline they adduce are the significant losses in membership of the several leading mainline denominations. Since 1965 the United Church of Christ membership has declined by 20 percent, the Presbyterian Church membership by 25 percent, the United Methodist Church by 18 percent, and the Episcopal Church membership by 28 percent.[3] On the face of it, the case for decline seems strong, especially in light of the increasing religious pluralism of the United States, with its rapidly growing numbers of Muslims, Buddhists, and Hindus. However, the Episcopal tradition has always been small, exercising social and cultural influence vastly disproportionate to its size. More than any other Protestant denomination, it has been identified with the national power structure and destiny. At the turn of the twentieth century, George Washington's hope for "a great church for national purposes" was realized in the dedication by Theodore Roosevelt of the new Washington National Cathedral, a powerful symbol of Episcopal influence, even if one with no officially sanctioned role or federal funding. Almost a century later, remarkably, that influence is still being asserted just as strongly by George Bush, who described the cathedral at its completion and consecration in the fall of 1990 as "a symbol of our nation's spiritual life overlooking the center of our nation's secular life."[4] Also, the Episcopal tradition has claimed more presidents historically than any other faith.[5] Today major indicators of this great influence continue unchanged: the current president of the United States is an Episcopalian, and Episcopalians and representatives of other liberal traditions continue to be overrepresented among Protestants in the United States Congress (although they lost some ground to the religious right in the 1990 congressional elections and the electoral politics of the 1980s).[6] A decrease in size, then, cannot account fully for the perceived decline of the Episcopal Church or for Episcopal concern about it. The question is: What does?

This chapter will argue that Episcopal concern about decline is being caused not simply by the decrease in church membership but by the changing anthropology of the church: both the changing composition of congregations and the shifts in meaning with regard to the identity of the church that this change is bringing. In particular, church membership increasingly is growing older, as a result even more heavily female, and to a much lesser but nonetheless significant degree gay and lesbian. The variables of age, gender, and sexuality are changing the face of the Episcopal Church and causing deep concern within it. Gender is especially prominent among these changes. Like many denominations, the Episcopal Church has always had a predominantly female membership.

What is new is the increasingly evident female makeup of congregations, a function to a significant degree of the aging of church membership. Moreover, as evident as they may be in terms of the laity, nowhere are both the changing face of the church and concern about it more evident than in relation to the question of religious leadership of the denomination: the Episcopal priesthood. It is with this question that we will begin, for it is at once the chief symbol and the main cause of Episcopal worries about decline.

Over the past decade and more, evidence of mounting worries in the Episcopal Church over the decline in the quality of candidates for ministry has grown. In July 1988, at the church's General Convention, the House of Bishops voted overwhelmingly to direct the Board for Theological Education to study the current procedures for the selection of candidates for the ministry and to make recommendations in 1991 for how to promote active recruitment of more able and younger people. This vote came in the midst of the continuing national trend for candidates for the Episcopal ministry entering diocesan ordination processes to be increasingly female, predominantly middle-aged, and, more frequently than in the past, openly homosexual. But in asking the Board for Theological Education to reform what the House of Bishops calls the "screening process" for ministry and to recruit younger candidates, the latter was implicitly concerned not only with who was in the candidate pool but also with who was *not* in it.[7] As often as it may be couched in terms especially of worry about the large number of female, older, and homosexual candidates for ministry, the fundamental concern about the Episcopal priesthood on the part of the church leadership, it will be argued, is actually concern not so much about the *presence* of these people as about the *absence* of the traditional ministerial candidates: young, usually married men.

More than anything else, in a tradition that symbolically and institutionally identifies masculinity with authority, it is the flight of young men from Episcopal leadership and from the laity more generally that seems to signal decline. This flight is a worry not at all far below the surface in the church, and it reveals how fundamentally the denomination has identified men with ministry. As an official of the Episcopal Divinity School, historically one of the major seminaries of the church, put it, when women enter the ministry, "pay scales go down, prestige goes down and the men get out."[8] Whether or not men are choosing not to enter the Episcopal priesthood because of the ordination of women, the fact is that the profession is failing to attract men and fear is rising that it is becoming structurally identified with femininity rather than masculinity. This fear was being voiced in the church as early as 1976, before the church voted to allow the ordination of women, when the General Ordination Examination, the official "licensing" examination of the denomination, offered the following statement regarding the nature of ministry as an essay subject: "In the future, the ordained ministry may become a profession chiefly for women, like nursing."[9]

Where have all the young men gone and where are they going? Contrary to a common argument, it is not women who are responsible for the male flight from religion. The figures show that young men began to choose other professional fields over religion well before women entered the graduate study of religion and theological education in sizable numbers. Religion, in fact, as a field has shrunk in size and significance in recent decades as a part of American higher education, a development that preceded the increasing enrollment of women in religion programs (and other professional schools) that began only in the late 1970s. According to Robert Wuthnow in his recent major study *The Restructuring of American Religion: Society and Faith since World War II,* it was between 1950 and 1970, when the professions as a whole were still overwhelmingly dominated by men, that the clergy fell from 4.2 to 2.2 percent of the new class of professionals.[10]

Ministry seemed in the decades of the 1950s and 1960s to lose prestige and the ability to compete successfully for the able young men who in those years constituted by far the majority entering (as well as already in) the professions, as the professions were emerging with new power in American society. (The same is true for scholarly careers in religion, which between roughly the same dates declined to half the percentage of all masters and doctoral degrees they had formerly represented.) This development in the profession of ministry is in sharp contrast to what was happening before World War II, when ministry kept pace with the other professions. Between 1910 and the late 1940s, the ratio of physicians to clergy actually fell slightly from 1.3:1 to 1.17:1, and the ratio of lawyers to clergy rose only from about even to 1.07:1. This declining interest of men in religion as a profession may be one important sign of the apparently enduring gender differences in religious commitment noted by Wuthnow. In stark contrast to the male flight from religion as a profession, once the bars to religious leadership began to fall, female enrollment in theological schools increased 223 percent between 1972 and 1980, while male enrollments increased only 31 percent.[11] In the

Episcopal Church, the flow of women into the ordination process continues to be heavy, despite the often not so subtle barriers to women that still exist.

But the flight of young men from the Episcopal Church is a larger question even than that of their increasing choice of other professions over those in religion, especially ministry. It is a more fundamental question of men's declining religious commitment and participation in general. One of the most important shifts in American religion since World War II has had to do with education. As both the general population of the United States and the religiously active public became more highly educated (and at the same time more liberal in orientation), the better-educated were by the 1980s no longer as active participants in religious organizations as they once were and no longer as "conventionally religious."[12] This was particularly true of the younger college-educated and particularly true of men. While the participation rates in religion of younger, better-educated people were declining overall, they were declining more among younger, better-educated men than women. Here again, this time in terms of the rank-and-file laity, there are important gender differences in religious commitment that do not seem to be disappearing—compared with their male peers, better-educated women are more likely to continue their religious participation:

> [H]igher levels of education and greater rates of participation in the labor force among women should presumably wipe out some of the differences in religious commitment that have been evident between women and men. When women with college educations are compared with men of similar educational attainment, however, the differences persist. Even when *younger* women with college educations are compared with younger, college educated men, no reduction is evident. Nor do the differences dissipate much when younger, college educated, full-time participants in the labor force are compared with their male counterparts.[13]

In relation to the decreasing religious participation of better-educated men and women, the Episcopal Church is in an especially vulnerable position. Always one of the traditionally better-educated denominations, along with the Presbyterian Church, it is being especially affected by this recent development. Both denominations are increasingly not attracting the liberal, college-educated that have been their characteristic populations, and not growing in membership overall. In fact, many of the better-educated who leave one Protestant denomination are not switching to the better-educated denominations but are giving up *any* denominational affiliation. The presiding bishop of the Episcopal Church, Edmond Browning, described Protestantism's loss of more highly educated, liberal people who leave the denomination: "Most Episcopalians who have left have not gone over to the conservative churches. They have gone nowhere."[14]

Within the church, then, decline is really understood to mean both declining membership overall and especially the decline in the quality of the denomination's religious leadership. More specifically, in both laity and clergy the pronounced decline being experienced by the Episcopal Church is the decline of men, particularly young men. It is this decline that is especially acutely perceived because symbolically and institutionally it represents within the denomination a decline not simply of male status but of authority itself. This decline threatens most visibly in the leadership of the denomination, both the clergy and potentially the ranks of higher denominational officials. To some extent it is already taking place; if current trends are not reversed, however, it will accelerate dramatically because of the retirement already under way of a whole generation of senior male clergy, bishops, and other denominational officials who have led the church since the years following World War II.

In sum, the center that is perceived as not holding in the declining Episcopal Church is the male center. The decline of male participation and male authority in the tradition, however little openly discussed, is being taken to mean the decline of the tradition itself. Why should this be so? Is this an accurate assessment of what is actually taking place? These are the questions with which the remainder of this chapter will be concerned. For if in fact the church is in decline, more precise analysis of the actual, as compared with the perceived, reasons for that decline may shed light on what is really happening, on the challenge that really faces the church and on what might be done to counteract the forces undermining the Episcopal tradition. The analysis may shed important light as well on the future of the tradition and its relationship to a changing society.

The first thing evident in the association of the loss of men and male authority with the decline of the Episcopal Church itself is the strength of the connection the church makes between masculinity and its institutional vitality. It is men who are being lost from the ranks of laity and clergy, and in particular it is *younger* men. There is at work here a set of anthropological assumptions linking gender, age, and vitality. To be specific, formulations of the problem of the Episcopal Church as one of decline are shaped by a set of assumptions about masculinity, age, and vitality. What is interesting but not well understood is the way in which these assumptions about the nature of human beings are linked with assumptions about institutional life and order. What is the meaning of the prevailing conception of vitality in the Episcopal ethos and what is its theological basis? To answer these questions, we must explore how it is that the loss of a certain kind of human being has become identified with the decline of institutional vitality and of the institution itself, or to put it positively, why the presence of men, especially young able men, is peculiarly identified with the vigor and health of the institution.

The male-centeredness of historical understanding of the Episcopal Church as an institution comes as no surprise, given the male-centeredness of the Christian tradition it serves. Here institutional order and divine order mirror one another. A body of scholarship that has developed in religion in recent decades examines precisely this coherence between the male-centeredness of Christian institutional history and Christian theology. This scholarship illuminates the interaction between religious life and thought, demonstrating how the normativity of the male in the anthropology embedded in Christian theology is related to the centrality of the male in institutional structures.

A critical assessment of whether and why the Episcopal Church is in decline, however, requires more detailed analysis of precisely this: how masculinity functions as a variable in Christianity in the connection between individual life, institutional patterns, and divine order. The first step is to recognize that masculinity functions as the chief variable linking all three because it has been the human norm in Christianity as traditionally interpreted. To be more exact, in Western Christianity, which has shaped North American Christianity, not only has male experience been universalized as human experience but what has been assumed to be normative for males has been the experience of privileged males. As a tradition, therefore, Christianity has helped fashion the fundamental cultural assumption shaping the dominant conceptions of human life and being in the West: that privileged white male being is human being. It is precisely this assumption that has made males, and particularly the normative experience of privileged males, central to the institutional life of the Episcopal tradition and Protestantism in general in the United States. It has done so first and foremost by identifying masculinity with authority, with the capacity to hold power and to influence.

An important second step in analyzing masculinity as a variable connecting individual life, institutional patterns, and divine order in the Episcopal Church, as in Western Protestantism at large, is recognizing that male normativity has had impact that goes beyond giving men a central place in institutional life. It has functioned further to shape the very life and order of institutions so that these reflect what is understood to be the fullness of human (male) being and experience. Hence, norms derived from male experience have come to be understood as normative as well for the *institutional structure* of the Church.

This recognition has important implications for understanding the problem of institutional decline and the conception of vitality to which it implicitly refers, for it takes account of the fact that in the anthropology of Christianity the "natural" hierarchy of sex is closely intertwined with a "natural" hierarchy of age.[15] Age is given its meaning for human life in relation to its function of organizing normative male experience. Understood broadly in this regard, age has to do not only with a particular period or time in an individual's life but also with the full span and meaning of the seasons of a life. In particular, it needs to be understood as the normative human life cycle that is perceived to order, and hence is derived from, the seasons of the normative male life.

As the normativity of the male in Christianity has made him central to the institutional church, so too his normative life cycle has powerfully shaped the institution's life and order. If male experience is made normative in Christianity and universalized as human experience, it needs also to be understood that that experience is *institutionalized* in the church. So not only have men been dominant in the institution in terms of official roles and authority but their experience and its patterns have also profoundly shaped the very nature of the institution. Institutional life and structure are not neutral but gendered. Of course, a chief expression of this fact in the Episcopal Church, as in other Christian traditions, has been the shape of the priesthood itself and the traditional notion (still hotly debated in some quarters) that it was made for men. Only very recently did the decision to allow the ordination of women to the Episcopal priesthood give women access to a role defined historically by men.

Age, the norms of time and life cycle that organize normative human (male) experience, is also a crucial variable organizing the institutional life and order of the Episcopal Church, and providing a framework of meaning within which both are interpreted. The importance of age within the church is evident in multiple ways: judgments about the vitality of the church and its own aging as an institution; the aging of the membership of the church; segregation by age of congregational activities; recruitment of clergy; and notions of the proper hierarchy of age in the church hierarchy. Age like gender, therefore, when taken as a category of analysis, reveals the ideology embedded in institutional structure; it reveals that the church as an institution is itself a theological text. To understand how the "natural" hierarchy of age, intertwined

IMAGES OF A NEW CHURCH

with that of sex, functions in profoundly shaping institutional life, we will turn next to a closer examination of age and attitudes toward aging in the Episcopal Church and Christianity more broadly.

A survey of contemporary Christian literature on aging and institutional efforts within Protestant denominations to address aging reveals the fundamental point that within Christianity and, more specifically, the Episcopal Church, age and aging are understood from a predominantly white, Western, male perspective.[16] Christian leaders, laity, and theologians who focus on aging see their analysis as objective. They assume that aging is a universal, historically constant human experience; one representative analysis by a leading theologian identifies time itself as "a general human-meaning factor."[17] In fact, however, the experience of aging commonly described or referred to is not universal but particular. Although most analysts think they examine aging as a human experience in contemporary church and society, they actually draw on the experience and perspectives of men as their primary source for definitions and interpretations of aging. There is little awareness of, or attention to, the distinctive experience of women and even less to that of racial and ethnic minority groups. In fact, aging is a socially constructed phenomenon and hence highly influenced by variables of sex, race, class, and culture. As I have shown elsewhere, examining at least one other kind of experience in American society, that of women, demonstrates that the model of aging drawn from the experience of men is *not* the human norm but particular to men—mainly privileged men.[18]

Embedded in this normative male view of aging is a conception of the cycle or rhythm of human life that is understood as a given, universal pattern. Notions of age and aging in Christianity carry powerful meaning in terms of what is perceived from the male perspective to be a natural ordering of human life, part of the larger natural order itself. This natural ordering is seen to provide a basic pattern or sequence to individual life and development.

Frequently referred to within (and outside) religion as the "peak/slope" model of human life, this life cycle is understood as a natural pattern of growth and decline, expansion and diminishment, creation and destruction. It is a pattern in which the meaning of human life is located in the possession of vigor and promise, and the time in which to fulfill the promise; in work that is central to existence and has significant consequences for self and others; and in the achievement of recognition, authority, and power. It is, in short, a pattern that has a heroic quality or at least the potential for that quality. Hence, the focal point of this "standard" human life cycle is midlife, a time when heroic striving for infinitude reaches its apex before beginning to be reversed by the reality of human finitude. The path of upward development that leads to independence and power, the goals of maturity, is followed by a downward path of decline toward death. So the developmental experience considered culturally normative for men is universalized as normative for all human beings: independence, freedom to pursue individual potential, power—and then the loss of all three.

The implications of this normative life cycle for our investigation of the problem of decline in the Episcopal Church are multiple. Perhaps the first is the way in which this "human" model functions to identify full humanity with the people who approximate it: men. In this framework, men are seen as the major potential for and midlife source of vitality and dynamism in church and society. Thus, the model functions to promote and defend male privilege, especially the power of privileged men in youth and the maturity of midlife. In the moral community of the church, as more broadly in American culture, it is such men that religion legitimizes as representing what anthropologist Clifford Geertz calls the "really real."[19]

No wonder, then, that the loss of men and particularly the loss of young men from the priesthood are interpreted within the framework of Christian anthropology as a sign of the decline of the Episcopal Church. If full humanity is located with men and especially their youthful potential, women are a secondary form of human being and no substitute. Neither are the older, midcareer people, particularly midcareer men, who have come to predominate in Episcopal seminaries and pools of candidates for ordination. The normative life cycle described above prescribes a normative professional model; the loss of this professional model is interpreted as further sign of institutional decline. A vital church should be attracting young men to its priesthood especially, as well as to the ranks of the laity, because these are the people formed in their youthful ministry by the church who will in midlife reach the peak of their powers and influence. In turn, the institution itself will be not only symbolized but fed by their dynamism and vitality. The young man fits properly as well into another aspect of institutional order created by the "natural" hierarchies of age and gender. Whether clergy or laity, he has not yet achieved the independence of midlife and is thus more susceptible to formation within the institution under the supervision and tutelage of senior male leaders. A midcareer or "second-career" candidate for ministry is too old to follow this professional developmental

320 IMAGES OF A NEW CHURCH

path within the church. Further, he may already have reached the peak of his powers in another profession and institution, and thus be coming to the church as he begins the decline of later maturity.

Another major implication of this normative life cycle embedded in Christian conceptions of human being is the negative assessment it bears of aging and old age in particular. Despite rich Christian resources and injunctions for a positive view of aging, Christian anthropology promotes negative images of elders and of aging itself. This contradiction within Christian theology and institutional life leads to a situation in which even clear motivation in the church to promote positive images and loving care of elders, to address the ageism of contemporary American religion and society, is systematically undermined. What undermines efforts to respond to the indignity and dishonor suffered by older people is the usually uncritically sustained theological view of aging as disease embedded in Christian anthropology. So, for instance, Pierre Teilhard de Chardin, a Christian thinker influential in Episcopal circles in the 1960s and 1970s, visualized human life as shaped by forces of growth and diminishment. He described aging in his writings as the overwhelming of the forces of creative power (activity) by those of disintegration (passivity): "that slow, essential deterioration which we cannot escape: old age little by little robbing us of ourselves and pushing us on towards the end."[20]

Aging is defined in Christian thought as a state of loss, loss not only of the component parts of personhood but also of personhood or humanity itself. Christian views of aging reflect and reinforce two cultural conceptions of human being. These two conceptions govern definitions of aging and are asymmetrical, representing differentially valued models of human being. Aging is understood as a life cycle that involves movement from the first, normative model of human being to the second, deficient model. The first of these models is presented as the ideal and the second as deviation from the ideal. The ideal model associates normative or "really real" human being with the following characteristics: independence, freedom, reason and creativity, action, mastery and achievement, participation in the public world, economic and social power, physical strength, sexual potency, and growth. The secondary model associates deficient or *not* "really real" human being with the opposite characteristics: dependence, limitation, lack of reason and mental activity, passivity, lack of competence, separation from the public world, economic and social marginality, physical weakness, sexual disinterest, and decline.

Nor is this negative view of aging or this peak/slope life-cycle pattern a recent one in Protestant religion in America. In "Sermon to Aged People," delivered in 1805, a preacher gave a startlingly similar description of both:

> Once we were *men;* now we feel ourselves to be but babes. Once we possessed active powers; now we have become impotent. Once we sustained our children and ministered to them with pleasure; now we are sustained by them. . . . Once we were of some importance in society; now we are sunk into insignificance. Once our advice was sought and regarded; now we are passed by with neglect and younger *men* take our place.[21]

And the American view of old age does not deviate from the Western Christian view in general. Rather, it has been profoundly influenced by the thought of major figures who shaped the history of Christianity out of which Protestantism came. For example, St. Augustine wrote in *De Vera Religione* (Of True Religion): "After the labors of young *manhood,* a little peace is given to old age. But it is an inferior age, lacking in lustre, weak and more subject to disease, and it leads to death. This is the life of *man* so far as *he* lives in the body"[22]

With regard to aging, then, the actual pattern of Christian churches is much like that of other social institutions, despite what some see as Christianity's unique resources for critically transforming the largely negative contemporary image and experience of aging. More than this, Protestantism itself may have helped shape these broader American social values and patterns with regard to age. In any case, a major implication of the negative assessment of aging that is part of Christian anthropology is that the very vitality of the Episcopal Church, like other denominations, is increasingly dependent on the inclusion and full participation of this growing and yet devalued population.

The church, like American society in general, is itself aging. In 1981, 56 percent of the membership of the Episcopal Church was age fifty or over. Although attention to aging as an institutional variable is so new to most Protestant denominations that recent and comparable statistics are not always available, we have some sense that the same thing is happening in the other major mainline traditions: 49 percent of the membership of the Methodist Church was fifty or over in 1983; 51 percent of the United Church of Christ was age fifty or over at the last national inventory conducted just prior to 1980; and more than 48 percent of the Presbyterian Church (U.S.A.) was age fifty or over in 1987.[23]

In a society that values youth more highly than old age, an institution whose membership is growing rapidly older is likely to be understood as in decline. All the more so because the very conception of old age at the heart of Christianity is one of declining vitality and possibility. A survey of Protestant denominations' literature on aging, which is largely a literature of advocacy, reveals the failure of these communities of faith to perceive the elderly as full participants in the spiritual, governing, pastoral, and social dimensions of their lives. Neither do these traditions typically view elders as resources for their larger mission in society. Elders frequently are seen, rather, as dependent, no longer actively contributing members of the church; as having lost much of their capacity for passionate engagement with issues, work, or other people. A congregation made up largely of older adults, as many already are and more will soon be, may even be viewed as a congregation in decline and therefore less attractive to ministers.

Examination of the "natural" hierarchies of sex and age in Christian anthropology, and the ways in which they are intertwined has shed important light on the judgment that the Episcopal Church is in decline. It has demonstrated the extent to which normative assumptions about sex and age, because they provide the criteria against which the institutional vitality of the church is being measured, are responsible for shaping the perception that the tradition is in decline. They are responsible too for identifying the *reasons* for that decline. Thus, while it may appear on the surface to be objective, based on membership numbers alone, the judgment of decline is actually a perspectival, gender-based assessment; an assessment made on the basis of the normativity of the privileged male and his life cycle. One problem with the perception of decline is that it *by definition* overlooks the vitality in the church represented by women and older people because its inherent bias does not allow full, purposeful humanity to be seen as located with them. But there is an even deeper problem represented by the judgment of decline.

Analysis of why the loss of male participation and male-centeredness is perceived as leading to the decline of the Episcopal Church reveals this deeper problem: the changing anthropology of the church as an institution is no longer consistent with the anthropology of its Christian theology. Within the church, that is, the changes taking place in North American society at large reflected in the church's membership and leadership are confronting ancient theological norms. Oddly enough, liberal religion is largely disinclined to come fully to grips with this development. Instead, it is for the most part looking the other way. This accounts for the inability of the Episcopal Church to see more clearly the real challenge it is facing and this very inability may well, in turn, be the real cause of its decline.

If there is evidence that the church is at a historical turning point and perhaps threatened with decline, that evidence is precisely the discontinuity between its actual institutional and its theological anthropology. Those seeking to address the current predicament of the church might choose from several possible responses to this situation. One response would be to try to restore the anthropological consistency by attempting to change the anthropology of the church back, if possible, to what it was. This in fact is the response many advocate, including those such as the members of the Episcopal Synod who take it to the extreme of arguing against the ordination of women (and noncelibate gay people) for the sake of "preserving the tradition." A second response would be to insist that men are not essential to the church, that women and elders represent the silent vitality of the church, and to press on to a future in which male participation declines even further. This response has its advocates as well.

But neither of these responses is adequate. The first, turning back the clock, is not only undesirable but unachievable as well. The second response fails to take seriously how fundamental gender and age have been as variables shaping the church. Like the first, it too hopes to leave Christian theology intact, but it fails to acknowledge the systematic limitations women and elders face in a church whose theology, in its structural as well as other forms of expression, goes unmodified. One example makes these limitations and the weight of this theology strikingly evident: how little the fact of women's entry into the priesthood is changing its nature. The case can in fact be made that women clergy, assigned as they often are in parishes especially to the pastoral dimension of Episcopal ministry, will increasingly emphasize that dimension over ministry's public and prophetic role.

There is a third and more adequate response, however. It begins with the recognition essential to any vital future for the church that the problem it faces is at root theological. Here theology must be understood in a new way, not as an abstract system merely of Christian thought— not as ideas by themselves. Rather, it must be understood as *fully* systematic: a discourse of meaning that finds structural as well as conceptual and liturgical expression. In particular, the theological problem of the church is the traditional anthropology embedded both in Christian thought and in Christian institutional structures and life. The third and more adequate response would take as a priority for the Episcopal Church (as for the Protestant mainline in general) the reinterpretation and reconstruction of this traditional Christian anthropology as it is articulated institutionally, theologically, and liturgically.

The starting point for this reinterpretation must be the fundamental assumptions about gender that shape that anthropology. These gender assumptions set the basic pattern of values that shape the lives of women and men, that define masculinity and femininity. In doing so, they also organize and symbolize the broader hierarchy of Christian values. Gender is associated inextricably with this entire hierarchy of values. We have only to look at the primary Christian values, truth and authority, to understand how this is so. It is precisely the traditional association of masculinity with these values and the negative association with them of femininity that has fashioned Christian understanding of authority itself, as well as of women and men and their proper religious and social roles. The whole debate in the church over the ordination of women, let alone the gender of God, testifies to the powerful role gender plays in mediating fundamental religious values.

There is an important reason revealed by the empirical facts of the Episcopal Church's current situation that this third response of systematic theological reconstruction alone is adequate if the Episcopal Church is to maintain its identity as a denomination and to have a future. If the Episcopal Church can be rightly understood to be facing the threat of decline, the real cause of that decline is not its failure to attract men, however problematic that may be. Rather, the larger problem is that the church, which has always been the better-educated church among North American Protestant denominations, is and has been failing in general to attract the better-educated in North American society.[24] It has been doing so because of the loss of plausibility, of interpretive and guiding power for modern life, of the tradition's religious symbols. It is this larger failure that will increasingly seal the church's fate, eroding further its distinctive identity as a denomination and accounting for the shrinkage of the size of its membership overall. It is this failure, furthermore, that results more than anything else in the failure of Christianity itself to attract the educated, liberal elite. It is this more highly educated and more liberal population for which the Episcopal Church, long a flagship of liberal Protestantism, seems to be losing its authority as an institution. The important question to ask is, why should this be so?

Religious systems of thought and practice do not have authority in any age, let alone the modern world, apart from their capacity to make sense of individual and collective experience, and to help shape it. The chief failure of the Episcopal Church (as of liberal Protestantism in general) is that it is fast losing for those whom it traditionally has served—institutionally and socially influential Protestants—the capacity to bring Christian theology to bear in a way that illuminates and guides contemporary experience. The liberal mainstream of Protestantism, rejecting conservative religious alternatives, perceives Christianity as no longer offering a plausible or valued model for individual and collective modern life. Why?

A major clue lies with what we have just seen: the changing anthropology of the church and the discontinuity between it and Christian theology as traditionally interpreted. But it is not this discontinuity *within* the church that is the larger theological problem the church faces. Rather, this internal discontinuity points to a larger disjunction between the anthropology of traditional Christianity and the changing anthropology of North American society itself. The plausibility of theology, of how value is presented and interpreted by religious symbols, hinges on its anthropological assumptions, particularly those regarding gender, race, age, and class. Anthropology, the representation of human being, is central to Christian theology. It provides the entry point into the tradition, allowing individuals to find there resources for understanding their own experience and the basic patterns of human life—the way it is and the way it should be—for religion tells people about the nature of the divine and the universe always in and through its description of the human. And because the human is a matter of male and female, a major point with which biblical religion itself begins, gender comes to play a central role in theology.

In relation always to such other variables as race, age, and class, gender encodes and mediates the values inherent in theological presentation of both the human and the divine. If Christianity is failing to provide a persuasive and illuminating account of both for better-educated liberal women and men, its contemporary crisis of plausibility is due in no small part to the outmoded anthropological inflectedness of its symbols. Its values are encoded in models of human life and divine reality that have been outstripped by modern experience. (The central example of this, discussed earlier, is the traditional identification in Christianity of the values of truth and authority with masculinity, an identification no longer perceived by the better-educated as illuminating on the level either of symbol or social institutions.) As a result, Christianity cannot speak effectively to the modern human condition. It is failing to interpret and guide both the attempts of these men and women to respond creatively in their personal lives to profound changes taking place in North American society, and their efforts to find insight and direction to bring to bear in interpreting and affecting the society around them.

Instead, it is the professions and particularly the policy fields under-girding them that appear to many to be equipped to take up the role of providing frameworks of interpretation and guidance. These are the discourses of meaning that appear to the better-educated, especially the younger better-educated and especially men, to offer the wisdom and vocabularies for understanding contemporary North American society, as well as the authority for shaping it.

Undoubtedly, the lure of professional fields other than ministry is not simply the capacity for authoritative response to society they appear to represent. Many, young and old, look to them for largely self-serving, materialistic reasons—for the status and economic benefits they provide. But not all of the professions are prestigious and lucrative; certainly public health, education, and governmental service are not commonly so. Neither are all or even most professionals rightly understood to be motivated mainly by material and selfish interests. Many have genuine, strong concern for helping others through their work and assisting in addressing the issues of modern public life. Nor can it be said that the professions and policy fields they draw on are more able than religion to command the loyalties and interest of the better-educated because they either are immune from or have completely surmounted the hurdles of anthropological change confronting the church. The discourses of policy in health, government, education, architecture and urban plan-ning, and even law, having been shaped by central anthropological as-sumptions profoundly influenced by religion, may ironically reflect assumptions shared with religion. Nevertheless, these fields hold sway because they are discourses profoundly connected and accountable to the swiftly changing realities of North American society in a way Prot-estant denominations have not shown themselves to be. These realities include new biological and social definitions of parenthood and family; shifting sex roles and changing sexual norms; rapidly increasing racial, ethnic, and religious pluralism; structural aging in society; and the need to redefine the relationship of human beings to the natural environment. Insofar as many of these changes have to do with sex, race, class, age, and cultural background, policy discourses have had no choice but to respond to the changing anthropology of the United States and its social institutions. Hence, they appear to have the power and the potential to guide the future of those institutions.

There is, however, yet another reason that policy fields appear to offer the better-educated (especially younger ones) more adequate frameworks of meaning and guidance, and more effective professional roles than do religion and ministry. To view modern society from the perspective of policy and professional expertise is to view it from a largely scientific perspective. It is this scientific basis, the quantitative methods of policy analysis and of management, that gives to policy fields the fundamental authority they appear to many to have. And there is persuasive evidence that in fact this scientific basis, although by no means wholly adequate to the task, is crucial and productive in many ways in addressing the ills that beset contemporary North American society. At the same time, there is ample evidence that what is not sufficiently developed in policy fields and practice are the ethical resources for guiding policy formulation, choices, and implementation. The inadequacy of policy fields as frameworks for interpretation and action in the modern world is their lack of a critical moral tradition and discourse for helping to shape the social goals they serve.

Where, then, are the resources for constructing humane and just visions of the present and future in North American society? Policy fields and the professions have failed so far to develop an ethical discourse that has kept pace and been integrated with their technical discourses. At the same time, the decline of liberal mainstream Protestantism signals the failure of liberal Christian thought, institutional life, and liturgy to keep pace with modern society, interpreting and bringing effectively to bear on our individual and collective experience its rich historical moral tradition. This failure, given especially the influential civic roles Episcopalians and other liberal Protestants have played historically, is a significant factor in the broader crisis of liberalism in American society and politics. It is this failure above all on which liberals who see in Christianity an important source of value and hope in contemporary life must focus.

There are indeed other religious and secular traditions, both conservative and liberal, that may offer the central moral resources for the life of the nation in future. They will certainly do so, and without the Episcopal Church, unless it and the larger mainstream Protestant tradition of which it is a part can summon the courage to face the loss of theological plausibility that is the root cause of its contemporary decline. The decline threatening liberal Protestantism is about what happens to a major religious tradition when the dominant influence of gender, race, and class—the influence of white, privileged men—that has shaped its religious symbols and institutional identity breaks down. Can the tradition reconstruct the model of human life and divine reality at is heart? What is left? Is there nothing or something?

Answering these questions will not be possible until the categories of gender, race, age, and class are made central to examination of the tradition's history and future. Because these variables have encoded the values of Christianity, employing them as significant categories of analysis will alone make possible reassessment and reinterpretation of those values. Only when that is done can the challenge of a *fully* systematic theological reconstruction of liberal Protestantism, one that is institutional as well as conceptual and liturgical, be taken up.

Notes

1. "Those Mainline Blues: America's Old Guard Protestant Churches Confront an Unprecedented Decline," *Time,* 22 May 1989, pp. 94–96.
2. For a discussion of the liberal establishment as a denominational, personal, and institutional network, see William R. Hutchison, "Protestantism as Establishment," in *Between the Times: The Travail of the Protestant Establishment in America 1900–1960,* ed. Hutchison (Cambridge: Cambridge University Press, 1989), pp. 3–18.
3. "Those Mainline Blues," p. 94.
4. *U.S. News and World Report,* 15 October 1990, p. 100.
5. "For the Capital Cathedral, a Slow Finishing," Ari L. Goldman, *New York Times,* 14 January 1990.
6. House of Bishops Resolution A183 *Journal of the General Convention of the Episcopal Church* (1988), p. 88. The Board for Theological Education sought financial assistance from the Lilly Endowment to support this study. In its successful proposal it wrote of the need to attract younger and more able candidates for ministry, quoting from a survey it had commissioned from the Hartford Center for Social and Religious Research, "Leadership and Theological Education in the Episcopal Church" (1987):

> In the section entitled, *Factors Contributing to the Need to Upgrade the Quality of Ordained Leadership,* they reported the following: "Within the bishop, deployment officer, and faculty groups only one in fifty (50) indicated that they did not believe the Church needed to upgrade the quality of its ordained leadership" (p. 28). The bishops responded saying that the most important contributing factor, 34%, was "not the right people." The second most important factor, 26%, was "screening not good" (p. 28). "The bishops' responses are typical of those of other groups with few exceptions" (p. 27).

8. *Newsweek,* 13 February 1989, p. 59.
9. 1976 General Ordination Examination, Set II, Part A.
10. Robert Wuthnow, *The Restructuring of American Religion: Society and the Faith since World War II* (Princeton: Princeton University Press, 1988), p. 160.
11. Ibid., p. 228.
12. Ibid., pp. 170–172.
13. Ibid., p. 226.

14. "Those Mainline Blues," p. 95.

15. The anthropology embedded in traditional Christianity links age with sex in its model of normative human experience and presents the model as according to natural law or God-given. This link is an assumption so fundamental in Western culture that we are only beginning to recognize and examine it. I am indebted to Clarissa W. Atkinson and her historical investigation of this link in a study of Christian motherhood for a deeper understanding of the "natural" basis of sex and age hierarchies. See her *The Oldest Vocation: Christian Motherhood in the Middle Ages,* Ithaca: Cornell University Press, 1991).

16. For a full discussion of this survey and aging in the Protestant denominations, see my "The Fall of Icarus: Gender, Religion, and the Aging Society" in *Shaping New Vision: Gender and Values in American Society,* ed. Clarissa Atkinson, Constance Buchanan, and Margaret Miles (Ann Arbor: UMI Press, 1987).

17. David Tracy, "Eschatological Perspectives on Aging," *Pastoral Psychology* 24 (Winter 1975): 119–134.

18. Buchanan, "The Fall of Icarus."

19. See Clifford Geertz, *The Interpretation of Cultures* (New York: Basic Books, 1973), pp. 123–124, for a discussion of the importance of religion as a source of notions of the "really real."

20. Pierre Teilhard de Chardin, *Le Milieu Divin: An Essay on the Interior Life* (London: Collins, 1960), p. 60.

21. Quoted in Carole Haber, *Beyond Sixty-Five: The Dilemma of Old Age in America's Past* (Cambridge: Cambridge University Press, 1983), p. 3 (emphasis added).

22. St. Augustine, *Of True Religion,* trans. J. H. S. Burleigh (Chicago: Regnery, 1964), p. 44 (emphasis added).

23. Methodist figure from Wade Clark Roof and William McKinney, *American Mainline Religion: Its Changing Shape and Future* (New Brunswick: Rutgers University Press, 1987), p. 152; Presbyterian figure from Stated Clerk of General Assembly, "Presbyterian Church (U.S.A.)—Age Demographics 12/31/87"; United Church of Christ figure from the United Church Board for Homeland Ministries, "Findings from the Church Membership Inventory" (1982); and Episcopal figures from the Episcopal Society for Ministry on Aging, "Aging and the Church: Promise, Performance, Potential."

24. Wuthnow, *The Restructuring of American Religion,* pp. 86, 171.

11

Theory, Theology, and Episcopal Churchwomen

Margaret R. Miles

Questions surrounding a theory of women's participation in past and present American Episcopal churches may take two foci. First, the particular question about the present: Why do—or, more pointedly, how can—women participate in the Episcopal·Church? The second focus is more general; it assumes that work on a particular content—women in Episcopal congregations—may also yield the possibility of a critique or nuancing of more wide-ranging theoretical questions, such as why women support patriarchal institutions. No doubt there are many problematic reasons for doing so, but are there any "good" reasons, and how can legitimate reasons be recognized and theorized? This essay will consider the second set of questions first, exploring some theoretical approaches to women's activities in established institutions. I will turn then to the particular question, asking whether the theories we have examined can contribute to understanding women's contemporary situation in the Episcopal Church.

I

Historically, the dominant Christian rhetoric defined the place of women in Christian communities as one of privileged subordination. The character traits to which women have been socialized in Christian societies—obedience, humility, submissiveness, and attentiveness to others' needs—are privileged, in devotional manuals, sermons, religious art, and theological treatises, as central to the "imitation of Christ" and thus to Christian behavior. Cultivation of these virtues may indeed have represented, for men, a correction of their socialization to aggressive and competitive self-interest. For women, however, they reinforced—rather than corrected—their socialized subordination to male authority. It would seem to follow that women, already socialized to humble acceptance of the roles and behavior to which they were assigned in male-designed and -administered societies, should have been recognized as ideal Christians. And so they were, when their self-abnegation assumed heroic proportions, as in asceticism and martyrdom.

Yet the attitudes and roles that were thought natural for women seem not to have been as appropriate for men to imitate as they should have been if they were really seen to represent ideal Christianity. Although many men were martyrs and ascetics, self-sacrifice was only *one* of the behavioral choices for Christian men; they could also achieve esteem as ecclesiastical leaders, as teachers, fighters, or thinkers. The *theologically* privileged position of subordination failed *practically* to empower women because they were, without alternatives, consigned to it. It must also be acknowledged, however, that by the exercise of individual creativity some women were able to use the condition of privileged subordination to play roles in the patriarchal church and in society that they might otherwise not have achieved. In Christian churches women have sometimes gained alternatives to the social and sexual arrangements in patriarchal societies. Nevertheless, Christian churches have usually displayed a wide disjunction between women's engagement, allegiance, and concrete support and their access to leadership roles in which the design and direction of the church as a social institution were debated and decided.

For example, women's associations have always existed in Episcopal churches. Often these organizations were task-oriented, but there were also study groups whose purpose was mutual support and learning. In these groups women frequently found both a form for their energies and considerable personal gratification. Women's groups have also provided crucial financial as well as emotional support for their churches. They have usually, however, achieved personal satisfaction and community esteem at the expense of suppressing a critical evaluation of their roles in churches that were grateful for their hard work but that offered them little formal institutional power. Traditional women's groups did not "rock the boat"; they "fit in." Neither did these groups—individually or communally—examine their own feelings of gratification in order to ascertain whether these feelings rested on socialized compliance with patriarchal domination.

It is important to say at the outset what I mean by *patriarchal,* whether I use that particular term or a synonymous phrase. Minimally, *patriarchy* is descriptive, indicating that Western Christian and post-Christian societies are and have been designed and administered by men. By *patriarchal,* I also mean, however, that the formal and informal institutions of these societies are designed to embody and support the agenda of male psyches.

In the early twentieth century Freud described the psychological roots of patriarchal domination in the relationship of the male infant to the mother. Freud's theory, though it should not be presumed to illuminate all historical and contemporary human interaction, suggests one interpretation of the intersubjective origin of male authority and control. He located the decisive dynamic in the dual and contradictory need of the infant on the one hand for recognition by the (m)other, and on the other hand for independence from the (m)other. He described male individuation as a difficult and dangerous process of creating a self-other distinction, a development in which "merging was a dangerous form of undifferentiation, a sinking back into the sea of oneness."[1] The male infant's task, then, was to resist the chimera of dependency by striving for omnipotence and control.[2] On the level of society, patriarchal institutions reflect the psychic agenda of the male infant: domination and control.[3]

Where do women "fit" in this scenario? The interplay between love and domination is a "two-way process, a system involving the participation of those who submit to power as well as those who exercise it."[4] For the dominated, "the pain that accompanies compliance is [often] preferable to the pain that attends freedom." Using Dostoevsky's "The Grand Inquisitor" as a paradigm of male dominance and female submission, Jessica Benjamin notes, "The awesome nearness of the ultimate power embodied in the Church makes pain tolerable, even a source of inspiration or transcendence. This ability to enlist the hope for redemption is the signature of the power that inspires voluntary submission . . . [a] power that inspires fear and adoration simultaneously."[5]

It is also possible, however, to understand women's allegiance to, and support for, institutions they neither designed nor administered without invoking female masochism. There can be no doubt that the "hope of redemption" offered by Christianity has been as attractive to women as to men. Moreover, women have supported patriarchal institutions because these institutions often provided the only *real* opportunities accessible to them.[6] To say that most women have accepted without question their exclusion from leadership roles in public institutions, their subordination, and the appropriation of their energies for male projects is not, I think, to honor sufficiently the integrity and creativity of historical women. The psychological explanation of a theory of intersubjectivity offers reasons for male domination, but it does not adequately explain women's complicity with the male project. It reiterates mothers' failure to require from their sons a parallel recognition of the mother's subjectivity as a result of societies' neglect in failing to affirm the mother as subject of her own experience—in the family as well as in social institutions. We must turn, then, to social theories of subjectivity.

II

A social theory of the subject must be preliminary to any effort to understand women in relation to institutions. Michel Foucault, Frigga Haug, Rom Harré, Bryan Turner, and others have argued convincingly that there is no preexisting entity called "the self" that is subsequently appropriated, trained, or manipulated to activities that maintain and reproduce society. Humans are fundamentally social beings whose "selves" are socially constructed. These authors describe the so-called repressive hypothesis, according to which "docile bodies" and behavior are engineered, as distorting without a parallel hypothesis that highlights the social *production* of motivation, desire, pleasure, and reward. According to these social theorists, although oppression of women existed, exists, and should not be underestimated, women are not *only* coerced by the male-designed institutions of "compulsory heterosexuality," family, and society; rather, the simultaneous processes of socialization, sexualization, and subjectification are also pleasurable learning processes in which effective social competencies are developed.[7] The gratification to be earned from progressively learning how to engage, control, and reap the rewards of the social order are inextricably linked to women's self-insertion into society.

These benefits, of course, are not undiluted. While women's attention has been on the increments of opportunity offered, for example by Christian churches, they have tended not to notice the continuity of the patriarchal project of domination and control across secular and ecclesiastical institutions. If the continuity of male-designed and -dominated institutions across historical and contemporary societies and religions were noticed and taken seriously, the conclusion might be, as Mary Daly has pointed out, that the establishment of patriarchy is itself the slenderly disguised agenda of both social and religious organizations.

Thus, a productivity hypothesis of women's socialization cannot simply replace the repressive hypothesis but, instead, must balance it by positing a continuum along which female socialization and subjectification occurs. At one end is the pleasurable sensation of empowerment by self-discipline and achievement; at the other end are the forceful forms of women's socialization—domestic and other forms of violence against women, and legal restriction of women's prerogatives and activities. Education, socialization, and force, Foucault argues, lie along a single continuum in which socialization is anticipatory force; it attempts, by training people to docile behavior, to forestall the necessity of coercion. Western institutions have affected women in oppressive as well as in productive ways that are seldom easy to distinguish and categorize. Social theories of the construction of subjectivity can help to account for women's complicity in supporting male domination and control without invoking female masochism. They describe some of the conditions women need in order to rectify present social arrangements, but they analyze neither the public sphere in which social arrangements are determined and maintained, nor do they identify any points of access for women to the public sphere. For this we must turn to feminist political theorists.

III

How do private and semipublic conversations and events relate to a broader sphere of public discourse? However misguided in theory and ineffective in practice the modern public sphere has been, it was nevertheless imagined as an ideal arena in which all men—at least—were granted voice. In the late twentieth century, however, mass communications have produced a "pseudopublic sphere" characterized by the "homogenizing and universalizing logic of the global megaculture of modern mass communication."[8] Another essay would be required to demonstrate that media communications inevitably reflect and reproduce the male interests that dominate the public sphere. Perhaps it is enough, for the present essay, to note that in a recent survey of images of women and men in a single issue of the *New York Times,* approximately 90 percent of the images of men appeared in news stories, and the same percentage of images of women appeared in advertising. These percentages reiterate ancient gender expectations in which men were assigned roles associated with rationality—thinking and acting—while women remain objects for the gaze of the male rational subject, achieving social esteem to the extent that they succeed in attracting that gaze.

Over and against pseudopublic spheres, groups with political, social, and religious concerns form what Rita Felski has recently called "counter-public spheres," or "critical oppositional forces."[9] In contemporary North American communication culture, a plurality of counter-public spheres, Felski says, "voice needs and articulate oppositional values which the 'culture industry' fails to address":

> These new sites of oppositionality are heterogeneous and do not converge
> to form a single revolutionary movement; the current plurality of public
> spheres is united only by a common concern to establish 'qualitatively
> new forms of social and political relations in which . . . mutuality, discus-
> sion, and concern with concrete needs predominate.' "[10]

To be effective, counter-public spheres must identify with clarity and precision what it is they oppose in the discourse of the public sphere. For example, several analyses have recently identified aspects of the public sphere that marginalize women. Iris Marion Young has reconstructed a modern concept of "public life" that emerged in the mid-eighteenth century. It was, she writes, characterized by the positing of a public sphere based on a universal impartial moral reason in contrast and opposition to the affectivity and desire predicated of the private realm. This dichotomy of reason and desire underlay the essential difference between public and private, directing masculinity to the criteria of impartial reason and identifying femininity with privatized desire and the private sphere to which women were confined.[11]

Neglecting to notice that, masked by a rhetoric of impartiality, desire also permeated and motivated discourse in the public sphere, this theory of public discourse simultaneously marginalized women and affectivity. In opposition, then, counter-public spheres expose and criticize the illusion of "transcendent impartiality" that has operated to exclude not only the expression of feeling but also the people associated with affectivity and desire from the public sphere. Seyla Benhabib has also discussed what she calls the "generalized other"[12] posited by the collective male subject who defines the public sphere. Because of the confinement of women's self-expression to the private sphere, because women did not represent themselves in the public sphere, the impartial universality of that sphere remained unchallenged by a "concrete other."

To these suggestions about the strategies by which women's experience and perspectives have been isolated from public discourse, a further consideration needs to be added. Because body and the natural world were identified with women and the private sphere, and contrasted with the "reason" that governed the public sphere, recognition of, and respect for, bodies—their pleasures and their sufferings—were not understood as central to public discourse. The result of this marginalization of bodies from the public sphere has been that the suffering entailed by wars, ecological crisis, economic injustice, and epidemic disease, as well as issues surrounding childbirth, abortion, and child care have been seen as peripheral to politics and government. Each of these issues has generated counter-public spheres in which attention to them has been, with varying effectiveness, carried to the public sphere.

The adversarial role of counter-public spheres should, however, not be emphasized at the expense of their constructive and reconstructive capacities. Ultimately, it is not a permanent condition of playing gadfly that defines the role of a feminist counter-public sphere but, rather, of weaving feminist critique and revision of the public sphere as it was inherited from earlier centuries into public discourse. The creation of a public discourse defined equally by women's and men's concerns, experiences, and perspectives should be the goal of a feminist counter-public sphere.

Integrated with Benjamin's intersubjective theory and with the social theories I have sketched, feminist political theory suggests new ways to envision women's participation in male-designed and -administered institutions. The contemporary question, then, is not whether women "should" support patriarchal institutions but, rather, whether there are ways in which already-existing institutions can work *for women* until they can be changed *by women* and men in the direction of an equality, mutuality, recognition of interdependence, and a distribution and circulation of power that can, at present, be envisioned only dimly and must eventually be worked out in myriad details and "on location." Instead of seeing women's leadership in patriarchal institutions as inevitably entailing the appropriation of women's time and energy for the reproduction of those institutions, a two-stage strategy of institutional change is needed.

In the first stage, women must achieve institutional positions in which they *can,* in the second stage, revise these institutions. This is a dangerous first step. Individuals, once they have achieved institutional power, have often succumbed to the pleasure of achievement and enjoyment of the rewards of such power and have forgotten their commitment to a project of reform. The only antidote to intoxication with such rewards is the ongoing support and critique of a self-critical community. Continuous and vigorous communal self-criticism can continuously monitor whether women's participation is effecting real change in the direction of *institutionalizing* equality.

Significant institutional change, it must be acknowledged, cannot be brought about by individuals but requires the construction of women's collective voice in the public sphere, a voice that women have gained only occasionally and briefly in the patriarchal Christian West. However, both of these critical terms—*collective voice* and *public sphere*—need further exploration.

Through talking and working together women are currently gathering—by induction rather than by deduction from an assumed and/or coerced "unity"—a feminist collective voice. Rooted in the diverse experiences of many women, collective voice need not mask the real differences among women in order to acknowledge the similarity of the subordinated experience of women as a "caste"[13] in patriarchal societies. This similarity of women's experience, however, must be a precisely defined, rather than a generalized, similarity. It refers specifically to the myriad social and sexual arrangements, customs, and laws by which women's access to self-representation in the public sphere has been, and continues to be, limited. Collective voice is constructed, then, by women's conversations, first with one another and eventually also with men in public or semipublic locations. In discussions in classrooms, churches, and interest and support groups, women learn simultaneously about the similarity and the diversity of one another's experience and begin through honest speaking and generous listening to identify with one another, not by pretending a universalizing impartiality but precisely by communicating the particular affectivity of their experiences. Suzanne R. Hiatt's account of the "irregular" ordinations of eleven women to the priesthood on July 29, 1974 emphasizes the process of gathering a self-critical collective voice in bringing about these ordinations that effectively forced the Episcopal Church to recognize women's ordination, and, by January 1977, to regularly ordain women to the priesthood.[14] The Episcopal Women's Caucus was organized in 1971 to organize and educate toward women's ordination; the caucus was itself the result of an earlier gathering of women in April 1970. Through building a network and an organization, this national group "built a groundswell of enthusiasm for women's ordination."[15]

In addition to the conversations of small groups of women and organizations of larger groups around issues of common concern, at least two other strategies for constructing collective voice are crucial. First, women in groups that tend to be composed of women of similar class and race must intentionally correct the ghetto assumptions that can be communicated and reinforced by conscious self-identification with women of other races, with battered women, poor women, sexually abused women. Groups on the model of the consciousness-raising groups of the 1970s can facilitate identification with women as a caste so that a response of identification with women with whom one may not be in face-to-face contact becomes spontaneous. Second, public events that acknowledge and celebrate women's public achievements are occasions on which collective voice is strengththened. The "irregular" ordination in 1974 was, for many women who attended or who heard descriptions of the event, such an occasion of joyous bonding. So was the consecration of Barbara Harris as Suffragan Bishop of Massachusetts in 1989. Let us now turn to examining the role of women in the Episcopal Church in relation to these theories of the social construction of the self and the public role of counter-public spheres.

IV

Is the Episcopal Church a valid form for women's energy? For many women, participation in Christian churches in general, and the Episcopal Church in particular, remains an ongoing question. Those who answer this question in the affirmative often feel that it would constitute a denial of their experience to withdraw from a community, a common story, and a practice that has—in addition to causing them much frustration and anger—provided and continues to provide challenge, support, encouragement, and comfort. If they no longer experienced spiritual and emotional nourishment in the Episcopal Church, they would be able to acknowledge with gratitude the role played in their lives by Christianity thus far and move beyond it. Nevertheless, in remaining in the Episcopal Church, they frequently examine their own intentions and motivations; they also ask whether the *effect* of their participation counts on the side of institutional change or on the side of maintaining the church as it is and has been. How long would they have waited, they ask themselves, for women's ordination to the priesthood before becoming convinced that the church is not in the process of coming to accept women's leadership? How long, they wonder, would they have waited for a woman bishop before deciding that institutional change is not occurring, or, if occurring, is happening as slowly as rocks grow when left in soil? It happens, Plotinus said, but don't expect to see it in a single human lifetime! Although the inertia of an establishment church continues to distress them, when they regard the developments of the past twenty years in the Episcopal Church in relation to women, they are forced to acknowledge that at least one form of institutional change—women's participation in leadership roles in the Episcopal Church—is advancing remarkably rapidly. The question concerning how women's leadership will *change* the church remains to be examined.

A global perspective makes it no easier to evaluate whether gains outweigh impediments and problems: on the one hand, the WASP and class affiliations of the American Episcopal Church are dramatically reversed in African Anglicanism; on the other hand, however, the Church of England, in spite of voting to "proceed toward" ordination of women to the priesthood, has not yet done so. The picture remains frustratingly mixed, and this ambivalence, many Episcopal women feel, is sustained on the global level.

In short, there are both concrete reasons for entertaining hope about the openness of the Episcopal Church to women's concerns and leadership, and reasons to despair. If we ask, then, what gender analysis reveals about the church rather than what the church says about gender, it is difficult to identify advantages for women without also noticing some dangers attached to and interwoven with these advantages. I will proceed, therefore, by discussing linked pairs of advantages and dangers.

First, the Episcopal Church in the United States, like Anglican churches throughout the world, has an institutional structure similar to the political structure of the American state. It is easy to locate power in this hierarchical structure. The clearly articulated distribution of power provides a ready-made strategy for establishing women in positions of leadership, authority, and power. This is not to say that a hierarchical distribution of power is desirable or unproblematic but only to recognize that it gives outsiders—such as women—a clear map as to which offices come first in the order of access. Although this refers mainly to clergywomen, not to laywomen who may seek to gain empowerment from the Episcopal Church for leadership in social and political spheres, laywomen benefit from the religious leadership of clergywomen who are in solidarity with their experience and concerns. The danger connected to the advantage of an explicit "ladder" or ecclesiastical power is obvious and need not be discussed at length: namely, the risk that having gained institutional validation, a woman may take on the institution's perspectives, forgetting that she has pursued power in order to redistribute it, to circulate it more widely and specifically to those who have formerly held lesser shares. A Spanish proverb warns, "You must change the world quickly, before it changes you." Women in leadership roles in patriarchal institutions must find that warning important to heed.

Second, the mainline Christian churches, in the context of Western culture, have consistently offered support and reinforcement for women's subordination. This agenda has been more subtle at some times than at others, but it is one of the most remarkable continuities of Christian theology and practice across the diverse societies of the Christian West.[16] From representational practices in which female nakedness symbolized and signaled sin to the massive witch persecutions of the sixteenth century, Christianity has accepted and reiterated women's secondary, derivative, and inferior nature in relation to men. In participating in the detection, exposure, and elimination of sexism within a mainstream Christian tradition, then, women can address male domination in one of its primary bastions, in a major social institution that maintains patriarchal society.[17] If sexism could be eradicated in Christian churches, patriarchy would lose one strong source of institutionalized support. On the other hand, the marginalization of Christian churches in secular society clearly means that the depatriarchalization of Christianity, if this can be achieved, will not affect society as much as the loss of ecclesiastical support would have done before a post-Christian age. Nevertheless, the dismantling of Christian sexism would certainly affect the culture as a whole and women in particular. The attendant danger is evident: it is the difficulty of distinguishing women's participation for purposes of changing an institution from support by the marginalized for a marginalizing structure.

A third reason for women to continue working within the Episcopal Church relates more directly to the possibility of constructing churches as counter-public spheres. A church can be understood and function as a semipublic arena in which women can construct the collective voice by which they can address and revise both the church as an institution and the secular public sphere. The intense, cumulative process by which women come to know—and say—what they think, listen to the perspectives of other women, and develop analyses, critiques, and plans for social action can occur in the context of a space that is simultaneously public and, in a post-Christian society, sheltered by its very marginalization from the assumptions, demands, and values of public life.

Male collective voice, informed by the male infant's project of domination and control of the (m)other, has governed the public sphere and its institutions. The conscious construction of alternative institutions will require another collective voice, a voice not automatically available from women who have been isolated from, and placed in competition with, one another in patriarchal institutions. Women's collective voice must be gathered in the process of speaking intimately, honestly, and at length with one another. This is a project that can begin in churches, moving out into home and society when sufficient strength and configuration have been gained. Churches that in the past have assimilated women's support and work without permitting them voice and leadership roles can now function as places to develop the individual and collective self-confidence necessary to come to voice, to analyze, criticize, and revise the patriarchal organization of church and society. Moreover, Christian churches, at present marginalized in a commercial and entertainment-oriented culture, could rediscover an ancient religious role of providing a countercultural or prophetic voice in relation to the values and interests of secular culture. Churches could become effective both in empowering members and in functioning as counter-public spheres.

Thus far I have been speaking primarily of Episcopal churches as instances of Christian churches in general. Now I would like to suggest that Episcopal churches in particular are "pregnable," even liable to women's revisionist participation. In "Feminist Theology and Anglican Theology," Owen Thomas argued that because Anglican theology has always tolerated—even encouraged—people with diverse theological perspectives held together by a common liturgical and sacramental *practice,* it is theoretically more open to feminist critique and revision.[18] Christian churches with a greater emphasis on confessional formulae, he says, find it more difficult to admit feminist revisions of the creeds that are seen as defining the character of these denominations. Although the religious "weight" may be somewhat more distributed in Anglican practice from language to ritual, however, it is still true that liturgy entails language. And it has not, thus far, proven easy to alter the androcentric language of the *Book of Common Prayer* and the mass. Nevertheless, the Episcopal emphasis on practice—on movement, posture and gesture, reading and listening, eating and drinking—does facilitate women's participation, rendering the verbal content of worship less crucial. Moreover, precisely because liturgy and sacraments have traditionally been the prerogative of an exclusively male priesthood, the exhilaration of hearing those words and seeing those gestures performed by a woman priest is—or can be—powerful and empowering for women.

Our exploration of several kinds of theories of social interaction—psychological, social, and political—has led to a theory of women's participation in Episcopal churches as one counter-public sphere in which collective voice can be developed as a base for challenging the "pseudopublic" sphere of mass communications.

If the persistent continuity of gendered socialization is to shift to mutuality in designing and administering a society in which opportunity and social roles are accessible to women and to currently marginalized men, however, the present plurality of counter-public spheres with their criticism and revision of publicly circulated values must continue to gather strength, voice, and courage to address—each group from its own collective voice—the communication media's limitations of the public sphere to the economic interests and class affiliation represented in mass communications. Theories, even those that are temporarily useful in imagining a more just society, must ultimately "collapse into immediacy,"[19] that is, they must be translated into the *practices* that make them concrete and move the concerns and values they represent beyond private conviction and into public attention. The communal practices— worship, discussion, social action—of Episcopal churches often bring together diverse people who would not otherwise speak with one another—women and men, people with different sexual orientations, the homeless and the affluent, educated and uneducated, to name only some of the most obvious diversities. Churches, as semipublic spheres, can become an arena in which counterpublic collectivities can be constructed.

Notes

1. Jessica Benjamin, *The Bonds of Love, Psychoanalysis, Feminism, and the Problem of Domination* (New York: Pantheon Books, 1988), p. 47. Benjamin criticizes Freud's analysis of infant development, proposing instead a theory of intersubjectivity in which the infant's task is to achieve a "paradoxical balance between recognition of the other and assertion of self." Struggle for domination and control, according to Benjamin, is not a "psychological inevitability" but the result of a specifically male-gendered process of psychic development.

2. The little girl, because she can grow up to be like the mother, need not, like the boy, struggle to control the mother. Freud did not theorize the dynamic of female psychic development beyond positing an opposite but parallel development in relation to the father. Benjamin, *The Bonds of Love,* revises Freud's theory and argues for a specifically female development.

3. For example, in a revealing passage in *City of God,* Augustine explicitly says that the Christian ruler—whether in household or state—should be mo-

tivated not by a "lust for domination" [*libido dominandi*] but, rather, by a "dutiful concern for the interests of others." He states in the same passage that "domestic peace" depends on an "ordered harmony about giving and obeying orders among those who live in the same house . . . husband gives orders to the wife, parents to children, and masters to servants." *City of God* XIX. 14, trans. Henry Bettenson (Middlesex, England: Penguin, 1972), p. 874.

4. Benjamin, *Bonds of Love,* p. 5.

5. Ibid.

6. Mary Daly's thesis that women's energy has always been usurped and used by patriarchal institutions (repressive hypothesis) does not recognize that energy is not a "thing" possessed by individuals and appropriated by power but is actually socially *produced* (productive hypothesis); see *Gyn/Ecology* (Boston: Beacon Press, 1990).

7. Frigga Haug, *Female Sexualization,* trans. Erika Carter (London: Verso, 1987), p. 166.

8. Rita Felski, *Beyond Feminist Aesthetics* (Cambridge: Harvard University Press, 1989), p. 166.

9. Ibid.

10. Ibid.

11. Iris Marion Young, "Impartiality and the Civic Public: Some Implications of Feminist Critiques of Moral and Political Theory," *Feminism as Critique,* ed. Seyla Benhabib and Drucilla Cornell (Minneapolis: University of Minnesota Press, 1986), pp. 57ff.

12. Seyla Benhabib, "The Generalized and the Concrete Other," in *Feminism as Critique,* ed. Benhabib and Drucilla Cornell (Minneapolis: University of Minnesota Press, 1986), pp. 77ff.

13. Mary Daly's term; the danger in speaking of women as a caste, or in invoking a women's "collective voice" is described in Iris Marion Young, "The Ideal of Community and the Politics of Gender," in *Feminism/Postmodernism,* ed. Linda J. Nicholson (New York: Routledge, 1990). Nevertheless, it is important not to glaze over women's similarities in recognizing and respecting their differences.

14. Suzanne R. Hiatt, "How We Brought the Good News from Graymoor to Minneapolis: An Episcopal Paradigm," *Journal of Ecumenical Studies* 20 1983):576–584. See also "The Episcopalian Story," in *Women of Spirit: Female Leadership in the Jewish and Christian Traditions,* ed. Rosemary Ruether and Eleanor McLaughlin (New York: Simon & Schuster, 1979), pp. 356–372.

15. Hiatt, "How We Brought the Good News," p. 579.

16. See my *Carnal Knowing: Female Nakedness and Religious Meaning in the Christian West* (Boston: Beacon, Press, 1989) for discussion of the figuration of women's bodies as symbol of sin, sex, and death in the textual and pictorial representational practices of the Christian West.

17. I do not agree with Bryan S. Turner (*The Body and Society* [Oxford: Basil Blackwell, 1984]) that "patriarchy," defined as legal and political oppres-

sion of women, no longer exists. Turner believes that the dismantling of women's subordination and oppression is gathering a momentum that will soon sweep away remaining vestiges of institutionalized sexism. He has not taken into account, however, the very class and gender variables that have always oppressed some women more than others; for example, most women—for financial, emotional, or other reasons—do not have access to the courts of law in which sexist situations may be examined and overturned.

18. Owen C. Thomas, "Feminist Theology and Anglican Theology," *Anglican Theological Review* 68, no. 2 (April 1986): 125–137.

19. Robin George Collingwood's phrase.

Afterword: Episcopal Women in the Context of American Religious Life

Dorothy C. Bass

To Harriet Beecher Stowe, daughter of the Yankee Protestant establishment, the Episcopal Church seemed a little out of place on the
American landscape. It was too festive and not quite morally earnest
enough; it was colorful and warm—"motherly," in contrast to the plain
and stern paternal character of the Beecher family's inherited Calvinism.
Yet how alluring it was! Even as she was writing her insightful portraits
of the Episcopal and Congregational churches of New England in her
1869 novel *Oldtown Folks,* Stowe was switching her own religious allegiance to the Episcopal Church.[1]

Now, as then, where to place Episcopalianism on the American religious landscape is a puzzling question—particularly for those of us who
are not Episcopalians. As many insiders know, this church possesses
internally much of the characteristic diversity of American religion itself:
WASPs and people of color, high and low liturgical preferences, regional
variations, and a notable socioeconomic range. Its external image, however, has often led other American Protestants to feel some of what
Harriet Beecher Stowe's fictional characters felt as they gazed at the
rich appointments and listened to the soothing chants of the Episcopal Church. Where does this fit in the larger picture of American
Protestantism?

The Episcopal Church has been an important institution within American religious life since colonial days. Though at first at odds with the dominant Puritanism of Stowe's native New England, it took early root in the southern and middle colonies and before long was strongly planted in New England as well. In 1783 Yale president Ezra Stiles predicted that most future Americans would belong to three religious parties: Congregational, Presbyterian, and Episcopal. As it turned out, he was mistaken.[2] Within a generation, the growth of new popular denominations, aided by the expansion of the United States into the West, was outpacing that of all three leading denominations of the colonial Eastern seaboard.

More recent efforts to identify the Episcopal Church's place on the religious map have lingered over neither Stowe's fascination with its liturgy nor Stiles's conviction of its prospects. Instead, they have placed it with a group of denominations identified by sociologists and historians as "mainstream Protestantism." The term is a controversial one: some commentators call these denominations "old line," others "centrist" or "conciliar." What the term seeks to describe, however, is a common history of cultural influence out of proportion to numerical strength, which arose from these denominations' early prominence and persistent cultural ease in American society. Usually included in this group, along with Episcopalians, are Presbyterians, Methodists, Congregationalists (now United Church of Christ), Disciples of Christ, and some parts of the Baptist and Lutheran communions.

A good case can be made for placing the Episcopal Church in this company. For one thing, membership decline has affected all these denominations since the 1960s, even while denominations of different character have grown; the Episcopal Church, in fact, is sometimes made the showcase of this common decline, as in a recent *Wall Street Journal* article on religious affiliation headlined "The Episcopalian Goes the Way of the Dodo."[3] The placement seems to work historically as well. The historian William R. Hutchison, who has analyzed changes in mainstream Protestant influence in American culture during the past century, gives the Episcopal Church a prominent position within the Protestant religious establishment that prevailed in 1900, whose structures are still visible today in spite of changes wrought by increasing pluralism.[4] In the field of sociology, Wade Clark Roof and William McKinney place Episcopalians with Presbyterians and Congregationalists at "the heart of the historic Protestant mainline." These three denominations, they argue, constitute a liberal Protestant religious family formed by the combination of modernist theological emphases with "strong Anglo-

American identity, . . . a culturally established status, . . . an ecumenical vision and public concern, a strong social consciousness, and a mediating posture toward matters of broad societal concern."[5] And policies of the Episcopal Church itself seem also to confirm the placement: it belongs to the flagship organizations of the Protestant mainline, the World Council of Churches and National Council of Churches, and participates with other mainstream denominations in the Consultation on Church Union.

And so the placement seems to fit. But does it? Episcopalians have a persistent sense of the distinctiveness of their church, and those of us who don't belong to it sense this too, as Harriet Beecher Stowe once did. This distinctiveness is apparent throughout this volume on Episcopal women.

First, the Episcopal Church stands out as more explicitly sacramental than other American Protestant churches. Although anthropologists might persuade scholars that ritual action operates in every church (including those explicitly hostile to ritual), and although liberal theologians might detect sacrament everywhere, laypeople's ability to embrace explicit ritual action and sacramental awareness clearly varies from church to church. In Episcopal women's accounts of their own religious experience, physical things matter: tasting the wine, polishing the brass, ironing the altar cloths, feeling the floor with one's knees. Here the concrete is numinous—more numinous than it is in the wordy, Bible-oriented ethos of most American Protestants. Indeed, in this regard Episcopalianism shows its kinship to Roman Catholicism.

Second, the Episcopal Church claims a connection to the Old World and fosters a love of Old World culture eschewed by most American Protestants. The term *Anglican,* which is today enjoying renewed popularity among Episcopalians, signals this connection, simultaneously reaching out to embrace cocommunicants throughout what was once the British Empire. While most of American Protestantism was taking its flavor from the Republic and the frontier (which were not without influence upon Episcopalians either), an urbane and aesthetic quality persisted among many Anglicans, even after the prayers for the royal family were deleted from the *Book of Common Prayer.*

Third, the Episcopal Church is more visibly hierarchical than other American Protestant churches. In fact, it is far from immune to the democratizing tendencies of modern American denominationalism: congregations do in fact have power, for example, and contemporary Episcopal theologians ordinarily celebrate the ministry of the whole people of God, as do other Protestant and post–Vatican II Catholic theologians. On the other hand, priesthood is understood differently than most Protestants understand ordained ministry, and bishops are more richly vested, in both apparel and esteem, than those in other non-Roman or non-Orthodox settings. These hierarchical assumptions help to shape the ethos of this denomination.

This church's placement on the American religious map is thus an ambiguous one. Though it shares with other mainstream Protestant denominations a common set of inheritances and present challenges, the Episcopal Church is also uniquely itself—as, indeed, is each of the other churches of mainstream Protestantism. Even in the midst of reports that the denominational loyalty of the American people is declining, denominational ethos persists.

The chapters in this volume focus on the histories, experiences, and images of women who were or are distinctively Episcopalian. Yet this very distinctiveness points beyond itself, providing an angle of vision that can open up new perspectives on the study of women in other churches as well, whether Catholic, Orthodox, or Protestant. Certain emphases have emerged in this volume because certain distinctive themes of Episcopalianism encourage them. Ironically, it is from these themes that scholars who would understand women's experiences in other denominations can learn the most.

The theme of religious life itself is the most significant of these. Neither beliefs, nor behaviors, nor stands taken, nor use of symbols, nor all of these together can comprehend this theme. Religious life, in which hearts reason and minds feel and hands worship, will never be adequately articulated; much less can scholars expect to describe it fully. But here, in this volume, a worthy attempt is made. The importance of religious life in the history and continuing reality of the churches can hardly be denied; yet it is nonetheless uncommon for scholars and other observers of American church life even to try to describe it in depth, as it occurs in persons, among friends, and within congregations.

This theme is strong in this volume partly because the sacramental emphasis of the Episcopal Church highlights an aspect of religious life that cannot be reduced to the more generic categories of morality and belief. But it also emerges because of the authors' feminist conviction that the perceptions and motivations of the women in the pews deserve attention. Their method, which here discloses the religious lives of Episcopal women, can and should be introduced into the study of other churches, and of men as well as of women, even though the content and styles of religiousness thereby discovered might vary greatly from those described here.

A second theme concerns the ambiguities of women's participation in a male-dominated church. Although these ambiguities are present in every denomination, distinctive characteristics of the Episcopal Church highlight their importance and complexity. As a liberal mainstream Protestant denomination, the Episcopal Church has a membership base heavily influenced by (and generally affirmative of) the modernization of gender relations in society. For instance, survey data show Episcopalians to be much more supportive of the public policies advocated by organized feminism than are the members of less liberal religious groups; also intriguing is the fact that feminists who are Episcopalian are more likely to attend church regularly than are nonfeminist Episcopalians or feminists who belong to other denominations.[6] In addition, better evidence than this that many Episcopal women find and have historically found satisfaction in church membership is in the chapters in this volume, which depict the range of women's commitment and involvement in congregational and denominational life.

Yet ambiguity is never far away when such evidence is introduced. For no matter how modernized gender relations have become and how many structures for involvement women have devised, the Episcopal Church is and has been a church governed almost entirely by men, symboled almost entirely through masculine imagery, and committed to patterns and purposes that do not seek the good of all women. This much could be said of virtually every church, of course. However, some of the distinctive features of the Episcopal Church have made it an exemplary case: sacramental emphasis, Old World allegiances, and hierarchical ethos have given a special fire to the Episcopal version of the widespread debate over women's participation in the churches. Change has here summoned up storms of remarkable intensity.

The tension between women's ecclesiastical subjection and women's creation of meaningful forms of participation runs throughout the history of the church universal, as it runs throughout this volume. Though universal, however, this tension can emerge only in specific historical forms. If scholars studying other denominations (or women seeking greater freedom within them) are to understand the ambiguities of women's ecclesiastical participation, they must learn to be alert to the specific dynamics operative therein. For example, the historian Jean Miller Schmidt has observed that distinctive features of Methodism—including its emphasis on preaching and its tradition of respect for the power of the Holy Spirit—differentiate the historical experience of women in the Wesleyan churches from those of their Episcopal cousins.[7]

These themes, highlighted by the Episcopal case, are of crucial importance to the study of American mainstream Protestantism itself. And they may also be of crucial importance to its renewal.

In this era of rapid change in the meaning of gender and in relations among men, women, children, and society, communities of faith necessarily play a central role in helping persons, families, and American culture itself to interpret the issues of gender. These issues are not abstract; they go to the root of personal identity and common life. Behind the highly visible controversies over sexuality and women's ordination, persons and families and communities are struggling with fundamental issues of a deeply religious nature. They are seeking wisdom and they are seeking grace, as they negotiate new terrain with their children, partners, parents, employers, and friends.

Churches with a heritage of theological openness, social awareness, and public service, including the Episcopal Church, currently face a historic opportunity for significant public leadership. Their challenge is to make available religious resources—wells of wisdom and gifts of grace—to a society and to persons sorely in need of them. The masculinist history and character of the existing churches have limited their ability to mediate such resources, to be sure. Therefore, criticizing accustomed images and constructing new ones will be a necessary part of the task that lies ahead. So will be comprehending the history of gender relations in the church, and listening carefully to the contemporary perceptions and experiences of women and men in the pews. This volume exemplifies some of the critical, reflective, and constructive work that lies ahead.

Far more is at stake in this than bringing the denominations to "correct" stands on relevant issues of polity and public policy. Though important, the struggles attending this political agenda often leave other matters neglected—matters such as helping the laity to reflect theologically upon their images of human well-being, or engaging in grass-roots ethical reflection on unsettling changes in sexual and reproductive practice, or devising forms of congregational life and care suitable for new familial arrangements. Changes in gender relations, in other words, bring spiritual as well as theological and institutional challenges. And often the mainstream Protestant churches, which characteristically prize personal privacy about religious experience and ethical choices, neglect this spiritual arena, when what they might bring to it is sorely needed conversation rather than the coercion favored by many religious groups.

In the midst of these historic challenges, and in light of the manifest hunger of the American people for wisdom and grace on issues related to gender, mainstream Protestant churches have an opportunity to serve the American public and, perhaps, to experience the renewal of their own spirituality. Liberating the redemptive message and power entrusted to the church from its historic bondage to limited versions of human and divine reality is the first step. The second, yet concurrent, step is offering this redemption to a world in need.

Notes

1. See Henry F. May, Introduction to *Oldtown Folks,* by Harriet Beecher Stowe, John Harvard Library ed. (Cambridge: Harvard University Press, 1966). Harriet's mother had been raised in the Episcopal Church, but she died when Harriet was only four years old.

2. Sidney E. Mead, *The Lively Experiment* (New York: Harper & Row, 1963), p. 107.

3. Wade Clark Roof, "The Episcopalian Goes the Way of the Dodo," *Wall Street Journal,* 20 July 1990, p. 1.

4. William R. Hutchison, ed., *Between the Times: The Travail of the Protestant Establishment in America, 1900–1960* (New York: Cambridge University Press, 1989), pp. 4, 11, 308.

5. Wade Clark Roof and William McKinney, *American Mainline Religion* (New Brunswick, N.J.: Rutgers University Press, 1987), pp. 85–86.

6. Roof and McKinney, *American Mainline Religion,* pp. 219–224; Robert Wuthnow, *The Restructuring of American Religion: Society and Faith since World War II* (Princeton: Princeton University Press, 1988), p. 229. Wuthnow reports that Presbyterian feminists also attend church in relatively large proportions.

7. Jean Miller Schmidt, comment delivered at a conference held in conjunction with the development of this volume, Princeton, N.J., 5 June 1990.

CONTRIBUTORS

Dorothy C. Bass is Associate Professor of Church History at Chicago Theological Seminary, and Director of the Lilly Project on Theological Education and Spiritual Formation in American Religious Communities at Valparaiso University. She is the author of a number of articles in American religious history, including "Ministry on the Margin: Protestants and Education," in *Between the Times: The Travail of the Protestant Establishment in America, 1900–1960,* ed. William R. Hutchison (Cambridge: Cambridge University Press, 1989).

Sandra Hughes Boyd is an Episcopal priest and Public Services Librarian at Dayton Memorial Library of Regis University in Denver, Colorado. She is coauthor (with Dorothy C. Bass) of *Women in American Religious History: An Annotated Bibliography and Guide to Sources* (Boston: G. K. Hall, 1986), and edited *Cultivating Our Roots: A Guide to Gathering Church Women's History* (Cincinnati: Forward Movement, 1984). She edits the newsletter of the Episcopal Women's History Project.

Irene Quenzler Brown is Associate Professor of Human Development and Family Relations at the University of Connecticut, Storrs. Among her most recent publications are the articles "Death, Friendship and Female Identity during New England's Second Great Awakening," *Journal of Family History* 12 (1987), and "Friendship and Spiritual Time in the Didatic Enlightenment," in *Autre temps, autre espace: an other time, an other space. Etudes sur l'Amerique preindustrielle,* ed. Elise Marienstras and Barbara Karsky (Nancy: Presses Universitaires de Nancy, 1986).

Constance H. Buchanan is Associate Dean and Director of Women's Studies in Religion at Harvard Divinity School. Her publications include

"The Fall of Icarus: Gender, Religion, and the Aging Society," in *Shaping New Vision: Gender and Values in American Culture*, vol. 2, Harvard Women's Studies in Religion series, which she edited with Clarissa W. Atkinson and Margaret R. Miles (Ann Arbor: UMI Press, 1987). She was also coeditor of the first volume of the same series, *Immaculate and Powerful: The Female in Sacred Image and Social Reality* (Boston: Beacon Press, 1985).

Mary Sudman Donovan is Lecturer in History at the University of Arkansas, Little Rock. She serves on the Board of Trustees of General Theological Seminary in New York City and is Vice-President of the Historical Society of the Episcopal Church. She has published widely in the field of Episcopal history. Her most recent books are *Women Priests in the Episcopal Church: The Experience of the First Decade* (Cincinnati: Forward Movement, 1988), and *A Different Call: Women's Ministries in the Episcopal Church, 1850–1920* (Wilton, Conn.: Morehouse-Barlow, 1986). She was one of the founding members of the Episcopal Women's History Project.

Marjorie Nichols Farmer is an Episcopal priest. Her current ministry is Episcopal chaplain in the Philadelphia Youth Study Center (the juvenile detention hall). As Vice-president of Clarence Farmer Associates, she is an educational, communications, and management specialist, and has served the community of Philadelphia in many capacities. She is former Executive Director for the English-Reading Curriculum of the School District of Philadelphia, and was a member of the Pay Equity Study for that city. Her services at the national level include the presidency of the National Council of Teachers of English, and consultancies to the U.S. Department of Education and the Educational Testing Service. She edited the volume *Teaching English: Consensus and Dissent* for the National Council of Teachers of English in 1986.

Joanna B. Gillespie has been a member of the faculty at Drew University and Visiting Professor at the College of William and Mary. Her publications include "The Clear Leadings of Providence: Pious Memoirs and Women's Self-Realization," *Journal of the Early American Republic* (1984); "What We Taught: Christian Education in the American Episcopal Church, 1920–1980," *Anglican and Episcopal History* 56 (March 1987); and "Carrie, or the Child in the Rectory: Nineteenth-century Episcopal Sunday School Prototype," *Historical Magazine* 51 (December 1982). She is a past president of the Episcopal Women's History Project.

Joan R. Gundersen is a member of the founding faculty of California State University, San Marcos. Previously she directed the Women's Studies program at St. Olaf College, where she was Professor of History. She has coauthored a number of books in American history; her articles include "Independence and Citizenship: Ideology and Women during the Era of the American Revolution," *Signs: Journal of Women in Culture and Society* 13 (1987), and "The Local Parish as a Female Institution: The Experience of All Saints Parish in Frontier Minnesota," *Church History* 55 (1986). She is a member of the Executive Board of the Episcopal Women's History Project.

Margaret R. Miles is Bussey Professor of Historical Theology at Harvard Divinty School. She held a Guggenheim Fellowship during the academic year 1982–1983. Her most recent books are *Desire and Delight: A New Reading of Augustine's "Confessions"* (New York: Crossroad Press, 1992); *Carnal Knowing: Female Nakedness and Religious Meaning in the Christian West* (Boston: Beacon Press, 1989); *Practicing Christianity: Critical Perspectives for an Embodied Spirituality* (New York: Crossroad Press, 1988); and *Image as Insight: Visual Understanding in Western Christianity and Secular Culture* (Boston: Beacon Press, 1985). She is a coeditor of the Harvard Women's Studies in Religion series.

Catherine M. Prelinger was a President of the Berkshire Conference of Women Historians. She served on the Advisory Committee of the Women's Studies in Religion Program at the Harvard Divinity School. Her publications include *Charity, Challenge and Change: Religious Dimensions of the Mid-Nineteenth Century Women's Movement in Germany* (Westport, Conn.: Greenwood Press, 1987); "The Female Diaconate in the Anglican Church: What Kind of Ministry for Women?" in *Religion in the Lives of English Women 1760–1930,* ed. Gail Malmgreen (London: Croom Helm; Bloomington: Indiana University Press, 1986); and "The Nineteenth-Century Deaconessate in Germany: The Efficacy of a Family Model," in *German Women in the Eighteenth and Nineteenth Centuries,* ed. Ruth-Ellen B. Joeres and Mary Jo Maynes (Bloomington: Indiana University Press, 1986). At the time of her death, she was on leave of absence from The Papers of Benjamin Franklin, Yale University, to edit this volume.

Rima Lunin Schultz is currently Fellow at the Newberry Library, Chicago. She is Project Director for Telling Women's Lives: A Chicago History Project sponsored by the Chicago Area Women's History Conference, producing an encyclopedia of Chicago women. She is author of *The Church and the City: A Social History of 150 Years at Saint James, Chicago* (Chicago: Cathedral of St. James, 1986). Her papers include "Kin, Credit, and Capital: Family Strategies in Booster Chicago, 1830–1860" (Social Science History Association conference, 1988), and "Businessmen, Bishops and the Church's Response to the City: The Diocese of Chicago, 1875–1940" (American Historical Association annual convention, 1986).

Elizabeth H. Turner is a member of the faculty at Queen's College, Charlotte, North Carolina. She is former Associate Editor of the *Journal of Southern History.* Her publications include "White-Gloved Ladies and 'New Women' in the Texas Woman Suffrage Movement," in *Southern Women: Histories and Identities,* ed. Virginia Bernhard, Betty Brandon, Elizabeth Fox-Genovese, and Theda Perdue (Columbia Miss.: University of Missouri Press, forthcoming), and "Women, Religion, and Reform in Galveston, Texas, 1880–1920," in *Urban Texas: Politics, Development, and Race,* ed. Char Miller and Haywood Sanders (College Station: Texas A&M University Press, 1989).

INDEX